Systems Thinkers

Magnus Ramage • Karen Shipp

Systems Thinkers

 Springer

Magnus Ramage
The Open University
Milton Keynes
United Kingdom

Karen Shipp
The Open University
Milton Keynes
United Kingdom

First published in 2009 by
Springer London

in association with
The Open University
Walton Hall, Milton Keynes
MK7 6AA
United Kingdom

This book forms part of the Open University course TU811 Thinking strategically: system tools for managing change and TU812 Managing systemic change: inquiry, action and interaction. Details of these and other Open University courses can be obtained from the Student Registration and Enquiry Service, The Open University, PO Box 197, Milton Keynes MK7 6BJ, United Kingdom (tel. +44 (0)845 300 60 90, email general-enquiries@open.ac.uk).

www.open.ac.uk

ISBN 978-1-84882-524-6   e-ISBN 978-1-84882-525-3
DOI 10.1007/978-1-84882-525-3
Springer Dordrecht Heidelberg London New York

Library of Congress Control Number: 2009933589

Printed on acid-free paper

Springer is part of Springer Science+Business Media (www.springer.com)

Contents

List of Figures

Introduction

This is a book about the people who shaped an idea – that to make sense of the complexity of the world, we need to look at it in terms of wholes and relationships rather than splitting it down into its parts and looking at each in isolation. In this book we call that idea systems thinking, although others have called it by other names (such as systems theory or systems sciences). Within this idea we include a number of areas which have independent origins but have tended over time to become interlinked while retaining their distinctiveness – general systems theory, cybernetics, complexity theory and system dynamics among others.

Our focus in the book is on people and how their personalities, lives and links with each other shaped these ideas. Other books have been written on the ideas as such, describing and classifying them in various ways, presenting a history of the ideas or arguing for the importance of one perspective or another. By focusing on the creators of the ideas, and by taking a broad look at a range of areas, we aim to shed a different light on systems thinking.

The people we write about are all fascinating, although in quite different ways. Some are widely known as the originators of one or another systems approach; some are very well known within the systems community but less so outside it; while others are well known figures who are less widely acknowledged as systems thinkers. Some are associated with a particular academic discipline, such as management, sociology or environmental studies, while others ranged widely across disciplines.

Each of the 30 authors in this book is discussed in a separate chapter, comprising two parts: first, a discussion of their life and work, and second, an extract from their writing. The extract, necessarily short (just a few pages) is intended to be a 'taster' to show the author's style of writing, their concerns and interests, and to encourage you to read more of their work. In many cases, we have edited it to bring out the author's main argument, while preserving their unique voice. It is not intended as a comprehensive guide to their key ideas – it is unlikely that by reading the extract in this book, you will be able to apply the author's ideas, but we hope it will give you a sense of why the ideas are so significant, and which of the authors you might want to find out more about.

Defining boundaries

One of the key concepts in many approaches to systems thinking is the *boundary*: how do you define what is within the system and what is outside of it? So it is perhaps no surprise that we have spent a considerable amount of time defining our own boundaries for this book.

Our goal in the book is to describe a set of thinkers whose work has been profoundly influential, and who collectively shaped the field of systems thinking. Our choice of thinkers is personal and partial, but it has been taken with great care and consideration. Inevitably you will find some exclusions that you may find puzzling or annoying, but we believe you will find that the thinkers we have included to be interesting and thought-provoking.

We are not seeking here to produce some sort of definitive canon of 'great systems thinkers'. Any such list would be flawed and necessarily incomplete, and would have to arise from a widespread effort rather than the work of a small group.

Two constraints affecting our choice were that we limited ourselves to 30 thinkers (for reasons of space) and that we made a deliberate choice to focus on individual authors rather than specific articles, schools of thought, or approaches. Our basic criteria for inclusion were that an author:

1. Explicitly identified themselves with one or more of the major traditions in systems thinking, by citing the works of previous authors within those traditions and/or working directly with earlier thinkers
2. Advanced systems concepts through their work and/or advanced another field through their application of systems concepts
3. Expressed their ideas in print

The first criterion is the most important. It required us to be explicit about our definition of 'systems traditions'. Initially, we took two major schools of thought as our starting point – general systems theory (GST) and cybernetics. Each has a single figure who can be identified as its founder (Ludwig von Bertalanffy and Norbert Wiener, respectively), as well as a number of others who made significant contributions to the field; each also has a clear historical point of creation as an explicit movement (the founding of the Society for General Systems Research in 1956 and the Macy Conferences on Cybernetics, 1946–1953).

There are few bodies of thought within systems thinking that cannot be explicitly traced back to one or both of these traditions. There are two exceptions to this, however. First, systems engineering, which essentially arose independently of general systems theory; however it later took on much of GST's language. Second, system dynamics, which despite its intellectual similarity to cybernetics (with its focus on feedback loops), does not pay any direct homage to that field in its official histories (e.g. Forrester 2007) – however it too has gradually taken on much of the concerns and language of both cybernetics and GST.

We see complexity theory as falling within our first criterion, with its strong links both to cybernetics and GST (as well as other sources); but operational research, with its somewhat different intellectual tradition, as falling outside of it.

The second criterion is intended to be relatively loose, simply stating our intention that the author should have developed the field of systems thinking, or applied systems thinking to another field in such an innovative way that that field has been significantly advanced. We take 'advance' to imply a significant contribution to the body of knowledge. With this criterion, we are explicitly excluding those who have used systems concepts in their work, often excellently and in very interesting ways, but have not fed back into the academic field. It is fair to say that the majority of those who have made significant contributions to systems thinking have simultaneously applied their contributions to other fields, although in a small number of cases the authors were sufficiently strongly self-identified with systems thinking (or one of its parts) that their main contribution has largely been within systems thinking.

The third criterion is intended to allow us only to include those who have explicitly described their contribution in a printed form. This does not necessarily include only academics – there are a number of practitioners on our list who participated in the various intellectual communities around systems thinking but wrote their ideas in a form others could use. It certainly does not include only academic-style writing: many of the authors we found most helpful are those who have written for a more popular audience. However, it does exclude those practitioners who have not published their work.

Inclusions and exclusions

Some issues in boundary setting arise from the choices discussed above and are worth exploring in further detail. First, our identified starting point of systems thinking as the explicit statements of GST and cybernetics by von Bertalanffy and Wiener, inevitably excludes those who preceded those authors. There are a number of important thinkers from the first half of the twentieth century who take an explicitly holistic line, in some cases explicitly discussing their work in terms of systems, such as Alexander Bogdanov and Jan Smuts; and philosophers who have influenced a number of major systems thinkers, such as John Dewey and Alfred North Whitehead. The same is true of thinkers from an earlier age, such as Aristotle (who first said that "the whole is greater than the sum of the parts") and Heraclitus. While all might be considered relevant, none of these thinkers are part of the tradition that is explicitly self-identified as systems thinking.

A trickier issue arises with Gestalt psychology with its emphasis on the relationship between wholes and parts; and indeed key people within the Gestalt movement, such as Wolfgang Köhler, were present at some of the Macy conferences. Nonetheless, given that Gestalt psychology arose prior to the founding of systems thinking, it is best thought of as a strongly-related precursor rather than explicitly part of the systems 'movement'. However, we have made a different choice in the case of the Gestalt-influenced thinker Kurt Lewin who was the originator of a number of ideas of great relevance to systems thinking including action research, the popular use of the term 'feedback', the founding of the field of organisational development, and (via Kolb) the concept of learning as a cyclical process.

A gap in this book is the absence of practitioners who have not chosen to describe their methods, ideas or applications in written form. This is not to say that such practitioners do not advance the discipline, given that much work within systems thinking is grounded in the cyclical relationship between theory and practice, but our focus in this book is on systems *thinking*, as expressed in writing.

Two other under-represented groups in our list of thinkers are women and those from outside of the Anglo-American tradition. We regret the lack of many women in this book (only three of our 30 thinkers are female), but this sadly reflects the history of systems thinking as a discipline, which as with many scientific disciplines has been male-dominated. We made a decision not to hide this fact by skewing our criteria to include more female writers. There are many women currently doing highly important work in systems thinking, so it is to be hoped that this balance may be different in future work.

Most of our thinkers are either from North America or Europe, and indeed most of the mainland European thinkers have worked in North America (many as part of the large migration by academics from central Europe in the 1930s and 1940s due to Nazi persecution and post-war hardship). Our stance partly reflects our need (due to our own limitations) for authors to have written or been translated into English, but also reflects the intellectual tradition we have considered, which largely arose in the USA with a significant British connection. There are many interesting systemic thinkers from outside this group, and the systems thinking traditions we discuss would be richer for hearing their voices, but this is not something we have been able to do in this work.

It is striking to compare our choices to those of others who have attempted a similar task, such as the three collections of papers edited by Emery (1969), Beishon and Peters (1972) and Midgley (2003). From their statements and lists of authors, we can see a fairly similar set of choices to those we have made. The historical points at which they start their collections are similar to ours and to each other – Emery includes a paper by Köhler (on open and closed systems) and Midgley includes an extract from Bogdanov's work on 'tektology' (and argues strongly in his introduction that it has as much right to appear there as von Bertalanffy's work, despite Bogdanov's weaker influence on the later systems thinking tradition); but otherwise the earliest major authors in each are von Bertalanffy and Wiener. Midgley (2003, p. xix) makes the useful point that "I do not believe it is possible to present a 'neutral' account of either systems thinking or its history ... interpretation is inevitable, and what appears central or peripheral depends on the purposes and assumptions of the person or people constructing the historical narrative".

An important distinction in our approach from the collections of papers mentioned above is that we have focused on people rather than ideas or papers. This has led to some significant choices. We have included those with especially interesting lives, and in a few cases have not included influential authors whose lives we have found less interesting. This has led us to omit certain areas important to the history of systems thinking which were not developed by clearly identifiable individuals, such as systems engineering. In a number of cases authors produced some of their most well-known works in collaboration with another author but we have chosen to focus on one of the authors – thus we write about Humberto Maturana but not Francisco Varela, about Howard Odum but not Eugene Odum, and about Eric Trist but not Fred Emery. A different book would include all of these authors.

There are many other authors we could have included in this book as well as those already mentioned, and have not, sometimes for the reasons discussed above but also simply for lack of space. These include Bela Banathy, Fritjof Capra, Bob Flood, Adam Kahane, David Kolb, Joanna Macy, James G. Miller, John Mingers, Ian Mitroff, Talcott Parsons, Gordon Pask, Anatol Rapoport and Ralph Stacey.

Groupings

We have grouped the thirty authors into seven categories (see Fig. 0.1). To some extent these groups exist simply as a device to make the book more manageable to read and understand. However they also reflect what to us are coherent groupings of authors. Some of them might be considered explicit schools of thought (such as system dynamics), while others group authors with connected ideas (such as learning systems). The choices we have made are intended to show clear connections between

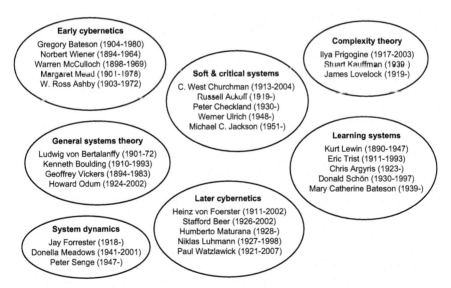

Fig. 0.1 The authors and groupings in this book

authors, and a few are deliberately unusual to provoke thought. The groupings were created from the starting point of our chosen authors, rather than schools of thought, and thus they do not represent a comprehensive guide to a particular school of thought (for example, there are many more thinkers who have contributed to general systems theory than the four we cover). The seven groupings are: early cybernetics, general systems theory, system dynamics, soft & critical systems, later cybernetics, complexity theory, and learning systems, and we will briefly introduce each in turn.

Early cybernetics is a highly influential approach based on the concepts of feedback and information, and the parallels between human and machine behaviour, applying these ideas to a wide range of disciplines. This grouping contains some of the pioneers who shaped the field of cybernetics (Gregory Bateson, Norbert Wiener, Warren McCulloch, Margaret Mead and Ross Ashby). Most of them were core participants in the Macy Conferences on Cybernetics (Ashby was not at most of these conferences, but his publication of the first textbook in the field had a deep influence). While Norbert Wiener coined the term 'cybernetics', and in many ways founded the field, we have chosen to write first about Gregory Bateson, as he represents the first flowering of cybernetics at its richest and broadest.

General systems theory is concerned with issues of open systems, emergence, boundary and hierarchy. The general systems movement championed interdisciplinarity long before it was widespread, with its goal of 'science in the service of humanity'. Our grouping contains four thinkers, two of whom can rightly be said to be the founders of general systems (Ludwig von Bertalanffy and Kenneth Boulding) and two slightly later thinkers who explicitly identified their work as being within general systems (Geoffrey Vickers and Howard Odum).

System dynamics focuses on computer modelling of systems with a high degree of feedback and circularity. It has its origins largely in the work of one man, Jay Forrester, and our grouping includes Forrester along with two of his students who have had enormous influence, Donella Meadows and Peter Senge. System dynamics is hugely important and interesting, but has been historically slightly isolated from other systems approaches; this section of the book shows some of the similarities and differences between system dynamics and other approaches.

Soft and critical systems is a highly applied approach that arises from the use of techniques from systems engineering and operational research to human systems, especially in management and public policy, and a sense of dissatisfaction with the capacity of those techniques to take account of the reality of human systems. These experiences led the thinkers in this section (C. West Churchman, Russell Ackoff, Peter Checkland, Werner Ulrich and Mike Jackson) to create a new set of methodologies that explicitly considered issues such as multiple perspectives, power and intractable problems with no simple solutions.

Later cybernetics is a grouping of several different authors who all have their roots in the work discussed in the 'early cybernetics' grouping, and thus form a second generation of cyberneticians, but who have each taken that work in somewhat different directions. The thinkers in this group are Heinz von Foerster,

Stafford Beer, Humberto Maturana, Niklas Luhmann and Paul Watzlawick. There is a considerable overlap with the 'second-order cybernetics' approach described by Heinz von Foerster – which takes into account the observer as well as the observed – but not all of the thinkers in this group sit neatly into that approach. All the thinkers in the group fall within the category we have elsewhere described as 'soft cybernetics', but so do some of the early cybernetics group, so we have chosen to describe this group in purely historical terms.

Complexity theory is an approach to the modelling of highly complicated and interconnected systems using techniques derived from the physical sciences, with a focus on self-organisation, emergence and nonlinearity. It takes inspiration both from general systems theory and cybernetics. Our grouping contains three scientists who have done crucial work in developing this approach to complex systems: Ilya Prigogine, Stuart Kauffman and James Lovelock. This grouping is slightly wider than complexity *science*, an approach initially developed at the Santa Fé Institute (where Kauffman is based); Prigogine and Lovelock take a somewhat similar approach in terms of computer modelling of complex systems and a focus on self-organisation, but the three thinkers developed their work largely independently of each other.

Learning systems is a broad group of thinkers with a common focus on the way people learn and the systems within which they learn. It begins with the important work of Kurt Lewin, who died young in the very early days of systems thinking but had a huge influence upon its developing work. The grouping continues with three thinkers who are strongly part of Lewin's tradition (as well as being influenced by other systems work) – Eric Trist, Chris Argyris and Donald Schön. The group ends with Mary Catherine Bateson, who presents one of the most refined and complete examples of a unified systems approach to learning and to life.

Acknowledgements

In conducting such a long and all-consuming project as this, we have been helped along the way by very many people, and while we can mention only a few of them, we are deeply grateful to everyone who has encouraged us through this journey.

The systems study group was a source of great support to us, and involved almost every member of the Systems Department at the Open University as well as several visitors. We particularly thank Rose Armson, Andrea Berardi, Chris Blackmore, Ray Ison, Bill Laidlaw, John Martin, Martin Reynolds, Sandro Schlindwein, Rupesh Shah and Roger Spear.

Bill Laidlaw, Tony Nixon, Becky Calcraft and Martin Reynolds were extremely helpful in reading drafts of various chapters and offering valuable advice on making them better.

The long gestation and production process of the book has been supported by a number of colleagues within the Open University and outside: Angela Walters and

Marilyn Ridsdale in our faculty; Teresa Kennard, David Vince, Giles Clark and Christianne Bailey of the university's Co-publishing department; Helen Desmond, Beverly Ford and Francesca Bonner at Springer. We are also grateful for additional information about some of the authors from Nancy Schön, Vanilla Beer, Dirk Baecker and Klaus Dammann; and for helpful conversations on several occasions with John Mingers.

Magnus would also like to thank personally his wonderful wife, Becky Calcraft, for her support, constant encouragement, long discussions and willingness to put up with late nights; and Alice, who hasn't had a single moment of her life when Daddy wasn't writing the book.

References

Beishon, R. J., & Peters, G. (1972). *Systems behaviour*. London: Harper and Row.
Emery, F. E. (1969). *Systems thinking: Selected readings*. Harmondsworth, UK: Penguin.
Forrester, J. W. (2007). System dynamics – A personal view of the first fifty years. *System Dynamic Review, 23*(2/3), 345–358.
Midgley, G. (Ed.) (2003). *Systems thinking (4 vols)*. London: Sage.

Early Cybernetics

Exploring parallels between the behaviour of cognitive and engineered systems, with a focus on feedback and information

Chapter 1
Gregory Bateson

Gregory Bateson, anthropologist and philosopher, was a deeply original thinker who crossed multiple disciplines, always sitting on the edge between them. He began only late in life to attempt to synthesise his many contributions. As Brockman (2004) wrote, "Bateson is not easy ... To spend time with him, in person or through his essays, was a rigorous intelligent exercise, an immense relief from the trivial forms that command respect in contemporary society." But his contributions were considerable, to a wide range of fields. He was perhaps the most wide-ranging and profound thinker in early cybernetics, and his work provides a foundation for much of the important work that followed, and a deep insight into the problems of the world today.

Practically every discussion of Bateson's work contains a different list of his disciplinary interests. He worked at one time or another in zoology, anthropology, cybernetics, communications theory, psychiatry, ethology (animal behaviour) and philosophy; and he also had a strong impact on family therapy, the environmental movement and organisational theory. His contribution to each of these fields was profound, but he was always ready to move on – as his biographer put it, he "posted himself to the margins of not one, but multiple disciplines from which he secluded and then absented himself" (Lipset 2005, p. 911).

Although he was an outsider in terms of disciplinary allegiance, he was part of a formidable intellectual dynasty. His grandfather, William Bateson, was a modernising Master of St Johns College, Cambridge. His father, also William, was a key early geneticist, who coined the word 'genetics' and brought the concepts of Gregor Mendel to wider attention. Gregory Bateson was married for more than a decade to the great anthropologist Margaret Mead, and their daughter, Mary Catherine Bateson, has herself become a celebrated anthropologist and systems thinker. His relationship with his father was not an easy one – Gregory was William Bateson's youngest son but both his elder brothers died (one in the First World War, the other through suicide) so that the considerable weight of his father's expectations fell upon Gregory – but he inherited a deep intellectual self-confidence as well as an admiration for influential outsiders (such as William Blake, a hero of both father and son). The important influence of father upon son is well summarised by Toulmin (1984, p. 3):

His strong physical presence – his great height and eagle profile – and the blend of intellectual confidence and personal diffidence that he inherited from the Cambridge tradition
of natural science (his father, William Bateson, was a founder of modern genetics) gave
him the personal and intellectual power to move in quietly on virtually any debate and
reshape it according to his own perspective. With his biological background, he was fully
aware of current scientific orthodoxy, but he treated it as a theme on which to compose
personal variations, and these, while sometimes eccentric, illuminated whatever they
touched.

Bateson was born in 1904 in Cambridge (England) and died in 1980 in San
Francisco. His list of institutional affiliations is long, including St Johns College
(Cambridge University), the University of California Medical School, the Veteran's
Administration Hospital in Palo Alto (California), the Oceanic Institute (Hawaii)
and the University of California at Santa Cruz. He also held many visiting professorships at other institutions. His research was carried out in a wide variety of
contexts – as an anthropologist, with peoples in New Guinea and Bali; during the
war, with the US Office of Strategic Services (forerunner to the CIA); with psychiatric
patients; with porpoises and dolphins; and on environmental issues.

However, perhaps Bateson's strongest 'institutional' affiliation was to a different
form of group: the Macy conferences on cybernetics, discussed in the chapters on
Wiener and McCulloch. He was a member of the core group at these conferences,
attending all ten conferences in the series and having a strong influence (along
with Margaret Mead) as a social scientist who took seriously the concept of
cybernetics as it unfolded. He had independently developed the concept of positive feedback, but the idea of negative feedback, and the general framework of
cybernetic ideas, was also of great importance to him. He later referred to the
Macy conferences as "one of the great events of my life" (quoted by Brockman
2004) and there are frequent references to cybernetics in most of his subsequent
writings.

Bateson's contributions to knowledge are almost as hard to summarise as his
disciplinary or institutional connections. Some of these can be found in specific
ideas, which have been important in various fields: the anthropological concept of
schismogenesis (positive feedback loops leading to increasing destruction of relationships); the psycho-therapeutic concept of the *double bind* (patterns of interaction where people are required to behave in two mutually incompatible ways
simultaneously); and the concept of *levels of learning* (observing that some forms
of learning are at a higher logical level than others, and form various ways of learning how to learn). To these we can add phrases which are widely quoted, such as
his definition of information as the "difference that makes a difference" (G. Bateson
1972, p. 453) and his use of the phrase (borrowed from Alfred Korzybski) that "the
map is not the territory" (G. Bateson 1972, p. 449). As Mead (1977, p. 171) summarised these ideas, they "have all been about relationships between individuals or
groups of individuals, elaborated and stylized by experience or culture". These are
important ideas, and they have had a significant impact – the concept of the double
bind was the foundation for the field of family systems therapy, and that of levels
of learning has directly contributed to organisational learning via the work of
Argyris and Schön.

However, if we were to take these concepts alone as an indicator of Bateson's thinking or his impact, we would lose most of its essence. In the final decade of his life, Bateson came to realise that in fact all his ideas were closely linked – that he "had not been merely blundering from field to field but had been struggling to develop a way of thinking that would be transferable, systematically, from one subject matter to another" (M.C. Bateson 2004, p. 50). In 1970, he gave the annual Korzybski lecture under the title "Form, Substance and Difference". This forms the most concise description of his thought as a whole, and our extract is taken from it. Later he wrote that in preparing this lecture (G. Bateson 1972, p. xvi):

> I found that in my work with primitive peoples, schizophrenia, biological symmetry, and in my discontent with the conventional theories of evolution and learning, I had identified a widely scattered set of bench marks or points of reference from which a new scientific territory could be defined.

What was the nature of this territory? It had several aspects, summed up in his conception of an "ecology of mind": the nature of information, the nature of mind and the nature of relationships between and among these two:

1. In the first of these aspects, he was concerned with issues of epistemology, which for him had become corrupted by centuries of Cartesian dualism with its split between the physical and the mental, and which needed to be reformed around the unity of these.
2. In the second aspect, Bateson was concerned with issues of cognition, which he viewed as a fundamental process in nature, spread across animals as much as humans, and even in humans not confined to events occurring in the brain.
3. In the third aspect, Bateson was concerned with the nature of relationship, of the patterns between mental and physical processes in different parts of nature (in referring to this as an ecology, he was writing as a biologist, and using the term to refer to a set of interacting entities in an environment, rather than the popular use of ecology to refer to issues around the survival of the natural environment).

This last aspect was summed up in his phrase "the pattern which connects". In his book *Mind and Nature* (G. Bateson 1979) this concept was used to explore the patterns which connect all living creatures – that is, the relationship between their similarities and differences. This pattern, he observed, has two major features – first, it is a 'metapattern', that is to say a pattern of patterns, which exists at a higher level of abstraction than simply the immediate similarities and differences between species; and second, it is dynamic rather than static – the relationships are constantly changing, forming "a dance of interacting parts only secondarily pegged down by various sorts of physical limits" (G. Bateson 1979, p. 13). As an illustration of the importance of relationships, he liked when giving talks to ask audiences to look at their hands and observe that as well as having five fingers, they could just as well be said to have four *relations between fingers*, and that this perspective was just as useful as the conventional one.

The range of different concepts that Bateson was able to draw patterns between in this way was quite dizzying, as described by Keesing (1974, p. 370): "What form of madness is it to see as similarly pattern the axial symmetry of marine organisms and Iatmul initiatory grades, or patterns of armament races and falling in love, or leaves and sentences, or mother-child interactions and a muddled telephone exchange, or the play of otters and Russell's Theory of Logical Types?" All these situations were fundamental to Bateson's interests – but so were the work of William Blake, the biblical Book of Job, the behaviour of people with schizophrenia, and the nature of thought and mind.

Bateson's eclectic mix of interests and his marginality led to a curious phenomenon during his life which has continued posthumously – he has been both lionized and ignored. As a reviewer of one of his books put it, "many who had personal knowledge of him speak of Bateson in terms of 'greatness', 'originality', 'distinction', 'uniqueness', and so on. ... And yet the corpus of his writing has had remarkably little impact beyond the range of a small coterie of devotees" (Nash 1981, pp. 409–410). As we have already shown, individual parts of his writing have had considerable impact upon a range of fields, but the whole pattern of his work has taken a long time to be understood and appreciated. There are some signs that this is happening – the centenary of his birth in 2004 led to a number of conferences and publications that brought together his work as a whole – but it is still a work in progress.

In the final decade of his life, Bateson's work took on a new focus. In 1968, Bateson wrote that "it may well be that consciousness contains systematic distortions of view which, when implemented by modern technology, become destructive of the balances between man, his society, and his ecosystem" (G. Bateson 1972, p. 440). This formed the basis of a conference he organised on the "Effects of Conscious Purpose on Human Adaptation" (M.C. Bateson 1972). Through this conference, Bateson came to the conclusion that the danger of environmental destruction – the risks of which were by then already apparent – arose from the deep-seated Western worldview that it is possible to make a separation between the organism, or species, and its environment.

This is a call to a new form of epistemology, which understands humanity within its environment, and Bateson's answer to it lay within his conception of an ecology of mind. As Mary Catherine Bateson (2000, p. xiv) wrote, "Bateson was haunted in his last years by a sense of urgency, a sense that the narrow definition of human purposes, reinforced by technology, would lead to irreversible disasters, and that only a better epistemology could save us". Perhaps it is only now, as ecological disaster becomes more and more pressing, that Bateson's originality and importance can begin to be fully appreciated.

Reading from G. Bateson's work

Bateson, G. (1972) *Steps to an Ecology of Mind*, pp. 448–465. With kind permission University of Chicago Press and Courtesy of the Institute for Intercultural Studies, Inc., New York.

We can now say – or at any rate, can begin to say – what we think a mind is. In the next 20 years there will be other ways of saying it and, because the discoveries are new, I can only give you my personal version. The old versions are surely wrong, but which of the revised pictures will survive, we do not know.

Let us start from the evolutionary side. It is now empirically clear that Darwinian evolutionary theory contained a very great error in its identification of the unit of survival under natural selection. The unit which was believed to be crucial and around which the theory was set up was either the breeding individual or the family line or the subspecies or some similar homogeneous set of conspecifics. Now I suggest that the last 100 years have demonstrated empirically that if an organism or aggregate of organisms sets to work with a focus on its own survival and thinks that that is the way to select its adaptive moves, its "progress" ends up with a destroyed environment. If the organism ends up destroying its environment, it has in fact destroyed itself. And we may very easily see this process carried to its ultimate *reductio ad absurdum* in the next 20 years. The unit of survival is not the breeding organism, or the family line, or the society.

The old unit has already been partly corrected by the population geneticists. They have insisted that the evolutionary unit is, in fact, not homogeneous. A wild population of any species consists always of individuals whose genetic constitution varies widely. In other words, potentiality and readiness for change is already built into the survival unit. The heterogeneity of the wild population is already one-half of that trial-and-error system which is necessary for dealing with environment.

The artificially homogenized populations of man's domestic animals and plants are scarcely fit for survival.

And today a further correction of the unit is necessary. The flexible environment must also be included along with the flexible organism because, as I have already said, the organism which destroys its environment destroys itself. The unit of survival is a flexible organism-in-its-environment.

Now, let me leave evolution for a moment to consider what is the unit of mind. Let us go back to the map and the territory and ask: "What is it in the territory that gets onto the map?" We know the territory does not get onto the map. That is the central point about which we here are all agreed. Now, if the territory were uniform, nothing would get onto the map except its boundaries, which are the points at which it ceases to be uniform against some larger matrix. What gets onto the map, in fact, is *difference*, be it a difference in altitude, a difference in vegetation, a difference in population structure, difference in surface, or whatever. Differences are the things that get onto a map.

But what is a difference? A difference is a very peculiar and obscure concept. It is certainly not a thing or an event. This piece of paper is different from the wood of this lectern. There are many differences between them – of color, texture, shape, etc. But if we start to ask about the localization of those differences, we get into trouble. Obviously the difference between the paper and the wood is not in the paper; it is obviously not in the wood; it is obviously not in the space between them, and it is obviously not in the time between them. (Difference which occurs across time is what we call "change".)

A difference, then, is an abstract matter.

In the hard sciences, effects are, in general, caused by rather concrete conditions or events – impacts, forces, and so forth. But when you enter the world of communication, organization, etc., you leave behind that whole world in which effects are brought about by forces and impacts and energy exchange. You enter a world in which "effects" – and I am not sure one should still use the same word – are brought about by *differences*. That is, they are brought about by the sort of "thing" that gets onto the map from the territory. This is difference.

Difference travels from the wood and paper into my retina. It then gets picked up and worked on by this fancy piece of computing machinery in my head.

The whole energy relation is different. In the world of mind, nothing – that which is *not* – can be a cause. In the hard sciences, we ask for causes and we expect them to exist and be "real". But remember that zero is different from one, and because zero is different from one, zero can be a cause in the psychological world, the world of communication. The letter which you do not write can get an angry reply; and the income tax form which you do not fill in can trigger the Internal Revenue boys into energetic action, because they, too, have their breakfast, lunch, tea, and dinner and can react with energy which they derive from their metabolism. The letter which never existed is no source of energy.

It follows, of course, that we must change our whole way of thinking about mental and communicational process. The ordinary analogies of energy theory which people borrow from the hard sciences to provide a conceptual frame upon which they try to build theories about psychology and behavior – that entire Procrustean structure – is non-sense. It is in error.

I suggest to you, now, that the word "idea", in its most elementary sense, is synonymous with "difference". Kant, in the *Critique of Judgment* – if I understand him correctly – asserts that the most elementary aesthetic act is the selection of a fact. He argues that in a piece of chalk there are an infinite number of potential facts. The *Ding an sich*, the piece of chalk, can never enter into communication or mental process because of this infinitude. The sensory receptors cannot accept it; they filter it out. What they do is to select certain *facts* out of the piece of chalk, which then become, in modern terminology, information.

I suggest that Kant's statement can be modified to say that there is an infinite number of *differences* around and within the piece of chalk. There are differences between the chalk and the rest of the universe, between the chalk and the sun or the moon. And within the piece of chalk, there is for every molecule an infinite number of differences between its location and the locations in which it *might* have been. Of this infinitude, we select a very limited number, which become information. In fact, what we mean by information – the elementary unit of information – is a *difference which makes a difference*, and it is able to make a difference because the neural pathways along which it travels and is continually transformed are themselves provided with energy. The pathways are ready to be triggered. We may even say that the question is already implicit in them.

There is, however, an important contrast between most of the pathways of information inside the body and most of the pathways outside it. The differences between the paper and the wood are first transformed into differences in the propagation of light or sound, and travel in this form to my sensory end organs. The first part of their journey is energized in the ordinary hard-science way, from "behind".

But when the differences enter my body by triggering an end organ, this type of travel is replaced by travel which is energized at every step by the metabolic energy latent in the protoplasm which *receives* the difference, recreates or transforms it, and passes it on.

When I strike the head of a nail with a hammer, an impulse is transmitted to its point. But it is a semantic error, a misleading metaphor, to say that what travels in an axon is an "impulse". It could correctly be called "news of a difference".

Be that as it may, this contrast between internal and external pathways is not absolute. Exceptions occur on both sides of the line. Some external chains of events are energized by relays, and some chains of events internal to the body are energized from "behind". Notably, the mechanical interaction of muscles can be used as a computational model.

In spite of these exceptions, it is still broadly true that the coding and transmission of differences outside the body is very different from the coding and transmission inside, and this difference must be mentioned because it can lead us into error. We commonly think of the external "physical world" as somehow separate from an internal "mental world". I believe that this division is based on the contrast in coding and transmission inside and outside the body.

The mental world – the mind – the world of information processing – is not limited by the skin.

References

Bateson, G. (1972). *Steps to an ecology of mind*. Toronto: Chandler.

Bateson, G. (1979). *Mind and nature: a necessary unity*. New York: Dutton.

Bateson, M. C. (1972). *Our own metaphor: A personal account of a conference on the effects of conscious purpose on human adaptation*. New York: Knopf.

Bateson, M. C. (2000). Foreword. In G. Bateson (Ed.), *Steps to an ecology of mind*, revised edition (pp. vii–xv). Chicago: University of Chicago Press.

Bateson, M. C. (2004). *Willing to learn: Passages of personal discovery*. Hanover, NH: Steerforth Press.

Brockman, J. (2004). Gregory Bateson: The Centennial 1904–2004. *Edge* 149. http://www.edge.org/documents/archive/edge149.html Accessed 13 Jan 2009.

Keesing, R. M. (1974). Review of *Steps to an ecology of mind. American Anthropologist, 76*(2), 370–372.

Lipset, D. (2005). Author and hero – rereading Gregory Bateson: The legacy of a scientist. *Anthropological Quarterly, 78*(4), 899–914.

Mead, M. (1977). End linkage: A tool for cross-cultural analysis. In J. Brockman (Ed.), *About Bateson* (pp. 169–231). New York: E.P. Dutton.

Nash, P. (1981). Connection and separation: Bateson's double bind. *Journal of Applied Behavioral Science, 17*(3), 409–417.

Toulmin, S. (1984). The evolution of Margaret Mead. *New York Review of Books, 31*(19), 3–9.

Chapter 2
Norbert Wiener

Norbert Wiener was a unique personality, a larger-than-life character famous for his very wide interests, extremely incisive mind and personal warmth, but also for his absent-mindedness, low self-esteem, and severe mood-swings. He was born in midwestern USA (Missouri) in 1894 to a Jewish family – his father had emigrated from Russia and his mother from Germany. Although the family were descended from the great twelfth century philosopher Moses Maimonedes, their Jewishness was hidden from Wiener during his childhood, due to the anti-semitism of the times, and he practised no religion until late in life.

Wiener was a child prodigy: he learned his alphabet at 18 months, obtained his bachelors degree at age 14 (from Tufts), and his PhD at age 18 (from Harvard). This was partly due to his own great ability, but also to the teaching regime of his father. Leo Wiener insisted on absolute correctness in all of young Norbert's work, responding indifferently to correct answers but with great anger to errors. When Norbert Wiener married in 1926, it was with much relief at gaining freedom from his father (Conway and Siegelman, 2005).

After postdoctoral work in Europe and a number of short-term jobs (many not judged suitable for Norbert by his father), Wiener took up a post as an instructor at the Massachusetts Institute of Technology (MIT) in 1919. He stayed at MIT for the rest of his life, becoming a full professor in 1931.

At MIT, Wiener was famous as a walker. He would walk around the corridors endlessly, talking to everyone he met (regardless of status or academic discipline), or absorbed in his own thoughts. His route was known as the *Wienerweg* (the German *weg* means walk or route) and he always took the path he insisted upon, regardless of what else was happening on it. Many anecdotes are told of Wiener's insistence on sticking to his route and his absent-mindedness. In one story, recounted by Heims (1980) among others, Wiener was said to have met a student around midday. After a long conversation, Wiener asked the student "can you tell me which way I was walking when we met – towards the canteen or away from it?" It was only the student's response that enabled Wiener to remember whether or not he had yet had lunch.

He was a traveller in many other ways. He was a visiting scholar at a number of universities outside his country, mostly notably in Cambridge (England), Göttingen (Germany) and Mexico City – in the 1920s in particular his mathematical work was

M. Ramage and K. Shipp, *Systems Thinkers,*   19
© The Open University 2009. Published in association with Springer-Verlag London Limited

better appreciated in Europe than in the United States. He also made significant academic visits to China, Russia and India, with big impacts on scientific work in each country. Indeed he died on one of these visits, of a heart attack on the steps of the Royal Institute of Technology, Stockholm, in 1964.

He also was an intellectual traveller. Although he always saw himself as a mathematician, he forged close working links with biologists, physiologists, engineers and social scientists. Two of his most important collaborations were with biologists, Arturo Rosenbleuth and Warren McCulloch, and these led directly to the founding of cybernetics. He later quarrelled with McCulloch for personal reasons, and never spoke to him again despite both working at MIT.

As a summary of Wiener's personality, one of his biographers (who worked with him on his later mathematical work) describes him as:

> Proverbially absent-minded, amusingly quirkish and idiosyncratic, he was fundamentally a gentle and humane soul. He was, however, given to recurrent manifestations of petulance, egoism, emotional instability, irrational insecurity and anxiety. His moods could swing from euphoria to gloom or vice versa on slight provocation (Masani 1990, p. 16)

Wiener's work can be approximately split into three areas: his mathematical work, his work in cybernetics, and his work as a social and political commentator, and we shall discuss each of these in turn.

It is tempting to think of Wiener largely as a cybernetician. This was not his own self-image, and indeed for the majority of his time at MIT, he was attached to the Department of Mathematics. Wiener's doctoral work was an extension of the logic of Bertrand Russell, then recently published in the great *Principia Mathematica* (1911). Following his doctorate, and still less than 20 years old, Wiener obtained a two year fellowship from Harvard to do postdoctoral work in England and Germany, with some of the great pure mathematical minds of his time – Russell himself and G.H. Hardy in Cambridge, and David Hilbert in Göttingen.

His key mathematical work, however, was in the field of applied mathematics, in which area he made many important contributions in the 1920s and 1930s. Perhaps most notable was his work in extending the theories of Lebesgue, Gibbs and Einstein to construct a technique for the statistical analysis of wave patterns, still known as the Wiener measure. He began this work in relation to Brownian motion (the semi-random movement of particles), leading ultimately to the statistical analysis of control systems and of communication which would be so important in the development of cybernetics. This work was also a major contributor to the theory of stochastic process, the foundation of modern probability theory.

Wiener's contribution to the founding of cybernetics cannot be overestimated, although many others played a part as well. He introduced the word 'cybernetics', a coinage from the Greek *kubernētēs*, 'steersman' (the navigator of a ship), as a term for "the entire field of control and communication theory, whether in the machine or in the animal" (Wiener 1948, p. 11). The term was also intended to refer back to the 'governor', the portion of an engine that ensures its effective operation (the word 'governor' is derived from a Latinized form of *kubernētēs*, and indeed Ampère used the term *cybernétique* to describe a theory of government in the nineteenth century, although Wiener was unaware of this when he coined the modern term). Through the publication of his book *Cybernetics* (1948) and the more popularly-focused *The Human Use of Human Beings* (1950), the concept became known rapidly to a wide public audience.

Wiener's definition of cybernetics contains two important paired concepts. He was clear that control (in physiological and engineering terms) and communication were highly related phenomena, and could be expressed in terms of *feedback*. He wrote that control and communication "centred not around the technique of electrical engineering but around the much more fundamental notion of the *message*, whether this should be transmitted by electrical, mechanical, or nervous means. The message is a discrete or continuous sequence of measurable events distributed in time" (Wiener 1948, p. 8). This concept of the message was crucial to the early development of communications theory, formalised on similar lines by Shannon and Weaver (1949), as was Wiener's definition of *information* as "a measure of [the] degree of organization" of a system (Wiener 1948, p. 11) and the mathematical negative of the entropy of that system – which he referred to as *negentropy*. Wiener regarded negative feedback as much more important and useful than positive feedback, leading to stability and effective control – he saw positive feedback as dangerous and unstable.

The other pair of concepts in Wiener's definition of cybernetics were the machine and the animal. In the 1930s and early 1940s, Wiener had conducted two major research projects – with Arturo Rosenbleuth on feedback within human and animal physiology; and with Julian Bigelow on the building of control systems for anti-aircraft weaponry (during World War II), again based on feedback principles. Rosenbleuth et al. (1943) put these projects together with the statement that "all purposeful behaviour may be considered to require negative feedback" (p. 19). This article is generally considered the founding document of cybernetics, sometimes along with an article by McCulloch and Pitts (1943), discussed in the chapter on McCulloch.

The parallel between human and machine activities was particularly important to the development of digital computers, then in its early stages. For this reason, cybernetics became rapidly identified in the public mind with these new technologies – hence the modern use of the term 'cyber' in compound words such as cyberspace. As Hayles (1999, p. 7) has written, "humans were to be seen primarily as information-processing entities who are *essentially* similar to intelligent machines". The equating of human and machine activities was to prove extremely important in a wide range of disciplines (including computing, psychology and management among others) but then was an almost entirely new concept, and it was the field of cybernetics which played a big part in making the concept widely known.

Wiener's final crucial contribution to cybernetics was his central role in the Macy conferences. This conference series – 10 two-day conferences from 1946 to 1953 – is frequently regarded as the founding event of cybernetics. Wiener was "the dominant figure at the conference series, in his role as brilliant originator of ideas and enfant terrible" (Heims 1980, p. 206). These conferences, organised and chaired by Warren McCulloch, at first had the rather clumsy (if descriptive) title of the Conference for Circular Causal and Feedback Mechanisms in Biological and

Social Systems. This title in itself expresses Wiener's range of concerns very clearly, and his role as the conceptual founding father of the conferences and the field. This role became even clearer at the sixth Macy conference (in 1949) when, at the suggestion of Heinz von Foerster, the title of the conference series was amended to the Conference on Cybernetics, a decision that moved Wiener greatly (von Foerster and Poersken 2002, p. 136).

Von Foerster's later introduction of the term 'second-order cybernetics' – the inclusion of the observer as a component of the cybernetic system under study – is often taken to exclude Wiener, to cast him on the 'wrong' side of a conceptual divide. This is not accurate, as a number of commentators have discussed. In a conversation with Gregory Bateson and Margaret Mead (both participants in the Macy conferences), discussing an input-output model with a box that encloses the feedback loops of a cybernetic system, Brand (1976) observed that "the engineer is outside the box ... and Wiener is inside the box" – that is, considering himself to be part of the system. Bernard-Weil (1994) has similarly argued that a number of the concepts key to second-order cybernetics, such as autonomy, dialogue and self-organization, can be found in Wiener's work, albeit not as central concerns.

Wiener's technical work in cybernetics continued long after the end of the Macy conferences. Although he refused to accept government or military research funding, he was involved in significant work on prosthetics (hearing aids and artificial arms) which fitted closely with his conception of cybernetics. However, in the final years of his life, he was most prominent in spreading the ideas of cybernetics and in warning about its impact upon society.

Wiener devoted much of his time in the last 20 years of his life to discussing the social and political implications of cybernetics, automation and the modern role of science. Although he had been actively involved in military research during World War II, he refused to co-operate with military work after the war, writing in a public statement that "the experience of the scientists who have worked on the atomic bomb has indicated that in any investigation of this kind the scientist ends by putting unlimited powers in the hands of the people whom he is least inclined to trust with their use" (Wiener 1947). From that point on, Wiener also refused to receive funding from military (and later government) sources and to participate in conferences sponsored by the military. The theme was one he would return to in many places; in the introduction to *Cybernetics*, he wrote that:

> Those of us who have contributed to the new science of cybernetics thus stand in a moral position which is, to say the least, not very comfortable. We have contributed to the initiation of a new science which, as I have said, embraces technical developments with great possibilities for good and for evil. We can only hand it over into the world that exists about us, and this is the world of Belsen and Hiroshima. (Wiener 1948, p. 28)

This stance gained him considerable public respect, but was a difficult one to take in the US of the late 1940s and early 1950s – not least because he was based at MIT, the bulk of whose research was funded by the military in that time. In the American political purges of the early 1950s led by Senator Joseph McCarthy, Wiener was investigated on a number of occasions by the FBI (partly for his stance on military funding and the role of cybernetics, partly for his friendship with eminent scientists who had a past involvement as Communists). Nonetheless, his public profile as an independent intellectual, separate from political processes, protected him and he escaped any persecution.

He also commented frequently on the effects of cybernetics upon the fabric of society. His book *The Human Use of Human Beings* (Wiener 1954), from which our reading is taken, describes the nature of the forthcoming cybernetic developments for a popular audience but also tempers them with a moral humanism, continuing his view that technologies can never be neutral. In his late work, he illustrated this by recounting stories about the literal-mindedness of technology (such as the *Sorcerer's Apprentice* with its many-dividing broom and the *Arabian Nights* tale of the genie released from captivity who vows to destroy its releaser). As Hayles (1999, p. 7) has written, although he was not always successful in his goal:

> For Wiener, cybernetics was a means to extend liberal humanism, not subvert it. The point was less to show that man was a machine than to demonstrate that a machine could function like a man.

Reading from Wiener's work

In giving the definition of Cybernetics in the original book (Wiener 1948), I classed communication and control together. Why did I do this? When I communicate with another person, I impart a message to him, and when he communicates back with me he returns a related message which contains information primarily accessible to him and not to me. When I control the actions of another person, I communicate a message to him, and although this message is in the imperative mood, the technique of communication does not differ from that of a message of fact. Furthermore, if my control is to be effective I must take cognizance of any messages from him which may indicate that the order is understood and has been obeyed.

It is the thesis of this book that society can only be understood through a study of the messages and the communication facilities which belong to it; and that in the future development of these messages and communication facilities, messages between man and machines, between machines and man, and between machine and machine, are destined to play an ever-increasing part.

When I give an order to a machine, the situation is not essentially different from that which arises when I give an order to a person. In other words, as far as my consciousness goes I am aware of the order that has gone out and of the signal of compliance that has come back. To me, personally, the fact that the signal in its intermediate stages has gone through a machine rather than through a person is irrelevant and does not in any case greatly change my relation to the signal. Thus the theory of control in engineering, whether human or animal or mechanical, is a chapter in the theory of messages.

Naturally there are detailed differences in messages and in problems of control, not only between a living organism and a machine, but within each narrower class of beings. It is the purpose of Cybernetics to develop a language and techniques that will enable us indeed to attack the problem of control and communication in general, but also to find the proper repertory of ideas and techniques to classify their particular manifestations under certain concepts.

The commands through which we exercise our control over our environment are a kind of information which we impart to it. Like any form of information, these commands are subject to disorganization in transit. They generally come through in less coherent fashion and certainly not more coherently than they were sent. In control and communication we are always fighting nature's tendency to degrade the organized and to destroy the meaningful; the tendency, as Gibbs has shown us, for entropy to increase.

Much of this book concerns the limits of communication within and among individuals. Man is immersed in a world which he perceives through his sense organs. Information. that he receives is coordinated through his brain and nervous system until, after the proper process of storage, collation, and selection, it emerges through effector organs, generally his muscles. These in turn act on the external world, and also react on the central nervous system through receptor organs such as the end organs of kinaesthesia; and the information received by the kinaesthetic organs is combined with his already accumulated store of information to influence future action.

Information is a name for the content of what is exchanged with the outer world as we adjust to it, and make our adjustment felt upon it. The process of receiving and of using information is the process of our adjusting to the contingencies of the outer environment, and of our living effectively within that environment. The needs and the complexity of modern life make greater demands on this process of information than ever before, and our press, our museums, our scientific laboratories, our universities, our libraries and textbooks, are obliged to meet the needs of this process or fail in their purpose. To live effectively is to live with adequate information. Thus, communication and control belong to the essence of man's inner life, even as they belong to his life in society.

[...]

For any machine subject to a varied external environment to act effectively it is necessary that information concerning the results of its own action be furnished to it as part of the information on which it must continue to act. For example, if we are running an elevator, it is not enough to open the outside door because the orders we have given should make the elevator be at that door at the time we open it. It is important that the release for opening the door be dependent on the fact that the elevator is actually at the door; otherwise something might have detained it, and the passenger might step into the empty shaft. This control of a machine on the basis of its *actual* performance rather than its *expected* performance is known as feedback, and involves sensory members which are actuated by motor members and perform the function of *tell-tales* or *monitors* – that is, of elements which indicate a performance. It is the function of these mechanisms to control the mechanical tendency toward disorganization; in other words, to produce a temporary and local reversal of the normal direction of entropy.

I have just mentioned the elevator as an example of feedback. There are other cases where the importance of feedback is even more apparent. For example, a gun-pointer takes information from his instruments of observation, and conveys it to the gun, so that the latter will point in such a direction that the missile will pass through the moving target at a certain time. Now, the gun itself must be used under all conditions of weather. In some of these the grease is warm, and the gun swings easily and rapidly. Under other conditions the grease is frozen or mixed with sand, and the gun is slow to answer the orders given to it. If these orders are reinforced by an extra push given when the gun fails to respond easily to the orders and lags behind them, then the error of the gun-pointer will be decreased. To obtain a performance as uniform as possible, it is customary to put into the gun a control feedback element which reads the lag of the gun behind the position it should have according to the orders given it, and which uses this difference to give the gun an extra push.

It is true that precautions must be taken so that the push is not too hard, for if it is, the gun will swing past its proper position, and will have to be pulled back in a series of oscillations, which may well become wider and wider, and lead to a disastrous instability. If the feedback system is itself controlled – if, in other words, its own entropic tendencies are checked by still other controlling mechanisms – and kept within limits sufficiently stringent, this will not occur, and the existence of the feedback will increase the stability of performance of the gun. In other words, the performance will become less dependent on the frictional load; or what is the same thing, on the drag created by the stiffness of the grease.

Something very similar to this occurs in human action. If I pick up my cigar, I do not will to move any specific muscles. Indeed in many cases, I do not know what those muscles are. What I do is to turn into action a certain feedback mechanism; namely, a reflex in which the amount by which I have yet failed to pick up the cigar is turned into a new and increased order to the lagging muscles, whichever they may be. In this way, a fairly uniform voluntary command will enable the same task to be performed from widely varying initial positions, and irrespective of the decrease of contraction due to fatigue of the muscles. Similarly, when I drive a car, I do not follow out a series of commands dependent simply on a mental image of the road and the task I am doing. If I find the car swerving too much to the right, that causes me to pull it to the left. This depends on the actual performance of the car, and not simply on the road; and it allows me to drive with nearly equal efficiency a light Austin or a heavy truck, without having formed separate habits for the driving of the two. [...]

It is my thesis that the physical functioning of the living individual and the operation of some of the newer communication machines are precisely parallel in their analogous attempts to control entropy through feedback. Both of them have sensory receptors as one stage in their cycle of operation: that is, in both of them there exists a special apparatus for collecting information from the outer world at low energy levels, and for making it available in the operation of the individual or of the machine. In both cases these external messages are not taken *neat*, but through the internal transforming powers of the apparatus, whether it be alive or dead. The information is then turned into a new form available for the further stages of performance. In both the animal and the machine this performance is made to be effective on the outer world. In both of them, their *performed* action on the outer world, and not merely their *intended* action, is reported back to the central regula-tory apparatus. This complex of behaviour is ignored by the average man, and in particular does not play the role that it should in our habitual analysis of society; for just as individual physical responses may be seen from this point of view, so may the organic responses of society itself. I do not mean that the sociologist is unaware of the existence and complex nature of communications in society, but until recently he has tended to overlook the extent to which they are the cement which binds its fabric together.

References

Bernard-Weil, E. (1994). The presence of Norbert Wiener in both order cybernetics. *Kybernetes*, *23*(6/7), 133–143.

Brand, S. (1976). For God's sake, Margaret: Conversation with Gregory Bateson and Margaret Mead. *CoEvolution Quarterly*, *10*, 32–44.

Conway, F., & Siegelman, J. (2005). *Dark hero of the information age: In search of Norbert Wiener, the father of cybernetics*. New York: Basic Books.

Hayles, N. K. (1999). *How we became posthuman: Virtual bodies in cybernetics, literature, and informatics*. Chicago: University of Chicago Press.

Heims, S. J. (1980). *John von Neumann and Norbert Wiener: From mathematics to the tech-nologies of life and death*. Cambridge, MA: MIT Press.

Masani, P. R. (1990). *Norbert Wiener, 1894–1964*. Basel, Switzerland: Birkhäuser Verlag.

McCulloch, W. S., & Pitts, W. (1943). A logical calculus of the ideas immanent in nervous activity. *Bulletin of Mathematical Biophysics*, *5*, 115–133.

Rosenbleuth, A., Wiener, N., Bigelow, J. (1943). Behavior, purpose and teleology. *Philosophy of Science*, *10*(1), 18–24.

Shannon, C. E., & Weaver, W. (1949). *The mathematical theory of communication*. Urbana, IL: University of Illinois Press.

Von Foerster, H., & Poersken, B. (2002). *Understanding systems: Conversations on epistemology and ethics*. Heidelberg, Germany: Carl-Auer-Systeme Verlag.

Wiener, N. (1947). A scientist rebels. *Atlantic Monthly*, *179*: 46.

Wiener, N. (1948). *Cybernetics: or control and communication in the animal and the machine*. Cambridge, MA: MIT Press.

Wiener, N. (1954). *The Human use of human beings: Cybernetics and society* (revised edition). Boston: Houghton Mifflin.

Chapter 3
Warren McCulloch

Warren McCulloch resembled an Old Testament prophet – he had a long beard, bright and intense eyes, great personal warmth but also great passion. Indeed Gregory Bateson (1991, p. 225) describes him as "like Moses, a leader who could and did bring us to the edge of the promised land, where he himself could never enter". His prophetic status can also be seen in a remark he frequently made, "Don't bite my finger, look where I am pointing" (quoted by Seymour Papert, introduction to McCulloch 1965, p. xxviii).

In very many ways McCulloch was, as Dupuy (2000, p. 112) says, "the leading figure of the cybernetics movement". Although the term 'cybernetics' was Wiener's, it was McCulloch who organised and chaired the celebrated Macy conferences, McCulloch who published the first logical model of the mind, and McCulloch who supported and acted as mentor to many of the key later figures of cybernetics. Yet as Dupuy (p. 111) also says, "McCulloch seems almost to have faded from view: even in the fields in which he made lasting contributions, many of the heirs to his legacy are unaware even of his name". By looking at McCulloch's intellectual and personal stances, we can learn just as much about the origins of cybernetics as by looking at those of Wiener. As McCulloch (1974, p. 13) characterised the distinction between the two, "he was a roundhead; I, a cavalier!" (The analogy is with the competing sides in the English Civil War – McCulloch was describing himself as flamboyant and easy-going, while Wiener was intense and serious.)

Warren Sturgis McCulloch was born in 1898 in New Jersey, and died in 1969. Although American himself, his family had Scottish roots, and he saw this connection as important to his personality. His initial training was in philosophy, psychology, logic and neurophysiology. It was in this last field – the study of the physiology of the nervous system – that he made his first contributions, working at Yale on the cerebral cortex of monkeys with the psychiatrist Dusser de Barenne, and from 1941 in the psychiatry department of University of Illinois. His core intellectual concern was a philosophical one, which he described in an anecdote about a conversation with an early mentor at the age of 19:

> That winter Rufus Jones called me in. "Warren," said he, "what is thee going to be?" And I said, "I don't know." "And what is thee going to do?" And again I said, "I have no idea; but there is one question I would like to answer: What is a number, that a man may know

it, and a man, that he may know a number?" He smiled and said, "Friend, thee will be busy as long as thee lives." I have been. (McCulloch 1965, p. 2)

This was indeed McCulloch's preoccupation for the whole of his life. He frequently characterised his work as 'experimental epistemology', the study of the nature of knowledge through understanding the nature of the brain within which it resides. He conducted this work at Illinois for ten years, moving to MIT's Research Laboratory for Electronics in 1952. Although a close colleague of Wiener's in the 1940s while cybernetics was becoming established, the two had fallen out by the time he moved to MIT, and they did not work together there. McCulloch's dedication to his research and frustration with the administrative aspects of academia can be seen in the fact that he was a full professor at Illinois, but in moving to MIT became simply a research associate, albeit head of a research group.

In other ways, McCulloch can be described as an early founder of cognitive science and the related field of artificial intelligence. We can see this in two ways.

First, he did significant work on the relationship between machines and minds – the process that Dupuy (2000), in the title of his book, calls the "mechanization of mind". A view that minds and machines are equivalent (now fairly commonplace but then a radical departure from a view of mind as something quite separate from physical reality) was at the core of McCulloch's thinking. In 1955 he wrote that "everything we learn of organisms leads us to conclude not merely that they are analogous to machines, but that they are machines. Man-made machines are not brains, but brains are a very ill-understood variety of computing machines" (McCulloch 1965, p. 163).

Second, McCulloch, working with Walter Pitts, constructed a logical model of the nature of mental activity, and in particular the computational behaviour of the neuron (McCulloch and Pitts 1943). This article proved important in the history of artificial intelligence (AI) research, as one of the first computational models of mind, although AI research took a different path for many years and it was not until the 1980s that neural networks became an important area within AI. By the time AI research became prominent, cybernetics was not very much in vogue and the connection with McCulloch was not stressed. John McCarthy, who coined the term 'artificial intelligence' in 1955, has written that "one of the reasons for inventing the term 'artificial intelligence' was to escape association with 'cybernetics'" (McCarthy 1988, p. 227).

As a person he was warm, energetic, and highly supportive of others – "the most loose and spontaneous, least machinelike of men" (Heims 1991, p. 39). He was famous for his bohemian lifestyle, with large summer gatherings of family, colleagues and friends at his farm in Connecticut. At the farm he "undertook crazy schemes – from constructing a sizable dam (referred to as a 'pond'), to building a quasi-cathedral (referred to as a 'barn')" (Beer 1999, p. 434). Heims relates that "in conversation he, more than most scientists, looked directly at the person talking with him, and his whole face became animated, his intense, blue eyes lighting up in discussion of technical points of any scientific problem or idea that caught his imagination" (1991, p. 38).

McCulloch was a very generous man, both in practical terms (helping out students and young colleagues financially and by having them stay at his house) and as an intellectual mentor. The list of younger colleagues who later described him as their mentor is a long one, and many important names are reflected there. As well as Walter Pitts, his close collaborator and almost an adopted son, the most notable people in terms of their later work were Heinz von Foerster, Gregory Bateson, Stafford Beer and Stuart Kauffman. McCulloch's influence can be strongly seen on the work of all four of these thinkers and through them on both cybernetics and complexity theory.

Despite this deep personal warmth, the mechanistic approach – the close analogy between humans and machines – remained important to McCulloch throughout his life. More than once, he made comparisons between machines and humans which demonstrated a certain preference for machines. In the Hixon symposium in 1948, the founding conference of cognitive science, he used the vivid image that by contrasting with early work in computing "for us in the biological sciences – or at least, in psychiatry – we are presented with an alien, or enemy's, machine. We do not know what the machine is supposed to do and certainly we have no blueprint of it" (Jeffress 1951, p. 32). Late in his life, he put the contrast even more starkly, saying that "Man to my mind is about the nastiest, most destructive of all the animals. I don't see any reason, if he can evolve machines that can have more fun that he himself can, why they shouldn't take over, enslave us, quite happily. They might have a lot more fun. Invent better games than we ever did." (M.C. Bateson 1972, p. 226)

Notwithstanding McCulloch's mechanistic approach, it was as a result of his work that the relativist approach to cybernetics which became known as second-order cybernetics began to form. This was partly due to his influence on Heinz von Foerster (the founder of second-order cybernetics) and on Gregory Bateson (with his work on communication, paradox and the distributed nature of mind). But McCulloch's focus on experimental epistemology made it a possibility that his understanding of the nature of knowledge would shift with his results, and this in fact did happen with the paper "What the Frog's Eye Tells the Frog's Brain" (Lettvin et al. 1959). Although the experimental work for this paper was done by Jerome Lettvin and Humberto Maturana, it was conducted in McCulloch's laboratory, he discussed its ideas as the paper was written, and he appears as a co-author. The paper argues that "the eye speaks to the brain in a language already highly organized and interpreted, instead of transmitting some more or less accurate copy of the distribution of light on the receptors" (Lettvin et al. 1959) – the frog's eye is constructing a model of reality as it views objects rather than reflecting an existing reality to the brain. These results would later form a key part of Maturana's view of the biology of cognition.

Perhaps McCulloch's greatest contribution to cybernetics was institutional. He instigated and chaired all ten of the celebrated conferences on cybernetics funded by the Macy Foundation, running from 1946 to 1953. These are often associated with Norbert Wiener, but it was McCulloch who was at their core. The list of participants in the conferences is extraordinary: simply among the more famous

ones are Gregory Bateson, Alex Bavelas, Heinz von Foerster, Ralph Gerard, Kurt
Lewin, Margaret Mead and John von Neumann (with guests including Claude
Shannon and Wolfgang Köhler). It was McCulloch who held this group together.

He was a strong chair of the conferences, who "exercised considerable control
over who was allowed to speak and who was not" (Hayles 1999, p. 57). Indeed,
Bateson and Mead in a dialogue remarked that "McCulloch had a grand design
in his mind ... on how the shape of the conversation would run over five years –
what had to be said before what else had to be said. ... He was very autocratic."
(Brand 1976)

By McCulloch's account, the early conferences were very argumentative:
"The first five meetings were intolerable. Some participants left in tears, never
to return. We tried some sessions with and some without recording, but nothing
was printable. The smoke, the noise, the smell of battle are not printable"
(McCulloch 1974, p. 12). The conferences were to lead to the foundation of
more than one new discipline, and to a much greater understanding between
participants of the possibilities and limits of interdisciplinarity: "we have
learned to know one another a bit better, and to fight fair in our shirt sleeves"
(McCulloch at the final conference in 1953, quoted by Heims 1991, p. 277).
The conferences were celebrated even as they were happening, and were one of
the chief reasons for the public awareness of cybernetics as a new (and mysterious) enterprise.

Of course, the Macy conferences did not happen in an intellectual void. As
Heims (1991) discusses, it was no accident that they took place post-war, given the
strong emphasis on team-working among scientists during the war (and consequent
blurring of disciplinary boundaries). It was also a time in the United States of growing social and political conservatism, which made the social sciences vulnerable to
colonisation by perspectives from biology, physics and mathematics. One of the
ongoing arguments at the Macy conferences was between the new mechanistic
psychology and more human-centred approaches such as psychoanalysis and
Gestalt psychology, both of which McCulloch strongly disagreed with. As Kay
(2001, p. 593) puts it, "the particular configurations of [McCulloch's conceptual]
tools and the premises governing their use bore the unmistakable marks of a new,
postindustrial episteme: an emergent technoculture of communication, control, and
simulation".

McCulloch was a paradox: the humanist who advocated mechanism; the realist
whose work led to relativism. He had a fascinating blend of intellectual ideas, and
his influence lives on in very many ways. At the end of his life, he described himself as follows (M.C. Bateson 1972, p. 24):

> I expected to be a theologian. I got seduced by mathematics. I got interested in the
> epistemic problems of all science, particularly mathematics. I majored in philosophy,
> minored in psychology, went to medical school in order to get the workings of a
> machine called a brain. I've been at it ever since. I have lived among brilliant youngsters
> who keep turning up new ideas all the time. I am very happy, very puzzled, very
> hopeful.

Reading from McCulloch's work

McCulloch, W.S. (1951) "Why the Mind is in the Head", in Jeffress, L.A. (ed.) *Cerebral Mechanisms in Behavior*, New York: John Wiley, pp. 42–57.

As the industrial revolution concludes in bigger and better bombs, an intellectual revolution opens with bigger and better robots. The former revolution replaced muscles by engines and was limited by the law of the conservation of energy, or of mass-energy. The new revolution threatens us, the thinkers, with technological unemployment, for it will replace brains with machines limited by the law that entropy never decreases. These machines, whose evolution competition will compel us to foster, raise the appropriate practical question: "Why is the mind in the head?"

Coming as I do between psyche anatomized and psyche synthesized, I must so define my terms that I can bridge the traditional gulf between mind and body and the technical gap between things begotten and things made.

By the term 'mind', I mean ideas and purposes. By the term 'body', I mean stuff and process. Stuff and process are familiar to every physicist as mass and energy in space and time, but ideas and purposes he keeps only in the realm of discourse and will not postulate them of the phenomena he observes. In this I agree with him. But what he observes is some sort of order or invariance in the flux of events. Every object he detects in the world is some sort of regularity. The existence of these objects is the first law of science. To detect regularities in the relations of objects and so construct theoretical physics requires the disciplines of logic and mathematics. In these fundamentally tautological endeavors we invent surprising regularities, complicated transformations which conserve whatever truth may lie in the propositions they transform. This is invariance, many steps removed from simple sensation but not essentially different. It is these regularities, or invariants, which I call ideas, whether they are theorems of great abstraction or qualities simply sensed. The reason for excluding them from physics is that they must not be supposed to be either stuff or process in the causal sequences of any part of the world. They are neither material nor efficient. So, to my mind Newton, Planck, and Jeans sin by introducing God as a sort of mind at large in the world to account for physical effects, like the action of gravity at a distance.

But let us now compel our physicist to account for himself as a part of the physical world. In all fairness, he must stick to his own rules and show in terms of mass, energy, space, and time how it comes about that he creates theoretical physics. He must then become a neurophysiologist (that is what happened to me), but in so doing he will be compelled to answer whether theoretical physics is something which he can discuss in terms of neurophysiology (and that is what happened to me). To answer 'no' is to remain a physicist undefiled. To answer 'yes' is to become a metaphysician – or so I am told.

But is that just? The physicist believes entropy to be somehow in or of physical systems. It may or must increase with time. But it is neither material nor efficient, in fact it is a number, namely, the logarithm of the probability of the state. It is, therefore, a measure of the disorder of an ensemble – or collection of systems. Now Norbert Wiener has proposed that information is orderliness and suggests that we measure it by negative entropy, the logarithm of the reciprocal of the probability of the state. Let us, for this argument, accept his suggestion. Ideas are then to be construed as information. Sensation becomes entropic coupling between us and the physical world, and our interchange of ideas, entropic coupling among ourselves. Our knowledge of the world, our conversation – yes, even our inventive thought – are then limited by the law that information may not increase on going through brains, or computing machines.

[...]

Let me define 'corruption' as the ratio of information in the input to that in the output. Each eye has something like a hundred million photoreceptors, each of which in a given millisecond can emit one or no impulse. In other words, it is an ensemble which can be in any one of $2^{100,000,000}$ possible states, or the amount of information it has is a hundred million units per millisecond.

[...]

What becomes of all the rest of the information? To answer that, conceive neurons as telegraphic relays. Each one may be tripped by some combination of signals provided these are very nearly synchronous. It detects the coincidence and only then emits a signal to subsequent relays. Now the threshold of the photoreceptors of the eye is always varying. At any one millisecond it may be tripped by a single photon, and, at another, fail to fire in response to many. By connecting many of these to a coincidence detector set to require a reasonable number of impulses simultaneously, we have a signal which corresponds to a statistically significant fraction of its receptors and so we wash out the random variation of threshold. Thus using the relayed information that fails to agree with other information, we achieve a high probability that what goes on through the nervous system does correspond to something in the world. Perhaps it will be clearer to say it this way. The logical probability that a neuron will have an impulse in one millisecond is ½, that two neurons of an ensemble in the same millisecond ½ × ½. The chance that both will fire by chance simultaneously is the product of their probabilities separately; that is, it is smaller; ¼. Therefore, in the nervous system, by repeatedly demanding coincidence we vastly increase the probability that what is in the output corresponds to something in the input. We pay for certainty with information. The eye relays to the brain about the hundredth part of the information it receives. The chance that what it does relay is due to chance is fantastically small, 2^{-100}, a billionth of a billionth of a billionth of a tenth of one per cent.

Here, then, is the first technically important difference between us and robots. In them we cannot afford to carry out any computations, no matter how simple, in a hundred parallel paths and demand coincidence. Consequently, no computing machine is as likely to go right under conditions as various as those we undergo.

[...]

A nervous impulse is also a signal. It is true if what it proposes is true, otherwise it is false. It is false if it arises from any cause other than the adequate, or proper, excitation of the cell. The threshold of the dark-adapted eye for light is about a photon in several seconds. Pressure applied to the eye will evoke impulses, but the energy required is many million times more. Press on the eye and you see light when there is no light. The signals are false. Thus nervous impulses are atomic signals, or atomic propositions on the move. To them the calculus of propositions applies provided each is subscripted for the time of its occurrence and implication given a domain only in the past. In terms of such a calculus applied to nervous nets, Pitts and I have been able to prove that even nets devoid of circles can realize any proposition which is a logical consequence of its input. As this is the most that *any* net *can* do it is obviously an adequate theory. We know, of course, that facilitation and extinction occur, and we showed that whatever these can effect can be done digitally, or discretely, by go, no-go devices. In our first essay, we were unable to obtain much more than the calculus of atomic propositions; but, by introducing circles in which a train of impulses patterned after some fact could circulate, we did get existential operators for time past.

[...]

There are other closed paths important in the origin of ideas, circuits which have 'negative feedback'. In terms of them reflexes were first defined as actions starting in some part of the body, setting up impulses to the central nervous system, whence they were reflected to those structures in which they arose, and there stopped or reversed the process that gave rise to them. All inverse feedbacks have this in common, that each establishes some particular state of the system, for they bring it back toward that state by an amount which increases with their deviation from that state. They are, as we say, error-operated. The state toward which they return the system is the goal, or aim, or end *in and of* the operation. This is what is meant by function. On these circuits Cannon founded his theory of homeostasis, and Rosenblueth and Wiener their theory of teleological mechanisms.

[...]

Neurons are cheap and plentiful. If it cost a million dollars to beget a man, one neuron would not cost a mill. They operate with comparatively little energy. The heat generated raises the blood in passage about half a degree, and the flow is half a liter per minute, only a quarter of a kilogram calorie per minute for 10^{10}, that is, 10 billion neurons. Von Neumann would be happy to have their like for the same cost in his robots. His vacuum tubes can work a thousand times as fast as neurons, so he could match a human brain with 10 million tubes; but it would take Niagara Falls to supply the current and the Niagara River to carry away the heat. So he is limited to about the thousandth part of man's computer. He has to be very careful to specify in detail which relays are to be connected to a given relay to trip it. That is not the case in human brains. Wiener has calculated that the maximum amount of information our chromosomes can convey would fill one volume of the *Encyclopaedia Britannica*, which could specify all the connections of ten thousand neurons if that was all it had to do. As we have 10^{10} neurons, we can inherit only the general scheme of the structure of our brains. The rest must be left to chance.

Chance includes experience which engenders learning. Ramon y Cajal suggested that learning was the growing of new connections.

I do not doubt that the cerebral cortex may be the most important place in primates. But it is certainly the most difficult place to look for change with use. Think of it as a laminated felt of fibers which serve to associate neighboring rough columns of cells nearly a hundred high and linked together vertically by their axons. These columns are then connected to distant columns by axons which dip into the white matter and emerge elsewhere into the cortex. These last connections I have studied for many years but have at best a general picture of how areas are related, certainly nothing that could give the detail necessary to distinguish between its connections before and after learning.

[…]

This brings us back to what I believe is the answer to the question: Why is the mind in the head? Because there, and only there, are hosts of possible connections to be formed as time and circumstance demand. Each new connection serves to set the stage for others yet to come and better fitted to adapt us to the world, for through the cortex pass the greatest inverse feedbacks whose function is the purposive life of the human intellect. The joy of creating ideals, new and eternal, in and of a world, old and temporal, robots have it not.

References

Bateson, G. (1991). *A sacred unity: Further steps to an ecology of mind*. New York: HarperCollins.

Bateson, M. C. (1972). *Our own metaphor: A personal account of a conference on the effects of conscious purpose on human adaptation*. New York: Knopf.

Beer, S. (1999). Let us now praise famous men – And women too (from Warren McCulloch to Candace Pert). *Systemic Practice and Action Research, 12*(5), 433–456.

Brand, S. (1976). For God's sake, Margaret: Conversation with Gregory Bateson and Margaret Mead. *CoEvolution Quarterly, 10*, 32–44.

Dupuy, J.-P. (2000). *The mechanization of the mind: On the origins of cognitive science*. Princeton: Princeton University Press.

Hayles, N. K. (1999). *How we became posthuman: Virtual bodies in cybernetics, literature, and informatics*. Chicago: University of Chicago Press.

Heims, S. J. (1991). *Constructing a social science for postwar America: The cybernetics group, 1946–1953*. Cambridge, MA: MIT Press.

Jeffress, L. A. (Ed.) (1951). *Cerebral mechanisms in behavior: the Hixon symposium*. New York: John Wiley.

Kay, L. E. (2001). From logical neurons to poetic embodiments of mind: Warren S. McCulloch's project in neuroscience. *Science in Context, 14*(4), 591–614.

Lettvin, J. Y., Maturana, H. R., McCulloch, W. S., Pitts, W. H. (1959). What the frog's eye tells the frog's brain. *Proceedings of the Institute for Radio Engineers, 47*(11), 1940–1959.

McCarthy, J. (1988). Review of *The Question of Artificial Intelligence. Annals of the History of Computing, 10*(3), 224–229.

McCulloch, W. S., & Pitts, W. H. (1943). A logical calculus of the ideas immanent in nervous activity. *Bulletin of Mathematical Biophysics, 5*, 115–133.

McCulloch, W. S. (1965). *Embodiments of mind*. Cambridge, MA: MIT Press.

McCulloch, W. S. (1974). Recollections of the many sources of cybernetics. *American Society for Cybernetics Forum, 6*(2), 5–16.

Chapter 4
Margaret Mead

Margaret Mead was one of the most well-known and well-respected social scientists of the twentieth century. She worked as an anthropologist, carrying out fieldwork over a number of years on a number of south Pacific islands. Her fame arose from the clarity of her writing, from her ability to express anthropological ideas in a way that the public could appreciate, and from the way she analysed her own culture (the United States) based on fieldwork elsewhere. She is not widely known as a systems thinker – yet she was deeply involved in the birth of the systems movement, and her work shows clear systemic elements.

Margaret Mead was born in 1901, in Philadelphia, and died in 1978, in New York. She was educated at Barnard College and Columbia University (both in New York). As an undergraduate (initially studying psychology), she took a course in anthropology with Franz Boas – the centre of a group working on a cultural approach to anthropology – and his student Ruth Benedict, and their ideas formed a basis for all her future work. Mead's primary institutional affiliation, where she was based for 50 years as curator and assistant curator, was the American Museum of Natural History in New York.

Mead was an active member of the Episcopal Church throughout her adult life, and highly motivated by an idea of service to humanity. In persuading her to leave psychology and devote her career to anthropology, Benedict told her that "Professor Boas and I have nothing to offer but an opportunity to do work that matters" (Mead 1972, p. 114), and the theme of "doing work that matters" is one that echoed throughout Mead's life.

Mead saw little separation between her work and her personal life (Howard 1984). Many of her deepest personal relationships were with people who she also worked closely with, both men and women. She was married three times (to Luther Cressman, Reo Fortune and Gregory Bateson) and also had long relationships with Ruth Benedict and Rhoda Metraux. She worked closely over a number of years with Fortune, Bateson, Benedict, Metraux and her daughter Mary Catherine Bateson.

Metraux (1980) has divided Mead's working life into four key phases. From 1925 to 1939, she was intensely involved in fieldwork, making five major trips and studying eight different peoples (all on the South Pacific islands). The first of these, which Metraux notes was her only solo field trip, was on Samoa, and resulted in her celebrated early book *Coming of Age in Samoa* (Mead 1928), which not only presented a detailed anthropological study in a way that was accessible to the general public but also formed a reflection on her own society (in relation to the status of young people). This style, of describing cultural patterns in another society with respect and in great detail, while relating these patterns to issues in American society, was one that Mead repeated through several further works. It brought her great distinction and public recognition, especially since the conclusions she was drawing often went beyond the expectations of her own society, but it also caused controversy and led to criticism of her work. During this period she published a total of nine books and (working with Gregory Bateson) made significant innovations in anthropological methods through the introduction of photography and film, which they subsequently closely analysed.

From 1939 to 1948, she was involved in public life on a series of applied problems relating to American society during World War II (notably the Committee on Food Habits on which she served with Kurt Lewin), when she "grasped how essential interdisciplinary thinking was in approaching these problems" (Metraux 1980, p. 266). During this time she also became a mother, to Mary Catherine Bateson, and typically approached Catherine's early life and upbringing in a spirit of inquiry, experiment and study. Mead (1972, p. 261) later wrote that "bringing up Cathy was an intellectual as well as an emotionally exciting adventure."

In a third phase of her life, from 1948 to 1953, she established (with Ruth Benedict) a series of projects on national cultures, again explicitly interdisciplinary. They designed a series of comparative studies of seven cultures, carried out over a number of years by a team which Mead coordinated following Benedict's death in 1948.

In the fourth phase of her life (1953–1978), Mead's diverse interests came together in a range of public settings. She taught in a number of institutions, took part in many conferences, served on several public policy committees, and published many books and articles accessible to both scholarly and popular audiences. She continued to carry out short periods of fieldwork in the South Pacific, observing the changes over the years in the cultures she had previously studied, but never again carried out a lengthy ethnographic study. She was a visiting professor at a number of universities. She also played a significant part as a public intellectual, writing widely in popular magazines to influence the thinking of the general public on a variety of issues arising from her interests. As Brand (1976) commented late in her life, "in public affairs she seems to have taken over the Eleanor Roosevelt niche".

While Mead spent a large part of her early life as a participant-observer in many different South Pacific cultures, in her subsequent life her ongoing passion was conversation and action, through conferences and through campaigns. Elise Boulding (1995) remarks that "there is hardly a social movement of the post-World War II decades that she did not personally touch". Mary Catherine Bateson (1984) has a photograph of Mead with the caption "portrait of Margaret reaching out to the world" (partly by contrast with Mead's ex-husband Gregory Bateson on a following page whose photograph is captioned "portrait of Gregory as onlooker").

Mead was very concerned with effecting positive large-scale social change, using the tools of anthropology to create harmony. Heims (1991, p. 270) remarks that she "treasured pluralism and diversity and abhorred the homogenization of cultures. ... Mead's active image of harmony with diversity was 'the orchestration of cultures'". Metraux (1980, p. 262) observed that: "she deeply believed that we, human beings, have the capacity and the cultural expectations necessary to keep our human enterprise going ... she committed herself with zest and humour, imagination and respect for hard facts, and above all continuing disciplined work ... to act on behalf of this enterprise."

Nonetheless, it must not be thought that Mead was concerned only with large-scale change. To take one example from her religious life: at the large-scale she was closely involved in the World Council of Churches. However she was also involved in smaller scale church ventures such as Emmaus House in Atlanta, which works to overcome poverty and racial segregation in that city. Throughout her life there was a constant theme of personal networks and of ways to build nurturing relationships that do not necessarily follow traditional patterns. Mary Catherine Bateson writes:

> Through my mother's writing echoes the question "What kind of world can we *build* for our children?" She thought in terms of building. She set out to create a community for me to grow up in ... and she built and sustained a network of relationships around herself, at once the shelter in which I rested and the matrix of her work and thought. (1984, p. 16)

We have already noted the criticism of some of her work that was made in response to her comparisons between American and other societies, some of this due to her socially liberal conclusions. After her death, she was publicly criticised by the Australian anthropologist Derek Freeman, who had also carried out fieldwork in Samoa, and who argued that Mead's methods had been insufficiently rigorous and led to some unwarranted conclusions. Freeman's criticism was widely spread through the popular media, and to some extent tarnished Mead's posthumous reputation. Other anthropologists have challenged Freeman's critiques and argued that they were largely unjustified.

Despite the widespread awareness of Mead's work in her own time and today, she is not widely known as a systems thinker – normally she is identified with her discipline, cultural anthropology. This is a curiosity: she played a big role in the establishment of systems thinking, and her work clearly demonstrates a strong systemic awareness. Elise Boulding (1995) observes that "studying microsocieties is an ideal way to get inside the dynamics of social process, and Mead made the most of her opportunities. She was always asking the questions: What makes things change? What makes things stay the same?"

Mead was deeply involved in the Macy conferences: she was one of a core group of social scientists (with Larry Frank and Gregory Bateson) who set them up alongside the physical scientists developing the mathematics of cybernetics. She edited the proceedings of the sixth to tenth conferences, with Heinz von Foerster. It was clear to her before the conferences that the world of social science was ready for the concepts of cybernetics – she said (citing Robert Merton) that "there wasn't a person in the country who was thinking hard about problems who didn't have a folder somewhere marked something like 'circular systems'" (Brand 1976).

Mead's involvement in the organisation of the systems movement continued after the Macy Conferences. She attended the founding meetings of the Society for General Systems Research (SGSR) and the American Society for Cybernetics (ASC), in 1954 and 1968 respectively. She continued to attend meetings of the SGSR, which were held until the early 1980s in conjunction with the American Academy for the Advancement of Science (Hammond 2003, p. 248) of which she was also a keen member. She was president of SGSR in 1972, immediately before her presidency of the AAAS. In the case of both the SGSR and the ASC she argued that the new society should apply its own principles to its organisation – "they [SGSR] could use their theory to predict the kind and size of society they wanted, what its laws of growth and articulation with other parts of the scientific community could be. I was slapped down without mercy. Of all the silly ideas, to apply the ideas on the basis of which the society was being formed to ITSELF!" (Mead 1968, p. 10).

Her commitment to social change can readily be linked to the SGSR's goal of "science in service of humanity". One of Mead's mostly widely-quoted phrases sums this up: "never doubt that a small group of thoughtful, committed people can change the world". The source for this is unknown, as discussed by the Institute of Intercultural Studies (2003b), but they comment that it bears a close resemblance to the ideas to be found in Mead (1964), where she discusses the dynamics of cultural evolution, and in particular argues that "our constructive imagination must be focused upon creating the conditions within which clusters containing highly gifted people are likely to form and, if they do, will make it possible for them to function well" (p. xxi).

Furthermore, Mead was conscious of the way that the use of cybernetics drifted away from its early potential. She was particularly critical of the popular use of the word 'feedback' as inherited from cybernetics and now in everyday language:

> Kurt Lewin (who died in 1947) took away from the first meeting [of the Macy conferences] the term "feedback". He suggested ways in which group processes, which he and his students were studying in a highly disciplined, rigorous way, could be improved by a "feedback process" as when, for example, a group was periodically given a report on the success or failure of its particular operations. In this very special form, feedback became part of the jargon of Group Dynamics. ... In this case, far from serving as a catalyzing, high-level theoretical tool, the term feedback has become a jargon-catchall for any kind of report back to government, management, the subjects of an experiment, subjects during an experiment, and so on. (Mead 1964, pp. 272–273)

Mead's view, as described by Miller (1996), was that "the other social sciences ... looked at only parts of a society but anthropology was concerned with the whole system so the emphasis on 'wholes' in systems theory was important". The Institute of Intercultural Studies (2003a) have also argued that: "as an anthropologist, Mead had been trained to think in terms of the interconnection of all aspects of human life. The production of food cannot be separated from ritual and belief, and politics cannot be separated from childrearing or art. This holistic understanding of human adaptation allowed Mead to speak out on a very wide range of issues".

However, it was unusual for her to explicitly use the *language* of systems in her scholarly writing. In essence, this seems to be because her anthropological understanding of holism was sufficient for her needs. She reflected at times on this lack of use of systems language, though she said it was common to most anthropological work. Commenting on cybernetics, she wrote that "anthropologists participated in the initial formulations and a few anthropologists have used the families of models that come from information and communication theory; but the use of such models has not penetrated the central core of the discipline" (Mead 1961, p. 479).

However, we can finally see Mead's overall view of the relation between anthropology – her core discipline – and systems ideas in an article that was published during her time as president of the SGSR:

> General systems theory has taken its impetus from the excitement of discovering larger and larger contexts, on the one hand, and a kind of microprobing into fine detail within a system, on the other. Both of these activities are intrinsic to anthropology to the extent that field work in living societies has been the basic disciplinary method. It is no revelation to any field-experienced anthropologist that everything is related to everything else, or that whether the entire sociocultural setting can be studied in detail or not, it has to be known in general outline. (Mead 1973, p. 8)

Reading from Mead's work

Reprinted by permission Mead, M. (1968) Cybernetics of cybernetics, In von Foerster, H. et al. (eds.), *Purposive Systems*, New York: Spartan Books. Institute of Intercultural Studies, Inc., New York.

I suppose that one of the reasons that I am contributing to this endeavor is that I myself was at the small Josiah Macy Foundation Conference on cerebral inhibition – in the middle of World War II – at which we began planning for the Macy Conferences which became the Conferences on Cybernetics (Mead et al. 1950–56). That first small conference was so exciting that I did not notice that I had broken one of my teeth until the conference was over.

I was a member of that first group as an anthropologist. The competence I had – and have comes from the intensive analysis of very small, relatively isolated, and intimately known communities which serve as living models from which one can sometimes develop larger, more formal models. Besides the anthropologists' experience with the small societies which are their laboratories, anthropologists have a second task: to interest themselves in what is happening in our own culture, to stand outside it and look at it as a whole.

As an anthropologist, I have been interested in the effects that the theories of cybernetics have within our society. I am not referring to computers or to the electronic revolution as a whole, or to the "implosion" and the end of dependence on script for knowledge, or to the way that dress has succeeded the mimeographing machine as a form of communication among the dissenting young. I specifically want to consider the significance of the set of cross-disciplinary ideas which we first called "feedback" and then called "teleological mechanisms" (Frank et al. 1948), and then called "cybernetics" – a form of cross-disciplinary thought which made it possible for members of many disciplines to communicate with each other easily in a language which all could understand. This was an important motive for those of us who worked in those first conferences at the end of the 1940s. We were impressed by the potential usefulness of a language sufficiently sophisticated to be used to solve complex human problems, and sufficiently abstract to make it possible to cross disciplinary boundaries. We thought we would go on to real interdisciplinary research, using this language as a medium. Instead, the whole thing fragmented. Norbert Wiener wrote his book *Cybernetics* (Wiener 1948). It fascinated intellectuals and it looked for a while as if the ideas that he expressed would become a way of thought. But they didn't.

I would now like to consider cybernetics as a way of looking at things and as a language for expressing what one sees. We might look at the history of thinking about the relations between the United States and the Soviet Union. There was a time about 20 years ago when the two countries were so preoccupied with each other that they acted as if they were the only two countries with any political significance on this planet. Specialists in each nation expended enormous energy trying to penetrate the secrets of the other system. The Soviets made a great many hypotheses about the way our system worked which were based on their own highly centralized form and which led to false conclusions, such as the assumption that both American political parties were run from "Wall Street" – a sort of capitalist counterpart of the Kremlin. This belief of theirs and our adverse views of the Kremlin have now coalesced in the present mythology of "the establishment" or "the industrial military complex". Twenty years ago, even 10 years ago, it was possible to think of the United States system and the Soviet system as two relatively self-contained and independent systems, coupled together by mutual suspicion, passionate attention, and intermittently successful espionage. It was even possible to propose – as I did a few years ago – that, if we wished for a more reliable form of knowledge and understanding between the two systems than espionage could provide, we should use cybernetics as a cross-cultural vocabulary for expressing the relevant differences between the two systems. I suggested this at a time when it seemed that cybernetics was ideologically free and was developing very rapidly in the Soviet Union. Many more young people there were learning about it than there were in this country, and it seemed that here was a possibility that two rival nations, with very different ideological premises, could develop a language in which their systems could be described in a way that was ideologically neutral. As there were many unadmitted occasions when the United States and the Soviet policy-makers did want to agree, such a language would have been useful.

Today there are new developments which make me less hopeful that such a venture could succeed. We have now developed an interest – and interest in Soviet affairs always contains a certain element of fear – in the possibility that the Soviet system may become totally cyberneticized, in the technical sense, as a way of controlling everything within its borders and possibly outside, with thousands of giant computers linked together in a system of prodigious and unheard-of efficiency. If this is so, or if we continue to discuss the computerization of the Soviet economy in terms of emulation and dread, cybernetics as a way of thought will cease to be ideologically free. There has also, however, been a marked decrease in the extent to which the United States and the Soviet Union are exclusively preoccupied with each other.

[...]

As the world scene broadens, there is a continuing possibility of using cybernetics as a form of communication in a world of increasing scientific specializations. The possibilities are fascinating if we can only get a large enough number of well-defined elements in large enough systems. It is argued, e.g., that Lake Erie is not only dead because there was no agency equipped to think ecologically about what was happening to its waters, but that, in fact, Lake Erie and its environs is too small a system to have been dealt with if, in fact, there had been any group or agency charged with preventing the Lake Erie disaster. It is further argued that if, instead, the whole Great Lakes region is considered together, then it might be possible to make the kind of predictions which could be tested in advance. In such a plan it should be possible to introduce correctives for too much linear and too little lateral planning, and linear planning is the besetting difficulty of most of the planning in the world today. It is argued that with large, inclusive, and well-analyzed systems we might be able to do a better job. There we find, on the one hand, tremendous hope about our capabilities to deal with complex systems if we can only identify the right system of the right size with the right variables. Although these are a great many ifs, they are not serious ifs. For we are free now from the superstition of some sociologists in the 1950s that we would never be able to deal with more than seven variables at once. And we have also gotten out from under the tyranny of the law of parsimony so that we can't be bullied quite so easily into thinking that the simplest solution to a problem is the best.

But, at the same time, I think we ought to look very seriously at the current state of American society within which we hope to be able to develop these very sophisticated ways of handling systems that are, indeed, in dire need of attention. Problems of metropolitan areas, the growth of such areas, and the choice of areas appropriate for planning certainly represent one such field. The interrelations between different levels of government, the efficient redistribution of income through procedures like the negative income tax, and the linkages necessary among parts of large industrial complexes that are widely separated in space are cases where a systems analysis is necessary. But the new kind of analysis of these complex systems on which predictions can be eased must be undertaken in a world which is made up of individuals who hold a great variety of positions of power within the various bureaucracies, in government, in industry, in the armed services. And these powerful people – who must order, provide for, and utilize such system analysis – are living in a world in which there are a large number of breakdowns in thinking. These breakdowns are of an order that I think should concern those of us who hope to promote the ability to think in cybernetic terms.

[...]

Yet it seems that interest in the human components of complex automated and computerized systems is decreasing rather than increasing. First we looked at men

and turned them into "human components", and then we stopped looking at them at all. We are educating the future human components, upon whose precision and accuracy and sense of responsibility the operation of future systems will depend, by training them to be trigger-happy in multiple-choice tests, by out-educating from their minds the fundamental human quality of responsibility based on accurate reasoning. I recently attended a large, expensive, and important conference on a subject of interest to many millions of people. The young and enthusiastic organizers, when queried about some of the arrangements they were making, simply replied: "We have decided we just have to risk failure". This is a form of ethical heroism appropriate perhaps in individual life but highly inappropriate in the design of national conferences on airport lighting, in fact in any of the increasing number of circumstances in which – as in parachute jumping – it is necessary to get it right the first time. We have not yet built into our educational system any recognition of the points where precision is essential, and yet we are living in a society where one mistake can dislocate the lives of thousands of people, wreck distribution systems, and distort life-history data, and subsequent career lines.
[…]

In World War II, anthropologists developed ways of thinking about old nations like Japan. Japanese culture was very easy to schematize in ways that were adequate for effective prediction. All that was needed was some hard work by experienced analysts. It was possible to probe and sample at anyone of many available points in order to get material for a systematic description. But new nations, amalgams of different cultures at different levels, within the present world framework, cannot be dealt with this way. We have no tools for doing a comparable analysis of Nigeria torn by civil war. We are dealing with new kinds of partial organization among areas of much higher and much lower organization which none of our theories take into account. In the past, it was possible to view opposing and organized systems in some degree of isolation. Today we are dealing with a sort of social metastasis in which there are fragments of formerly highly organized behavior which are unsystematically related to each other. We have no way of thinking about this.

If we think of the steps through the early interdisciplinary development of cybernetic models, through general systems theory and our growing willingness to include more and more complex systems, I think that now we have to take another step and develop ways of thinking about systems that are still bounded but within which there are loci of very contrasting degrees of organization and disorganization. If we approach them with our former methods, if we treat some of these organized pieces in isolation, we may get something that can be treated as a system, but we learn nothing about the way in which it is embedded in intractable ways in some larger and less organized context, and we may also do a great deal of harm.

References

Bateson, M. C. (1984). *With a daughter's eye: A memoir of Margaret Mead and Gregory Bateson.* New York: William Morrow.

Boulding, E. (1995). Feminist inventions in the art of peacemaking. *Peace and Change, 20*(4), 408–438.

Brand, S. (1976). For God's sake, Margaret: Conversation with Gregory Bateson and Margaret Mead. *CoEvolution Quarterly, 10,* 32–44.

Frank, L. K. et al. (1948). Teleological mechanisms. *Annals of the New York Academy of Sciences, 50*(4), 187–278.

Hammond, D. (2003). *The science of synthesis: Exploring the social implications of general systems theory.* Boulder: University Press of Colorado.

Heims, S. J. (1991). *Constructing a social science for postwar America.* Cambridge, MA: MIT Press.

Howard, J. (1984). *Margaret Mead: A life.* New York: Fawcett Crest.

Institute of Intercultural Studies (2003a). Margaret Mead: An anthropology of human freedom. http://www.interculturalstudies.org/Mead/biography.html. Accessed 13 Jan 2009.

Institute of Intercultural Studies (2003b). Frequently asked questions about Mead/Bateson. http://www.interculturalstudies.org/faq.html. Accessed 13 Jan 2009.

Mead, M. (1928). *Coming of age in Samoa: A psychological study of primitive youth for western civilization.* New York: William Morrow.

Mead, M., Teuber, H. L., von Foerster, H. (Eds.) (1950–1956). *Cybernetics,* 5 vols. New York: Josiah Macy, Jr. Foundation.

Mead, M. (1961). Anthropology among the sciences. *American Anthropologist, 63*(3), 475–482.

Mead, M. (1964). *Continuities in cultural evolution.* New Haven, CT: Yale University Press.

Mead, M. (1968). Cybernetics of cybernetics. In H. von Foerster et al. (Eds.), *Purposive systems: Proceedings of the first annual symposium of the American Society for Cybernetics* (pp. 1–11). New York: Spartan Books.

Mead, M. (1972). *Blackberry winter: My earlier years.* New York: William Morrow.

Mead, M. (1973). Changing styles of anthropological work. *Annual Review of Anthropology, 2,* 1–26.

Metraux, R. (1980). Margaret Mead: A biographical sketch. *American Anthropologist, 82*(2), 262–269.

Miller, J. L. (1996). A look back at the systems society. *Behavioral Science, 41*(4), 263–269.

Wiener, N. (1948). *Cybernetics: or control and communication in the animal and the machine.* Cambridge, MA: MIT Press.

Chapter 5
W. Ross Ashby

Ross Ashby was a deeply original thinker, who produced innovative work in a number of different areas. He was a psychiatrist by training, and his core concern was in understanding how the mind and brain worked, to find "what principles must be followed when one attempts to restore normal function to a sick organism that is, as a human patient, of fearful complexity" (Ashby 1956, p. vii). The pursuit of this goal led him to advance the field of cybernetics very significantly. His influence on the field, both in his own time and to the present day, has been considerable.

Ashby was one of the first people to work explicitly in the field of cybernetics. He produced one of the very earliest papers in cybernetics, wrote the first textbook in the field, developed a much-discussed working model of an electronic brain, and invented the term 'self-organisation'. He formulated one of the most widely-accepted fundamentals of cybernetics, the Law of Requisite Variety. As Pickering (2005, p. 234) has written, "in the cybernetic pantheon, Ashby ranked second only to Wiener; in the field of self-organisation he ranked first". He was also closely involved in the General Systems movement and in work that would lead to the birth of complexity theory.

William Ross Ashby was born in 1903 in London, and died in 1972 near Bristol. He was educated at Cambridge University and St. Bartholomew's Hospital in London. He worked largely as a practising psychiatrist for the early part of his career, at mental hospitals in London and Northampton, although he published a number of research articles on medical topics from 1930 onwards. In 1947, he became the director of research at Barnwood House Hospital in Gloucester, where he remained until 1959 and where much of his early work on cybernetics was conducted. After a brief spell as director of the Burden Neurological Institute in Bristol, he moved in 1961 to the University of Illinois, to work as a professor in the Biological Computing Laboratory of Heinz von Foerster. He retired from Illinois in 1970, already very ill, and returned to the United Kingdom. In the final years of his life, he was made an honorary professorial fellow at the University of Wales in Cardiff and a Fellow of the Royal College of Psychiatrists.

Ashby was a very private person. Stafford Beer, who admired his work greatly and drew upon it in a number of his own works, described Ashby as "very much his own man, and difficult to know" (Beer 1973, p. 2). He was a precise and rigorous

M. Ramage and K. Shipp, *Systems Thinkers,*
© The Open University 2009. Published in association with Springer-Verlag London Limited

thinker, who "could be infuriating in his habit of stopping people in mid-sentence to demand exact definitions, and he would not hesitate to declare that an utterance was a mere concatenation of words bearing no meaning whatsoever" (Beer 1973, pp. 1–2). Nonetheless, he could be highly enthusiastic and inspiring to those with whom he worked. Conant (1974), a former student, says that "his grave and somewhat forbidding demeanour gave way, when he was engaged in a conversation or lecture, to an animated style in which his unique keen wit and knack for viewing the commonplace from unusual perspectives would soon turn the discourse into a startling stream of surprises". Throughout his life (starting in 1928 and continuing until his death), he wrote a journal in which he first developed all of his ideas, the entire text of which has been made available online by his family (Ashby 1928–1972).

Ashby's first major contribution to the field of cybernetics can be seen in his paper "Adaptiveness and Equilibrium" published in 1940, three years *before* the two articles generally regarded as the founding papers of cybernetics (McCulloch and Pitts 1943; Rosenbleuth et al. 1943). In this paper, Ashby described the process of a chain of variables where one has an impact on the next (which he called a 'functional circuit'). He had a clear concept of both negative and positive forms of feedback, the results of which he referred to as stable and unstable equilibrium respectively – he remarked that "if we find that a system persists, in spite of the usual small disturbances which affect every physical body, then we may draw the conclusion with absolute certainty that the system must be in stable equilibrium" (Ashby 1940, p. 482). He went on to draw a close parallel between the concept of stable equilibrium (i.e. a system controlled by negative feedback) and adaptive behaviour of animal and humans to their environment – in effect, a model of learning which he would develop in later work.

That Ashby should have written in terms of feedback in 1940 is not entirely surprising: as discussed in the chapter on Margaret Mead, the concept of circular systems was quite widespread in the period. Indeed, a decade later Ashby was to be a member of the Ratio Club, an informal group of young scientists whose membership was limited to those "who had Wiener's ideas before Wiener's book appeared" (a phrase of the club's founder John Bates, quoted in Wheeler et al. 2002, p. 95) – other members of the club included the great mathematician and computer scientist Alan Turing and W. Grey Walter who created an early robot known as the 'mechanical turtle', among many others later influential in various scientific fields. Nonetheless, the clarity and explicitness with which Ashby discussed these ideas was unusual, as was his link to adaptive behaviour.

Ashby developed his model of stability and adaptation further through the building of an experimental machine which became greatly famous, the Homeostat. It was designed as an electronic model of the process of homeostasis in the brain, and the way in which a machine could achieve stability by its own activity. As Pickering (2002, p. 417) has remarked, it was one of the very first examples of "a real machine that would randomly ... reconfigure itself in response to its inputs" and as such quite revolutionary among the machines of the late 1940s. The Homeostat even featured in *Time* magazine, which referred to it as "the thinking machine", and describing Ashby's view as being that the machine "takes action on its own, according to any change in situation affecting it" (*Time* 1949).

The Homeostat and its design formed the basis of the first of Ashby's two highly significant books, *Design for a Brain* (first published in 1952, with a much revised second edition in 1960). His goal in this book was to consider in more depth the question of adaptive behaviour, and its working in the brain, and "to show that a system can be both mechanistic in nature and yet produce behaviour that is adaptive" (Ashby 1960, p. 1). That is, he sought to create a mechanistic model of the brain and its ability to learn. The Homeostat formed the experimental evidence for this work, while cybernetics (and information theory) formed the theoretical basis. In many ways the book is now a historical curiosity – while there are still many theorists with the same goal as Ashby, especially within cognitive science, the methods they use have changed – it was an important early attempt to work in this way.

The book also introduced his concept of ultrastability, a generalisation of the self-regulating property of the Homeostat. He describes this mechanism as 'double feedback', and argues that the mechanism must always be present in any system which has adaptive behaviour altered by interaction with its environment. This concept would later form the basis of Argyris and Schön's (1978) distinction between single- and double-loop learning.

Ashby's second book, *Introduction to Cybernetics*, had a wider and more lasting impact than his first. For many years it was the major text in the field of cybernetics, and had a strong impact. He described cybernetics as a theory of machines, within which category he included living organisms and their brains as much as machines built by humans (a common view among many early cyberneticians). He argued that cybernetics is a general field of study of theoretical validity in its own right (see the reading from his work below).

The generality which Ashby applied to systems through his use of cybernetics was close in its goals to that of general systems theory (GST). Ashby became very interested in this approach, and was closely involved in the early days of the Society for General Systems Research – he attended its founding conference in 1955, and was president of the society from 1962 to 1964. However, his approach to general systems theory was somewhat at odds with that of many others within GST, notably Ludwig von Bertalanffy. Ashby viewed von Bertalanffy's method as being essentially empirical, one that "takes the world as we find it, examines the various systems that occur in it – zoological, physiological, and so on – and then draws up statements about the regularities that have been observed to hold" whereas his method "goes to the other extreme, considers the set of 'all conceivable systems', and then reduces the set to a more reasonable size" (Ashby 1958). For his part, von Bertalanffy "objected to [Ashby's] basic definition of a system as a 'machine with input', because it only applied to closed systems" (Hammond 2003, p. 120).

The tools which Ashby presents in *Introduction to Cybernetics* are largely mathematical, but at a level such that they are quite accessible. He treats cybernetics in terms of a theory of transformation – the identification of difference, "either that two things are recognisably different or that one thing has changed with time"

(Ashby 1956, p. 9). The *state* of a system at any given time (i.e. the present value of its variables, for Ashby required any system must be definable in terms of quantifiable variables) is a crucial part of this analysis.

Deriving from the concept of state, in Ashby's work, is the concept of *variety*: the number of possible states that a system can have, which in a system with more than a small number of variables will be a very large number. As Beer (1974) argues, variety can thus be taken as a measure of the complexity of a system.

Ashby applied the concept of variety to the question of regulation (i.e. the control, governance or management of a larger system by a smaller system), considering the relationship between the variety in the regulator and in the system being regulated. He concluded, in his famous Law of Requisite Variety, that the regulator must contain as much variety as the system being regulated. That is to say, if there is insufficient variety in the regulator, the only solutions are either to increase the variety in the regulator or to decrease the variety in the system being regulated. It is not the case that the variety of the regulator must be identical to the variety of the system being regulated, but there is a strict mathematical (logarithmic) relationship between the two, and the regulator must contain sufficient variety to cope.

Variety was not the only way in which Ashby was interested in complex systems. As he argues, cybernetics "offers a method for the scientific treatment of the system in which complexity is outstanding and too important to be ignored" (Ashby 1956, pp. 4–5). A key part of the modern understanding of complexity is the concept of self-organisation, a term coined by Ashby (1947), where he argues that "a machine can be at the same time (a) strictly determinate in its actions, and (b) yet demonstrate a self-induced change of organisation" (p. 125), although in later work he argued that the concept is highly complex and needs great care if it is not to be interpreted glibly.

Most of the work described above was conducted while Ashby was working at Barnwood House Hospital. In 1961, as described, he moved to work at the University of Illinois, a decade that "was in his own estimation the most fruitful period of his career" (Conant 1974). His work in that period, on detailed questions of the mathematics of cybernetics, has had considerable impact on his colleagues and students of the time (including Stuart Kauffman, who developed Ashby's ideas in complexity theory) but less impact beyond those colleagues than did his earlier work. Ashby was an important part of the active research and teaching community at Illinois, but his role was not entirely obvious there. Pangaro (1988, p. 11) reports a story of Heinz von Foerster that "Ashby's students came to him, Heinz, as head of the laboratory, to complain of how simple the material was that their teacher, Ashby, was presenting. When Ashby was told this, his eyes lit up with pleasure as he replied, 'It has taken me twenty years to make these ideas seem simple'."

Ashby was a deeply original thinker, who laid the foundations for much of the later work in cybernetics and complexity theory, both as a theorist and as a builder of machines. Stafford Beer summarised his work as follows:

> Ross Ashby had the great gift of continual innovation. Whenever he spoke, what he said was new. And always (for me at least) it was wildly exciting. He was in continual onslaught

of the frontiers of knowledge until the last, and it will be many years until his latest work is disseminated and understood. (Beer 1973, p. 1)

Reading from Ashby's work

W. Ross Ashby, *An Introduction to Cybernetics*, Chapman & Hall, London, 1956.
Internet (1999): http://pcp.vub.ac.be/books/IntroCyb.pdf
Copyright © 1956, 1999 by the Estate of W. Ross Ashby
Extract from pages 1–6.

Cybernetics was defined by Wiener as "the science of control and communication, in the animal and the machine" – in a word, as the art of *steermanship*, and it is to this aspect that the book will be addressed. Co-ordination, regulation and control will be its themes, for these are of the greatest biological and practical interest.

We must, therefore, make a study of mechanism; but some introduction is advisable, for cybernetics treats the subject from a new, and therefore unusual, angle. [...] The new point of view should be clearly understood, for any unconscious vacillation between the old and the new is apt to lead to confusion.

The peculiarities of cybernetics

Many a book has borne the title "Theory of Machines", but it usually contains information about *mechanical* things, about levers and cogs. Cybernetics, too, is a "theory of machines", but it treats, not things but *ways of behaving*. It does not ask "what *is* this thing?" but "*what does it do?*" Thus it is very interested in such a statement as "this variable is undergoing a simple harmonic oscillation", and is much less concerned with whether the variable is the position of a point on a wheel, or a potential in an electric circuit. It is thus essentially functional and behaviouristic.

Cybernetics started by being closely associated in many ways with physics, but it depends in no essential way on the laws of physics or on the properties of matter. Cybernetics deals with all forms of behaviour in so far as they are regular, or determinate, or reproducible. The materiality is irrelevant, and so is the holding or not of the ordinary laws of physics. [...] *The truths of cybernetics are not conditional on their being derived from some other branch of science.* Cybernetics has its own foundations. It is partly the aim of this book to display them clearly.

Cybernetics stands to the real machine – electronic, mechanical, neural, or economic – much as geometry stands to a real object in our terrestrial space. There was a time when "geometry" meant such relationships as could be demonstrated on three-dimensional objects or in two-dimensional diagrams. The forms provided by the earth – animal, vegetable, and mineral – were larger in number and richer in properties than could be provided by elementary geometry. In those days a form which was suggested by geometry but which could not be demonstrated in ordinary space was suspect or inacceptable. Ordinary space *dominated* geometry.

Today the position is quite different. Geometry exists in its own right, and by its own strength. It can now treat accurately and coherently a range of forms and spaces that far exceeds anything that terrestrial space can provide. Today it is geometry that contains the terrestrial forms, and not vice versa, for the terrestrial forms are merely special cases in an all-embracing geometry.

The gain achieved by geometry's development hardly needs to be pointed out. Geometry now acts as a framework on which all terrestrial forms can find their natural place, with the relations between the various forms readily appreciable. With this increased understanding goes a correspondingly increased power of control.

Cybernetics is similar in its relation to the actual machine. It takes as its subject-matter the domain of "all possible machines", and is only secondarily interested if informed that some of them have not yet been made, either by Man or by Nature. What cybernetics offers is the framework on which all individual machines may be ordered, related and understood.

Cybernetics, then, is indifferent to the criticism that some of the machines it considers are not represented among the machines found among us. In this it follows the path already followed with obvious success by mathematical physics. This science has long given prominence to the study of systems that are well known to be non-existent – springs without mass, particles that have mass but no volume, gases that behave perfectly, and so on. To say that these entities do not exist is true; but their non-existence does not mean that mathematical physics is mere fantasy; nor does it make the physicist throw away his treatise on the Theory of the Massless Spring, for this theory is invaluable to him in his practical work. The fact is that the massless spring, though it has no physical representation, has certain properties that make it of the highest importance to him if he is to understand a system even as simple as a watch.

The biologist knows and uses the same principle when he gives to *Amphioxus*, or to some extinct form, a detailed study quite out of proportion to its present-day ecological or economic importance.

In the same way, cybernetics marks out certain types of mechanism as being of particular importance in the general theory; and it does this with no regard for whether terrestrial machines happen to make this form common. Only after the study has surveyed adequately the *possible* relations between machine and machine does it turn to consider the forms actually found in some particular branch of science.

In keeping with this method, which works primarily with the comprehensive and general, cybernetics typically treats any given, particular, machine by asking not "what individual act will it produce here and now?" but "what are *all* the possible behaviours that it can produce?"

It is in this way that information theory comes to play an essential part in the subject; for information theory is characterised essentially by its dealing always with a *set* of possibilities; both its primary data and its final statements are almost always about the set as such, and not about some individual element in the set.

This new point of view leads to the consideration of new types of problem. The older point of view saw, say, an ovum grow into a rabbit and asked "why does it do this – why does it not just stay an ovum?" The attempts to answer this question led to the study of energetics and to the discovery of many reasons why the ovum should change – it can oxidise its fat, and fat provides free energy; it has phosphorylating enzymes, and can pass its metabolises around a Krebs' cycle; and so on. In these studies the concept of energy was fundamental.

Quite different, though equally valid, is the point of view of cybernetics. It takes for granted that the ovum has abundant free energy, and that it is so delicately poised metabolically as to be, in a sense, explosive. Growth of some form there will be; cybernetics asks "why should the changes be to the rabbit-form, and not to a dog-form, a fish-form, or even to a teratoma-form?" Cybernetics envisages a set of possibilities much wider than the actual, and then asks why the particular case should conform to its usual particular restriction. In this discussion, questions of energy play almost no part – the energy is simply taken for granted. Even whether the system is closed to energy or open is often irrelevant; what *is* important is the extent to which the system is subject to determining and controlling factors. So no information or signal or determining factor may pass from part to part without its being recorded as a significant event. Cybernetics might, in fact, be defined as *the study of systems that are open to energy but closed to information and control* – systems that are "information-tight".

The uses of cybernetics

After this bird's-eye view of cybernetics we can turn to consider some of the ways in which it promises to be of assistance. I shall confine my attention to the applications that promise most in the biological sciences. The review can only be brief and very general. Many applications have already been made and are too well known to need description here; more will doubtless be developed in the future. There are, however, two peculiar scientific virtues of cybernetics that are worth explicit mention.

One is that it offers a single vocabulary and a single set of concepts suitable for representing the most diverse types of system. Until recently, any attempt to relate the many facts known about, say, servo-mechanisms to what was known about the cerebellum was made unnecessarily difficult by the fact that the properties of servo-mechanisms were described in words redolent of the automatic pilot, or the radio set, or the hydraulic brake, while those of the cerebellum were described in words redolent of the dissecting room and the bedside – aspects that are irrelevant to the *similarities* between a servo-mechanism and a cerebellar reflex. Cybernetics offers one set of concepts that, by having exact correspondences with each branch of science, can thereby bring them into exact relation with one other.

It has been found repeatedly in science that the discovery that two branches are related leads to each branch helping in the development of the other. [...] The result is often a markedly accelerated growth of both. The infinitesimal calculus and astronomy, the virus and the protein molecule, the chromosomes and heredity are examples that come to mind. Neither, of course, can give *proofs* about the laws of the other, but each can give suggestions that may be of the greatest assistance and fruitfulness. [...] Here I need only mention the fact that cybernetics is likely to reveal a great number of interesting and suggestive parallelisms between machine and brain and society. And it can provide the common language by which discoveries in one branch can readily be made use of in the others.

The complex system

The second peculiar virtue of cybernetics is that it offers a method for the scientific treatment of the system in which complexity is outstanding and too important to be ignored. Such systems are, as we well know, only too common in the biological world!.

In the simpler systems, the methods of cybernetics sometimes show no obvious advantage over those that have long been known. It is chiefly when the systems become complex that the new methods reveal their power.

Science stands today on something of a divide. For two centuries it has been exploring systems that are either intrinsically simple or that are capable of being analysed into simple components. The fact that such a dogma as "vary the factors one at a time" could be accepted for a century, shows that scientists were largely concerned in investigating such systems as *allowed* this method; for this method is often fundamentally impossible in the complex systems. Not until Sir Donald Fisher's work in the 1920s, with experiments conducted on agricultural soils, did it become clearly recognised that there are complex systems that just do not allow the varying of only one factor at a time – they are so dynamic and interconnected that the alteration of one factor immediately acts as cause to evoke alterations in others, perhaps in a great many others. Until recently, science tended to evade the study of such systems, focusing its attention on those that were simple and, especially, reducible.

In the study of some systems, however, the complexity could not be wholly evaded. The cerebral cortex of the free-living organism, the ant-hill as a functioning society, and the human economic system were outstanding both in their practical importance and in their intractability by the older methods. So today we see psychoses untreated, societies declining, and economic systems faltering, the scientist being able to do little more than to appreciate the full complexity of the subject he is studying. But science today is also taking the first steps towards studying "complexity" as a subject in its own right.

Prominent among the methods for dealing with complexity is cybernetics. It rejects the vaguely intuitive ideas that we pick up from handling such simple machines as the alarm clock and the bicycle, and sets to work to build up a rigorous discipline of the subject. For a time (as the first few chapters of this book will show) it seems rather to deal with truisms and platitudes, but this is merely because the foundations are built to be broad and strong. They are built so that cybernetics can be developed vigorously, without the primary vagueness that has infected most past attempts to grapple with, in particular, the complexities of the brain in action.

Cybernetics offers the hope of providing effective methods for the study, and control, of systems that are intrinsically extremely complex. It will do this by first marking out what is achievable (for probably many of the investigations of the past attempted the impossible), and then providing generalised strategies, of demonstrable value, that can be used uniformly in a variety of special cases. In this way it offers the hope of providing the essential methods by which to attack the ills – psychological, social, economic – which at present are defeating us by their intrinsic complexity. [This book] does not pretend to offer such methods perfected, but it attempts to offer a foundation on which such methods can be constructed, and a start in the right direction.

References

Argyris, C., & Schön, D. A. (1978). *Organizational learning: A theory of action perspective.* Reading, MA: Addison-Wesley.

Ashby, W. R. (1928–1972). Journal (25 vols). Online version 2008, The W. Ross Ashby Digital Archive. http://www.rossashby.info/journal. Accessed 13 Jan 2009.

Ashby, W.R. (1940). Adaptiveness and equilibrium. *Journal of Mental Science, 86*, 478–484.

Ashby, W.R. (1947). Principles of the self-organizing dynamic system. *The Journal of General Psychology, 37*, 125–128.

Ashby, W. R. (1956). *An introduction to cybernetics.* London: Chapman & Hall.

Ashby, W. R. (1958). General systems theory as a new discipline. *General Systems, 3*, 1–6.

Ashby, W. R. (1960). *Design for a brain: The origin of adaptive dehaviour* (2nd edition). London: Chapman & Hall.

Beer, S. (1973). Obituary: Professor W. Ross Ashby. *Operational Research Quarterly, 24*(1), 1–2.

Beer, S. (1974). *Designing freedom.* Chichester: John Wiley.

Conant, R. (1974). W. Ross Ashby. *International Journal of General Systems, 1*, 4–7.

Hammond, D. (2003). *The science of synthesis: Exploring the social implications of general systems theory.* Boulder, CO: University Press of Colorado.

McCulloch, W. S., & Pitts, W. (1943). A logical calculus of the ideas immanent in nervous activity. *Bulletin of Mathematical Biophysics, 5*, 115–133.

Pangaro, P. (1988). New order from old: The rise of second-order cybernetics and implications for machine intelligence. Unpublished manuscript. http://www.pangaro.com/NOFO/index.html. Accessed 13 Jan 2009.

Pickering, A. (2005). A gallery of monsters: Cybernetics and self-organisation, 1940–1970. In S. Franchi and G. Güzeldere (Eds.), *Mechanical bodies, computational minds: Artificial intelligence from automata to cyborgs* (pp. 229–245). Cambridge, MA: MIT Press.

Pickering, A. (2002). Cybernetics and the mangle: Ashby, Beer and Pask. *Social Studies of Science, 32*(3), 413–437.

Rosenbleuth, A., Wiener, N., Bigelow, J. (1943). Behavior, purpose and teleology. *Philosophy of Science, 10*(1), 18–24.

Time (1949). The thinking machine. *Time*, 24 Jan 1949.

Wheeler, M., Bullock, S., Di Paolo, E., Noble, J., Bedau, M., Husbands, P., Kirby, S., Seth, A. (2002). The view from elsewhere: Perspectives on a life modeling. *Artificial Life, 8*(1), 87–100.

General Systems Theory

General characteristics of systems, with a focus on emergence, boundary, hierarchy, and the system in relation to its environment

Chapter 6
Ludwig von Bertalanffy

Ludwig von Bertalanffy was the creator of general systems theory (GST) – he coined the term, developed it in detail in his many writings, and was a key part of the group which took it forward and spread the concept. Indeed, the systems movement would not have taken the form it did without Bertalanffy – for while holistic thinking has arisen in many places, it was Bertalanffy's language and concepts that took hold as the core of systems thinking. He was ahead of his time, always far beyond conventional views, and for the second half of his life never quite found a place where he fitted in. A fellow-founder of GST describes him as "kindly, shy, [with] a curious mixture of confidence that he was saying something important and diffidence that grew out of the lack of people to receive it" (Boulding 1983, p. 19). His biographer describes him as "the least known intellectual titan of the twentieth century" (Davidson 1983, p. 9).

Bertalanffy was as much a biologist as he was a systems thinker. In the 1920s, when biology was very largely an experimental science, he championed the role of theoretical biology, and developed quantitative models for it. He was one of the key early advocates of an 'organismic' conception of biology (focusing on the whole system of an organism). He also later carried out crucial experimental work on the diagnosis of cancer via cellular screening. Bertalanffy's work on GST arose as an extension of his ideas in biology, of the organism as a whole and its openness to its environment, and while it may be too strong to say that GST is a "biological metaphor in disguise" (Morgan 1986, p. 45), it clearly has its roots in Bertalanffy's biological work.

(Karl) Ludwig von Bertalanffy was born in 1901 near Vienna to a Catholic family, and died of a heart attack in 1972 in the United States. His roots were in the Hungarian nobility (*von* signifies nobility in German), and he could trace his origins back to the mid-sixteenth century. He grew up and had his education in Vienna, where he lived until 1948, experiencing both the deep benefits and troubles of Austria in the first half of the twentieth century. The Vienna in which he was reared was still the intellectual and cultural heart of Europe, and he gained hugely from it. On the other hand, his family's savings were destroyed by the economic collapse of the 1920s, his country was annexed by Nazi Germany, and large parts of the city (including his home) destroyed at the end of the Second World War. He married Maria in 1924, and they remained devoted to each other until his death – "the story

M. Ramage and K. Shipp, *Systems Thinkers,*
© The Open University 2009. Published in association with Springer-Verlag London Limited

of Ludwig von Bertalanffy became the story of Ludwig and Maria from the time of their first meeting" (Davidson 1983, p. 51).

Bertalanffy took his PhD in physics and philosophy at the University of Vienna. His supervisor was Moritz Schlick, founder of the celebrated Vienna Circle who developed and championed the theory of logical positivism (which argued that empirical science was the only valid form of knowledge, and that discussion of values had no place in science). The Circle was also committed to a 'unified science' with a common language in which all scientific principles could be expressed. Bertalanffy came to reject the reductionism and value-neutrality of the Vienna Circle, but was strongly influenced by the goal of unified science. On receiving his PhD in 1926, he became a professor at the University of Vienna, where he remained until 1948.

He had a sabbatical in 1937–1938 in the US (where he gave his first public presentation on GST, at the University of Chicago), and hoped to remain there but was unable to get a further grant as the Nazis had by then annexed Austria and American funds for visiting scholars were being allocated to Jewish refugees. Bertalanffy therefore returned to Vienna where he spent the war years as an academic – he was regarded by the Third Reich as somewhat of a subversive, being against the use of biology to justify racism, but suffered no direct harassment.

After the war, Austria's economy was almost destroyed and Bertalanffy suffered considerable hardship. In addition, many of his own manuscripts were lost in the destruction caused by the retreating Nazis. He managed to move in 1948 to Switzerland, funded by a publisher, to complete his book *Das Biologische Weltbild* (*Problems of Life*), which was the fullest outline of his organismic biology. Through a biologist who had been highly influenced by his earlier work, Joseph Woodger, he obtained a year's stay at the University of London Medical School. While in London he received a grant to move to Canada as a professor of biology at the University of Ottawa, becoming a Canadian citizen in 1954. Crucially, he had a year's fellowship in 1954–1955 at the Centre for Advanced Studies in the Behavioural Sciences (CASBS) at Stanford, California, where he came together with the group who with him founded the Society for General Systems Research (the story of this founding is discussed further in the chapter on Kenneth Boulding). This society, later the International Society for the Systems Sciences, was never large but was highly influential in its development and propagation of GST. Bertalanffy served as its muse, and co-edited its annual journal from the society's inception in 1956 until his death.

After the CASBS, he moved every few years for the rest of his life to a different research institution – the Mt Sinai Hospital in Los Angeles (co-director of biological research) in 1955, at the Menninger Foundation (for psychiatry) in Kansas in 1958, at the University of Edmonton (Alberta) from 1961 to 1969, lastly at the State University of New York. Bertalanffy received considerable acclaim late in life and after his death, with a two volume *Festschrift* (celebration of his work), a nomination for the Nobel Prize in 1972 (though he died before the nomination could be considered), and a conference at the University of Vienna in 2001 on the centenary of his birth (that university now hosts the Bertalanffy Center for the Study of

Systems Science). During his life, he was highly insecure about where his next job would be found, although he never let his GST colleagues know this: as Kenneth Boulding said, "if he had, some of us would have made an effort to get him a good, steady position ... I don't think anybody of my acquaintance ever knew the difficulties he was in" (quoted by Davidson 1983, p. 64).

Bertalanffy's organismic biology, on which he first published in the mid-1920s, "emphasises consideration of the organism as a whole or system, and sees the main objective of biological sciences in the discovery of the principle of organisation at its various levels" (von Bertalanffy 1973, p. 10). The key aspects of this definition – the importance of the *whole system*, and the idea that the distinction between a system and a collection of parts is that the system has some form of *organisation* of its parts – would recur many times in his work. Organismic biology stood against the prevailing mechanistic consensus in biology – treating biological phenomena as entirely explainable through physics and chemistry. It also rejected the major alternative view of biology, vitalism, which argued that there was some mysterious underlying force to explain the complexity of life, which Bertalanffy argued was insufficiently powerful and still grounded in a reductionist worldview. Bertalanffy did however draw upon some concepts developed by the vitalist Hans Driesch, notably equifinality which observes that the same end point (in the development of an organism) may be reached in various different ways from different starting points.

Bertalanffy's work on organismic biology developed further in his use in 1932 of the concept of the organism as an open system, an idea he took originally from thermodynamics. An open system has a clear boundary, and thus a distinction between the inside of the system and the outside (its environment), but it is possible for both matter and energy to cross the boundary; by contrast, in a closed system it is only possible for energy to cross the boundary. von Bertalanffy (1950, p. 23) wrote that "living systems are open systems, maintaining themselves in exchange of materials with environment, and in continuous building up and breaking down of their components".

Such a system is not in a traditional state of equilibrium, in that it is constantly changing, and yet it retains its basic form. Bertalanffy referred to this situation as 'dynamic equilibrium' (the original German term was *Fliessgleichgewicht*), although in one of his mostly widely-read English-language articles on the subject (von Bertalanffy 1950), he used the term 'steady state'. For Bertalanffy, the dynamism and evolution of this state was the crucial part, but many critics (then and now) have connected this with conventional forms of static equilibrium, which emphasise continuity and conservatism. The concept of dynamic equilibrium – that a system needs to constantly change its component parts to maintain its basic form of organisation – is a highly important one. Bertalanffy developed this concept in very precise mathematical form, which has been used by a number of other authors, notably the complexity theorist Ilya Prigogine in his later work on non-equilibrium thermodynamics (discussed in the chapter on Prigogine).

It was the application of the idea of the open system to wider situations that led Bertalanffy to develop GST, his aim being "to determine principles that applied to systems in general, to classify logically different types of systems, and to work out mathematical models for describing them, with the ultimate aim of unifying science" (Hammond 2003, p. 117). He initially presented these ideas in a seminar while visiting the University of Chicago in 1937; the cool reception to the ideas led him not to write them up for publication until 1945, although the building of the journal to which he submitted the paper was lost in the troubled end of the war, and in fact it took until 1949 before his ideas appeared in print. By this time, the concept of the whole system was much more common and acceptable, not least through the wide use of interdisciplinary teams in wartime.

The term 'general system theory' (the use of the plural 'systems' came later) was coined by Bertalanffy as a translation, with which he was later unhappy, of his German term *Allgemeine Systemlehre*. The German term implies a theory of systems which is applicable in many different fields, while the English term is more ambiguous and can be taken to imply that there is such an entity as a 'general system' about which he was presenting a theory. In fact, his goal was a general theory of systems as opposed to a theory of general systems. Indeed, Pouvreau and Drack (2007) note that the term arose as a generalised version of the *Systemlehre* (theory of systems) presented in 1927 by the Gestalt psychologist Wolfgang Köhler, who had a considerable influence on Bertalanffy's ideas. This is not purely a semantic issue, but is in fact crucial to a common misunderstanding of Bertalanffy's work: he was not seeking to present an all-encompassing theory of everything, but rather a set of common principles that could be applied in different places.

Bertalanffy's ideas, especially those of open systems, dynamic equilibrium and organisation, were applied by very many others working in biology, psychology, management and physics (see, for example, the chapters of this book on Eric Trist and Ilya Prigogine). More controversially, his ideas were picked up in the 1950s and 1960s by the developers of techniques of systems analysis/engineering and made the intellectual foundation for that work, whose origins lay in military and industrial planning. As these techniques had considerable influence in ways that critics saw as dehumanising, Bertalanffy's ideas gained a degree of negative association.

In fact, this association was very unfair. Bertalanffy's own worldview was strongly humanistic, and from his early days as a critic of the Vienna Circle he was a strong advocate of the role of values and ethics in science. He also did considerable work on applying his ideas to psychology, challenging what he frequently referred to as the 'robot model' of behaviourist psychology and functionalist sociology. He wrote that: "if the principle of homeostatic maintenance is taken as a golden rule of behaviour, the so-called well-adjusted individual will be the ultimate goal, this is a well-oiled robot maintaining itself in optimal biological, psychological, and social homeostasis" (von Bertalanffy 1973, p. 115).

This critique of homeostasis (negative feedback) was also central to Bertalanffy's keenness to differentiate GST from cybernetics, which emphasised homeostasis and thus in Bertalanffy's view was at risk of promoting social conservatism. While this is undoubtedly true for some applications of cybernetics, other researchers have used cybernetic principles in the service of social change (such as Margaret Mead and Gregory Bateson). Indeed, Norbert Wiener himself had a highly humanistic outlook, somewhat at odds with the mechanistic approach often taken by the movement he developed (as discussed in the chapter on Wiener). Bertalanffy acknowledged cybernetics and systems analysis as legitimate parts of a wider systems movement – essentially as special cases of GST – but felt the need to distance himself from some of their ideas.

As his work on GST developed, Bertalanffy became more aware of the wider philosophical implications of his work. He argued that GST was best considered as a new paradigm in thinking, with profound epistemological implications. In particular, he believed that GST demonstrated the obsolescence of the logical positivists' view that it is possible to reduce all knowledge to physics. He wrote that knowledge "is an interaction between knower and known, this dependent on a multiplicity of factors of a biological, psychological, cultural, linguistic, etc., nature. ... This lead to a 'perspective' philosophy for which physics, fully acknowledging its achievements in its own and related fields, is not a monopolistic way of knowledge" (von Bertalanffy 1973, p. xxi).

It is hard to over-estimate the importance of Ludwig von Bertalanffy to the development of systems thinking. He was one of the first thinkers to explicitly identify the importance of thinking in terms of systems, across all disciplines and all types of system. He gave the field its basic name, many of its core concepts and a common language (although more in terms of words than the mathematics he sought to use). Bertalanffy was never an easy or comfortable man, but he was a profound and important thinker. Hammond (2003, p. 133) sums up his work as follows:

> Bertalanffy's GST was an attempt to articulate a more inclusive and global perspective. In his view, the most important characteristic of open, living systems was their capacity for creativity and self-transcendence. While seeking patterns of organisation that were applicable at different levels of organisation, Bertalanffy still preserved a place for the individual and the particular as an essential component for social organisation.

Reading from Bertalanffy's work

von Bertalanffy, L. (1955), "General Systems Theory", *Main Currents in Modern Thought*, 11, pp. 75–83.

Modern science is characterized by its ever-increasing specialization, necessitated by the enormous amount of data, the complexity of techniques and of theoretical structures within every field. Thus science is split into innumerable disciplines continually generating new subdisciplines. In consequence, the physicist, the biologist, the psychologist and the social scientist are, so to speak, encapsulated in their private universes, and it is difficult to get word from one cocoon to the other.

This, however, is opposed by another remarkable aspect. Surveying the evolution of modern science, we encounter a surprising phenomenon. Independently of each other, similar problems and conceptions have evolved in widely different fields.

It was the aim of classical physics eventually to resolve natural phenomena into a play of elementary units governed by "blind" laws of nature. This was expressed in the ideal of the Laplacean spirit which, from the position and momentum of particles, can predict the state of the universe at any point in time. This mechanistic view was not altered but rather reinforced when deterministic laws in physics were replaced by statistical laws. According to Boltzmann's derivation of the second principle of thermodynamics, physical events are directed toward states of maximum probability, and physical laws, therefore, are essentially "laws of disorder", the outcome of unordered, statistical events. In contrast to this mechanistic view, however, problems of wholeness, dynamic interaction and organization have appeared in the various branches of modern physics. In the Heisenberg relation and quantum physics, it became impossible to resolve phenomena into local events; problems of order and organization appear whether the question is the structure of atoms, the architecture of proteins, or interaction phenomena in thermodynamics. Similarly biology, in the mechanistic conception, saw its goal in the resolution of life phenomena into atomic entities and partial processes. The living organism was resolved into cells, its activities into physiological and ultimately physicochemical processes, behavior into unconditioned and conditioned reflexes, the substratum of heredity into particulate genes, and so forth. In contradistinction, the organismic conception is basic for modern biology. It is necessary to study not only parts and processes in isolation, but also to solve the decisive problems found in the organization and order unifying them, resulting from dynamic interaction of parts, and making the behavior of parts different when studied in isolation or within the whole. Again, similar trends appeared in psychology. While classical association psychology attempted to resolve mental phenomena into elementary units – psychological atoms as it were – such as elementary sensations and the like, gestalt psychology showed the existence and primacy of psychological wholes which are not a summation of elementary units and are governed by dynamic laws. Finally, in the social sciences the concept of society as a sum of individuals as social atoms, e.g., the model of Economic Man, was replaced by the tendency to consider society, economy, nation as a whole superordinated to its parts. This implies the great problems of planned economy, of the deification of nation and state, but also reflects new ways of thinking.

This parallelism of general cognitive principles in different fields is even more impressive when one considers the fact that those developments took place in mutual independence and mostly without any knowledge of work and research in other fields.

There is another important aspect of modern science. Up to recent times, exact science, the corpus of laws of nature, was almost identical with theoretical physics. Few attempts to state exact laws in non-physical fields have gained recognition. However, the impact of and progress in the biological, behavioral and social sciences seem to make necessary an expansion of our conceptual schemes in order to allow for systems of laws in fields where application of physics is not sufficient or possible.

Such a trend towards generalized theories is taking place in many fields and in a variety of ways. For example, an elaborate theory of the dynamics of biological populations, the struggle for existence and biological equilibria, has developed, starting with the pioneering work by Lotka and Volterra. The theory operates with biological notions, such as individuals, species, coefficients of competition, and the like. A similar procedure is applied in quantitative economics and econometrics. The models and families of equations applied in the latter happen to be similar to those of Lotka or, for that matter, of chemical kinetics, but the model of interacting entities and forces is again at a different level. To take another example: living organisms are essentially open systems, i.e., systems exchanging matter with their environment. Conventional physics and physical chemistry dealt with closed systems, and only in recent years has theory been expanded to include irreversible processes, open systems, and states of disequilibrium. If, however, we want to apply the model of open systems to, say, the phenomena of animal growth, we automatically come to a generalization of theory referring not to physical but to biological units. In other words, we are dealing with generalized systems. The same is true of the fields of cybernetics and information theory which have gained so much interest in the past few years.

Thus, there exist models, principles, and laws that apply to generalized systems or their subclasses, irrespective of their particular kind, the nature of their component elements, and the relations or "forces" between them. It seems legitimate to ask for a theory, not of systems of a more or less special kind, but of universal principles applying to systems in general.

In this way we postulate a new discipline called *General System Theory*. Its subject matter is the formulation and derivation of those principles which are valid for "systems" in general.

The meaning of this discipline can be circumscribed as follows. Physics is concerned with systems of different levels of generality. It extends from rather special systems, such as those applied by the engineer in the construction of a bridge or of a machine; to special laws of physical disciplines, such as mechanics or optics; to laws of great generality, such as the principles of thermodynamics that apply to systems of intrinsically different nature, mechanic, caloric, chemical or whatever. Nothing prescribes that we have to end with the systems traditionally treated in physics. Rather, we can ask for principles applying to systems in general, irrespective of whether they are of physical, biological or sociological nature. If we pose this question and conveniently define the concept of system, we find that models, principles, and laws exist which apply to generalized systems irrespective of their particular kind, elements, and the "forces" involved.

A consequence of the existence of general system properties is the appearance of structural similarities or isomorphisms in different fields. There are correspondences in the principles that govern the behavior of entities that are, intrinsically, widely different. To take a simple example, an exponential law of growth applies to certain bacterial cells, to populations of bacteria, of animals or humans, and to the progress of scientific research measured by the number of publications in genetics or science in general. The entities in question, such as bacteria, animals, men, books, etc., are completely different, and so are the causal mechanisms involved. Nevertheless, the mathematical law is the same. Or there are systems of equations describing the competition of animal and plant species in nature. But it appears that the same systems of equations apply in certain fields in physical chemistry and in economics as well. This correspondence is due to the fact that the entities concerned can be considered, in certain respects, as "systems", i.e., complexes of elements standing in interaction. The fact that the fields mentioned, and others as well, are concerned with "systems", leads to a correspondence in general principles and even in special laws when the conditions correspond in the phenomena under consideration.

In fact, similar concepts, models and laws have often appeared in widely different fields, independently and based upon totally different facts. There are many instances where identical principles were discovered several times because the workers in one field were unaware that the theoretical structure required was already well developed in some other field. General system theory will go a long way towards avoiding such unnecessary duplication of labor.

System isomorphisms also appear in problems which are recalcitrant to quantitative analysis but are nevertheless of great intrinsic interest. There are, for example, isomorphies between biological systems and "epiorganisms" (Gerard) like animal communities and human societies. Which principles are common to the several levels of organization and so may legitimately be transferred from one level to another, and which are specific so that transfer leads to dangerous fallacies? Can societies and civilizations be considered as systems?

It seems, therefore, that a general theory of systems would be a useful tool providing, on the one hand, models that can be used in, and transferred to, different fields, and safeguarding, on the other hand, from vague analogies which often have marred the progress in these fields.

There is, however, another and even more important aspect of general system theory. It can be paraphrased by a felicitous formulation due to the well-known mathematician and founder of information theory, Warren Weaver. Classical physics, Weaver said, was highly successful in developing the theory of unorganized complexity. Thus, for example, the behavior of a gas is the result of the unorganized and individually untraceable movements of innumerable molecules; as a whole it is governed by the laws of thermodynamics. The theory of unorganized complexity is ultimately rooted in the laws of chance and probability and in the second law of thermodynamics. In contrast, the fundamental problem today is that of organized complexity. Concepts like those of organization, wholeness, directiveness, teleology, and differentiation are alien to conventional physics. However, they pop up everywhere in the biological, behavioral and social sciences, and are, in fact, indispensable for dealing with living organisms or social groups. Thus a basic problem posed to modern science is a general theory of organization. General system theory is, in principle, capable of giving exact definitions for such concepts and, in suitable cases, of putting them to quantitative analysis.

References

Boulding, K. (1983). Introduction. In M. Davidson (Ed.), *Uncommon sense: The life and thought of Ludwig von Bertalanffy (1901–1972), Father of General Systems Theory* (pp. 17–19). Los Angeles: JP Tarcher.

Davidson, M. (1983). *Uncommon sense: The life and thought of Ludwig von Bertalanffy (1901–1972), Father of General Systems Theory.* Los Angeles: JP Tarcher.

Hammond, D. (2003). *The science of synthesis: Exploring the social implications of general systems theory.* Boulder, CO: University Press of Colorado.

Morgan, G. (1986). *Images of organization.* London: Sage.

Pouvreau, D., & Drack, M. (2007). On the history of Ludwig von Bertalanffy's "General Systemology", and on its relationship to cybernetics. *International Journal of General Systems, 36*(3), 281–337.

von Bertalanffy, L. (1950). The theory of open systems in physics and biology. *Science, 111*(2872), 23–29.

von Bertalanffy, L. (1955). General systems theory. *Main Currents in Modern Thought, 11,* 75–83.

von Bertalanffy, L. (1973). *General system theory: Foundations, development, applications.* London: Penguin (original American publication 1968).

Chapter 7
Kenneth Boulding

Kenneth Boulding was an economist and one of the founders of general systems theory. He led a long and varied life, being involved in the founding of peace studies as well as general systems, writing volumes of poetry as well as many academic books, and making a significant contribution to ecology and social theory as well as his original field of economics. He was a broad-minded and diverse thinker who did much both to embody a systems approach across his many disciplines, and to influence systems thinking through his work. Elise Boulding (1995, p. 259), his wife, wrote that:

> Kenneth delighted in life. Nothing was too small to escape his absorbed attention. He always carried a tiny but powerful magnifying glass in his pocket so he could absorb details invisible to the naked eye of any object. By the same token, nothing was too large or too far away to escape his interest. At night he would mount his trusty telescope on the porch and lose himself in the stars. ... Ironically, his way of seeing things was so unique that what people remember best about Kenneth was the unexpectedness of his observations, the unusual connections his mind was always making. Kenneth's mind at work was a mind at *play*.

Despite the range of academic fields Boulding influenced, he always regarded himself as an economist, and his academic posts were always based in that discipline. Indeed in 1949 he received the American Economics Association's highly prestigious Clark medal, awarded every second year to the most outstanding economist under the age of 40. However, his shift to general systems (with its strong biological base in the work of Ludwig von Bertalanffy) was treated with great suspicion by the economics establishment. As noted by Mott (2000, p. F440), "while having established sound credentials as an economist, economists in general took note of him as a profound thinker, though few took his work seriously in the sense of incorporating his ideas into their own writings". Boulding recalled meeting a young man at a conference who said, "my professor warned me about you – you sold your soul to the biologists" to which he replied, "well I didn't sell it cheap" (Boulding 1985a, p. 4). In this chapter we will show the kind of bargain he made with 'the biologists' (von Bertalanffy and others) with whom he joined in founding general systems theory.

Kenneth Ewart Boulding was born in 1910 in Liverpool, growing up in a comparatively poor working-class family. He was able to obtain scholarships to school in Liverpool and then to university in Oxford, where he took a degree in Philosophy, Politics and Economics in 1931. Also in 1931, he joined the Religious Society of Friends (Quakers), of which he was an active member for the rest of his life. Obtaining a Commonwealth Fellowship, he studied economics for three years at the University of Chicago (initially towards a Ph.D., though he never gained that qualification). Returning to the UK, he taught for three years at the University of Edinburgh. In 1937 he was offered a job at Colgate University, in upstate New York, and never again resided in the UK, taking American citizenship in 1948.

In 1941, Boulding married Elise Biorn-Hansen, a Norwegian-turned-American, who herself became a very significant academic within sociology (of families) and peace studies. Kenneth and Elise were to have five children together, and became key supporters of each others' academic work. A colleague from Boulding's middle years (Singer 1998) remarks that:

> He and Elise were – to use Karl Deutsch's phrase – towers of strength, whose goodness, integrity, generosity and energy sustained many of us. Their home was a little chaotic, with a steady flow of visitors, local friends of all stripes, professions, and ages, exciting discussions, frequent potluck suppers, and an irresistible mix of goodwill and serious purpose.

For most of the 1940s, the Bouldings moved around various parts of North America: to Princeton where Kenneth worked for a year with the economic and financial section of the League of Nations (from which he resigned during a controversy over a public statement he wrote on disarmament); then to Fisk University for a year; and to Iowa State College from 1943–1949 (with an interlude at McGill University). In 1949, Boulding settled for almost 20 years at the University of Michigan, just then beginning to be an important centre for the social sciences. His main post was in Economics, but during much of the 1960s he also was director or co-director of the newly-established Centre for Research on Conflict Resolution. In 1968, Boulding moved to the University of Colorado, where he was based for the rest of his life. He retired in 1980, but was an emeritus professor at Colorado until his death in 1993.

As well as these full-time posts, he also had a number of visiting fellowships and chairs. The most important of these from a systems perspective was a year (1954–1955) at the Centre for Advanced Study in the Behavioural Sciences in Stanford, California, during which time the ideas which led to the founding of general systems germinated. Other visiting positions included universities in Jamaica, Tokyo and Texas. After his retirement he held many visiting positions in universities around the world. He received honorary degrees from 36 universities; he was a fellow of the American Academy of Arts and Sciences, the American Philosophical Society, the (US) National Academy of Sciences, and the British Academy. Most unusually, he was nominated for both the Nobel prizes in economics and peace.

Boulding published a large collection of writing on many themes, publishing 30 books (most of them single-authored) and so many articles that his *Collected Papers* runs into six volumes. His first book was published in 1941 (when he was aged 31), and his last after his death. Many of his books were dictated and then subsequently typed with little revision, leading to a highly discursive writing style. As well as his academic writing, he published four books of sonnets and several pamphlets and books on religious themes; and a collection of his aphorisms, sketches and short poetry was edited by a former student (Beilock 1980).

His work in economics moved him from fairly conventional Keynsianism in the 1930s to reject a mechanistic approach to economics based on the theory of the equilibrium, and rather to develop an open systems and evolutionary perspective on economics. As Dopfer (1994, p. 1202) remarks: "he developed a vision of the economy which, on the one hand, was imbedded in a broad ecological context and, on the other hand, stressed the asymmetry of time and the global irreversibility of economic processes". He was also a key founder of peace studies as a field of academic study (along with other pioneers of systems thinking, notably Anatol Rapoport), and of the *Journal of Conflict Research* in 1957.

Our focus here, however, is primarily on Boulding's contributions to the development of general systems theory as a discipline. These can be thought of as fourfold: the importance of level, his part in founding general systems as a field, the addition of a phenomenological perspective, and work on the integration of the social sciences.

First, Boulding was the originator of the modern concept of the systems hierarchy, identifying a series of levels under which one could analyse systems, with the suggestion that systems at one level could be regarded as subsystems embedded within the higher levels. Boulding (1956a), in a manifesto paper on general systems that has been widely republished and is the source of the extract from Boulding's work in this chapter, first described the concept of level as an approach to general systems theory "through the arrangement of theoretical systems and constructs in a hierarchy of complexity, roughly corresponding to the complexity of the 'individuals' of the various empirical fields". In this paper, Boulding identifies nine levels of system – these are detailed in the reading in this chapter. While others would later create more comprehensive frameworks, notably the very detailed work of James G. Miller (1978), Boulding was the first to introduce the concept of a systems hierarchy and his approach had great influence in subsequent work in systems thinking.

Second, Boulding was a co-founder of the Society for General Systems Research (SGSR). He was one of the four people who met at a celebrated lunch in the autumn of 1954 at the Centre for Advanced Study in the Behavioural Sciences (the others being Ludwig von Bertalanffy, Anatol Rapoport and Ralph Gerard), which led to a meeting the following year at the American Association for the Advancement of Science (which 70 people attended) and in 1956 to the founding of the SGSR. Boulding was the Society's president for its first two years. In fact, Boulding had corresponded with Bertalanffy for the previous two years, and Hammond (1995, p. 286) suggests that Boulding was responsible for Bertalanffy being asked to be a fellow at the Centre for Advanced Study. Hammond also describes a letter from Boulding to Bertalanffy in November 1953 asking "whether or not he though the time was ripe for the formation of a society to promote General System Theory".

In the words of Banathy (1995, p. 257), the SGSR had two initial questions at its heart: "what would happen if science could be redefined by crossing disciplinary boundaries and forging a unified theory of scientific inquiry?" and "how can we place science in the service of society?" Both of these questions strongly reflect Boulding's concerns up to that point, and "science in service of humanity" was the SGSR's initial slogan.

Boulding's third major contribution to systems thinking was his introduction of a phenomenological perspective. This was developed in his book *The Image* (Boulding 1956b), written at the end of his year at the Centre for Advanced Study in the Behavioural Sciences – it was dictated in just nine days, one chapter per day (Mott 2000, p. F436). In this book, he advances a theory of knowledge which says that all our experiences of the world are mediated through the mental filter of our understanding. He writes that: "for any individual organism or organization, there are no such things as 'facts'. There are only messages filtered through a changeable value system" (Boulding 1956b, p. 14). His concern is not with the truth or otherwise of our mental images, rather the process by which they are built up – his work could thus be said to belong to the sociology of knowledge rather than to philosophy. However, his book discusses the way in which mental images are developed within the individual and the group across a range of fields (organizations, biology, society, economics, politics, history etc.). The book had little direct impact at the time of its publication, but considerable subsequent impact upon soft systems thinking through the work of Geoffrey Vickers and Peter Checkland, who introduced a phenomenological perspective into a field – systems engineering – previously dominated by a mechanistic worldview.

A final systemic strand of Boulding's work, which became particularly pronounced in his later writing, concerned the integration of the social sciences. In Boulding (1985a, p. 3) he argued, half-jokingly, that "general systems divided into two branches just a little way up the trunk: one, special general systems, which went in for mathematical modelling; and the other, general general systems ... with its interest in homology and the perception of structural similarities in different parts of the empirical world". He suggested that his own work fell into the latter category and that it "comes out of ecology, economics and evolutionary theory, and looks at the world as a set of ecological interactions, populations of different species under conditions of constantly changing parameters". In books such as *Ecodynamics* (Boulding 1978) and *The World as a Total System* (Boulding 1985b), he took a very broad perspective on systems behaviour at many levels and from many conceptual perspectives. In successive chapters of this latter book he considered the world variously as a physical, biological, social, economic, political, communication and evaluative system.

Within economics, this work led him to be one of the key founders of two active sub-disciplines: ecological economics and evolutionary economics, both of which trace their routes back to Boulding's work. The systemic economist Hazel Henderson (1995, p. 275) summarises his work in *Ecodynamics* as follows:

> Boulding fearlessly attacks the central problems of epistemology and taxonomy: where to place boundaries in modelling systems, how to account for different system levels and dimensions and portray interdependencies; when to aggregate and when to dis-aggregate data, i.e. what are appropriate levels of detail in all such models – while recognizing that they all imply an observer with a specific position and vantage point in the universe.

In this way we can see Boulding's work drawing together all its various strands – general systems, radical economics, phenomenology and even peace studies. As Hammond (1995, p. 289) describes the combination: "his work highlights the importance of perception and his emphasis on integration is critical given the increasing fragmentation and polarization in the contemporary world".

Kenneth Boulding was full of joy and optimism. In a memorial piece after his death, his wife Elise quoted one of his sonnets, written just months before his death (E. Boulding 1995, p. 260)[1]:

Joy is Outrageous. Here we are on a cliff
  In a cloud; and we know there is a brink
  That well may be closer than we think.
We could be over it in just a jiff.
Over all broods the silent sound of 'if'
  And even where we stand we sense a stink
  Of pain and human misery – we shrink
And then comes, almost like a clown saying 'Piff',
Absurd joy to the world, the Lord is come
  Like fresh sap rising in a withered tree
  A flame of praise, rising exultantly
Beyond all reason in a world so glum.
There is a vast refreshment in the sky –
What matters cliffs indeed to those who fly!

Reading from Boulding's work

Reprinted by permission, Boulding, K. E. General Systems Theory – The Skeleton of Science, *Management Science*. ©1956, The Institute for Operations Research and the Management Sciences (INFORMS), 7240 Parkway Drive, Suite 300, Hanover, MD 21076 USA.

Two possible approaches to the organization of general systems theory suggest themselves, which are to be thought-of as complementary rather than competitive, or at least as two roads each of which is worth exploring. The first approach is to look over the empirical universe and to pick out certain general phenomena which are found in many different disciplines, and to seek to build up general theoretical models relevant to these phenomena.

[...]

A second possible approach to general systems theory is through the arrangement of theoretical systems and constructs in a hierarchy of complexity, roughly corresponding to the complexity of the 'individuals' of the various empirical fields. This approach is more systematic than the first, leading towards a 'system of systems'. It may not replace the first entirely, however, as there may always be important theoretical concepts and constructs lying outside the systematic framework. I suggest below a possible arrangement of 'levels' of theoretical discourse.

---

[1] Sonnet by Kenneth Boulding, quoted from Boulding (1995), 'Introduction to Special Issue: Kenneth Boulding', *Systems Research* 12(4):259–260. Reproduced with permission of John Wiley and Sons Ltd.

(i)   The first level is that of the static structure. It might be called the level of *frameworks*. This is the geography and anatomy of the universe – the patterns of electrons around a nucleus, the pattern of atoms in a molecular formula, the arrangement of atoms in a crystal, the anatomy of the gene, the cell, the plant, the animal, the mapping of the earth, the solar system, the astronomical universe. The accurate description of these frameworks is the beginning of organized theoretical knowledge in almost any field, for without accuracy in this description of static relationships no accurate functional or dynamic theory is possible. Thus the Copernican revolution was really the discovery of a new static framework for the solar system which permitted a simpler description of its dynamics.

(ii)   The next level of systematic analysis is that of the simple dynamic system with predetermined, necessary motions. This might be called the level of *clockworks*. The solar system itself is of course the great clock of the universe from man's point of view, and the deliciously exact predictions of the astronomers are a testimony to the excellence of the clock which they study. Simple machines such as the lever and the pulley, even quite complicated machines like steam engines and dynamos fall mostly under this category. The greater part of the theoretical structure of physics, chemistry, and even of economics falls into this category. [...]

(iii) The next level is that of the control mechanism or cybernetic system, which might be nicknamed the level of the *thermostat*. This differs from the simple stable equilibrium system mainly in the fact that the transmission and interpretation of information is an essential part of the system. As a result of this the equilibrium position is not merely determined by the equations of the system, but the system will move to the maintenance of any *given* equilibrium, within limits. Thus the thermostat will maintain *any* temperature at which it can be set; the equilibrium temperature of the system is not determined solely by its equations. The trick here of course is that the essential variable of the dynamic system is the *difference* between an 'observed' or 'recorded' value of the maintained variable and its 'ideal' value. If this difference is not zero the system moves so as to diminish it; thus the furnace sends up heat when the temperature as recorded is 'too cold' and is turned off when the recorded temperature is 'too hot'. The homeostasis model, which is of such importance in physiology, is an example of a cybernetic mechanism, and such mechanisms exist through the whole empirical world of the biologist and the social scientist.

(iv)   The fourth level is that of the 'open system', or self-maintaining structure. This is the level at which life begins to differentiate itself from not-life: it might be called the level of the *cell*. Something like an open system exists, of course, even in physico-chemical equilibrium systems; atomic structures maintain themselves in the midst of a throughput of electrons, molecular structures maintain themselves in the midst of a throughput of atoms. Flames and rivers likewise are essentially open systems of a very simple kind. As we pass up the scale of complexity of organization towards living systems, however, the property of self-maintenance of structure in the midst of a throughput of material becomes of dominant importance. An atom or a molecule can presumably exist without throughput: the existence of even the simplest living organism is inconceivable without ingestion, excretion and metabolic exchange. Closely connected with the property of self-maintenance is the property of self-reproduction. It may be, indeed, that self-reproduction is a more primitive or 'lower level' system than the open system, and that the gene and the virus, for instance, may be able to reproduce themselves without being open systems. It is not perhaps an important question at what point in the scale of increasing complexity 'life' begins. What is clear, however, is that by the time we have got to systems which both reproduce themselves and maintain themselves in the midst of a throughput of material and energy, we have something to which it would be hard to deny the title of 'life'.

(v)   The fifth level might be called the genetic-societal level; it is typified by the *plant*, and it dominates the empirical world of the botanist. The outstanding characteristics of these systems are first, a division of labor among cells to form a cell-society with differentiated and mutually dependent parts (roots, leaves, seeds, etc.), and second, a sharp differentiation between the genotype and the phenotype, associated with the phenomenon of equifinal or 'blue-printed' growth. At this level there are no highly specialized sense organs and information receptors are diffuse and incapable of much throughput of information – it is doubtful whether a tree can distinguish much more than light from dark, long days from short days, cold from hot.

(vi) As we move upward from the plant world towards the animal kingdom we gradually pass over into a new level, the 'animal' level, characterized by increased mobility, teleological behaviour, and self-awareness. Here we have the development of specialized information-receptors (eyes, ears, etc.) leading to an enormous increase in the intake of information; we have also a great development of nervous systems, leading ultimately to the brain, as an organizer of the information intake into a knowledge structure or 'image'. Increasingly as we ascend the scale of animal life, behaviour is response not to a specific stimulus but to an 'image' or knowledge structure or view of the environment as a whole. This image is of course determined ultimately by information received into the organism; the relation between the receipt of information and the building up of an image however is exceedingly complex. It is not a simple piling up or accumulation of information received, although this frequently happens, but a structuring of information into something essentially different from the information itself. After the image structure is well established most information received produces very little change in the image – it goes through the loose structure, as it were, without hitting it, much as a sub-atomic particle might go through an atom without hitting anything. Sometimes however the information is 'captured' by the image and added to it, and sometimes the information hits some kind of a 'nucleus' of the image and a reorganization takes place, with far reaching and radical changes in behaviour in apparent response to what seems like a very small stimulus. The difficulties in the prediction of the behaviour of these systems arises largely because of this intervention of the image between the stimulus and the response.

(vii) The next level is the 'human' level, that is of the individual human being considered as a system. In addition to all, or nearly all, of the characteristics of animal systems man possesses self consciousness, which is something different from mere awareness. His image, besides being much more complex than that even of the higher animals, has a self-reflexive quality – he not only knows, but knows that he knows. This property is probably bound up with the phenomenon of language and symbolism. It is the capacity for speech – the ability to produce, absorb, and interpret *symbols*, as opposed to mere signs like the warning cry of an animal – which most clearly marks man off from his humbler brethren. Man is distinguished from the animals also by a much more elaborate image of time and relationship; man is probably the only organization that knows that it dies, that contemplates in its behaviour a whole life span, and more than a life span. Man exists not only in time and space but in history, and his behaviour is profoundly affected by his view of the time process in which he stands.

(viii) Because of the vital importance for the individual man of symbolic images and behaviour based on them it is not easy to separate clearly the level of the individual human organism from the next level, that of social organizations. In spite of the occasional stories of feral children raised by animals, man isolated from his fellows is practically unknown. So essential is the symbolic image in human behaviour that one suspects that a truly isolated man would not be 'human' in the usually accepted sense, though he would be potentially human. Nevertheless it is convenient for some purposes to distinguish the individual human as a system from the social systems which surround him, and in this sense social organizations may be said to constitute another level of organization. The unit of such systems is not perhaps the person – the individual human as such – but the 'role' – that part of the person which is concerned with the organization or situation in question, and it is tempting to define social organizations, or almost any social system, as a set of roles tied together with channels of communication. The interrelations of the role and the person however can never be completely neglected – a square person in a round role may become a little rounder, but he also makes the role squarer, and the perception of a role is affected by the personalities of those who have occupied it in the past. At this level we must concern ourselves with the content and meaning of messages, the nature and dimensions of value systems, the transcription of images into a historical record, the subtle symbolizations of art, music, and poetry, and the complex gamut of human emotion. The empirical universe here is human life and society in all its complexity and richness.

(ix) To complete the structure of systems we should add a final turret for transcendental systems, even if we may be accused at this point of having built Babel to the clouds. There are however the ultimates and absolutes and the inescapable unknowables, and they also exhibit systematic structure and relationship. It will be a sad day for man when nobody is allowed to ask questions that do not have any answers.

References

Banathy, B. H. (1995). Guest editorial: Kenneth E. Boulding 1910–1993. *Systems Research, 12*(4), 257–258.

Beilock, R. P. (Ed.) (1980). *Beasts, ballads and Bouldingisms*. New Brunswick, NJ: Transaction Books.

Boulding, E. (1995). Introduction to special issue: Kenneth Boulding. *Systems Research, 12*(4), 259–260.

Boulding, K. (1956a). General systems theory – the skeleton of science. *Management Science, 2*(3), 197–208.

Boulding, K. (1956b). *The image: Knowledge in life and society*. Ann Arbor, MI: University of Michigan Press.

Boulding, K. (1978). *Ecodynamics: A new theory of societal evolution*. Beverly Hills, CA: Sage.

Boulding, K. (1985a). The next thirty years in general systems. *General Systems Yearbook, 29*, 3–5.

Boulding, K. (1985b). *The world as a total system*. Beverly Hills, CA: Sage.

Dopfer, K. (1994). Kenneth Boulding: A founder of evolutionary economics. *Journal of Economic Issues, 28*(4), 1201–1204.

Hammond, D. (1995). Perspectives from the Boulding files. *Systems Research, 12*(4), 281–290.

Henderson, H. (1995). An appreciation of Kenneth Boulding. *Systems Research, 12*(4), 273–279.

Miller, J.G. (1978). *Living systems*. New York: McGraw-Hill.

Mott, T. (2000). Kenneth Boulding, 1910–1993. *The Economic Journal, 110*(464), F430–F444.

Singer, J. D. (1998). Boulding at Michigan: General systems and peace research. *Online Journal of Peace and Conflict Research*, 1.2. http://www.trinstitute.org/ojpcr/1_2sing.htm. Accessed 13 Jan 2009.

Chapter 8
Geoffrey Vickers

Sir Geoffrey Vickers was a lawyer and manager, and provides an outstanding example of deep reflection after a long and varied career. He produced a series of important and thought-provoking works in retirement, which had a strong influence upon the developing use of systems thinking in management, decision-making and politics. He had such an impact upon the work of the Systems group at the Open University that its seminar room for many years had a large photograph of Vickers gazing down upon all discussions. Indeed, Open University students are still introduced to systems thinking with Vickers' analogy between the lobster trap which creatures enter but cannot leave and thinking traps into which people fall: "a trap is a trap only for the creatures which cannot solve the problems it sets. Man traps are dangerous only in relation to the limitations of what men can see and value and do" (Vickers 1972, p. 15).

The general systems pioneer Kenneth Boulding, who Vickers knew well and who had a strong influence on Vickers' work, summed up his ideas as follows (Boulding 1983, p. 8):

> Vickers' experience taught him that the real world is an endless dynamic flux, that all goals are transient, that equilibrium is a figment of the human imagination, even though a useful one, and that our images of facts and of evaluations are inextricably mixed and are formed mainly in an interactive learning process which he calls 'appreciation'.

Sir Charles Geoffrey Vickers was born in 1894 to a family of Nottingham lace merchants – he grew up in Vickers St, named after an ancestor; and was educated at the public school Oundle and at the University of Oxford. Shortly after he arrived at Oxford, the First World War was declared and he was made an officer, fighting in a number of key battles and being awarded the Victoria Cross and the Belgian Croix de Guerre. He was even considered brave enough that his portrait appeared on a cigarette card. After the war, he trained as a lawyer and worked for 15 years as a partner in an influential London law firm, Slaughter and May. It was only when the Second World War arrived that he became a manager, as Director of Economic Intelligence at the Ministry of Economic Warfare.

Following the Second World War, Vickers spent ten years as a director of the National Coal Board (NCB), first as legal adviser but for most of his time as "board member in charge of manpower, training, education, health and welfare"

(Blunden 1985, p. 108) – in modern terms, the director of human resources. At the time the NCB, then just established following the nationalisation of the coal industry in the post-war Labour government under Clement Attlee, was one of the largest employers in the UK, with nearly 800,000 staff. It was a time of great change in the industry – as Blunden (1985, p. 108) says, "the industry was riddled with entrenched and divisive attitudes between colliery managers and miners formed during the last years of private industry, what Vickers called 'that thirty years of decline when men were cheap' ". The task was immense.

Vickers retired in 1955. The rest of his life was spent reflecting on his working life, building up a body of ideas about management, governance and systems which stands, according to Blunden (1985), alongside such great management practitioners-turned-thinkers as Chester Barnard and Henri Fayol. He was never formally affiliated to a university – his institutional affiliation on one paper (Vickers 1978) is simply shown as "Little Mead, Goring on Thames, Reading, Great Britain", the house where he lived. However in his later years he had close connections with the Systems group at the Open University (through whom a number of his books were edited or republished), and held a visiting professorship at Lancaster University. He received recognition from the systems community both during and after his life. He was president of the Society for General Systems Research in 1977 (now the International Society for the Systems Sciences), and their Vickers Memorial Award is still given annually to the best student paper at their conference. He received the first gold medal of the UK Systems Society. He died in 1982 – his last book (Vickers 1983) was completed in 1981 when he was aged 86, and published after his death.

His writing style is lucid but dense, very much the style of an educated Englishman of his time. Unlike many other prominent systems thinkers (though by no means all), he made little use of diagrams in his work, being entirely focused on words as a means of description and analysis. While deeply embedded in English culture, he was keenly aware of its limitations. Ison reports a conversation with Donald Schön about whether the concept of reflective practice had cross-cultural applicability. Schön replied with a anecdote from Vickers, who "had suggested that reflective practice might be difficult for an English gentleman because he would find it difficult to say what he thought to your face, but would have no problems stabbing you in the back in private" (Ison 2005, p. 282).

For someone who was so much part of the British Establishment, he was a very approachable and humane person. Blunden (1985, p. 108) describes him as "a man of great personal charm and unusual classlessness, he once confessed to feeling more at home with the national executive of the National Union of Mineworkers than with his fellow Board members". His grandson remembers him as follows (Miller 2005, p. 347):

> My memories of Geoffrey are of someone who listened quietly and spoke with a careful choice of words. He was driven by an underlying feeling of wonder in the world, and saw himself as a modest part of an amazing whole. He was able to appreciate the very small and the very large and had an enormous appreciation of history and human experience.

Vickers' work in systems thinking was always focused on the nature of human systems and decision-making, at many different levels: managerial, political and societal. He applied his ideas to many areas of human systems involving judgement, at organisational, social and global levels. His ideas were positive, open and democratic, as described by John Forester (1994, p. 72):

> Sir Geoffrey Vickers never pretended that his analyses could be the last word. Rather, the remarkable freshness, insight, and productive and hopeful character of his writing lies precisely in its clear sense that here he is posing pressing questions for others to refine and pursue to enable further planning dialogue and the democratisation of policy-making.

In addressing these issues, he made a number of other important contributions to systems thinking. Three contributions stand out. First, he emphasises the key importance of *relationships* between people (or things) as a way of understanding systems. For Vickers, the heart of all human activity (especially in organisations) involves maintaining human relationships rather than seeking goals as in the traditional models of management. This was not intended as a soft or easy concept – he emphasised that individuals need to take personal responsibility for maintaining these relationships and for the stability of society, a view which as Adams et al. (1987) observe is at odds with the widespread idea of the 'autonomous individual'. In an extraordinary letter written in 1924 to his son Burnell at the age of two (to be read to him later), Vickers argued that:

> Human contacts are dangerous [because] they matter so much, and no one knows how much they matter. Even the most trivial meeting makes a difference, slight or lasting, to one or both. Intimate contacts make heaven and hell, they can heal and tear, kill and raise from the dead.
> These contacts are the fields in which we succeed or fail. I believe that they matter far more than anything else in life. What we are is written on the people whom we have met and known, touched, loved, hated and passed by. It is the lives of others that testify for or against us, not our own. (quoted by Blunden 1984, p. 9).

Second, he argued that systems should be thought of as *tools of understanding* rather than a precise description of reality. It is only once we have a sense of the system as a device for understanding rather than a statement about the nature of the world, that it becomes possible to look at systems from multiple perspectives and to respect all of those perspectives as equally valid. Vickers was thus one of the first originators within systems thinking of the turn to a phenomenological perspective. Blunden (1985, p. 108) argues that "years before management thinkers such as Checkland were to apply phenomenology to management, Vickers urged that it was not actions, but the meaning which men saw in actions, that was significant". In doing this he drew explicitly upon the phenomenological work of Boulding (1956), but also upon his strong practical background in management and public life.

Vickers' third and probably his most significant contribution was the concept of the *appreciative system*, a description of the ongoing process of sense-making over time. The individual has an understanding of the world which arises from their experiences and actions; this understanding feeds back into those experiences and actions, and changes over time as a result of the interaction of these. The concept of appreciation is hard to grasp, and as Blackmore (2005, p. 337) notes, Vickers "contextualized it differently in his different writings". Nonetheless, in general he used the term to refer to a "combined judgement of value and fact" – "for facts are relevant only by reference to some judgement of value and judgements of value are meaningful only in regard to some configuration of fact" (Vickers 1968, p. 198). This concept was important to Vickers because it formed an epistemological basis for the nature of 'judgement' (that is, of decision-making in organisations and social policy) which goes well beyond the rationalist approach to decision-making that was so prevalent in his time. An appreciative system is "a set of readinesses to distinguish some aspects of the situation rather than others and to classify and value these in this way rather than that … they seem to be organized as a whole, so inter-related that a change in one part of the system is likely to affect and be dependent on changes elsewhere" (Vickers 1965, p. 67).

Appreciative systems had a considerable effect upon the development of the Soft Systems Methodology by Peter Checkland and others. Checkland and Casar (1986) discussed at length the importance of appreciative systems, and constructed a model of the process of appreciation (see Fig. 8.1). The flux of events and ideas (shown at the top of the model) unfolds and changes over time, and the process of appreciation is that of perceiving reality and making judgements about it, which leads to actions that become part of the stream of events. They argue that in the process of appreciation, we are constantly perceiving reality and making judge-ments about it, although "the epistemology of the judgement-making will be one of relationship-managing rather than goal-seeking" (Checkland and Casar 1986, p. 5). This judgement-making stems from standards about the nature of the world, and about values as to what is good and bad within it. These standards become modified as a result of previous acts of appreciation.

We have largely discussed in this chapter Vickers' contribution to management and to systems thinking, as a practitioner and as an academic. He had many other aspects to his professional and intellectual life, notably in the area of law and public

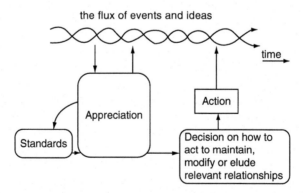

Fig. 8.1   Diagram of Vickers' appreciative systems model, from Checkland, P.B. and Casar, A. (1986) 'Vickers' concept of an appreciative system: a systemic account', *Journal of Applied Systems Analysis* 13: 3–17 (diagram appears on p. 6). Permission granted by Wiley-Blackwell UK

affairs. Blunden (1984, p. 9) notes that "of his four careers – lawyer, soldier, public administrator, and academic – only one, the law, was in Vickers' own eyes a Class A success". In a similar vein Churchman (1984, p. v) argues that "the tradition he selected could be called 'the law', but with an emphasis on the ethical implications of legal processes". As well as the ethical implications noted by Churchman, Vickers also had considerable concern for the social implications of various legal and political processes. The range of his interests and the scope of his work can be sampled from the titles of some of Vickers' papers in a posthumous collection edited at our own university (Open Systems Group 1984): "population policy, its scope and limits"; "the future of morality"; "violence, war and genocide"; "what sets the goals of public health?"; "ecology, planning, and the American dream"; "community medicine"; "industry, human relations, and mental health"; "the changing nature of the professions".

Vickers' work has similarly been applied in a wide range of fields after his death. In management and systems thinking his concept of appreciative systems has been especially influential (Checkland 2005), but his work has been taken up in fields including learning and environmental decision making (Blackmore 2005); post-liberalism (Blunden 1994); city planning (Forester 1994); moral philosophy (Williams 2005); and international conflict (Dando 1994). The breadth of fields to which Vickers' work is applicable shows both his own wide range of interests and the general nature of his theories.

Geoffrey Vickers was a remarkable man whose insights and interests continue to be highly relevant to today's intellectual and practical problems. His personality and concerns were summed up in an introduction to another collection of his papers by American colleagues:

> This was a man who cared – he cared about the concrete events and circumstances of the *lived-in* world of daily life, as well as the larger questions of the human enterprise. And he cared with a depth and exuberance and authenticity which was apparent, no doubt, to virtually everyone who spent any time in his presence. ... It is fitting [that] his most durable intellectual legacy should be the concept of the appreciative system. His own appreciative system was one of the keenest, most refined, and most thoroughly integrated of any human being that we have had the pleasure to know. (Adams et al. 1987, p. xiii).

Reading from Vickers' work

Vickers, G. (1983) *Human Systems are Different*, London: Harper and Row. Material provided with permission from the Vickers family and the Open University.
Extract from pages 12–17.

The most essential characteristic of an open system is that its *form* is more enduring than the presence of the substances which constitute it at some moment of time. The Greek philosopher who said that we never step twice into the same river was, I think, being wilfully perverse in presenting an important truth. For he surely knew as well as anyone that a river is the name we give to a form; not to the water which happens to constitute it at some moment of time. All the other characteristics of open systems flow from this basic concern with form, rather than substance.

[...]

Of course the substances are conserved. The water which flows through the river will ultimately find its way back into the atmosphere through evaporation or transpiration in the course of a passage in which it may have been part of many forms, including animal and vegetable forms. The forms, by contrast, are far from indestructible. On the other hand, if they survive, they tend to become more complex. The questions are how they endure long enough to earn a name; and how some of them elaborate their forms with the passage of time.

Some forms are imposed almost wholly by independent factors external to themselves – as the river is largely determined by the contours of its catchment area and the volume and distribution of its supply of water from rain and springs. Some sustain their form largely by internal directives and regulators, such as those which determine the growth and form of an animal and the levels of its internal heat and chemical constituents. Some owe their form to both factors, as where external factors are themselves changed by the behaviour of the form and react upon it to change it, as with men in a market place or on a battlefield. All these questions concerning the ways in which open systems preserve their form even through change are questions of *regulation*, the second focus of interest which naturally arises in the study of form.

An open system seldom preserves its form absolutely unchanged even for a brief period. One major reason for this is that its regulation consists partly in correcting deviations from its 'normal' state and some deviation is usually required to signal the need for a regulatory act. But apart from this, no open system lasts for ever. Its stability can never be taken for granted; it fluctuates and it may at any time escape from even the minimal regulation needed to sustain it and dissolve or change into something else. The animal dies, the skater falls, the business goes into liquidation, the community is absorbed by another or scattered or destroyed by natural forces (like Pompeii) or more frequently by human forces (like Carthage). So the third focus of interest, a counterpart of the second, is *stability*, or rather the whole dimension from maximal stability to dissolution. With this we must associate a concern with *growth*. For growth involves change both within a system and in the relations between it and its surround and these changes are bound to affect stability unless the regulative process takes care of them. The growth of a human organism from a single cell into the immense complexity of its adult form could not be achieved except by a marvel of internal regulation including most refined timing. There is a radical difference between cancerous and organic growth.

Open systems, by definition, do not exist in isolation. They depend on complex exchanges with their surround; exchanges of matter, of energy, of information, and of other communications not conveniently included in the useful but very narrow concept of information. The variety and reliability of these exchanges vary vastly. The giant sloth does not ask much of its surround or offer much to it, by comparison with his human fellow creatures in cabinets and boardrooms.

The progress towards greater interdependence which comes with growth involves limitations as well as enlargements, for it involves both mutual and, far more, complementary constraints and commitments. For example, the rights and duties of parent to child, teacher to taught, even buyer to seller, are not identical with the converse rights and duties of the other members of each pair, except for a few, such as honesty, respect, and compassion, which are regarded by the culture as the rights and duties of all. Moreover, as the individual and the systems to which he belongs become engaged in an increasingly complex net of interdependence, both the constraints and the commitments tend to impose more contradictory imperatives. Organization can mitigate this but not remove it. We must then add to our list of concerns the words *interdependence, limitation* and *organization*.

It is sobering to reflect that even three or four decades ago it was still possible for intelligent people to debate whether a 'whole' could possibly be more than the sum of its 'parts', and if so how. Today it is perfectly apparent, though not yet completely accepted, that every whole must necessarily be both more and less than the sum of its parts. It is less because its parts are constrained by being organized. They can no longer do some things which were open to them in their unorganized state. For example, the constituents of a dead body are free to combine in other forms, once the discipline of the living organism is relaxed. But they are also more than their sum because, when organized, they can do what they could not do alone or as an unorganized aggregate.

Thus the study of systems has validated the concept of organization and established what was regarded as a heresy in the heyday of reductionism. At every new level of organization constraints and enablements emerge which could not have been detected or even predicted from a study of their constituent parts in isolation. Vitalism, the theory that the origin and phenomena of life are due to a vital principle or life force, as distinct from a purely chemical or physical force, was once a dreaded heresy; it is seen today as a name for one of the many steps in organization. Organisms do indeed behave differently from inorganic systems. They do not defy or elude or contradict the laws which govern their constituents but they add other and new regularities which are functions of their new level of organization. And this would remain no less true if we could synthesize them from their inorganic components.

Of what then do systems consist? They consist of relationships. Surely there must be objects, entities which support these relationships? It seems probable to me that the relationships are more basic than the entities related; that we abstract or infer these entities solely from our experience of relationships. To avoid such metaphysical speculations let us agree that there are entities to be related. But they are curiously elusive and relative to the concerns which draw our attention to them. [...]

Take a more elaborate example. To an architect a school is a building designed to accommodate and facilitate specified activities. Its siting is irrelevant except for physical features of the actual site. To a planner it is a service to a community and its location is important to its utility and convenience. To an educator it is a community of teachers and students assembled for a number of related purposes.

To an individual teacher it is a workplace, a responsibility, an opportunity, and a step in a teaching career. To the local sanitary engineer it is one among many generators of sewage of which he has to dispose. He is not concerned with what else goes on there. But his concern with sewage disposal may make him sensitive to some factor which is irrelevant to most or all of the others – for example, to its height above sea level relative to the contour on which his sewage disposal works is situated. And if this concern were anticipated, it might even have affected the activities of the planner in siting the school, through the medium of the local authority's finance committee, concerned with the cost of providing services. How many kinds of fragmented entity is a school? Of how many wholes is it a part? How far is it itself a whole or many different wholes?

These are unreal problems, derived from our habit of attaching labels to 'entities' and thus exaggerating their integrity. It is, however, possible and important to draw a distinction between those internal relations which enable any assembly to sustain its 'form' (any of its forms) and those which enable it to act as a whole on its surround. From the viewpoint of parents, teachers, and students the school remains not only a school but *the* familiar school so long as teaching, attendance and activities proceed 'as usual', even though teachers and students change. A host of internal relationships have to be maintained if this is to happen. Teachers must attend and teach; students must attend and keep their disruptive activities below whatever threshold has become acceptable. A host of external relationships must also be maintained between the school as a whole and its surround, the physical support systems (including the drains already mentioned), the arrangements for recruiting trained teachers to replace those who leave or are promoted, the payment of salaries, the maintenance of structures, even the minimal good will of the parents (if they are to be regarded as wholly 'external', as in England they so often are). All these relationships, both internal and external, have limits beyond which they cannot be pushed without escalating instability which may result in irreversible change or even dissolution of the system. Within these limits change can be accommodated sometimes almost unnoticed, sometimes welcomed. Unhappily it is often difficult to predict where these limits lie until they have been passed.

So the relation between wholes and parts begins to become clearer. An organization is a whole in so far as it acts as a whole on its surround. These external relations can be sustained only so long as its internal relations support them. This relation between inner and outer is not a simple dichotomy; for systems may be related hierarchically.

[…]

One further important point remains to be noted. Forms are indeed often related hierarchically and it is this which encourages us to differentiate them as wholes and parts. Cells, each a complex marvel of organization, combine to form organs which together create organisms which support persons, which combine in societies. But relations are not necessarily arranged hierarchically, as the example of the school has shown. Many 'entities' form part of many different systems which are not themselves related in any hierarchic fashion, though events may raise one or other to a status of overriding importance. Few urban activities, for example, can continue for long if the sewage system stops working. Yet whilst it works, it is taken for granted as one of many physical support systems.

In the chapters which follow I will develop some of these ideas further; but I hope this introduction has made the basic ideas as I see them sufficiently clear to be summarized.

1. Systems are nets of *relations* which are sustained through *time*. The processes by which they are sustained are the process of *regulation*. The limits within which they can be sustained are the conditions of their *stability*.
2. Open systems depend on and contribute to their surround and are thus involved in *interdependence* with it as well as being dependent on the interaction of their internal relationships. This interdependence imposes *constraints* on all their constituents. *Organization* can mitigate but not remove these constraints which tend to become more demanding and sometimes even more contradictory as the scale of organization rises. This places a limit, though usually not a predictable one, on the possibilities of organization.
3. Open systems cannot, by definition, be 'wholes' if this is taken to mean systems wholly independent of their surround. But in so far as any open system acts as a whole in relation to its surround it is useful to distinguish the *internal relations* which enable it to do so from the *external relations* which it thus sustains. It is thus both legitimate and necessary to move freely from the consideration of a system as a whole to the consideration of it as part of a larger system; it is equally legitimate and necessary to realize that its constituents may also be constituents of other systems.
4. Systems are thus *tools of understanding* devised by human minds for understanding situations, including situations in which human beings appear as constituents. They are not *arbitrary* constructs. They must include the minimum number of relationships needed to constitute the situation which is to be understood. But this is defined by its relevance to the *concerns* of some human minds.

References

Adams et al. (1987). Preface. In G. Vickers (Ed.), *Policymaking, communication, and social learning* (pp. xi–xiv). New Brunswick, NJ: Transaction Publishers.

Blackmore, C. (2005). Learning to appreciate learning systems for environmental decision making: A 'Work-in-Progress' perspective. *Systems Research and Behavioral Science, 22*(4), 329–341.

Blunden, M. (1984). Geoffrey Vickers – An intellectual journey. In Open Systems Group (Ed.), *The Vickers papers* (pp. 3–42). London: Harper & Row.

Blunden, M. (1985). Vickers' contribution to management thinking. *Journal of Applied Systems Analysis, 12*, 107–112.

Blunden, M. (1994). Vickers and postliberalism. *American Behavioral Scientist, 38*(1), 11–25.

Boulding, K. (1956). *The image: Knowledge in life and society*. Ann Arbor, MI: Michigan University Press.

Boulding, K. (1983). Foreword. In G. Vickers (Ed.), *Human systems are different*. London: Harper and Row.

Checkland, P. B. (2005). Webs of significance: The work of Geoffrey Vickers. *Systems Research and Behavioral Science, 22*(4), 285–290.

Checkland, P.B., & Casar, A. (1986). Vickers' concept of an appreciative system: A systemic account. *Journal of Applied Systems Analysis, 13*, 3–17.

Churchman, C. W. (1984). Preface. In Open Systems Group (Ed.), *The Vickers papers* (pp. v–vi). London: Harper & Row.

Dando, M. (1994). The management of international conflict. *American Behavioral Scientist, 38*(1), 133–152.

Forester, J. (1994). Judgment and the cultivation of appreciation in policy-making. *American Behavioral Scientist, 38*(1), 64–74.

Ison, R. L. (2005). Geoffrey Vickers 2004: Contemporary applications and changing appreciative settings. *Systems Research and Behavioral Science, 22*(4), 277–284.

Miller, P. (2005). Memories of Geoffrey. *Systems Research and Behavioral Science, 22*(4), 347–348.

Open Systems Group (Ed.) (1984). *The Vickers papers*. London: Harper & Row.

Vickers, G. (1965). *The art of judgment: A study of policy making*. London: Harper and Row.

Vickers, G. (1968). *Value systems and social processes*. London: Tavistock Publications.

Vickers, G. (1972). *Freedom in a rocking boat*. London: Penguin.

Vickers, G. (1978). Practice and research in managing human systems – Four problems of relationship. *Policy Sciences, 9*(1), 1–8.

Vickers, G. (1983). *Human systems are different*. London: Harper and Row.

Williams, G. (2005). Geoffrey Vickers: Philosopher of responsibility. *Systems Research and Behavioral Science, 22*(4), 291–298.

Chapter 9
Howard Odum

This is a tale of two brothers, Howard and Eugene Odum, and how they introduced ideas from general systems theory and cybernetics into the field of ecology, in the process coming to dominate ecology as an academic discipline for decades. While both drew on systems ideas, our focus is on the younger brother, Howard, as it was he who more explicitly brought these ideas into ecology and was more closely aligned with systems organisations. The importance of the Odum brothers' contribution has been summed up by a former student of Howard's, who wrote that they "were not only among the first to educate generations of scholars and the public about ecology but also pioneers in uniting the human and social aspects of environmental issues with their ecological and natural dimensions" (Gunderson et al. 2002).

Howard Thomas Odum was born in 1924 in North Carolina, USA and died in 2002 in Florida. His father, Howard Washington Odum, was a distinguished sociologist who worked on the regional characteristics of the American South, and was a notable early white proponent of black rights; his influence ensured that "understanding the relationship between humans and their immediate environment was something of a family tradition" (Madison 1997, pp. 209–210). Because he shared his father's first name, Howard Thomas Odum was usually referred to as Tom or HT (the latter being his own preference). HT's brother Eugene was ten years older than him, born in 1913, and was a pioneer of ecology; he had a huge influence on the field through his textbook *Fundamentals of Ecology* (first published in 1953), which was the major textbook in the field for many years and appeared in several editions, most with HT's involvement. Eugene Odum also died in 2002, just one month before his younger brother.

HT Odum took his first degree in zoology, graduating in 1947 from the University of North Carolina. His studies were interrupted by the Second World War, and he spent the time in the US Air Force as a tropical meteorologist, which gave him early experience of modelling and the role of energy in natural systems, both of which would become major themes in his later work. He did his graduate work at Yale in the field of biogeochemistry, studying the global strontium cycle and completing his Ph.D. in 1951. His supervisor at Yale was G. Evelyn Hutchinson, a participant in the Macy conferences on cybernetics who was a boyhood friend of Gregory Bateson and was one of the first to incorporate feedback concepts in ecology. Hutchinson "criticized ecological principles that maintained a dualism between living formations and their physical conditions – climate, soil and so on – and he worked to integrate biological and physical processes in a practical program of ecology" (Taylor 2005, p. 56).

After his time at Yale, Odum moved to the University of Florida where he spent four years. Between 1954 and 1970 he was based in four different universities – Duke University in North Carolina, and the universities of Texas, Puerto Rico and North Carolina – each broadening his awareness of different types of ecosystems and deepening his theoretical work. In 1970 he returned to the University of Florida where he spent the rest of his career, in the department of Environmental Engineering Sciences. He introduced several important concepts to ecology (discussed further below), such as a focus on energy, the maximum power principle and 'emergy'; and he developed a powerful set of diagrams mapping energy flows in a range of ecological systems. He was notable for the range of his fieldwork as an ecologist – freshwater springs, coral reefs, large ocean bays, tropical rain forests, agriculture, swamps and others. He was also a leader, along with others, in founding the fields of systems ecology, ecological economics and ecological engineering, each now major areas.

The Odum brothers were responsible for the widespread use of the concept of the ecosystem, a unit that includes all living organisms in a given location and their natural environment, under the view that these are "inseparably inter-related and interact upon each other" (EP Odum 1971, p. 8). The word 'ecosystem' has a history going back to 1935 when it was coined by the British biologist Arthur Tansley, but it was through the Odums' work that it came to popular use. Their understanding of ecosystems was described clearly after their deaths by Gunderson et al (2002):

> In response to Aldo Leopold's contention that we need to "think like a mountain" to understand ecology, the Odums would have argued that we need [to] think like a system. Their world view was one of systems, i.e., components, connections, and complexity. They fought long and hard to develop a science that was not just about dissecting and understanding parts, but about understanding and unraveling the dynamics of the whole.

HT Odum was a highly innovative thinker, who taught his many students through extensive experience of fieldwork as well as through theory. At his memorial service, "many generations of his students spoke of his influence and stature as a genius" (Gunderson et al. 2002) while others described "his kindness, for his ability to bring out the best in everyone, his mentoring, and his care for the 'underdog'" (Brown et al. 2004, p. 4). After his death, one student recalled an experience of being taught in a fieldwork setting by Odum: "We're trekking around the marshes at Cedar Key [in Florida] … the mosquitoes are really, really bad. HT has his head down in the root zone; someone comments on the mosquitoes that are getting to him. And, of course, he says: 'the real issue is to ask and understand what the mosquitoes are doing for this system'. And that captures his gift: asking the key question, at the key moment, and at the key scale that most of us don't think about" (Gilliland 1994, p. 89).

Odum wrote a number of important papers and books that took forward the field of ecology, perhaps most notably *Environment, Power and Society* (HT Odum 1971), described as "a book that changed the lives of many who read it" (Brown et al. 2003, p. 294) and still highly relevant today. The development of systems ecology, set out in his book of the same name (HT Odum 1983), was perhaps the greatest single contribution that Odum made. It arose from the application of ideas from both general systems theory and cybernetics to the field of ecology. He described this approach as the use not of a microscope but rather a 'macroscope' and noted that:

> Bit by bit the machinery of the macroscope is evolving in various sciences and in the philosophical attitudes of students. ... Whereas men used to search among the parts to find mechanistic explanations, the macroscopic view is the reverse. Men, already having a clear view of the parts in their fantastically complex detail, must somehow get away, rise above, step back, group parts, simplify concepts, interpose frosted glass, and thus somehow see the big patterns. (HT Odum 1971, p. 10).

This macroscopic approach, of studying large-scale systems of great complexity, was at the heart of systems ecology. As early as 1957, in a monograph describing a widely-read early study of a river ecosystem in Silver Springs, Florida, Odum described his goal as "the complete quantitative determination of the states and flow [in the situation] as well as the control mechanisms by which such a picture is sustained" (HT Odum 1957, p. 59) – a goal clearly influenced by cybernetics. Influenced by the biogeochemical approach of his doctoral work, HT Odum – and his brother Eugene – came to see *energy* as the most useful way of describing both ecosystems and their control mechanisms. In this they were heavily drawing on ideas from thermodynamics, in which field the concept of energy is central, just as Ludwig von Bertalanffy had done in forming the basic ideas of general systems theory.

The central method for Odum in understanding the behaviour of an ecosystem at any scale was to follow its energy flows: the way in which energy was transferred and transformed from one part of the system to another. This approach gave him the capacity to follow the behaviour of a system closely, and to create general principles about its behaviour. Three of these principles stand out from his work. First was the *maximum power principle*, which states that ecosystems tend to evolve to a state that maximises their power output rather than their efficiency. Second was his concept of *embodied energy*, "the work previously required to generate a product or service" (HT Odum 1996, p. vii), which he argued must be taken into account to ascertain the true cost of something. Third, he developed a detailed method for drawing *energy systems diagrams*, a highly stylised form of circuit diagram including elements such as energy sources, sinks and stores, which allowed for detailed modelling of ecosystems that did not require the user to have a knowledge of mathematics. There are clear parallels between Odum's diagram work and the system dynamics modelling of Jay Forrester – each used quite similar symbols, drawing upon physical analogies to model social and natural systems. Odum was aware of these parallels but there has been no significant collaboration between users of the approaches.

Based on his analysis of energy flows, Odum vividly argued that the agricultural revolution had been badly misunderstood as being driven by efficiency gains, although in fact it was very dependent on oil use, an idea which is still very relevant given today's widespread concern about carbon emissions and the environmental impact of food production and transportation (HT Odum 1971, pp. 115–116):

> The great conceit of industrial man imagined that his progress in agricultural yields was due to new know-how in the use of the sun. A whole generation of citizens thought that the carrying capacity of the earth was proportional to the amount of land under cultivation and that higher efficiencies in using the energy of the sun had arrived. This is a sad hoax, for industrial man no longer eats potatoes made from solar energy; now he eats potatoes partly made of oil.

Odum understood his work as being in the area of general systems theory, writing in *Systems Ecology,* that "in this book we seek to understand the principles of general systems theory along with the reality of environmental systems" (HT Odum 1983, p. 4). He was chair of the International Society for Systems Sciences (the successor to the Society for General Systems Research which von Bertalanffy and Boulding had founded) in 1991 and his work had a clear ethical basis in line with the Society's founding principle of "science in service of humanity". While aspects of his work resemble other areas within systems thinking – his focus on feedback being close to cybernetics, and his diagram-based modelling being close to system dynamics – the systems community with which he was most closely connected was that of general systems theory.

In later life, both HT and Eugene Odum were to gain considerable recognition for their work. They jointly received several important international prizes, most significantly the Crafoord Prize from the Royal Swedish Academy of Sciences in 1987, considered to be the equivalent of the Nobel Prize in a number of fields, including ecology, where Alfred Nobel did not establish an award. The Academy's citation for the award said that the brothers "initiated a new epoch in the history of ecology ... they have laid a firm foundation for systems ecology, the study of how the different ecosystems are built up and how they function" (Royal Swedish Academy of Sciences 1987).

The work of the Odum brothers was not uncontroversial, both in their time and to the present day – they have been criticised by ecologists, general systems theorists and sociologists. From an ecological perspective, the Odums were seen as advocating a view that ecosystems necessarily exist in equilibrium (strictly speaking, in what von Bertalanffy called dynamic equilibrium or a 'steady state'). However, as Partridge (2005) has argued, while the Odums did focus on equilibrium in their early work, they shifted their position with the rest of the scientific community, and in late work Eugene Odum wrote (citing the work of Ilya Prigogine) that "an ecosystem is a thermodynamically open, far from equilibrium, system" (EP Odum 1992, p. 542).

From a general systems perspective the main criticisms have been two-fold. First, they have been criticised for the reductionist step of representing all systems in terms of energy flows, thus "reinforcing a utilitarian and managerial view of the relationship between humans and nature" (Hammond 1997, p. 198), although in his defence we have seen that HT Odum with his macroscopic perspective saw this as essentially a form of abstraction. Second, they have been criticised for not taking multiple perspectives into account, in particular when they move from purely natural systems to those involving human beings – Kenneth Boulding wrote of the Odums' work that "the basic error is the failure to recognise that all values are human values created by human valuations. Social systems cannot be reduced to physical descriptions whether in terms of energy, entropy, or any other kind of physical or engineering efficiency concepts" (Boulding 1977, quoted by Hammond 1997, p. 202).

HT Odum has been criticised from a sociological perspective for his "technocratic optimism" (Taylor 2005, p. 53) – the view that all the problems of the world could be solved by technology, if it were only harnessed correctly by intelligent people. In fact, Odum was often against the introduction of technology into ecosystems (as we have seen in his criticism of oil use) – Taylor's criticism relates rather to Odum's modelling of ecosystems using tools from engineering such as circuit diagrams, and the rationality that goes with that.

These criticisms aside, it is clear that Howard Thomas Odum was a highly creative and influential thinker who did a huge amount to bring systems ideas into the field of ecology and the environment. His legacy was summed up during his lifetime as follows: "H.T. Odum sees nature in a fundamentally new and incredibly important way. His greatest gift has been to give biologists, ecologists and engineers a new set of eyes with which to view the living world. He is like a master painter confronting a huge blank canvas. ... He is altering our perception of nature, design and the future" (Todd 1994, p. 104).

Reading from Odum's work

Systems Ecology: an Introduction, Odum, H.T. New York: John Wiley Copyright © 1983. Reproduced with permission of John Wiley & Sons Inc.
Extract from pages 17–19.

An environmental system is a network of component parts and processes on the scale of the environment. Environmental systems usually include some area of the earth's land or water. Examples are forests, lakes, seas, farms, cities, regions, countries, and the biosphere as a whole. These tend to be comprised of living organisms, chemical cycles, water flows, components of the earth, and so on. The components often include humans and human-manufactured machines, units, or organization such as industry, cities, economic exchanges, social behavior, and transportation, communication, information processing, politics, and many others. Each of these components is a complex subsystem of the larger environmental systems. Biological community subsystems control the detailed performances of the many species of living organisms. What is a system, and what is a subsystem is an arbitrary characteristic of one's point of view. One person's system is another person's subsystem. There are apparently similar laws of function and mechanism operating at all levels of scale and size.

The word 'ecosystem' is a short expression for 'ecological system'. To some people, 'ecological system' has become a synonym for 'environmental system'. Others use the word 'ecosystem' only for those systems of nature that generally do not include humans. In this book we use the terms 'ecosystem' and 'environmental system' interchangeably. An organized system of land, water, mineral cycles, living organisms, and their programmatic behavioral control mechanisms is called an *ecosystem.*

Examples of large ecosystems are whole forested regions, the seas, and the biosphere as a whole. Examples of small ecosystems are such associations of organisms and microenvironments, as ponds, coral heads, and aquaria in school classrooms. Small ecosystems are subsystems within the larger ones. In the broadest modern usage, systems that include humans, such as farms, industries, and cities, are also regarded as ecosystems, and there is a growing recognition that humans are incomplete without the life support of self-maintaining natural ecosystems. All these systems develop structures and processes adapted to the environmental inputs available to them.

In time through the process of trial and error, complex patterns of structure and process have evolved, the successful ones surviving because they use materials and energies well in their own maintenance, competing well with other patterns that chance interposes. The parts of successful ecosystems are organized by exchanges of minerals, food chains, economic transfers, and other work services that act among the components. These pathways of work can be diagrammed to show the designs of ecosystems [e.g. Fig. 9.1]. The engineering of new ecosystems designs is a new field that uses systems that are mainly self-organizing. Ecosystems will require delicate and intelligent measures for effective use.

With our growing knowledge of ecological design, management of the ecosystems by human interactions is one of the bright hopes for humans if their large, rich sources of energy supporting their present complex urban system begins to wane.

Example of an environmental system

Figure 9.1 is a diagram of a typical environmental system that has several energy sources, each of a different quality and a coarse aggregation of components to show organization in the characteristic hierarchical pattern.

In qualitative translation into English, the diagram in Fig. 9.1 expresses energy inflows in (1) sunlight, (2) accompanying rain, and (3) geologic uplift. These develop soils and interact to operate production by environmental life support systems (natural areas without humans) and production by agriculture and forestry. These supply products and services to the urban areas along with imports that are obtained by purchases with money. The money for purchasing imports comes from sale of exports. The urban systems send wastes back to the environmental system and services of labor, fertilizer, equipment, and so on, to the agriculture and forestry sector. A switching unit controls the harvest of products for shipment to the urban

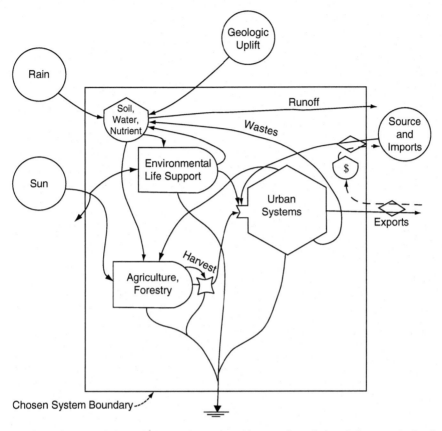

Fig. 9.1 Diagram of an environmental system with use of symbols of the energy circuit language

systems. The life-support systems help build soils. Outflows include the exports; the runoff; and the used, degraded energy.

Cycle of materials

A characteristic of systems is their recycling of materials, especially those that have few inflows. Forests and plankton ecosystems recycle phosphorus, human economies recycle steel and aluminum, the biosphere recycles water, the mountain building systems recycle sediment materials, and so on. Diagrams of systems usually show this important feature; for instance, Fig. 9.1 shows a recycle of wastes (Lotka 1925).

Material flows as energy flows

Sometimes there is confusion about the energy associated with flows of materials. Since any concentration of a substance relative to its environment constitutes a small potential energy storage, all recognizable flows of materials carry an energy content. The energy is sufficient to drive the degrading diffusion of that substance away from its concentrations.

Although the actual concentrations of energy are small, the embodied energy of successive work in developing the concentrations may be very large. For example, large solar energies are used to develop the food chains to guano birds, which in turn develop island phosphate deposits. The solar energy embodied in phosphate deposits is large. The energy transformation ratio is the ratio of solar calories per calorie of phosphate concentration. [...] Generally, the more critical and important a material is as a limiting factor, the more embodied energy it carries. The energy is of high quality.

[...]

Information flows as energy flows

As one passes from abundant low-quality energy through successive transformations in chains or webs [...] the actual calorie flows decline, but the embodied energy and energy quality increases as already described. Where the sequence of transformations is very long, only tiny fractions of the original quantity of calories is still contained, but the energy transformation ratios are very large. Customarily people don't regard these flows as energy, but usually call them *information*. Flows of genes, books, television communications, computer programs, human culture, art, political interactions, and religious communications are examples of information. However, these all have very large embodied energies and high ratios of calories of solar energy per calorie of information. It is still appropriate to consider the calories of potential energy in information, since this is what drives the depreciation and loss of information as with losses of other kinds of storage. Information cannot be stored without some concentration of substance or energy fields relative to the environment. For example, words on a page are concentrations of ink, memory on a computer disk is a concentration of magnetic field, and information in biological genes is a storage of DNA form relative to the environment.

The flows of information carry the most embodied energy and also have the greatest amplifier and control effects per calorie. They are the feedbacks of highly embodied energy that provide systems with specialized services, feeding back positive actions that 'repay' their webs for the energy dispersed in the development of the information. [...] Information pathways are energy pathways also and are drawn in energy language as regular pathways, but usually feeding back from the far right side of the diagrams.

Money is a special kind of information flow that controls through its circulation as a countercurrent with exchange rates according to human behavior programs for reacting to prices. Energy circuit language uses dashed lines or color to help recognize this component web.

Structure and function

Understanding structure and function is an often stated objective of system sciences. Structure is in the pattern of connections and in the storages. To simplify models, the patterns of connections of complex diagrams may be combined as a single storage in aggregating detail. Functions are flows and changes of state as energy passes through network structure. Processes are located at points of energy transformation usually at intersections.

References

Brown, M. T. et al. (2003). Prof. Howard T. Odum, 1924–2002. *Energy, 28*(3), 293–301.

Brown, M. T., Hall, C. A. S., Jørgensen, S. E. (2004). Eulogy. *Ecological Modelling 178*(1/2), 1–10.

Gilliland, M. W. (1994). Letter to the editor. *Ecological Engineering, 3*(2), 89.

Gunderson, L., Folke C., Lee M., Holling C. S. (2002). In memory of Mavericks. *Conservation Ecology, 6*(2), article 19. http://www.consecol.org/vol6/iss2/art19/. Accessed 13 Jan 2009.

Hammond, D. (1997). Ecology and ideology in the general systems community. *Environment and History, 3*(2), 197–207.

Lotka, A. (1925). *Elements of physical biology*. New York: Williams and Wilkins.

Madison, M. (1997). 'Potatoes made of oil': Eugene and Howard Odum and the origins and limits of American agroecology. *Environment and History, 3*(2), 209–238.

Odum, E. P. (1971). *Fundamentals of ecology* (3rd edition). Philadelphia: W.B. Saunders.

Odum, E. P. (1992). Great ideas in ecology for the 1990s. *Bioscience, 42*(7), 542–545.

Odum, H. T. (1957). Trophic structure and productivity of Silver Springs, Florida. *Ecological Monographs, 27*(1), 55–112.

Odum, H. T. (1971). *Environment, power, and society*. New York: Wiley-Interscience.

Odum, H. T. (1983). *Systems ecology: An introduction*. New York: John Wiley.

Odum, H. T. (1996). *Environmental accounting: EMERGY and environmental decision making*. New York: John Wiley.

Partridge (2005). "Disequilibrium ecology" – much ado about nothing. Group meeting of the International Society for Environmental Ethics. http://gadfly.igc.org/ecology/APA-ISEE.htm. Accessed 13 Jan 2009.

Royal Swedish Academy of Sciences (1987). Press release: The Crafoord prizewinners 1987 Eugene P. Odum and Howard T. Odum. http://www.kva.se/en/Press_room/Press-releases/The-Crafoord-Prizewinners-1987-Eugene-P-Odum-and-Howard-T-Odum/.

Taylor, P. J. (2005). *Unruly complexity: Ecology, interpretation, engagement*. Chicago: University of Chicago Press.

Todd, J. (1994). Letter to the editor. *Ecological Engineering, 3*(2), 104.

System Dynamics

Revealing the underlying dynamics of organisational, societal and global systems through computer modelling

Chapter 10
Jay Forrester

Jay Wright Forrester is an American engineer and management thinker. He is the founder of System Dynamics, an approach based on computer modelling which arguably has done more than any other method to provide a practical and realistic analysis of change processes in systems. System Dynamics (SD) has been taken up across the world, initially by Forrester's students and colleagues, but increasingly by a much wider community. It has had profound and influential applications in a range of fields, most prominently organisational management, urban planning and environmental policy. Forrester summed up his concerns and his understanding of SD in an 'elevator pitch' (a statement short enough to be spoken in an elevator ride) on an email list:

> System dynamics deals with how things change through time, which includes most of what most people find important. It uses computer simulation to take the knowledge we already have about details in the world around us and to show why our social and physical systems behave the way they do. System dynamics demonstrates how most of our own decision-making policies are the cause of the problems that we usually blame on others, and how to identify policies we can follow to improve our situation. (Forrester 1997).

Jay Forrester was born in 1918 in rural Nebraska, in the midwestern United States. He grew up on a cattle ranch where he had the experience that "in an agricultural setting, life must be very practical. It is not theoretical; nor is it conceptual without purpose. It is full-time immersion in the real world" (Forrester 2007, p. 345). Although he considered continuing in agriculture, he took his undergraduate degree in electrical engineering at the University of Nebraska, graduating in 1939. This study gave him a further important lesson – in his view electrical engineering was "about the only academic field with a solid, central core of theoretical dynamics" (Forrester 2007, p. 345).

These two aspects of his character – a focus on results and on being practical combined with a theoretical interest in dynamics – have shaped his work ever since. One colleague describes him as "quiet, imposingly tall and faultlessly courteous. He speaks slowly and in an assured way, producing analyses of a complexity seldom found in conversation. ... He is direct and unambiguous in what he wishes to convey, firmly and consistently supportive of people and ideas he approves of. Of those he does not support he can be trenchant and devastating, or nuanced and delicate, seemingly depending on the approach that he judges will be most effective in delivering his message" (Lane 2007, p. 110).

In 1939, Forrester moved to the Massachusetts Institute of Technology, where he spent his entire career, formally retiring in 1989, and is still a professor emeritus and active researcher. His initial work was in the Servomechanisms Laboratory, founded by Gordon Brown who was to become his mentor over 50 years, "substantially responsible for helping me develop my career" (Forrester 1996, p. 350). Brown was Forrester's employer as a research assistant during the years of the Second World War; he supervised Forrester's Masters thesis (passed in 1945); and it was even through Brown that Forrester met his wife, Susan. Moreover, the "feedback system theory that I learned in his Servomechanisms Laboratory became the foundation for the field of system dynamics" (Forrester 1996, p. 350).

Servomechanisms are mechanical devices which control the behaviour of a larger system through feedback. A classic example is the thermostat controlling the boiler of a heating system. During the war, Brown and Forrester worked on servomechanisms to control the behaviour of radar antennae and gun mounts. Following the war, Forrester began work on the design of an early aircraft flight simulator. The simulator was intended to be based on an analogue computer, but ended up as one of the very first digital computers, Whirlwind, which in due course evolved into SAGE (Semi-Autonomous Ground Environment), an air defence system.

Whirlwind, for which Forrester was project leader (it began operation in 1951), was ground-breaking: it was the first digital computer to operate in real time and to use video displays for output. A further important innovation in the Whirlwind project was Forrester's invention of magnetic core memory, for many years the dominant form of computer memory. A key employee on this work was Ken Olsen, the founder of the Digital Equipment Corporation, on whose board Forrester served for many years.

By 1956, Forrester felt that "the pioneering days in digital computers were over" (Forrester 1989, p. 4). He remained at MIT but moved to its School of Management (later the Sloan School), founded in 1952 with a large grant from Alfred Sloan, head of General Motors. This was less of a large shift than it might seem – as head of the Whirlwind project, he had already experienced several years as a manager of a very large scale project, involving negotiation and contracting with several partner organisations. His initial goal in moving to the School of Management was to apply the lessons he had learned about technology to issues of management. In doing so he created the field of system dynamics.

Forrester's first study involved fluctuations in levels of sales, inventory and employees in household appliances at General Electric (GE). The company was going through inexplicable cycles, apparently unrelated to normal business demand, where sometimes their workers would be terribly over-stretched and at other times the company would have to sack people. Forrester was able to model the cycles and observe that they created positive feedback loops arising from delays in interactions between different departments of the company. Initially he modelled these using paper and pencil, but he was convinced of the importance of computers for enhancing management decision-making, and as part of the project a colleague built a compiler that allowed the direct entry of the feedback equations into a computer. This compiler later developed into DYNAMO, which was used for many years as the basis of simulation models within system dynamics. The model of GE's inventory control, and especially the delay between different departments, was later re-expressed in terms of beer production by Forrester's graduate students and became the basis of a classic simulation game used in many introductory courses, the MIT Beer Game.

Forrester published his first results as an article in the *Harvard Business Review* (Forrester 1958), later expanded to a book (Forrester 1961) – both with the title of 'Industrial Dynamics' which served as the name of the field for its first decade. As he presented it, the work rests on four foundations: feedback control theory, an understanding of decision-making processes, simulation, and the use of digital computers to enable mathematical modelling. Of these, he believed the first to be the most important, directly arising from work on servomechanisms. He wrote that from this theory we learnt about "the effect of time delays, amplification, and structure on the dynamic behaviour of a system ... [and] that the interaction between system components can be more important the components themselves" (Forrester 1961, p. 14).

The first ten years of work on system dynamics resulted in a solid theoretical core which continues to be the basis of the field to this day. In 1968, Forrester published a textbook which outlined the main concepts and methods of system dynamics (Forrester 1968a). He was very clear that SD was driven by the *structure* of systems and that the structure was described by a set of interlocking feedback loops. Importantly, "a model of a system is formulated by starting with the loop structure, not by starting with components of loops" (Forrester 1968b, p. 407). The interaction between these loops produces the behaviour of the system. These loops were made up of two different kinds of variables, referred to as *levels* (those which define the state of the system) and *rates* (those which define the flow between levels).

SD's strong emphasis on feedback and control suggests close parallels with cybernetics, and indeed the early development of both approaches was largely done at MIT. However, it is clear from Forrester's account that he took his understanding of feedback from quite different sources, largely that of servomechanisms, and had no connection with cybernetics. Richardson (1991), a former student of Forrester's, identifies two parallel threads of the use of feedback ideas in social sciences (the servomechanisms thread and the cybernetics thread) with important distinctions, placing Forrester along with a number of economists who applied feedback in their work, most notably Herbert Simon who later won the Nobel prize for his work on management decision-making. In particular, Richardson argues that those in the cybernetics thread (in which he also includes general systems theory) treat feedback as a "tool for controlling systems in the face of [external] disturbances" while those in the servomechanisms thread see feedback loops "as an internal aspect of the structure of social systems" (Richardson 1991, p. 164).

As well as being in a position to clarify the nature of the SD approach, 1968 saw Forrester and his colleagues – by then a well-established group at MIT – beginning to branch out to other fields beyond management. This was especially inspired by the outgoing mayor of Boston becoming a one year visiting professor at MIT, with an office next to Forrester's. Through this contact, Forrester became interested in the modelling of urban issues, and was able to assemble a group of those who understood the nature and problems of cities. The result was a detailed SD model of a city, published in the book *Urban Dynamics* (Forrester 1969). The book's conclusion was controversial: "that all of the major urban policies that the United States was following lay somewhere between neutral and highly detrimental, from the viewpoint either of the city as an institution, or from the viewpoint of the low-income, unemployed residents" (Forrester 1989, p. 8). Its methodology was no less controversial – instead of drawing upon existing literature on urban planning, it worked entirely from a computer model. The book tended to polarise opinions, some very positive and others very negative. The ideas in Forrester's book were later taken up (in the late 1980s) as the basis for a highly successful computer game, SimCity, which simulated the behaviour of a number of cities and allowed players to control aspects of their design and management.

Forrester's urban modelling also led directly to the most famous application of SD, the modelling of the world economy and ecosystem. This work was carried out through the Club of Rome, an informal and small group of influential people in business, academia and politics, founded by Aurelio Peccei, an Italian business executive. Learning of Forrester's urban work, Peccei invited him to join the Club and to attend a meeting in Switzerland in 1970. The Club had been offered a grant from the Volkswagen Foundation if they could propose a clear research project to tackle what they called the '*problématique humaine*': the interlocking issues of global population, crime, pollution, resource depletion, terrorism etc (Kleiner 1996). After listening to a series of debates that were proving increasingly unsatisfactory, Forrester proposed the development of an SD model of the world problems, and invited the Club to visit MIT to explore the approach and its potential. The bulk of the modelling work was carried out within the MIT SD group by a team led by one of Forrester's former students, Dennis Meadows. Forrester wrote a further book based on this work, *World Dynamics* (Forrester 1971) which was a surprise best-seller and highly controversial, even being reviewed on the front pages of some newspapers; the more popular book which followed, *Limits to Growth* (Meadows et al. 1972) sold still better and was still more controversial. This work is discussed in greater depth in the chapter on Donella Meadows. It was during the Club of Rome project that Forrester's group started to use the term 'system dynamics' rather than 'industrial dynamics', given that the focus of the work was much broader than industrial applications (Meadows 2002).

The work around urban and world dynamics led Forrester in a further direction: the SD National Model, a project to build a detailed model of the US economy with the ability to predict as well as describe economic phenomena. This began in the early 1970s and was the subject of a large amount of research by Forrester and his colleagues over a number of years. The group published early descriptions of the national model, but no definitive description of the project. However, Forrester

(2007, p. 352) reported that he was writing a book on the subject, then with the planned title of "A General Theory of Economic Behavior". Forrester has also actively pursued the use of SD in education at all levels – clearly at university and post-experience level, but also with a particular interest in the possibility of teaching it to school-children.

Two other aspects of Forrester's further development of SD are especially interesting. First, he has overseen its development at MIT over the past 50 years, and actively led a large research group for most of that time, from whom have come such figures as Donella Meadows, John Sterman and Peter Senge among many others. As one indication of the level of activity, over a period of 47 years, the SD group produced almost 5,000 working papers.

Admirably, however, Forrester has made no attempt to create an 'official' version of system dynamics and prevent others from developing their ideas within the field. In fact, the ownership of SD as a field is now held by the System Dynamics Society, founded as an international society in 1983 and now with more than 1,100 members in 58 different countries (Lane 2007). This society holds an annual conference and publishes a successful journal. Forrester was its founding president, and is recognised and honoured as the founder of the field, but his voice as to the future is only one of many.

The second striking aspect of Forrester's later work has been his treatment of models. Computer-based modelling is central to system dynamics, and the chief criticisms of the field often arise from this, assuming that the models are used in a simplistic way. Forrester takes a basically realist position on model-building, explicitly positioning himself against Checkland and arguing that "in system dynamics, we have a set of principles, incomplete as they may be, that I believe do represent the actual nature of physical and social reality" (Forrester 1994, p. 250). There are subtler issues involved, however. As SD has developed, it has become clear that the modelling *process* is as important as the resulting model. As Sterman (2002, p. 521) has written, citing a much earlier paper of Forrester's, "because all models are wrong, we reject the notion that models can be validated in the dictionary definition sense of 'establishing truthfulness', instead focusing on creating models that are useful ... we argue that focusing on the process of modelling rather than on the results of any particular model speeds learning and leads to better models, better policies, and a greater chance of implementation and system improvement". Given this attitude to modelling, Lane has argued that it is meaningless to situate SD as a 'hard systems thinking' approach; rather it has a "much more participative and contingent relationship between a model and those working with it" (Lane 2000, p. 18).

In creating system dynamics, Jay Forrester built more than a method or theory – he created a whole new form of thinking. While focused on computer-based modelling and thus expert-driven, it is highly practical and oriented towards real change in real situations. As Morecroft and Homer (2007, p. 20) have written, Forrester has "established for [system dynamics] an analytic paradigm that combines boldness and broad vision with rigor and depth". In doing so he has made a great and long-lasting contribution.

Reading from Forrester's work

Forrester, Jay Wright 1975 from "Counterintuitive Behaviour of Social Systems", in Chapter 14
of *Collected Papers of Jay W. Forrester*. Waltham, MA: Pegasus Communications.

Computer models of social systems

People would never send a space ship to the moon without first testing prototype models and making computer simulations of anticipated trajectories. No company would put a new household appliance or airplane into production without first making laboratory tests. Such models and laboratory tests do not guarantee against failure, but they do identify many weaknesses which can be corrected before they cause full-scale disasters.

Social systems are far more complex and harder to understand than technological systems. Why then do we not use the same approach of making models of social systems and conducting laboratory experiments before adopting new laws and government programs? The customary answer assumes that our knowledge of social systems is not sufficient for constructing useful models.

But what justification can there be for assuming that we do not know enough to construct models of social systems but believe we do know enough to directly redesign social systems by passing laws and starting new programs? I suggest that we now do know enough to make useful models of social systems. Conversely, we do not know enough to design the most effective social policies directly without first going through a model-building experimental phase. Substantial supporting evidence is accumulating that proper use of models of social systems can lead to far better systems, laws, and programs.

Realistic laboratory models of social systems can now be constructed. Such models are simplifications of actual systems, but computer models can be far more comprehensive than the mental models that would otherwise be used.

Before going further, please realize that there is nothing new in the use of models to represent social systems. Each of us uses models constantly. Every person in private life and in business instinctively uses models for decision making. The mental images in one's head about one's surroundings are models. One's head does not contain real families, businesses, cities, governments, or countries. One uses selected concepts and relationships to represent real systems. A mental image is a model. All decisions are taken on the basis of models. All laws are passed on the basis of models. All executive actions are taken on the basis of models. The question is not to use or ignore models. The question is only a choice among alternative models.

Mental models are fuzzy, incomplete, and imprecisely stated. Furthermore, within a single individual, mental models change with time, even during the flow of a single conversation. The human mind assembles a few relationships to fit the context of a discussion. As debate shifts, so do the mental models. Even when only a single topic is being discussed, each participant in a conversation employs a different mental model to interpret the subject. Fundamental assumptions differ but are never brought into the open. Goals are different but left unstated.

It is little wonder that compromise takes so long. And even when consensus is reached, the underlying assumptions may be fallacies that lead to laws and programs that fail. The human mind is not adapted to understanding correctly the consequences implied by a mental model. A mental model may be correct in structure and assumptions but, even so, the human mind – either individually or as a group consensus – is apt to draw the wrong implications for the future.

Inability of the human mind to use its own mental models becomes clear when a computer model is constructed to reproduce the assumptions contained in a person's mental model. The computer model is refined until it fully agrees with the perceptions of a particular person or group. Then, usually, the system that has been described does not act the way the people anticipated. There are internal contradictions in mental models between assumed structure and assumed future consequences. Ordinarily assumptions about structure and internal governing policies are more nearly correct than are the assumptions about implied behavior.

By contrast to mental models, system dynamics simulation models are explicit about assumptions and how they interrelate. Any concept that can be clearly described in words can be incorporated in a computer model. Constructing a computer model forces clarification of ideas. Unclear and hidden assumptions are exposed so they may be examined and debated.

The primary advantage of a computer simulation model over a mental model lies in the way a computer model can reliably determine the future dynamic consequences of how the assumptions within the model interact with one another. There need be no doubt about a digital computer accurately simulating the actions that result from statements about the structure and policies in a model.

In some ways, computer models are strikingly similar to mental models. Computer models are derived from the same sources; they may be discussed in the same terms. But computer models differ from mental models in important ways. Computer models are stated explicitly. The 'mathematical' notation used for describing the computer models is unambiguous. Computer simulation language is clearer, simpler, and more precise than spoken languages. Computer instructions have clarity of meaning and simplicity of language syntax. Language of a computer model can be understood by almost anyone, regardless of educational background. Furthermore, any concept that can be clearly stated in ordinary language can be translated into computer-model language.

There are many approaches to computer models. Some are naive. Some are conceptually inconsistent with the nature of actual systems. Some are based on methodologies for obtaining input data that commit the models to omitting major relationships in the psychological and human areas that we all know to be crucial. With so much activity in computer models and with the same terminology having different meanings in the different approaches, the situation is confusing to a casual observer. The key to success is not in having a computer; the important thing is how the computer is used. With respect to models, the key is not to computerize a model, but, instead, to have a model structure and decision-making policies that properly represent the system under consideration.

I am speaking here of system dynamics models – the kind of computer models that are only now becoming widely used in the social sciences. System dynamics models are not derived statistically from time-series data. Instead, they are statements about system structure and the policies that guide decisions. Models contain the assumptions being made about a system. A model is only as good as the expertise which lies behind its formulation. A good computer model is distinguished from a poor one by the degree to which it captures the essence of a system that it represents. Many other kinds of mathematical models are limited because they will not accept the multiple-feedback-loop and nonlinear nature of real systems.

On the other hand, system dynamics computer models can reflect the behavior of actual systems. System dynamics models show how difficulties with actual social systems arise, and demonstrate why so many efforts to improve social systems have failed. Models can be constructed that are far superior to the intuitive models in people's heads on which national social programs are now based.

System dynamics differs in two important ways from common practice in the social sciences and government. Other approaches assume that the major difficulty in understanding systems lies in shortage of information and data. Once data is collected, people have felt confident in interpreting the implications. I differ on both of these attitudes. The problem is not shortage of data but rather inability to perceive the consequences of information we already possess. The system dynamics approach starts with concepts and information on which people are already acting. Generally, available information about system structure and decision-making policies is sufficient. Available information is assembled into a computer model that can show behavioral consequences of well-known parts of a system. Generally, behavior is different from what people have assumed.

Counterintuitive nature of social systems

Our first insights into complex social systems came from corporate work. Time after time we went into corporations that were having severe and well-known difficulties. The difficulties would be obvious, such as falling market share, low profitability, or instability of employment. Such difficulties were known throughout the company and were discussed in the business press.

One can enter a troubled company and discuss what people see as the causes and solutions to their problems. One finds that people perceive reasonably correctly their immediate environments. They know what they are trying to accomplish. They know the crises which will force certain actions. They are sensitive to the power structure of the organization, to traditions, and to their own personal goals and welfare. When interviewing circumstances are conducive to frank disclosure, people state what they are doing and can give rational reasons for their actions. In a troubled company, people are usually trying in good conscience and to the best of their abilities to help solve the major difficulties. Policies are being followed that they believe will alleviate the difficulties. One can combine the stated policies into a computer model to show the consequences of how the policies interact with one another. In many instances it emerges that the known policies describe a system which actually causes the observed troubles. In other words, the known and intended practices of the organization are sufficient to create the difficulties being experienced. Usually, problems are blamed on outside forces, but a dynamic analysis often shows how internal policies are causing the troubles. In fact, a downward spiral can develop in which the presumed solutions make the difficulties worse and thereby cause greater incentives to redouble the very actions that are the causes of trouble.

The same downward spiral frequently develops in government. Judgment and debate lead to a program that appears to be sound. Commitment increases to the apparent solution. If the presumed solution actually makes matters worse, the process by which degradation happens is not evident. So, when the troubles increase, the efforts are intensified that are actually worsening the situation.

References

Forrester, J. W. (1958). Industrial dynamics: A major breakthrough for decision makers. *Harvard Business Review, 36*(4), 37–66.

Forrester, J. W. (1961). *Industrial dynamics*. Cambridge, MA: MIT Press.

Forrester, J. W. (1968a). *Principles of systems*. Cambridge, MA: MIT Press.

Forrester, J. W. (1968b). Industrial dynamics – After the first decade. *Management Science, 14*(7), 398–415.

Forrester, J. W. (1969). *Urban dynamics*. Cambridge, MA: MIT Press.

Forrester, J. W. (1971). *World dynamics*, Cambridge, MA: Wright-Allen Press.

Forrester, J.W. (1989). The beginning of system dynamics. System Dynamics Society, Stuttgart, 13 July 1989. http://sysdyn.clexchange.org/sdep/papers/D-4165-1.pdf. Accessed 13 Jan 2009.

Forrester, J.W. (1994). System dynamics, systems thinking, and soft OR. *System Dynamics Review, 10*(2–3), 245–256.

Forrester, J.W. (1996). Obituary: Gordon Stanley Brown (1907–1996). *System Dynamics Review, 12*(4), 350.

Forrester, J.W. (1997). System dynamics in the elevator. System-dynamics email list. http://www.ventanasystems.co.uk/forum/viewthread.php?tid=1787#pid1964. Accessed 13 Jan 2009.

Forrester, J.W. (2007). System dynamics – A personal view of the first fifty years. *System Dynamics Review, 23*(2/3), 345–358.

Kleiner, A. (1996). *The age of heretics: Heroes, outlaws, and the forerunners of corporate change.* London: Nicholas Brealey.

Lane, D.C. (2000). Should system dynamics be described as a 'Hard' or 'Deterministic' systems approach? *Systems Research and Behavioral Science, 17*(1), 3–22.

Lane, D.C. (2007). The power of the bond between cause and effect: Jay Wright Forrester and the field of system dynamics. *System Dynamics Review, 23*(2/3), 95–118.

Meadows, D.H., Meadows, D.L., Randers, J., Behrens, W.W. (1972). *The limits to growth: A report for the club of Rome's project on the predicament of mankind.* New York: Universe Books.

Meadows, D.L. (2002). Dana Meadows: Asking hard questions, speaking simple truths. *System Dynamics Review, 18*(2), 111–119.

Morecroft, J., & Homer, J. (2007). The 2006 Jay Wright Forrester Award. *System Dynamics Review, 23*(1), 19–20.

Richardson, G. P. (1991). *Feedback thought in social science and systems theory*. Philadelphia: University of Pennsylvania Press.

Sterman, J. (2002). All models are wrong: Reflections on becoming a systems scientist. *System Dynamics Review, 18*(4), 501–531.

Chapter 11
Donella Meadows

Donella Meadows – known as Dana to her many friends – was an environmental scientist and activist. She was a prolific writer, best known for a single book, *The Limits to Growth* (Meadows et al. 1972) which sold millions of copies, but she was also the author of several other books and a widely-read weekly newspaper column. As an activist, she lived the life she advocated, working as an organic farmer and living in a sustainable community. As a colleague said of her, "she talked sustainable development, and walked it" (Hafkamp 2001).

Meadows was born in 1941 in Illinois. Her education was solidly scientific – she took a BA in chemistry from Carleton College in Minnesota in 1963, and a Ph.D. in biophysics from Harvard in 1968. She began work as a postdoctoral researcher in biophysics at Harvard, taking a year off for an overland trip through Asia. She returned from the trip to Harvard but shortly thereafter left to work at MIT for two years on the Club of Rome world modelling project. In 1972, she moved to Dartmouth College where she taught environmental studies and system dynamics until she resigned her post in 1985 to concentrate on environmental activism. She founded several environmental institutes, wrote extensively, lived life as simply and close to the land as possible, and worked as a visiting scholar and fellow in a number of different academic and non-governmental organisations. She died from bacterial meningitis, after a short illness, in New Hampshire in 2001.

Her long trip to Asia in the late 1960s had a powerful impact on her personal and academic life. She visited a series of countries, including Turkey, Iran, Afghanistan, Pakistan, and India – as she wryly commented much later, "in those days Americans were welcome in all those countries" (DH Meadows 2002, p. 109) – living as simply as the people in the villages they visited, consuming no meat or alcohol, cut off from television and newspapers for weeks at a time, even finding hot showers to be a luxury. Returning to the US was a major shock: "Looking with Asian eyes, we couldn't believe how much stuff people had. We saw how little the stuff had to do with happiness. We also had strong memories of the poverty, the erosion, the deforestation, and the hunger we had seen. The world was very real to us. We resolved to live our lives in a way more consistent with the whole of it" (DH Meadows 2002, p. 109). This experience led her to move to an organic farm in New Hampshire, and to embrace an idea of self-sufficiency. Meadows' integrity, the consistency between her lifestyle and the ideas she advocated, was extraordinary – as one tribute following her death said:

> More than anyone I have ever met, Dana lived by the famous systems credo, 'Think Globally, Act Locally'. In her columns she wrote of the damage to the earth and its inhabitants caused by pesticides, herbicides, and factory farming. At home she was an organic farmer. From her sheep came wool she carded, dyed, spun, and knit into beautiful sweaters, socks, mittens, and more. The farm yielded a bounty of the most delicious food; the waste made compost and fed the chickens; their eggs nourished the people; the chicken manure enriched the garden. She truly closed the loop. (Sterman 2002, p. 103).

She became involved in the project that made her famous almost by accident. After returning from Asia, her husband Dennis (who had taken his Ph.D. in the System Dynamics group at MIT) returned to MIT and quickly became involved in the Club of Rome world modelling project, whose origins are described in the chapter of this book on Jay Forrester. Hearing about the project and noticing that "it sounded like a much more sophisticated version of the connections we had been making as we bumped over the roads of Asia" (DH Meadows 2007, p. 192), she postponed her return to her Harvard postdoctoral fellowship to attend the two-week seminar Forrester ran for the Club of Rome members. Her enthusiasm for the project was so great that she resigned her Harvard fellowship and worked on it without pay for the next two years. The system dynamics model, based on Forrester's original model, was known as World3. Each model was built up of five sectors – population, industry, agriculture, natural resources, and the environment. The project team consisted of seventeen researchers, led by Dennis Meadows. Donella's role was to write the population sector of World3, "integrating biological, social, cultural and economic factors in an endogenous account of fertility, aging, and mortality; in my view the best demographic model of its time, and still worthy of study today" (Sterman 2002, p. 102).

Eight months into the project, a meeting was held with the Club of Rome to present the project's initial findings. At that meeting, Jay Forrester argued strongly that the primary cause of the cluster of global problems being studied was *growth*, "exponential growth of energy use, material flows, and population against the earth's physical limits. That which all the world sees as the solution to its problems is in fact a cause of those problems" (DH Meadows 2007, p. 193). Linking her experiences in Asia with this argument, Meadows came to feel that "this fixation on growth … was a boastful, bullying, living thing, with its own malignant needs" (Kleiner 1996, p. 212). The Club of Rome's members heard this view and the initial results of the model respectfully, but their talk was still of different, albeit more benevolent, forms of growth as solutions to the world's problems. Frustrated, Meadows felt that the best route was to express these ideas more clearly, with little recourse to technical data. She produced a short paper for the Club of Rome, which gradually grew over the course of 1971 in response to comments from Club members. The project team intended to produce a detailed and highly technical report, but seeing this paper – now grown to the length of a short book – the Club of Rome's founder and president, Italian industrialist Aurelio Peccei, told the Meadows that "the technical report is fine, but what we really need is Dana's little memo as a book" (Kleiner 1996, p. 214).

The book was published early the following year, as *The Limits to Growth* (Meadows et al. 1972). The effect of the book was extraordinary. It was well-publicised – the publisher was a think-tank, Potomac Associates, who as a matter of course sent copies of their publications to politicians and policy-makers around the world, and organised a one-day symposium at the Smithsonian Institute in Washington DC, with several television crews present. Forrester's earlier book on the world model (Forrester 1971) had already been a bestseller, and this new book was even more widely read. *Limits to Growth* went on to be published in 30 languages and to sell around ten million copies.

The book discussed the nature and problems of exponential growth, describing and drawing on the World3 model. It presented three major conclusions (Meadows et al. 1972, pp. 23–24):

1. If the present growth trends in world population, industrialization, pollution, food production, and resource depletion continue unchanged, the limits to growth on this planet will be reached sometime within the next 100 years. The most probable result will be a rather sudden and uncontrollable decline in both population and industrial capacity.
2. It is possible to alter these growth trends and to establish a condition of ecological and economic stability that is sustainable far into the future. The state of global equilibrium could be designed so that the basic material needs of each person on earth are satisfied and each person has an equal opportunity to realize his individual human potential.
3. If the world's people decide to strive for this second outcome rather than the first, the sooner they begin working to attain it, the greater will be their chances of success.

It is important to realise that these conclusions were established and backed up by very rigorous computer-based modelling. Of course, *Limits to Growth* was not the first widely-read book to argue that humanity was living beyond its collective means that argument had been made by many authors, ranging from Henry David Thoreau to Rachel Carson. However, it was one of the first books to make this argument with such a strong scientific basis, and that added greatly to the book's impact. As well as being widely read, the book was somewhat controversial – as Kleiner (1996, p. 214) puts it, "economists and economic writers turned on [it] throughout America and Europe, setting off a firestorm that would inflame the debate about economic growth for another twenty years". Twenty years after the publication of the original book, three of the original project team re-ran the model and found that "many resource and pollution flows had grown beyond their sustainable limits" (Meadows et al. 1992, p.xiv). It seems clear that these limits have by now been exceeded even further.

Following the Club of Rome project, Meadows moved in 1972 to work at Dartmouth College, a prestigious but traditional university where she was the first woman ever to gain tenure. She was a well-regarded and influential teacher. One of her students was John Sterman, later Jay Forrester's successor as head of the system dynamics group at MIT, who moved into the subject specifically to learn from her.

Dennis Meadows later described her as "a brilliant teacher – dedicated, creative, caring, and effective" (DL Meadows 2002, p. 202) and also noted that she taught through her writing, calling it "a treasure chest for those of us trying to understand the field, increase our own mastery, teach our skills to others, or enhance our effectiveness in communicating our results to others" (DL Meadows 2002, p. 204).

While at Dartmouth, Meadows published a number of books on environmental issues, co-founded the Balaton Group (an international network of sustainability researchers and practitioners), and, as previously mentioned, worked as an organic farmer. She also wrote a highly insightful book on the nature of modelling which examined in detail the nature and implications of several well-established computer models. She and her co-author concluded this book by arguing that:

> Modellers can see themselves as well-meaning but basically powerless pawns in the system of political shoving, at the mercy of clients and funders who are bent on trivial purposes and who are not likely to follow any advice that is different from what they already thought. They can see themselves as removed, objective, purified by the truth as revealed within social statistics and high R^2 values. ... Or modellers can see themselves as responsible not to parochial, short-term interests, but to all humankind. They can see themselves as simplifiers, clarifiers, and fellow-explorers. They can listen more than they talk, ask the questions people really want asked, draw forth visions, designs, and experiments. They can be comfortable with the fact that they have glands, hearts, values, beliefs, moral stands, and blind spots. They can be willing to be wrong, vulnerable, caring, and idealistic. They can hold the highest intellectual standards of scientific hypothesis-formation and disproof, along with the highest human standards of integrity, compassion, and truthfulness. (Meadows and Robinson 1985, p. 433).

In 1985, she left Dartmouth, although she remained an adjunct professor there and connected to other universities. Her main role for the rest of her life was as an environmental activist, constantly urging people to think and to live better. In particular, she began a weekly newspaper column, *The Global Citizen*, on environmental issues from a systems perspective, producing more than 800 columns and published by newspapers throughout the United States. In her final column, published just three weeks before her death, she wrote that "if we believe that it's effectively over, that we are fatally flawed, that the most greedy and short-sighted among us will always be permitted to rule, that we can never constrain our consumption and destruction, that each of us is too small and helpless to do anything, that we should just give up and enjoy our SUVs while they last, well, then yes, it's over" (DH Meadows 2001).

While she emphasised the crucial importance of personal action in the face of environmental disaster, Meadows also took the view that this and related issues such as global poverty and war had to be addressed at a higher systemic level. In what turned out to be the final years of her life, Meadows developed her ideas on the nature of systemic development into a coherent view that united individual and collective change. In particular she wrote a brilliant paper on places to intervene in a system (DH Meadows 1999), where she presents twelve possible 'leverage points', from specifics such as transport networks or the structure of information flows to more fundamental issues like the mindset underlying a system. At the time of her death she was working on a book along these lines which remained unfinished, *Thinking in Systems*, from which the extract below is taken. Warshall (2001, p. 39) described Meadows' combination of individual and structural change as "a compassionate path – to remove blame from individuals and focus human energy on useful leverage points and correcting system perversities ... creative destruction of harmful patterns was central".

Donella Meadows spent 30 years living the life she felt was needed for the world, and inspiring others to live and work in ways that also would change the world. She inspired very many through her teaching, writing and life. The hope she felt and displayed can be seen in much of her writing but vividly in the following passage:

> It is difficult to speak of or to practice love, friendship, generosity, understanding, or solidarity within a system whose rules, goals, and information streams are geared for lesser human qualities. But we try, and we urge you to try. Be patient with yourself and others as you and they confront the difficulty of a changing world. Understand and empathize with inevitable resistance; there is some resistance, some clinging to the ways of unsustainability, within each of us. Include everyone in the new world. Everyone will be needed. Seek out and trust the best human instincts in yourself and in everyone. Listen to the cynicism around you and pity those who believe it, but don't believe it yourself. (Meadows et al. 1992, p. 234).

Reading from Meadows' work

Meadows, D. H. (2001), Dancing with Systems, *Whole Earth*, Issue 106, pp. 58–63. With permission Whole Earth.

People who are raised in the industrial world and who get enthused about systems thinking are likely to make a terrible mistake. They are likely to assume that here, in systems analysis, in interconnection and complication, in the power of the computer, here at last, is the key to prediction and control. This mistake is likely because the mindset of the industrial world assumes that there is a key to prediction and control. I assumed that at first too. We all assumed it, as eager systems students at the great institution called MIT. [...]

But self-organizing, nonlinear, feedback systems are inherently unpredictable. They are not controllable. They are understandable only in the most general way. The goal of foreseeing the future exactly and preparing for it perfectly is unrealizable. The idea of making a complex system do just what you want it to do can be achieved only temporarily, at best. We can never fully understand our world, not in the way our reductionistic science has led us to expect.

[...]

Systems thinking leads to another conclusion, however – waiting, shining, obvious as soon as we stop being blinded by the illusion of control. It says that there is plenty to do, of a different sort of 'doing'. The future can't be predicted, but it can be envisioned and brought lovingly into being. Systems can't be controlled, but they can be designed and redesigned. We can't surge forward with certainty into a world of no surprises, but we can expect surprises and learn from them and even profit from them. We can't impose our will upon a system. We can listen to what the system tells us, and discover how its properties and our values can work together to bring forth something much better than could ever be produced by our will alone.

We can't control systems or figure them out. But we can dance with them!

I already knew that, in a way before I began to study systems. I had learned about dancing with great powers from whitewater kayaking, from gardening, from playing music, from skiing. All those endeavors require one to stay wide awake, pay close attention, participate flat out, and respond to feedback. It had never occurred to me that those same requirements might apply to intellectual work, to management, to government, to getting along with people.

But there it was, the message emerging from every computer model we made. Living successfully in a world of systems requires more of us than our ability to calculate. It requires our full humanity – our rationality, our ability to sort out truth from falsehood, our intuition, our compassion, our vision, and our morality.

I will summarize the most general 'systems wisdoms' I have absorbed from modeling complex systems and hanging out with modelers. These are the take-home lessons, the concepts and practices that penetrate the discipline of systems so deeply that one begins, however imperfectly, to practice them not just in one's profession, but in all of life.

The list probably isn't complete, because I am still a student in the school of systems. And it isn't unique to systems thinking. There are many ways to learn to dance. But here, as a start-off dancing lesson, are the practices I see my colleagues adopting, consciously or unconsciously, as they encounter systems.

1   Get the beat

Before you disturb the system in any way, watch how it behaves. If it's a piece of music or a whitewater rapid or a fluctuation in a commodity price, study its beat. If it's a social system, watch it work. Learn its history. Ask people who've been around a long time to tell you what has happened. If possible, find or make a time graph of actual data from the system. Peoples' memories are not always reliable when it comes to timing. [...]

2   Listen to the wisdom of the system

Aid and encourage the forces and structures that help the system run itself. Don't be an unthinking intervener and destroy the system's own self-maintenance capacities. Before you charge in to make things better, pay attention to the value of what's already there. [...]

3 Expose your mental models to the open air

Remember, always, that everything you know, and everything everyone knows, is only a model. Get your model out there where it can be shot at. Invite others to challenge your assumptions and add their own. Instead of becoming a champion for one possible explanation or hypothesis or model, collect as many as possible. Consider all of them plausible until you find some evidence that causes you to rule one out. That way you will be emotionally able to see the evidence that rules out an assumption with which you might have confused your own identity. [...]

4 Stay humble. Stay a learner

Systems thinking has taught me to trust my intuition more and my figuring-out rationality less, to lean on both as much as I can, but still to be prepared for surprises. Working with systems, on the computer, in nature, among people, in organizations, constantly reminds me of how incomplete my mental models are, how complex the world is, and how much I don't know. [...]

5 Honor and protect information

A decision-maker can't respond to information he or she doesn't have, can't respond accurately to information that is inaccurate, can't respond in a timely way to information that is late. I would guess that 99% of what goes wrong in systems goes wrong because of faulty or missing information. [...]

6 Locate responsibility in the system

Look for the ways the system creates its own behavior. Do pay attention to the triggering events, the outside influences that bring forth one kind of behavior from the system rather than another. Sometimes those outside events can be controlled (as in reducing the pathogens in drinking water to keep down incidences of infectious disease). But sometimes they can't. And sometimes blaming or trying to control the outside influence blinds one to the easier task of increasing responsibility within the system. [...]

7 Make feedback policies for feedback systems

[...] You can imagine why a dynamic, self-adjusting system cannot be governed by a static, unbending policy. It's easier, more effective, and usually much cheaper to design policies that change depending on the state of the system. Especially where there are great uncertainties, the best policies not only contain feedback loops, but meta-feedback loops – loops that alter, correct, and expand loops. These are policies that design learning into the management process.

8   Pay attention to what is important, not just what is quantifiable

Our culture, obsessed with numbers, has given us the idea that what we can measure is more important than what we can't measure. You can look around and make up your own mind about whether quantity or quality is the outstanding characteristic of the world in which you live. […] No one can (precisely) define or measure justice, democracy, security, freedom, truth, or love. No one can (precisely) define or measure any value. But if no one speaks up for them, if systems aren't designed to produce them, if we don't speak about them and point toward their presence or absence, they will cease to exist.

9   Go for the good of the whole

Don't maximize parts of systems or subsystems while ignoring the whole. As Kenneth Boulding once said, don't go to great trouble to optimize something that never should be done at all. Aim to enhance total systems properties, such as creativity, stability, diversity; resilience, and sustainability – whether they are easily measured or not. […]

10   Expand time horizons

The official time horizon of industrial society doesn't extend beyond what will happen after the next election or beyond the payback period of current investments. The time horizon of most families still extends farther than that – through the lifetimes of children or grandchildren. […] When you're walking along a tricky, curving, unknown, surprising, obstacle-strewn path, you'd be a fool to keep your head down and look just at the next step in front of you. You'd be equally a fool just to peer far ahead and never notice what's immediately under your feet. You need to be watching both the short and long terms – the whole system.

11   Expand thought horizons

[…] Seeing systems whole requires more than being 'interdisciplinary', if that word means, as it usually does, putting together people from different disciplines and letting them talk past each other. Interdisciplinary communication works only if there is a real problem to be solved, and if the representatives from the various disciplines are more committed to solving the problem than to being academically correct. They will have to go into learning mode, to admit ignorance and be willing to be taught, by each other and by the system. It can be done. It's very exciting when it happens.

12   Expand the boundary of caring

Living successfully in a world of complex systems means expanding not only time horizons and thought horizons; above all it means expanding the horizons of caring. There are moral reasons for doing that, of course. And if moral arguments are not sufficient, systems thinking provides the practical reasons to back up the moral ones. The real system is interconnected. No part of the human race is separate either from other human beings or from the global ecosystem. It will not be possible in this integrated world for your heart to succeed if your lungs fail, or for your company to succeed if your workers fail, or for the rich in Los Angeles to succeed if the poor in Los Angeles fail, or for Europe to succeed if Africa fails, or for the global economy to succeed if the global environment fails. [...]

13   Celebrate complexity

Let's face it, the universe is messy. It is nonlinear, turbulent, and chaotic. It is dynamic. It spends its time in transient behavior on its way to somewhere else, not in mathematically neat equilibria. It self-organizes and evolves. It creates diversity, not uniformity. That's what makes the world interesting, that's what makes it beautiful, and that's what makes it work. [...]

14   Hold fast to the goal of goodness

Examples of bad human behavior are held up, magnified by the media, affirmed by the culture, as typical. [...] The far more numerous examples of human goodness are barely noticed. They are Not News. They are exceptions. Must have been a saint. Can't expect everyone to behave like that.

And so expectations are lowered. The gap between desired behavior and actual behavior narrows. [...] We know what to do about eroding goals. Don't weigh the bad news more heavily than the good. And keep standards absolute. [...]

References

Forrester, J. W. (1971). *World dynamics*. Cambridge, MA: Wright-Allen Press.

Hafkamp, W. (2001). A tribute to Dana Meadows, from the Balaton Group. Address at Donella Meadows memorial service, American Academy of Arts & Sciences, 22 April 2001. http://www.sustainer.org/meadows/BostonSpeeches.html. Accessed 13 Jan 2009.

Kleiner, A. (1996). *The age of heretics: Heroes, outlaws, and the forerunners of corporate change*. London: Nicholas Brealey.

Meadows, D. H., Meadows, D. L. Randers, J., Behrens, W. W. (1972). *The limits to growth: A report for the club of Rome's project on the predicament of mankind*. Washington, DC: Potomac Associates.

Meadows, D. H., &Robinson, J. M. (1985). *The electronic oracle: Computer models and social decisions*. Chichester, UK: John Wiley.

Meadows, D. H., Meadows, D. L., Randers, J. (1992). *Beyond the limits: Confronting global collapse, envisioning a sustainable future*. Post Mills, VT: Chelsea Green.

Meadows, D. H. (1999). *Leverage points: Places to intervene in a system*. Hartland, VT: The Sustainability Institute.

Meadows, D. H. (2001). Polar bears and three-year-olds on thin ice. The Global Citizen, 2 February 2001. http://www.pcdf.org/Meadows/arctic.html. Accessed 13 Jan 2009.

Meadows, D. H. (2002). Living lightly and inconsistently on the land. *System Dynamics Review*, *18*(2), 109–110.

Meadows, D. H. (2007). The history and conclusions of *The Limits to Growth*. *System Dynamics Review*, *23*(2/3), 191–197.

Meadows, D. L. (2002). Dana Meadows: Asking hard questions, speaking simple truths. *System Dynamics Review*, *18*(2), 111–119.

Sterman, J. D. (2002). Dana Meadows: Thinking globally, acting locally. *System Dynamics Review*, *18*(2), 101–107.

Warshall, P. (2001). Donella Meadows. *Whole Earth*, *104*, 38–39.

Chapter 12
Peter Senge

Peter Michael Senge is a management academic and consultant. He has been principally responsible for drawing together and popularising the concept of the learning organisation. Through his work he has brought systems thinking (or at least a particular form of it) to the attention of a very wide audience. His ideas have primarily been applied in business organisations, but they have taken an increasingly wider dimension in recent years. He has described himself as an 'idealistic pragmatist', and his goal is idealistic: "to change the world by helping people change deeply" (Dumaine 1994).

Senge (generally pronounced Sen-gee) was born in 1947 in Los Angeles where he also spent his childhood. He attended university at Stanford, studying engineering, graduating in 1970. As a student he "became interested in population growth, a topic that got him thinking about the world and big issues like overpopulation, hunger, and the environment" (Dumaine 1994). This concern led him to graduate study at the Massachusetts Institute of Technology (MIT) in the system dynamics group, taking an MSc in social systems modelling in 1972. He continued at MIT as a researcher, completing his Ph.D. in 1978, on a comparison between an aspect of economic modelling through the System Dynamics National Model (see Chapter 10 on Jay Forrester) with the way the same issue is handled in neoclassical economic modelling. Although he was working in Jay Forrester's group and regarded Forrester as his intellectual mentor, Senge's Ph.D. was supervised by a rising young academic (a near contemporary) who later became an investment banker, Nathaniel Mass. Following his Ph.D., Senge began work as a lecturer at MIT, where he still works – he is currently a senior lecturer in the Sloan School of Management.

The first steps towards Senge's conception of the learning organisation came in the mid-1970s. While still working on his Ph.D., Senge developed a training event, the Leadership and Mastery seminar, along with Charlie Kiefer (a management consultant) and Robert Fritz (a composer and researcher). The seminar, intended to train senior managers in issues of system dynamics, personal mastery and shared vision, has been run many times – Senge has talked of having led the seminar more than 250 times (Scharmer 1996). This seminar formed the basis of Senge, Kiefer and Fritz's consultancy firm Innovation Associates, where much of Senge's key work developed.

© The Open University 2009. Published in association with Springer-Verlag London Limited

The combination of modelling experience through system dynamics and management development experience was to prove crucial to the development of his work on the learning organisation. The latter also arose from Senge's personality. His colleague Robert Fritz (2005) describes him as "a brilliant shining light. I am awed by his ability to bring people into higher levels of perspective, much higher than most of us are able to envision on our own. Having known him for a long time, I know this is part natural talent, but also part discipline, part self-generated growth, and also true intellectual integrity". Senge has been a Zen Buddhist for many years and regularly meditates. In most of his writing his religious perspective is tacit and demonstrates itself in calls for personal mastery and the importance of discipline, although in his recent work, he has taken a more explicitly spiritual focus.

Through the 1980s, Senge developed his ideas further, through work both at Innovation Associates, and at MIT, where he became director of the Systems Thinking and Organizational Learning programme. As well as Forrester, his key intellectual influences were Chris Argyris (who had developed the concept of organisational learning, along with Donald Schön), W. Edwards Deming (the founder of total quality management, strongly influenced by systems thinking) and David Bohm (a quantum physicist who worked extensively on the importance of dialogue). Through his consultancy, he also became highly influenced by a group of senior executives of considerable wisdom, whose ideas and experiences he draws on extensively in his work, most notably including Arie de Geus, head of planning at the Royal Dutch/Shell group (and a key developer of scenario planning) and William O'Brien, chief executive of Hanover Insurance (an American general insurance company).

These elements in Senge's work – system dynamics, his consultancy and especially the Leadership and Mastery seminar, his inspiration from a set of key academics, and his relationship with business leaders – came together in his conception of the learning organisation. He expressed that synthesis in a book: *The Fifth Discipline*, where he described a learning organisation as one where "people continually expand their capacity to create the results they truly desire, where new and expansive patterns of thinking are nurtured, where collective aspiration is set free, and where people are continually learning how to learn together" (Senge 1990, p. 3). It is hard to over-stress the importance of the book. It has sold over one million copies worldwide, it has launched a whole new industry in management development and consultancy, and it is quoted by almost everyone subsequently writing on organisational learning.

The development of *The Fifth Discipline* as a book went through several phases. Originally, Senge planned to co-author a book with Arie de Geus, who in 1988 wrote a celebrated article under the title 'Planning as Learning' in which he argued that "the ability to learn faster than competitors may be the only sustainable competitive advantage" (de Geus 1988, p. 71). After two years of work Senge and de Geus decided to produce separate books. To complete his book, Senge turned for help to Art Kleiner, a journalist who acted as an editor and writing coach. Because Kleiner has acted as a 'ghostwriter' for several bestselling books, there have long been rumours that *The Fifth Discipline* was ghostwritten, something Kleiner denies:

"Peter Senge wrote his own book. ... I made suggestions, helped reframe the outline, taped some conversations, drafted some segments, suggested the title, and edited the draft. Then he laboriously rewrote everything again" (Kleiner 1998, p. 26). Kleiner also helped to clarify Senge's ideas in one very important respect:

> "The idea of disciplines emerged in conversations with Art. He kept after me to express the essential message of the book in just one sentence. Finally I realized that everything in my life in which I had been deeply interested was a discipline, and that discipline was the thread that ran through everything I had to say in the book" (Senge, interviewed by Galagan 1991, p. 38).

The five disciplines of the book are systems thinking, personal mastery, mental models, shared vision and team learning. Each of these rests upon important work carried out previously by others. The discipline of *mental models* draws on Argyris and Schön's work on action science and reflective practice. *Team learning* draws on Argyris' work on organisational defensive routines, and also the work of the physicist David Bohm on ways of fostering dialogue within groups as a form of learning. The disciplines of *personal mastery* and *shared vision* come from Senge's work with Innovation Associates in the Leadership and Mastery seminar. Finally, *systems thinking* in Senge's book is a modified form of system dynamics based on describing systems with diagrams which show a series of interlocking feedback loops. These diagrams frequently fall into a set of standard patterns called system archetypes. Systems thinking is described as the fifth discipline because it is "the discipline that integrates the disciplines, fusing them into a coherent body of theory and practice" (Senge 1990, p. 12).

Senge's use of the term 'systems thinking' in the book has proved controversial. The term was already in widespread use to refer to a large variety of systems approaches, but Senge restricts it solely to his modified form of system dynamics. The success of *The Fifth Discipline* has led to Senge's use of the term becoming widespread, especially in the United States. As Lane (1995, p. 1160) puts it, the risk of Senge's use of the term is that it "so easily leads people to believe that there is no difference between the works of Forrester and those of, say, Beer and Checkland". The problem in this view is not that Senge uses the term 'systems thinking' but that he solely equates it to his particular approach, with no mention of other approaches. Wolstenholme (1999) suggested the term "qualitative system dynamics" for Senge's approach, but this phrase has not gained popularity. In fact, Lane (1995, p. 1159) quotes Senge as having said to a system dynamics conference that "I gravitated naively to the term 'systems thinking' ... I never intended to be disrespectful", and in later books he refers to other forms of systems thinking as well as his own. However, the use of the term solely to refer to Senge's qualitative system dynamics is still commonplace, causing some confusion.

In fact, the mainstream system dynamics (SD) community has been somewhat disquieted by the way that Senge has developed their ideas, and especially the fact that he presents lessons from SD without the use of simulation models. As Jay Forrester himself has written, "The danger comes from encouraging people to believe that systems thinking is the whole story. ... It is only from the actual simulations that inconsistencies within our mental models are revealed. Systems thinking can be a first step toward a dynamic understanding of complex problems, but it is far from sufficient" (Forrester 2007, p. 355). Nonetheless, it is clear that Senge has brought considerable publicity and interest to SD, and that many people, inspired by his work, have gone further into the more detailed simulation-based approach – the success of Sterman's (2000) thorough textbook on SD is one indication of this.

We have mentioned the extent to which Senge drew upon others' ideas (giving them proper credit) in weaving together the different parts of *The Fifth Discipline*. Indeed, he has said explicitly that "the book was a byproduct of about 15 years of working by several persons including me. The Western idea that a person owns an idea is bizarre – ideas are very much a product of our lifetime and of all the people who influence us directly and indirectly" (Senge, interviewed by Fulmer and Keys 1998, pp. 34–5). As the popularity of the book spread, this community became more explicitly defined. Senge had worked for some years with senior managers at MIT, in what became the Organisational Learning Center (OLC), and with consultants at Innovation Associates. The OLC had close involvement from managers in nineteen large companies, but was constrained by its being aligned to a particular university and in a single geographical setting. In 1997, the OLC became independent of MIT as the Society for Organisational Learning (SoL), an international organisation composed of academics, consultants and business leaders, with Senge as its founding chairperson. SoL was designed to enable organisational learning through its structures as well as its activities, and was intended to be distributed and decentralised in its power structures; it was inspired by the work of Dee Hock, founder of the highly distributed Visa credit card network (Fulmer and Keys 1998). SoL now has established groups in ten countries as well as emerging groups in many more.

A further expression of the community of practitioners around Senge has been the publication of three books aimed at practitioners, which take further the ideas of *The Fifth Discipline*. Each of the three books has Senge has its lead author (and leader of the process which produced them) but was written by a large group of practitioners in the ideas discussed. The first of these, *The Fifth Discipline Fieldbook*, was intended for those who asked the question "This is great, but what do we do Monday morning?" (Senge et al. 1994, p. 5). It was written by over 70 contributors although unlike *The Fifth Discipline*, Art Kleiner (1998) happily acknowledges it as being an exercise in ghostwriting, as he shaped the book through writing up discussions with the contributors involved. The *Fieldbook*, which is full of short and practical articles, was highly successful among practitioners, with one describing the way he kept "two copies, one intact and the other separated into loose leaf form" (Godfrey 1999). Two further books along the same lines followed – *The Dance of Change* (Senge et al. 1999) looked at ways to solve the consultants' dilemma that so many well-meant change processes fail; and *Schools that Learn* (Senge et al. 2000) took the idea of the learning organisation, already popular among educators, and applied it quite explicitly to the needs of educational institutions.

Senge's work in the first decade of the twenty-first century has become increasingly concerned with profound change in the world, both in spiritual terms and in terms of sustainability. In *Presence* (Senge et al. 2005), written in a quite different style from the *Fieldbook* and its successors, he and his co-authors address how fundamental change can occur in individuals and organisations. They equate this change, a deeper kind of organisational learning, with presence, "being fully conscious and aware in the present moment ... deep listening, [being] open beyond one's preconceptions and historical ways of making sense" (Senge et al. 2005, p. 13). They argue that this change is necessary both for individuals and for large organisations to enable the planet to survive in the face of climate change and environmental destruction. The book is quite explicitly spiritual in its focus, drawing on those religious traditions which emphasise mystical and holistic practices, especially Buddhism (the book is dedicated to the Buddhist cognitive scientist Francisco Varela, whose work is discussed in the chapter of this book on Maturana) but also other religions. Senge also continues to work with leaders of large organisations in building significant change in them as individuals and in the organisations they run.

An interesting question about Senge is the extent to which he can be called a 'management guru' (as he is described by some). In many ways, he is a quintessential guru – he is an academic who has published bestselling books, given inspirational speeches to large conferences (for large fees), worked comfortably with leaders of large companies, and drawn on his consultancy experiences to write further works. Yet he is committed to a much deeper level of personal and organisational change than many of those called management gurus, and as Brad Jackson (2001, p. 155) argues, he "projects a studiously anti-guru persona through his soft-spoken, high-pitched voice and donnish attire". Moreover, he has not sought an ongoing leadership role in the organisations he has established, preferring "to be loosely linked with numerous organizations in which he assumes a comparatively lower profile role and works in a collaborative mode" (Jackson 2001, p. 148).

Peter Senge has made extraordinary changes to individual and collective understanding of the way organisations learn, and the way that systems thinking can help this learning. He advocates profound change and is unafraid to exhibit it in his own way of working. In his interest in building learning communities, he has built an extensive community of practitioners and scholars working to help organisations learn and to change for the better.

Reading from Senge's work

Today's problems come from yesterday's 'solutions'

[…] Often we are puzzled by the causes of our problems; when we merely need to
look at our own solutions to other problems in the past. […] Police enforcement
officials will recognize their own version of this law: arresting narcotics dealers on
Thirtieth Street, they find that they have simply transferred the crime centre to
Fortieth Street. Or, even more insidiously, they learn that a new citywide outbreak
of drug-related crime is the result of federal officials intercepting a large shipment
of narcotics – which reduced the drug supply, drove up the price, and caused more
crime by addicts desperate to maintain their habit.

Solutions that merely shift problems from one part of a system to another often
go undetected because [those] who 'solved' the first problem are different from
those who inherit the new problem.

The harder you push, the harder the system pushes back

In George Orwell's *Animal Farm*, the horse Boxer always had the same answer to
any difficulty: "I will work harder", he said. At first, his well-intentioned diligence
inspired everyone, but gradually, his hard work began to backfire in subtle ways.
The harder he worked, the more work there was to do. What he didn't know was
that the pigs who managed the farm were actually manipulating them all for their
own profit. Boxer's diligence actually helped to keep the other animals from seeing
what the pigs were doing. Systems thinking has a name for this phenomenon:
'Compensating feedback': when well intentioned interventions call forth responses
from the system that offset the benefits of the intervention. We all know what it
feels like to be facing compensating feedback – the harder you push, the harder the
system pushes back; the more effort you expend trying to improve matters, the
more effort seems to be required. […]

Behaviour grows better before it grows worse

[…] Compensating feedback usually involves a 'delay', a time lag between the
short-term benefit and the long-term disbenefit. […] In complex human systems
there are always many ways to make things look better in the short run. Only eventually does the compensating feedback come back to haunt you.

The key word is 'eventually'. The delay [...] explains why systemic problems are so hard to recognize. A typical solution feels wonderful, when it first cures the symptoms. Now there's improvement; or maybe even the problem has gone away. It may be 2, 3, or 4 years before the problem returns, or some new, worse problem arrives. By that time, given how rapidly most people move from job to job, someone new is sitting in the chair.

The wasy way out usually leads back in

[...] We all find comfort applying familiar solutions to problems, sticking to what we know best. [...] After all, if the solution were easy to see or obvious to everyone, it probably would already have been found. Pushing harder and harder on familiar solutions, while fundamental problems persist or worsen, is a reliable indicator of nonsystemic thinking – what we often call the 'what we need here is a bigger hammer' syndrome.

The cure can be worse than the disease

Sometimes the easy or familiar solution is not only ineffective; sometimes it is addictive and dangerous. [...] The long-term, most insidious consequence of applying nonsystemic solutions is increased need for more and more of the solution. [...] The phenomenon of short-term improvements leading to long-term dependency is so common, it has its own name among systems thinkers – it's called "Shifting the Burden to the Intervenor". [...]

Shifting the Burden structures show that any long-term solution must, as [Donella] Meadows says, "strengthen the ability of the system to shoulder its own burdens" (Meadows 1982). Sometimes that is difficult; other times it is surprisingly easy. A manager who has shifted the burden of his personnel problems onto a Human Relations Specialist may find that the hard part is deciding to take the burden back; once that happens, learning how to handle people is mainly a matter of time and commitment.

Faster is slower

[...] For most American business people the best rate of growth is fast, faster, fastest. Yet, virtually all natural systems, from ecosystems to animals to organizations, have intrinsically optimal rates of growth. The optimal rate is far less than the fastest possible growth. When growth becomes excessive – as it does in cancer – the system itself will seek to compensate by slowing down; perhaps putting the organization's survival at risk in the process. [...]

When managers first start to appreciate how these systems principles have oper-
ated to thwart many of their own favorite interventions, they can be discouraged and
disheartened. The systems principles can even become excuses for inaction – for
doing nothing rather than possibly taking actions that might backfire, or even make
matters worse. The real implications of the systems perspective are not inaction but
a new type of action rooted in a new way of thinking – systems thinking is both
more challenging *and* more promising than our normal ways of dealing with
problems.

Cause and effect are not closely related in time and space

Underlying all of the above problems is a fundamental characteristic of complex
human systems: 'cause' and 'effect' are not close in time and space. By 'effects',
I mean the obvious symptoms that indicate that there are problems – drug abuse,
unemployment, starving children, falling orders, and sagging profits. By 'cause'
I mean the interaction of the underlying system that is most responsible for generating
the symptoms, and which, if recognized, could lead to changes producing lasting improvement. Why is this a problem? Because most of us assume they *are* –
most of us assume, most of the time, that cause and effect *are* close in time
and space.

When we play as children, problems are never far away from their solutions – as
long, at least, as we confine our play to one group of toys. [...] The root of our difficulties is neither recalcitrant problems nor evil adversaries – but ourselves. There is a
fundamental mismatch between the nature of reality in complex systems and our
predominant ways of thinking about that reality. [...]

Small changes can produce big results – but the areas of highest leverage – are often the least obvious

Some have called systems thinking the 'new dismal science' because it teaches that
most obvious solutions don't work – at best, they improve matters in the short run,
only to make things worse in the long run. But there is another side to the story.
For systems thinking also shows that small, well-focused actions can sometimes
produce significant, enduring improvements, if they're in the right place. Systems
thinkers refer to this principle as 'leverage'.

Tackling a difficult problem is often a matter of seeing where the high leverage
lies, a change which – with a minimum of effort would lead to lasting, significant
improvement. [...]

There are no simple rules for finding high-leverage changes, but there are ways
of thinking that make it more likely. Learning to see underlying 'structures' rather

than 'events' is a starting point. [...] Thinking in terms of processes of change rather than 'snapshots' is another.

You can have your cake and eat it too – but not at once

Sometimes, the knottiest dilemmas, when seen from the systems point, of view, aren't dilemmas at all. [They] appear in a whole new light once you think consciously of change over time.

For years, for example, American manufacturers thought they had to choose between low cost and high quality. "Higher quality products cost more to manufacture", they thought. "They take longer to assemble, require more expensive materials and components, and entail more extensive quality controls." What they didn't consider was all the ways the increasing quality and lowering costs could go hand in hand, over time. What they didn't consider was how basic improvements in work processes could eliminate rework, eliminate quality inspectors, reduce customer complaints, lower warranty costs, increase customer loyalty, and reduce advertising and sales promotion costs. They didn't realize that they could have both goals, if they were willing to wait for one while they focused on the other. [...]

Many apparent dilemmas [...] are by-products of static thinking. They only appear as rigid 'either-or' choices, because we think of what is possible at a fixed point in time. Next month, it may be true that we must choose one or the other, but the real leverage lies in seeing how both can improve over time.

Dividing an elephant in half does not produce two small elephants

Living systems have integrity. Their character depends on the whole. The same is true for organizations; to understand the most challenging managerial issues requires seeing the whole system that generates the issues. [...]

Seeing 'whole elephants' does not mean that every organizational issue can be understood only by looking at the entire organization. Some issues can be understood only by looking at how major functions such as manufacturing, marketing, and research interact; but there are other issues where critical systemic forces arise within a given functional area; and others where the dynamics of an entire industry must be considered. The key principle, called the 'principle of the system boundary', is that the interactions that must be examined are those most important to the issue at hand, *regardless* of parochial organizational boundaries. [...]

Sometimes people go ahead and divide an elephant in half anyway. You don't have two small elephants then; you have a mess. By a mess, I mean a complicated problem where there is no leverage to be found because the leverage lies in interactions that cannot be seen from looking only at the piece you are holding.

There is no blame

We tend to blame outside circumstances for our problems. 'Someone else' – the competitors, the press, the changing mood of the marketplace, the government – did it to us. Systems thinking shows us that there is no outside; that you and the cause of your problems are part of a single system. The cure lies in your relationship with your 'enemy'.

References

De Geus, A.P. (1988). Planning as learning. *Harvard Business Review, 66*(2), 70–74.

Dumaine, B. (1994). Mr Learning Organization. *Fortune, 130*(8), 147–157.

Forrester, J.W. (2007). System dynamics – A personal view of the first fifty years. *System Dynamics Review, 23*(2/3), 345–358.

Fritz, R. (2005). Review of *Presence*. http://www.presence.net/fritz.html. Accessed 13 Jan 2009.

Fulmer, R.M., & Keys, J. B. (1998). A conversation with Peter Senge: New developments in organizational learning. *Organizational Dynamics, 27*(2), 33–42.

Galagan, P.A. (1991). The learning organization made plain. *Training and Development, 45*(10), 37–44.

Godfrey, B. (1999). The dance of change. Learning-org mailing list posting LO20884. http://www.learning-org.com/99.03/0124.html. Accessed 13 Jan 2009.

Jackson, B. (2001). *Management gurus and Management fashions: A dramatistic inquiry.* New York: Routledge.

Kleiner, A. (1998). The visible ghost. *Across the Board, 35*(10), 26.

Lane, D.C. (1995). Trying to think systematically about 'Systems Thinking'. *Journal of the Operational Research Society, 46*(9), 1158–1162.

Meadows, D.H. (1982). Whole earth models and systems. *CoEvolution Quarterly, 34*, 98–108.

Scharmer, C. O. (1996). Closing the feedback loop between matter and mind: Conversation with Dr. Peter M. Senge. *Dialog on Leadership.*
http://www.dialogonleadership.org/interviews/Senge.shtml. Accessed 13 Jan 2009.

Senge, P. M. (1990). *The fifth discipline: The art and practice of the learning organization.* New York: Doubleday.

Senge, P. M., Kleiner, A., Roberts, C., Ross, R. B., Smith, B. J. (1994). *The fifth discipline fieldbook: Strategies and tools for building a learning organization.* London: Nicholas Brealey.

Senge, P. M., Kleiner, A., Roberts, C., Ross, R. B., Roth, G., Smith, B. J. (1999). *The dance of change: The challenges of sustaining momentum in learning organizations.* New York: Currency Doubleday.

Senge, P. M., Cambron-McCabe, N., Lucas, T., Smith, B. J., Dutton, J., Kleiner, A. (2000). *Schools that learn: A fifth discipline fieldbook for parents, educators, and everyone who cares about education.* New York: Currency Doubleday.

Senge, P. M., Scharmer, C. O., Jaworski, J., Flowers, B. S. (2005). *Presence: Exploring profound change in people, organizations and society.* London: Nicholas Brealey.

Sterman, J. D. (2000). *Business dynamics: Systems thinking and modeling for a complex world.* Boston: Irwin/McGraw-Hill.

Wolstenholme, E.F. (1999). Qualitative vs quantitative modelling: The evolving balance. *Journal of the Operational Research Society, 50*(4), 422–428.

Soft and Critical Systems

Methodologies for systemic intervention in organisations and government, addressing intractable problems, multiple perspectives and power

Chapter 13
C. West Churchman

Charles West Churchman was a philosopher of systems and management, who did more than anyone to bring ethical considerations into the field of systems thinking. He was a pioneer in several academic fields, always driven by what he described as his "moral outrage" (Churchman 1982, p. 17) that the human intellect is capable of organising society to solve the great problems of the world, such as malnutrition, poverty and war, and yet humanity allows these problems to persist. This moral outrage drove him to establish new fields, develop a range of influential theoretical concepts, and to work as a consultant to a number of important organisations. He was also a highly gifted teacher and developed in his students an acute critical and ethical awareness in his approach to systems thinking. A former student summed up his philosophy and personality, as well as his lasting contribution as follows:

> West Churchman has devoted his life and his philosophy to securing improvements in the human condition by means of the human intellect. His is a calling that demands from us the most in compassion and consciousness. He pursues it with dignity fortified with contagious passion. (Mason 1988, p. 374).

Churchman was deeply religious. He was born in 1913 as a Catholic in Philadelphia, Pennsylvania – a distant ancestor travelled to the United States on the same ship as the founder of the state, William Penn. Churchman attended a Quaker school, learning there that "you can have a life dedicated to humanity – that was the best thing one could do" (quoted in van Gigch et al. 1997, p. 732). As a youth, he seriously considered becoming a Benedictine monk, but he found the monastic life was not appropriate for him. His religious background contributed to his moral outrage and his belief that systems thinking should be "committed to ascertaining not simply whether the decision maker's choices lead to his desired ends, but whether they lead to ends that are ethically defensible" (Churchman 1979, p. 65). Van Gigch and McIntyre-Mills (2006, p.xiii) describe his defining characteristics as "humility and compassion".

At the age of 17, as an undergraduate at the University of Pennsylvania, Churchman recorded in his journal that his life would be dedicated to bettering humanity (van Gigch et al. 1997). The only question was what field would best allow him to do this. His initial answer was philosophy, as the subject that was at the heart of knowledge, and he took all his degrees in philosophy, at the University

© The Open University 2009. Published in association with Springer-Verlag London Limited

of Pennsylvania (graduating with his Ph.D. in 1938) where he then became a faculty member. He became strongly influenced at Pennsylvania by the work of Edgar Singer (who had been a student of William James, the founder of the American pragmatist school of philosophy). As Churchman (1979, p. 9) later wrote, "Singer's philosophical position had the theme of comprehensiveness, so that all aspects of the natural world were to be 'swept in' ... he undertook to include values in explicit ways". In keeping with Singer's focus on values, Churchman also became an opponent of the then widely-held philosophical doctrine of logical positivism which sought to deny the importance of values in science.

Soon after taking his Ph.D., the Second World War began, and he spent five years working on statistical methods for quality control at an arms factory, the Frankford Arsenal. This experience led him further in the direction of applied philosophy – as he later recorded, he felt that "the enemy was Hitler and his successful armies, and not the logical positivists. Hitler was highly dangerous, while the positivists just sounded silly. This philosophical mind began to realize that philosophy should be used to study serious problems like war, security, and human living" (Churchman 1994, p. 100). During the war, he also began a long collaboration with Russell Ackoff, initially his Ph.D. student but subsequently a colleague – for a period of about 20 years they worked so closely together that letters were sometimes addressed to "C. West Ackoff and Russell L. Churchman" (Ackoff 1988, p. 355).

Following the war, he returned to the University of Pennsylvania, and sought to take forward the application of philosophy, especially Singer's pragmatism, to social issues (such as urban planning and organisational management). Feeling increasingly frustrated with the possibility of doing this at Pennsylvania, he left in 1948 to work at Wayne State University in Detroit. Churchman received further recognition for his philosophical work in 1948, becoming editor of a prestigious journal, *Philosophy of Science* (which he edited until 1958). Nonetheless, he felt increasingly isolated in the philosophical community – well-regarded but unable to carry out his work on social change, viewed by his colleagues as too far outside the mainstream of the field. This continued to be a problem at Wayne, and after two years he left to join a new department in a new field: operations research, at the Case Institute of Technology in Cleveland, Ohio. He did however meet his wife Gloria while living in Detroit, and they married in 1954.

Churchman's years at Case, from 1951 to 1958, were crucial in the establishment of operations research (OR) as an academic discipline. OR had developed during the war, as the application of scientific principles to the management of military operations. It quickly developed a body of practical techniques which proved to be highly useful, and after the war these began to be applied to industrial management. Despite its practical success, OR had little academic basis, and it was Churchman's great contribution to develop the field academically. In his years at Case, Churchman (working closely with Russell Ackoff who had also moved to Case) established the first Masters and Ph.D. programmes in OR, ran a series of influential annual conferences, built up a group which grew to twenty academic staff, and published the first textbook in the field, *Introduction to Operations Research* (Churchman et al. 1957). He was also involved in the establishment of the parallel field of management science (MS), and founding editor of the journal *Management Science*. The success of the textbook led Churchman to a new post in 1958, as professor at the University of California, Berkeley, where he remained for the rest of his career (until 1996).

Despite Churchman's clear success in establishing operations research and management science as academic disciplines, these fields gradually moved away from his vision of a life dedicated to humanity and towards an emphasis on the details of the mathematical methods used in the fields. As Ulrich (2004, p. 211) described it, comparing the situation with Churchman's experience in philosophy, the OR and MS community "honoured its pioneer but did not really hear him". As his work at Berkeley developed, Churchman thus gradually shifted from OR and MS towards general systems theory, although in many ways, a systems approach was already present in his work, with the influence of Singer's concept of comprehensiveness combined with his own concern for practical action. He was later to refer to his approach as 'social systems design'.

In the 1960s, many of the most widely-used systems methods (such as systems analysis and systems engineering) had exactly the same flaws as Churchman had previously found in OR and MS: too great a faith in the power of rational planning, too little concern for values and ethics, and an over-focus on mathematical models. Through Churchman's work, many of these shortcomings were addressed, and he began a shift towards the approaches later called soft and critical systems. He early on introduced a scepticism towards the power of rational planning: in his first major book on systems thinking, published in 1968 and selling over 200,000 copies, he wrote that "however a systems problem is solved – by planner, scientist, politician, anti-planner, or whomever – the solution is wrong, even dangerously wrong" (Churchman 1968, p. 229). He did, however, argue in the same book that "the systems approach is not a bad idea" (Churchman 1968, p. 232), intending both to imply that systems approaches can be helpful and that they can be ethical.

He took these ideas forward in two further major books, which between them form the basis for a critical and ethical approach to systems: *The Design of Inquiring Systems* (Churchman 1971) and *The Systems Approach and its Enemies* (Churchman 1979). These books are so full of insights that they are hard to summarise. The first, which is deeply philosophical but has been found to be highly relevant to information systems design, is a tour through the work of a number of key philosophers, and their implications for designing systems. Churchman's approach is to consider systems design as being one of making 'whole system judgements' – of making decisions as to what is part of the system and what is outside of it (an approach later termed 'boundary judgements' by Ulrich, discussed in chapter 16). A key part of this judgement process is the *Weltanschauung* (worldview) of the person making the judgement, a concept Churchman (1971) introduced into systems thinking from the philosophy of Immanuel Kant and was later to be drawn upon by a number of others.

Reynolds (2004, p. 542) describes the process of making whole systems judgements as follows: "after initially being concerned with the holistic attempt at *sweeping in* all relevant values and perspectives pertaining to a systems design, a *process of unfolding* draws out the implications of making the necessary and inevitable boundary judgements required for further purposeful action". These related activities of sweeping-in and unfolding, which derive from Singer's ideas, have been taken up by a number of systems authors using a critical approach.

Although Churchman's view of systems to this point was broad, it did not yet take the full critical perspective implied by his earlier concerns. He incorporated this perspective by considering the prevalent view of systems as a process of rational planning (similar to that which Checkland would later term 'hard systems thinking'), which omits the consideration of four key areas he termed its 'enemies' – politics, morality, religion and aesthetics. He discussed the relationship between each of these and the rational systems approach as a dialectical process – one where the two opposing views are contrasted and then combined in a new approach, a process he referred to as "being one's own enemy" (Churchman 1979, p. 204). As he puts it, "the resultant being is neither a loose dreamer nor a hard thinker; to be the enemy means to release the bonds of hard rationality" (Churchman 1979, p. 205). In this work we can see the basis for much that followed in the critical approach to systems thinking – although some scholars would argue that Churchman's work does not go far enough in its consideration of issues of power and inequality, Churchman gave considerable impetus and background to later work in this area.

While we have emphasised Churchman as a scholar, writing was not his only way of transmitting his ideas. Given his strong concern for social change, he worked with a number of government agencies and other organisations to improve their systems, including NASA, the Systems Development Corporation, the U.S. Department of Energy, the U.S. Office of Education and the U.S. Fish and Wildlife Service. Perhaps the most notable of these was his work with NASA, for whom he directed a Social Science Programme at Berkeley from 1963 to 1971 to study its ways of working in the Apollo programme and to draw lessons for other organisations' management. While these various consultancy appointments influenced Churchman's ideas considerably, he seldom presented them as complete case studies in his writing, instead concentrating on the ideas and illustrating them with examples from his consultancy work.

A further key way in which Churchman disseminated his ideas was through his teaching. Churchman taught for over 50 years, especially graduate students and working managers. Students who would go on to have a strong influence on systems thinking included Werner Ulrich, Ian Mitroff and Robert Mason, as well as Russell Ackoff. His teaching radically changed the lives and careers of his students. His influence was broad and significant: "today, West's students can be found working in health sciences, in military service, in finance and accounting, in education, in architecture and urban planning, in information systems and in universities worldwide" (Koenigsberg and van Gigch 1994, p. 2).

Churchman was famous for conducting academic discussions while knitting, as recounted by one former student (Heiner Müller-Merbach, quoted in Koenigsberg and van Gigch 1994, p. 4) in a way that demonstrates much of Churchman's democratic and supportive character:

He returned with a sweater-in-progress, dark blue with little bright yellow animals, mythical ones included. West commented on the mythical ones by mumbling something about random numbers. He continued knitting while participating actively in the discussion, carefully listening and sometimes intervening. ... This activity contributed in a remarkable way to the group's social climate that night. It did not draw the group's attention that much, yet all of us recognized every single stitch. West somehow conducted the discussion invisibly with his needle.

West Churchman carried on working to secure improvements in the human condition until the end of his life. When he reached the age of 70, instead of retiring he moved into an emeritus professorship at Berkeley in peace and conflict studies. He only finally left this post in 1996, aged 83, but even then carried on working on 'global ethical management', and although seriously ill with Parkinson's disease, he was writing until his death in California in 2004.

It is hard to summarise the work of such an intellectual and moral pioneer, so much loved by so many people, but his life and ideas were very well described a decade before his death by a former student, Ian Mitroff (1994, p. 98):

West Churchman is a moral and intellectual beacon of hope and inspiration to those who have been privileged to know and to work closely with him. He has taught us to think deeply about science and management. He has schooled us in the systems approach. He has shown us how to rise above the narrow and unethical concerns of the prevailing disciplines. He has annoyed us with his questions about the obvious. Even more, he has amazed us with his insights. Beautiful ideas flow from sources deep within him that contemporary management and science cannot even begin to understand, let alone talk about.

Reading from Churchman's work

From *The Design of Inquiring Systems* by C West Churchman © 1971 by Basic Books, Inc.
   Reprinted by permission of BASIC BOOKS, a member of Perseus Books Group.
Extract from pages 5–8.

On design (preliminary statement)

The introductory remarks of this chapter themselves suggest some of the salient characteristics of design. First of all, design belongs to the category of behavior called teleological, i.e., 'goal seeking' behavior. More specifically, design is thinking behavior which conceptually selects among a set of alternatives in order to figure out which alternative leads to the desired goal or set of goals. In this regard, design is synonymous with planning, optimizing, and similar terms that connote the use of thought as a precursor to action directed at the attainment of goals.

Each alternative, ideally, describes a complete set of behavior patterns, so that someone equipped with the same thought processes as the designer will be able to

convert the design into a specific set of actions. Consequently, as a first approximation, design has the following characteristics:

1. It attempts to distinguish in thought between different sets of behavior
   patterns.
2. It tries to estimate in thought how well each alternative set of behavior patterns
   will serve a specified set of goals.
3. Its aim is to communicate its thoughts to other minds in such a manner that they
   can convert the thoughts into corresponding actions which in fact serve the goals
   in the same manner as the design said they would.

It will be noted that these specifications contain the phrases 'attempts to',
'tries to', and 'aim'; the point is that the designer tries to do these three things,
but may not succeed. If the phrases had been omitted, then we should have
been caught in the awkward position of saying that design behavior occurs
only when it is completely successful, i.e., never. Indeed, it is important at the
outset to recognize that there are degrees of design, depending on a person's
interest in the three efforts, as well as the amount of success he attains
in them.

There is a fourth characteristic of design behavior that is important for the subsequent discussion. This is the goal of generality, or, as many would put it, methodology; the designer strives to avoid the necessity of repeating the thought process
when faced with a similar goal-attainment problem by delineating the steps in the
process of producing a design.

In a sense, this design goal consists in communicating with another designing
mind faced with similar problems. Once the designer has had some success in this
fourth effort, he can say that he can tell *why* a design is good, in addition to telling
the *what*, *when*, and *how*, which the first three efforts attempt to accomplish. The
broader the class of problems that a design methodology can be used to solve, the
deeper the 'explanation' of the design.

It is evident that some 'other mind' is critical for the designer, whether it be his
own mind later on or some different person. This other mind transforms thoughts
into action (3) or into other designs (4). In understanding the design process it
would be very convenient to have a standard 'other mind', which the student of
design could use to test the effectiveness of various design processes. A recently
developed mind, the digital computer, is a likely candidate. We can defer for later
argument the question whether a computer 'has' a mind. For the present, it appears
to be a good candidate for a standard because (a) its processes belong under the
category of thinking, and (b) in principle one can test whether a set of ideas have
been adequately transmitted to it.

So our question is whether it is possible to tell a computer how to design an
inquiring system, or, in other terms, teach a computer to conduct research. The
purpose is not to design an 'automated' researcher, but rather to discover what in
the research process is truly the 'lonely' part, the part that cannot be designed, at
least relative to a standard computer.

[...]

On the design of systems

We are specifically interested in the design of systems, i.e., of structures that have organized components. As we move into the discussion in greater depth, we shall have to say a great deal about the concept of a system, but one central problem of all systems design can easily be illustrated. For example, the designer of a home for a family is designing a system. Narrowly, he may think of a particular instance of a design as the specification of a physical house, designated by a complete set of architectural drawings and specifications. In this case, the components may be the rooms, and the relations between the components may be the geometrical scheme of the house in three-dimensional space. But the architect may ask himself a broader question: whether the house is not a component of a larger system, consist-ing of the family (or its activities) and the house. When he does ask himself this question, he may wonder whether his design task should include the design of a part of the family's activities. For example, he may wonder whether he can change the family's typical way of using the kitchen facilities. Still more broadly, he may ask whether the house plus family is not a component of an urban social system, and whether he ought not to consider alternative designs of this entire community. If he perceives his task in the narrowest sense, then he tells himself that the larger system is not his concern; how the family behaves is entirely up to them, or how the com-munity is planned is entirely up to the planners and politicians. In such a case, he believes that the maximum size of the system is the house (plus, say, its location on the land). He may believe that there is a larger system that may concern some other designer; such a larger system may be the city in which the house is to be placed. But as far as he is concerned, larger systems are not relevant to the effectiveness of his choices.

Thus, one system design problem of central importance is to decide how large the system is, i.e., its boundaries and environment. A closely related problem is one of determining the basic components, i.e., the components that do not contain sub-components. For example, the architect may decide that there are ultimate choices he can make from a catalogue: he cannot or should not consider alternative ways of putting together the parts of a window, since this is entirely up to the window manu-facturers. In this case, he regards the system to have a smallest component.

All men are system designers, and each man tries to determine what, in his world, is the largest system and the smallest. For each human, the system he designs is his life, i.e., his self. The question all of us face is what is the largest and smallest system which constitutes the self? Where does self designing begin and end?

The trouble with such a question is that it is so confusing. The intent is clear enough in each specific case, however. A man must decide whether to pay attention to his own survival and welfare only, or his family's, or his city's, or his nation's, or the world's, or of 'space'. He must decide whether to 'take' what is offered in terms of goods and money, or to create his own. In either direction he looks for the broadest and the deepest limits of his world of system design. But to translate these familiar problems of human living into a form that can receive sensible general answers is the difficult task.

As we proceed in the discussion of the design of inquiring systems, we shall find that we must face the question of the largest and smallest system: what is the largest set of components the designer of inquiring systems must consider, and what are the fundamental components that cannot be further analyzed into systems? To illustrate, is it enough to consider just the acts of formulating hypotheses and testing hypotheses? If this is essentially all that an inquirer can be expected to do, then such matters as generalizations from theories or the communication of results are taken to be outside the purview of the inquirer, and hence matters of concern to other systems. Likewise, if the human being is regarded as essential for inquiry but the process by which he creates new ideas is taken to be forever beyond the scope of analysis, then the human creator is regarded as a fundamental component, one lower bound of the hierarchy of components.

To the four characteristics of design given above, we must therefore add a fifth which is specific to the design of systems: the systems designer attempts to identify the whole relevant system and its components; the design alternatives are defined in terms of the design of the components and their interrelationships.

References

Ackoff, R. L. (1988). C. West Churchman. *Systems Practice, 1*(4), 351–355.

Churchman, C. W., Ackoff, R. L., Arnoff, E. L. (1957). *Introduction to operations research.* New York: John Wiley.

Churchman, C. W. (1968). *The systems approach.* New York: Dell Publishing.

Churchman, C. W. (1971). *The design of inquiring systems: Basic concepts of systems and organization.* New York: Basic Books.

Churchman, C. W. (1979). *The systems approach and its enemies.* New York: Basic Books.

Churchman, C. W. (1982). *Thought and wisdom.* Seaside, CA: Intersystems Publications.

Churchman, C.W. (1994). Management science: Science of managing and managing of science. *Interfaces, 24*(4), 99–110.

Koenigsberg, E., & van Gigch, J.P. (1994). In celebration of the 80th birthday of C. West Churchman, Born Mount Airy, Pennsylvania, August 29, 1913. *Interfaces, 24*(4), 1–4.

Mason, R. (1988). Exploration of opportunity costs and consideration for future generations: Two lasting contributions to systems thinking. *Systems Practice, 1*(4), 367–375.

Mitroff, I. (1994). The cruel science of world mismanagement: An essay in honour of C. West Churchman. *Interfaces, 24*(4), 94–98.

Reynolds, M. (2004). Churchman and Maturana: Enriching the notion of self-organization for social design. *Systemic Practice and Action Research, 17*(6), 539–556.

Ulrich, W. (2004). In memory of C. West Churchman (1913–2004): Reminiscences, retrospectives, and reflections. *Journal of Organisational Transformation and Social Change, 1*(2–3), 199–219.

Van Gigch, J. P., & McIntyre-Mills, J. (2006). Preface to a new book series: C. West Churchman legacy and related works. In J. McIntyre-Mills (Ed.) *Rescuing the enlightenment from itself: Critical and systemic implications for democracy* (pp. xiii–xv). New York: Springer.

Van Gigch, J.P., Koenigsberg, E., Dean, B. (1997). In search of an ethical science: An interview with C. West Churchman, an 80th birthday celebration. *Journal of Business Ethics, 16*(7), 731–744.

Chapter 14
Russell Ackoff

Russell Ackoff (usually known as 'Russ') is a pioneer of the application of systems approaches to management, both through theoretical developments and through a deep and practical engagement with many different organisations. He is a passionate advocate of the need for systems approaches to take full account of the complexity of inter-related problems and not simply to present glib technical solutions.

Ackoff is notable as a theorist, having been responsible for many key innovations in operations research (a field to which he helped to give academic respectability) and systems thinking. He is equally strong in working as a consultant, although he dislikes the term, preferring to call himself an educator: "A consultant goes in with a solution. He tries to impose it on a situation. An educator tries to train the people responsible for the work to work it out for themselves. We don't pretend to know the way to get the answer" (Stern 2007). He has also made significant innovations in formal university teaching, introducing radical new curricula in both operations research and systems thinking. He is a strong and able communicator, in speech and writing – his articles uses many vivid devices, such as anecdotes (especially his collection known as "Ackoff's fables"), aphorisms (e.g. "a bureaucrat is one who has the power to say 'no' but none to say 'yes'" – Ackoff et al. 2007, p. 91) and pithy, well-argued opinions. As Kirby and Rosenhead (2005, pp. 132–133) put it, "his writing style is both muscular and readable (paralleling his outstanding skills as a public speaker)".

Russell Ackoff was born in 1919 in Philadelphia – his grandparents were Russian immigrants but had their children in the United States. He studied at the University of Pennsylvania – an interest in design processes and an uncle who was an architect led him to take his BA in architecture, but during his final undergraduate year he fell under the spell of West Churchman and took his Ph.D. in philosophy with Churchman (and Churchman's mentor, the pragmatist philosopher E.A. Singer), graduating in 1947. As was allowed by Pennsylvania's rules, Ackoff's Ph.D. dissertation was jointly authored by Ackoff and Churchman, and when asked which parts had been written by Ackoff they simply selected chapters at random. This led to Ackoff passing his Ph.D. but failing to have his teaching fellowship renewed.

M. Ramage and K. Shipp, *Systems Thinkers*,
© The Open University 2009. Published in association with Springer-Verlag London Limited

As Ackoff was unable to get a position at Pennsylvania, he moved to Wayne State University in Detroit, where he spent four years, moving in 1951 to the Case Institute of Technology. At Case he co-founded, with Churchman, its Operations Research (OR) Group, the first in the world, and was a co-author of the first text-book in OR (Churchman et al. 1957). Ackoff directed the OR group after Churchman moved to Berkeley in 1958. He was also president of the OR Society of America in 1956.

In 1964, he returned to Pennsylvania as a professor at its business school (Wharton), along with many of the Case OR group; he stayed there until his retire-ment in 1986. In the mid-1970s, he devised and ran the Social Systems Sciences postgraduate programme at Wharton. On retiring from Wharton, he subsequently headed a consultancy firm, Interact: the Institute of Interactive Management. In 2000 the University of Pennsylvania established the Ackoff Center for Advancement of Systems Approaches in his honour. He has published more than 20 books, both scholarly and popular, and numerous articles.

Ackoff is a forceful and passionate thinker and practitioner. In describing their close collaboration, Churchman (1990, p. 130) wrote "if the story of my early years with Russ sounds like they were years of battle, then the sound is correct". One of his key industrial collaborators, August Busch III of the Anheuser-Busch brewing company, refers to his "argumentative and sometimes even combative approach to problem solving ... both the company and Russ developed as a result of the sharp and intensive way he defended his position" (Busch 1990, p. 147). On the other hand, as his close colleague at Wharton and Interact, Jamshid Gharajedaghi (2002) has written, "to be accepted as a friend by Russ, is to become the subject of his incisive and unrelenting critique ... at the same time, he is equally tireless in pro-moting you as nothing but the very best".

He has worked with a large number of organisations as a consultant-educator. Two of the most significant have taken very different forms. First, he has worked for more than 30 years as a consultant to Anheuser-Busch (makers of Budweiser among many other brands), which had a strong influence on his thinking and the issues he considered. He conducted research for them in areas as diverse as logis-tics, marketing, corporate planning, environmental issues, alcoholism and corporate organisation. In this time, the company's market share of US beer sales grew from 7% to 41%, and "although it is impossible to trace precise causal relationships, it is a straightforward and relatively simple task to show that Ackoff's contribution to this growth was real and considerable" (Busch 1990, p. 146). His experiences with Anheuser-Busch fed directly into several of Ackoff's books; they also supported his research projects financially for many years.

He had a very different, but equally important, experience in a project in a deprived black area of Philadelphia, Mantua which began in 1968. Based on com-munity leaders' slogan of "plan or be planned for", the project involved the local community in planning for the future development of the neighbourhood, using the resources and skills of the university but clearly driven by the community. This was a highly participative view of research: "we, the researchers, designed a relation with the 'subjects' in which the subjects conducted research on us. It was the community members' task to find out how to use the University and our Center effectively, and, by so doing, to solve the researchers' problem of determining how to be useful" (Ackoff 1970, p. 768). Ackoff drew lessons from this project which influenced his later work considerably, in particular the importance of OR taking social responsibility seriously and going beyond a technical perspective, and the need for widespread participation in planning processes. In an article discussing the project he contrasted this experience with planning in large organisations: "the effective ghetto leader has a knowledge of and concern with his environment that few governmental or industrial leaders have ... however limited his effect on the larger environment may be, the ghetto leader uses all his power to push it in a direction that is compatible with his aspirations for his neighbourhood. He believes in active intervention in the larger community and its future because he knows that his neighbourhood cannot thrive unless the larger community thrives" (Ackoff 1970, p. 771). The Mantua project was also to form the inspiration for later British work in 'community OR' (Jackson 1990).

Ackoff has had a long and interesting relationship with the field of operations research. In Kirby's (2003) terms, Ackoff shifted from being an OR apostle to an OR apostate, in a process lasting 30 years. As already mentioned, Ackoff was involved very closely in the establishment of OR as an academic discipline, in his work with Churchman at Case. His influence on the development of academic OR in Britain was also considerable, with several visits including acting as a "marriage broker" (Jackson 1990, p. 178) between the Tavistock Institute and the Operational Research Society, in the formation of the Institute of Operational Research at the Tavistock.

However, Ackoff became increasingly disillusioned with OR as a discipline. He had always been "concerned to widen the scope of the discipline far beyond the tactical problems of industry and commerce" (Kirby 2003, pp. 1131–1132), had made frequent critiques of the narrow technical nature of OR and written about its need for social responsibility (based on experiences such as the Mantua project). His dissatisfaction culminated in a famous pair of papers in which he argued that "Operational Research was once an outrageous idea. It no longer is. Today it is an idea dressed in a sombre dark suit, a bowler on its head, a black umbrella on its arm and an attaché case in its hand" (Ackoff 1979, pp. 198–199). The influence of Ackoff's views was considerable in the UK, forming a key part of the drive towards a broader, more strategic form of OR known as 'soft OR'; but in the US he was treated very differently and "his direct influence is now hard to find in the academic OR community ... it is as if he has been written out of the official OR canon" (Kirby and Rosenhead 2005, pp. 133).

His frustration with OR led Ackoff, as it did Churchman, in the direction of systems thinking (particularly general systems theory). He argued that we have left the machine age, with its concept of the universe as a mechanism and its consequent focus on analytical thinking and reductionism; and instead are entering the systems age, with a focus on synthetic (systemic) thinking and expansionism, the idea "that all objects, events, and experiences of them are parts of larger wholes" (Ackoff 1974, p. 12). A crucial part of Ackoff's approach to systems thinking was his introduction of the concept of a *mess*: a system of problems recognising the fact that "no problem ever exists in complete isolation; every problem interacts with other problems and is therefore part of a set of interrelated problems" (Ackoff 1974, p. 21). In particular, it is insufficient and indeed counter-productive to break a mess down into its constituent elements, which can even lead to the mess becoming worse. A key example for Ackoff are the different aspects of urban life, such as health, crime, education, transport and racial tensions, which can only be made better if treated collectively (today's list would be longer and perhaps include environmental issues and religious tensions, but the need for systemic thinking is the same).

Instead of looking for simple-minded solutions, we need an effective process of what Ackoff calls 'mess management'. He argues that the way to handle messes (in both community and organisational settings) is through planning, and specifically a participatory and systemic method he calls *interactive planning* (by contrast with three weaker, less systemic means of planning – inactive, reactive and proactive). This method, and the related concept of interactive management, has formed the basis of Ackoff's work in systems thinking from the 1970s onwards. It derives partly from his experiences in the Mantua project and their slogan "plan or be planned for", which forms the subtitle of the key book on the process (Ackoff 1981).

Interactive planning works on the principle of 'idealized redesign' of a system: "a design of the system with which the designers would replace the existing system now if they were free to do so" (Ackoff 1979, p. 191). Importantly, this redesign must consider the whole system, in all its parts, simultaneously; and it must involve the participation of all key stakeholders. Participation, crucial to the commitment of stakeholders to the change that is devised, is enabled by the democratic nature of this redesign process – it does not require experts. Ackoff (1981) identifies five stages of interactive planning: formulating the mess (understanding the problems and opportunities involved), ends planning (designing the desirable future), means planning (finding ways to reach the desirable future), resource planning (deciding what human, financial and other resources are required and how to obtain them), and design of implementation and control (the details of how to put the changes into place and check that they have actually happened).

As well as the development of interactive planning/management, Ackoff made important contributions to teaching systems thinking. The Social Systems Science (S^3) programme at Wharton, which he established in the mid-1970s along with others disillusioned with OR, was designed on the principle that an effective degree programme should not be "made up of an aggregation of independently given and taken courses that leave the difficult task of their synthesis to be performed by the student alone; the principal instruments of education are Learning and Research Cells which are collective efforts at synthesis, not analysis" (Ackoff 1979, p. 197). S^3 was highly successful, with large numbers, and highly effective in teaching systems ideas, although its methods were too unorthodox to make it popular with Ackoff's colleagues at the Wharton School.

Ackoff is not universally popular, given the forthrightness of his views and his keenness to critique established ideas in a range of situations. Nonetheless, he is widely respected for the range of his innovations, the extent to which he has brought democratic principles to organisational and national planning via systems thinking, and his insistence on going beyond narrow technical solutions. He is a man of passion and vision. Ultimately, as a long-term colleague at Anheuser-Busch put it (Pritzker 1990, p. 152):

> Russ has not been the model of the cool, aloof, dispassionate, and 'objective' scientist. Rather he has been intensely involved in the 'messes' and problems with which he has been asked to deal. He has been the model of the committed, partisan investigator.

Reading from Ackoff's work

Ackoff, R. L. On Passing through 80, *Systemic Practice and Action Research*. New York: Aug 1999. Vol. 12, Iss. 4; p.425–430. With kind permission of Springer Science and Business Media

For me there has never been an amount of money that makes it worth doing something that is not fun. So I'm going to recall the principal sources of the fun that I have experienced.

First, the fun derived from denying the obvious and exploring the consequences of doing so. In most cases, I have found the obvious to be wrong. The obvious, I discovered, is not what needs no proof, but what people do not want to prove. [...]

Here is a very small sample of the obvious things I have had great fun denying.

- *That improving the performance of the parts of a system taken separately will necessarily improve the performance of the whole.* False. In fact, it can destroy an organization, as is apparent in an example I have used ad nauseam: installing a Rolls Royce engine in a Hyundai can make it inoperable. This explains why benchmarking has almost always failed. Denial of this principle of performance improvement led to a series of organizational designs intended to facilitate the management of interactions: the circular organization, the internal market economy, and the multidimensional organization.
- *That problems are disciplinary in nature.* Effective research is not disciplinary, interdisciplinary, or multidisciplinary; it is transdisciplinary. Systems thinking is holistic; it attempts to derive understanding of parts from the behaviour and properties of wholes rather than derive the behaviour and properties of wholes from those of their parts. Disciplines are taken by science to represent different parts of the reality we experience. In effect, science assumes reality is structured and organized the way universities are. This is a double error. First, disciplines do not constitute different parts of reality; they are different aspects of reality, different points of view. Any part of reality can be viewed from any of these aspects. The whole can

be understood only by viewing it from all the perspectives simultaneously. Second, the separation of our different points of view encourages looking for solutions to problems with the same point of view from which the problem was recognized. Paraphrasing Einstein, we cannot deal with problems as effectively as possible by employing the same point of view as was used in recognizing them. When we know how a system works, how its parts are connected and interact to produce the behaviour and properties of the whole, we can almost always find one or more points of view from which better solutions to the problem can be found than can be found from the point of view from which the problem was recognized. For example, we do not try to cure a headache by brain surgery, but by putting a pill in the stomach. We do this because we understand how the body, a biological system, works. When science divides reality up into disciplinary parts and deals with them separately, it reveals a lack of understanding of reality as a whole, as a system. [...]

- *That the best thing that can be done to a problem is to solve it.* False. The best thing that can be done to a problem is to dissolve it, to redesign the entity that has it or its environment so as to eliminate the problem. Such a design incorporates common sense and research and increases our learning more than trial-and-error or scientific research alone can.

My second source of fun has been the revelation that most large social systems are pursuing objectives other than the ones they proclaim and that the ones they pursue are wrong. They try to do the wrong thing righter and this makes what they do wronger. It is much better to do the right thing wrong than the wrong thing right, because when errors are corrected it makes doing the wrong thing wronger, but the right thing righter.
A few examples: [...]

- *The educational system is not dedicated to produce learning by students, but teaching by teachers, and teaching is a major obstruction to learning.* Witness the difference between the ease with which we learned our first language without having it taught to us, and the difficulty with which we did not learn a second language in school. Most of what we use as adults we learned once out of school, not in it, and what we learned in school we forget rapidly – fortunately. Most of it is either wrong or obsolete within a short time. Although we learn little of use by having it taught to us, we can learn a great deal by teaching others. It is always the teacher who learns most in a classroom. Schools are upside down. Students should be teaching, and teachers at all levels should learn no matter how much they resist doing so.

A student once asked me in what year I had last taught a class on a subject that existed when I was a student. A great question. After some thought, I told him 1951. "Boy", he said, "You must be a good learner. What a pity you can't teach as well as you can learn." He had it right.

- *The principal function of most corporations is not to maximize shareholder value, but to maximize the standard of living and quality of work life of those who manage the corporation.* Providing the shareholders with a return on their investments is a requirement, not an objective. As Peter Drucker observed, profit is to a corporation as oxygen is to a human being: necessary for existence, not the reason for it. A corporation that fails to provide an adequate return for their investment to its employees and customers is just as likely to fail as one that does not reward its shareholders adequately.

The most valuable and least replaceable resource is time. Without the time of employees, money can produce nothing. Employees have a much larger investment in most corporations than their shareholders. Corporations should be maximizing stakeholder, not shareholder, value.

My third source of fun derives from producing conceptual order where ambiguity and confusion prevail. Some examples:

- *Identifying and defining the hierarchy of mental content which, in order of increasing value, are data, information, knowledge, understanding, and wisdom.* However, the educational system and most managers allocate time to their acquisition that is inversely proportional to their importance. Few individuals, and fewer organizations, know how to facilitate and accelerate learning – the acquisition of knowledge – let alone understanding and wisdom. It takes a support system do to so.

All learning ultimately derives from mistakes. When we do something right we already know how to do it; the most we get out of it is confirmation. Mistakes are of two types: commission (doing what should not have been done) and omission (not doing what should have been done). Errors of omission are generally much more serious than errors of commission, but errors of commission are the only ones picked up by most accounting systems. Then since mistakes are a no–no in most corporations, and the only mistakes identified and measured are ones involving doing something that should not have been done, the best strategy for managers is to do as little as possible. No wonder it prevails in American organizations.

- *Identifying and defining the three basic types of traditional management: the reactive or reactionary, the inactive or conservative, and the preactive or liberal.* Then showing that a fourth type, the interactive or radical, denies the assumptions common to the three traditional types and, therefore, constitutes a radical transformation of the concept of management. The interactive manager plans backward from where he wants to be ideally, right now, not forward to where he wants to be in the future, or past.

The interactive manager plans backward because it reduces the number of alternative paths he must consider, and his destination is where he would like to be now ideally, because if he did not know this, how could he possibly know where he will want to be at some other time?

- *Identifying and defining the ways we can control the future: vertical integration, horizontal integration, cooperation, incentives, and responsiveness.* These are seldom used well. Corporations tend to collect activities that they do not have the competence or even the inclination to run well. They also tend more to adversarial relationships with employees, to encourage competition between parts of the corporation and conflict with competitors. As Peter Drucker pointed out, there is more competition within corporations than between them, and it tends to be less ethical. In many cases managers unintentionally create incentives that result in activities diametrically opposed to their best interests – for example, rewarding themselves for short-term performance, ignoring the long term, or paying commission based on the amount of a sale rather than its profitability. This encourages the sale of underpriced, hence usually unprofitable, items.

Few organizations are ready, willing, and able to change in response to unanticipated internal or external changes; they lack the responsiveness of a good driver of an automobile, who gets to where he wants to go without forecasts of what he will encounter but the ability to cope with whatever occurs.

My fourth source of fun has been the *disclosure of intellectual con men* – for example, propagators of TQM, benchmarking, downsizing, process reengineering, and scenario planning. Management is incurably susceptible to panacea peddlers. They are rooted in the belief that there are simple, if not simple-minded, solutions to even the most complex of problems. And they do not learn from bad experiences. Managers fail to diagnose the failures of the fads they adopt; they do not understand them. Most panaceas fail because they are applied antisystemically. They need not be, but to do otherwise requires an understanding of systems and the ability to think systemically. The perceived need to learn something new is inversely proportional to the rank of a manager. Those at the top feel obliged to pretend to omniscience and, therefore, refuse to learn anything new even if the cost of doing so is success.

Finally, my fifth source of fun has derived from designing organizations that can avoid the kinds of traps I have described here, for example, the designs of a democratic hierarchy, an internal market economy, a multidimensional organizational structure, and learning and adaptation support systems. But I have derived the most fun working with others on the design of INTERACT, the Social Systems Sciences Graduate Program at The Wharton School, and the Operations Research Graduate Programs at Case and Penn.

I am indebted to all who have made my 'work' a continuous source of fun.

References

Ackoff, R.L. (1970). A black Ghetto's research on a University. *Operations Research, 18*(5), 761–771.

Ackoff, R. L. (1974). *Redesigning the future: A systems approach to societal problems.* New York: John Wiley.

Ackoff, R.L. (1979). Resurrecting the future of operational research. *Journal of the Operational Research Society, 30*(3), 189–199.

Ackoff, R.L. (1981). *Creating the corporate future.* New York: John Wiley.

Ackoff, R.L. (1999). On passing through 80. *Systemic Practice and Action Research, 12*(4), 425–430.

Ackoff, R. L., Addison, H. J., Bibb, S. (2007). *Management F-laws: How organizations really work.* Axminster, UK: Triarchy Press.

Busch, A. (1990). Russell L. Ackoff and Anheuser-Busch. I. The influence of the man on the organization. *Systems Practice, 3*(2), 145–150.

Churchman, C.W. (1990). Ackoff comes of age. *Systems Practice, 3*(2), 125–130.

Churchman, C. W., Ackoff, R. L., Arnoff, E. L. (1957). *Introduction to operations research.* New York: John Wiley.

Gharajedaghi, J. (2002). Russell Ackoff. International Society for the Systems Sciences. http://projects.isss.org/Russell_L_Ackoff. Accessed 13 Jan 2009.

Jackson, M. (1990). Russell Ackoff's Jerusalem. *Systems Practice, 3*(2), 177–182.

Kirby, M. (2003). The intellectual journey of Russell Ackoff: From OR apostle to OR apostate. *Journal of the Operational Research Society, 54*(11), 1127–1140.

Kirby, M., & Rosenhead, J. (2005). IFORS' operational research hall of fame: Russell L. Ackoff. *International Transactions in Operational Research, 12*(1), 129–134.

Pritzker, L. (1990). Russell L. Ackoff and Anheuser-Busch. II. The influence of the organization on the man. *Systems Practice, 3*(2), 151–158.

Stern, S. (2007). Anti-guru of joined-up management. *The Daily Telegraph*, 8 Feb 2007, Appointments Section p.3.

Chapter 15
Peter Checkland

Peter Bernard Checkland has had a huge influence on systems thinking, especially in the fields of management and information systems, although his ideas have been taken up in a wide range of fields. He is most notable for the development of Soft Systems Methodology (SSM), deriving from an action research programme lasting more than 30 years. As well as methodological innovations, Checkland introduced a number of key conceptual developments, in particular his distinction between 'hard' and 'soft' systems thinking, and his championing of the soft approach. As Mingers (2000, p. 747) notes, "SSM has reoriented an entire discipline and touched the lives of literally thousands of people … [soft] thinking is now completely taken for granted within the systems discipline".

Checkland was born in 1930 in Birmingham, where he also grew up and went to school. Following national service, he went to Oxford University to study chemistry, graduating with a first-class degree in 1954. He decided not to take a Ph.D., on the grounds that only four or five people around the world were actually likely to read his results. He remarks that "suddenly it seemed absurd to be devoting intense intellectual activity to something which only a tiny handful of people would care about" (Checkland 2000b, p.S61).

He resolved instead to dedicate himself to applied science, an approach he would follow throughout his career. He went straight from Oxford to ICI Fibres where he worked from 1954 to 1968 on the applications of nylon and polyester, progressing through various levels of management. As a scientist and a manager, he became aware of the field of management science, but was deeply disappointed by its irrelevance to his practice, later remarking that "in 14 years as a manager, I personally was continually puzzled by the irrelevance of text-book management science to my real problems" (Checkland 1980, p. 320).

He had made considerable use of systems ideas in his work at ICI, and in 1969 moved to Lancaster University to apply these ideas to management problems, working in the department of Systems Engineering, which later changed its name simply to 'Systems'. He remained at Lancaster until his retirement in 1997 and is still an emeritus professor there, although he has been a visiting professor at various other universities. He has received various awards and honorary doctorates from several universities, and was president of the Society for General Systems Research in 1986.

Peter Checkland married his wife Glenys in 1955, and remained married until her death in 1990; they have two daughters. Of Glenys, Checkland (2000b, p.S59) wrote: "Loving her for the forty-three years I knew her is the best thing that's happened to me in my life; losing her, the worst. Since I lost her, whenever I've faced any dilemma I've asked myself what her advice would have been, and I've always known the answer".

Flood (2000, p. 723) has described him as a "man of passion and structure", noting that "Checkland is a person with a love of English literature, jazz, and rock climbing. Both jazz and rock climbing involve passion and structure. These two qualities are key ingredients that readers of his books soon encounter" (Flood 2000, p. 724).

On joining Lancaster University, Checkland began a programme of action research "to see if systems ideas could help us to tackle the messy problems of 'management'" (Checkland 2000a, p.S11). This work was to last 30 years until his retirement, and carries on to the present day through his and others' work. The Department of Systems Engineering had been established at Lancaster in 1966 by Gwilym Jenkins, the first Systems department in a UK university. The department's teaching consisted of a one year Masters programme that included a five month project applying systems ideas in a real-world setting. The annual cycle of these projects, along with consultancy work and doctoral research, formed the testing ground for successive iterations to the methodology being developed at Lancaster, that would eventually become SSM.

The basis for the work, systems engineering, developed in industry through the need to build large and complex physical systems (such as chemical plants or telephone networks). Systems engineering was well developed when Checkland started on the research, involving a process of defining the problem, its surrounding system and constraints; building a model of the system (usually computer-based); using that model to investigate possible changes to the system; and implementing a redesigned system incorporating changes identified through the model.. This approach had been seen to work well in a range of industrial settings, and continues to be crucial in such applications to the present day.

However, when applied to management problems, Checkland rapidly found that systems engineering was inadequate. It took for granted too much about the nature of the system and its objectives, whereas defining those things often proves to be highly problematic in complex social settings such as management. A key case study that informed this change was consultancy work for the British Aircraft Corporation on the Concorde project, running late and over-budget. Ostensibly, the objectives of the project were clear: to build an aircraft that met the technical specification within time and cost requirements and would gain safety approval. However, it was clear that a larger set of objectives also existed, notably political ones – the project, as an Anglo-French joint venture, could readily be seen as a means of demonstrating British sincerity at a time Britain was applying for membership of the European Community in the face of the veto of President de Gaulle of France. This led to a clear and important lesson: that "it was necessary to declare both a world-view which made a chosen model relevant, and a world-view which would then determine the model content ... there would always be a number of models in play, never simply one model purporting to describe 'what is the case'" (Checkland 2000a, p.S15).

These lessons – the importance of worldviews (for which Checkland adopted the German term *Weltanschauungen* from West Churchman), and the related issue of multiple views of reality – would form the basis of the thinking behind SSM. After ten years of work, Checkland (1981) drew together the ideas in a book, *Systems Thinking, Systems Practice*, probably still the mostly widely cited of his works. He distinguished between two forms of systems thinking – hard and soft. As described in the 1981 book (as we will see later, his understanding of the distinction developed over time), hard systems thinking referred to approaches such as systems engineering and operational research, which take as given the problem or need; in soft systems approaches, the true nature of the problem arises from the process of the systems study.

Soft Systems Methodology was described in Checkland (1981) as a seven-stage process, an expression of the methodology he was later to drop for his own use but which is still widely used in secondary texts, especially for teaching purposes. It is important to note here that Checkland has never seen SSM as a method – a single set of steps which can be followed in order – but rather as a methodology, "a set of ongoing principles which can be adapted for use in a way which suits the specific nature of each situation in which it is used" (Checkland and Poulter 2006, p. 6). The seven stages form one expression of the methodology, and Checkland would later create other expressions (such as the set of principles found in the reading from his work below). The original seven stages were: (1) enter a problem situation, understood in an unstructured way; (2) express the problem situation in a more formal manner, especially its structure and process; (3) formulate a set of "root definitions" of relevant systems (a clear statement of the nature of the system); (4) build a set of "conceptual models" of activities which fulfil those root definitions and form an ideal state of the system; (5) compare the conceptual models with the earlier description of the problem situation; (6) given this comparison, decide on possible changes which are both systemically desirable and culturally feasible to help reach this ideal state; and (7) take action to improve the problem situation through the implementation of these changes.

As well as introducing a methodology with the seven-step version of SSM, Checkland (1981) also brought to wide attention a set of tools that the Lancaster group had developed which were used at the different stages of SSM. In particular, rich pictures and root definitions have proved useful in many settings beyond the explicit use of SSM. Rich pictures are perhaps the most widely used: they are a pictorial representation (usually hand-drawn) of the key elements in a problem situation, including issues of structure and process but without expressing these in terms of systems. Root definitions are a means of defining the nature of a particular system, to express it as 'a system to ...' – as part of deciding upon a root definition, the CATWOE framework (customers, actors, transformation, worldview, owner, environment) serves as a mnemonic to ensure the most important elements are included.

Through the 1980s and 1990s, Checkland developed SSM and its related ideas considerably. Crucially, he came to express the distinction between hard and soft systems thinking in terms of whether systems were considered to be a part of the world (hard) or a part of our way of understanding the world (soft), which he later described as a "shift of systemicity (or 'systemness') from the world to the process of inquiry into the world" (Checkland 2000a, p.S17). This shift is a key part of Checkland's highly influential reorientation of the field of systems thinking in line with the philosophical school of interpretivism, which looks at the social world in terms of multiple perspectives, rather than the previously-dominant approach of functionalism (or positivism) which holds that a single view of the world is the 'real' one. While Checkland was influenced by a number of others' work in this regard, notably Geoffrey Vickers and his concept of appreciative systems, Checkland was one of the first thinkers to put an interpretivist approach to systems thinking into practice.

Related to the shift to interpretivism was Checkland's developing argument that soft systems represented a shift from a focus on optimisation and goal-seeking to a focus on learning. Checkland increasingly came to view SSM as a learning system, and argued that "SSM is doubly systemic – it is itself a cyclic learning process; and it uses systems models within that process" (Checkland 1985, p. 764). This conception of SSM led Checkland to understand it in a much more abstracted form than the seven-step version – he described the seven-step version as 'mode 1 SSM' and outlined as well an internalised, situation-driven version of SSM, 'mode 2 SSM', which in use by expert practitioners drew on the same principles but used very different steps.

We have largely described Checkland's individual journey through soft systems, but an important aspect of his work was that it arose through collaboration with many other people at Lancaster – students, colleagues and fellow consultants. One of Checkland's key contributions was to lead and to draw together this community who in many ways collectively developed SSM. As part of this role, he was an accomplished teacher, especially of students on Lancaster's one year Masters programme (as well as Ph.D. students). A significant proportion of present-day influential UK academics in systems thinking, information systems and operational research studied the Lancaster Masters programme. One former student wrote that "Peter's lectures were some of the best I have ever experienced, both because they addressed my fundamental concerns and issues about people in organizations and because Peter was incredibly incisive and articulate, always peppering his lectures with provocative and stimulating insights" (Mingers 2000, p. 735).

SSM has been applied to all sorts of organisations and to all sorts of issues, but it has had a particular applicability in the field of information systems (IS). From the earliest days of the development of the methodology, many of the case studies involved the development of some sort of information system, and for a time the Masters degree at Lancaster had a specific IS focus. The generic nature of the methodology meant that it needed little explicit tailoring to work in this context, but it was clear that important lessons were learned from this process. Accordingly, Checkland and Holwell (1998a) devoted a whole book to exploring the use of SSM in information systems, with the aim of bringing greater conceptual clarity to a field which implies systems thinking in its title but is often deeply confused about the meaning and implications of this connection.

Checkland has long conceived of the programme of developing SSM and its related ideas as being one of action research, the approach first introduced by Kurt Lewin, and as part of this programme he has developed a clear understanding of the nature of action research. In Checkland (1985) he introduced a concept of inquiry as being in three parts: an intellectual framework (F), a methodology for using that framework (M), and an area of application (A) in which the methodology is used. Checkland and Holwell (1998b, p. 14) argue that "it is essential to declare in advance the elements FMA … without that declaration, it is difficult to see how the outcome of [action research] can be more than anecdotal". It is undoubtedly the case that much work labelled as action research is lacking in intellectual rigour, and Checkland's work provides a basis for treating action research in a rigorous manner.

His ideas are not without their critics. Most notably, the 'critical systems thinking' school of thought, discussed in the chapter on Michael Jackson grew out of a sense that SSM was inherently reformist, and in its recognition of multiple perspectives did not allow for enough of a consideration of power and conflict between those perspectives. The result in SSM is said to be one that too often favours the powerful.

An equally fundamental, but quite different, criticism has been made by John Mingers, who has argued against Checkland's stance on shifting systemicity from the world to the process of enquiry (as discussed above). By doing this, Mingers argues that Checkland "reduces the force of systems thinking" and notes that for the early systems thinkers, concepts such as system, feedback and the nature of equilibrium "were genuine explanatory concepts in that the existence of such systemic processes in the world was necessary to explain the phenomena that were observed; to deny reality to systems concepts is to reduce them to an essentially arbitrary language game" (Mingers 2000, p. 749).

Peter Checkland has had a considerable and lasting impact upon the systems movement, as a thinker, practitioner, methodology builder and teacher. He has suggested that a highly skilled practitioner of SSM has the following characteristics: "sensitivity to people and situations: a readiness to see the world through the eyes of another; an ability to think with clarity; above all, an ability to inspect and think about your own thinking" (quoted in Winter 2000, p. 383). Checkland's own ability to think with clarity, his passion and structure, have led to long-lasting change in the way we think about systems.

Reading from Checkland's work

- We all live in the midst of a complex interacting flux of changing events and ideas which unrolls through time. We call it 'everyday life', both personal and professional. Within that flux we frequently see situations which cause us to think: 'Something needs to be done about this, it needs to be improved.' Think of these as 'problematic situations', avoiding the word 'problem' since this implies 'solution', which eliminates the problem for ever. Real life is more complex than that!
- Soft Systems Methodology (SSM) is an organized way of tackling perceived problematical (social) situations. It is action-oriented. It organizes thinking about such situations so that action to bring about improvement can be taken.
- The complexity of problematical situations in real life stems from the fact that not only are they never static, they also contain multiple interacting perceptions of 'reality'. This comes about because different people have different taken-as-given (and often unexamined) assumptions about the world. This causes them to see it in a particular way. One person's 'terrorism' is another's 'freedom fighting'; one person sees a prison in terms of punishment, another sees it as seeking rehabilitation. These people have different *worldviews*. Tackling problematical situations has to accept this, and has to pitch analysis at a level that allows worldviews to be surfaced and examined. For many people worldviews are relatively fixed; but they can change over time. Sometimes a dramatic event can change them very quickly.
- All problematical situations, as well as containing different worldviews, have a second important characteristic. They always contain people who are trying to act *purposefully*, with intention, not simply acting by instinct or randomly thrashing about – though there is always plenty of that too in human affairs.
- The previous two points – the existence of conflicting worldviews and the ubiquity of would-be purposeful action – lead the way to tackling problematical situations. They underpin the SSM approach, a process of inquiry which, through social learning, works its way to taking 'action to improve'. Its shape is as follows:

1. Find out about both the problematical situation and the characteristics of the intervention to improve it: the issues, the prevailing culture and the disposition of power within the overall situation (its politics). Ways of doing these things are provided.
2. From the finding out, decide upon some relevant purposeful activities, relevant that is to exploring the situation deeply, and remembering that the ultimate aim is to define and take 'action to improve'. Express these relevant purposeful

activities as activity *models*, each made to encapsulate a declared worldview, the model being a cluster of linked activities which together make up a purposeful whole. (For example, one model could express in terms of activities the notion 'prison' as if it were only 'a punishment system', another could express it as 'a rehabilitation system'.) Such models never describe the real world, simply because they are based on one pure worldview. They are devices, or tools, to explore it in an organized way. Techniques for building and using such models have been developed.

3. Use the models as a source of questions to ask of the real-world situation. This provides a coherent structure to a discussion or debate about both the situation and how it might be changed, a discussion which will surface worldviews and generate ideas for change and improvement.

4. In the course of the discussion, continually bring together the results of the 'finding out' in (1) and the ideas for change in (3). The purpose now is to find changes which are both arguably *desirable* (given those models) but also culturally *feasible* for these people in this particular situation with its particular history, culture and politics. This is a process of seeking accommodations between different worldviews. That is to say, it is a process of finding versions of the to-be-changed situation which different people with conflicting worldviews could nevertheless *live with*. (Don't expect the worldviews to go away, nor wish that they would. Clashing worldviews, always present in human affairs, stimulate energy and ideas for change.)

- The elements (1) to (4) above constitute a *learning cycle*. They have necessarily been described linearly here but in use there is much iteration within the cycle as learning occurs. It is never followed in the flat-footed way in which it has been laid out here for explanatory purposes. Also it is apparent that it is essentially a group process leading to *group learning*. It is best carried out by people in the problematical situation itself, not left to an outside 'expert', though knowledgeable people can facilitate the process.

- Taking action to improve a problematical situation will of course itself change that situation, so that the learning cycle could in principle begin again. In any case the changing flux of everyday life will itself bring new events and new ideas, so that no human situation could ever be rendered static. In this sense SSM's learning cycle can be seen as never-ending. It ultimately offers a way of continuously managing any ongoing human situation. It does this by helping understanding of complex situations, encouraging multiple perspectives to be taken into account, and bringing rigour to processes of analysis, debate and taking 'action to improve'.

The seven points made above are presented pictorially in Fig. 15.1.

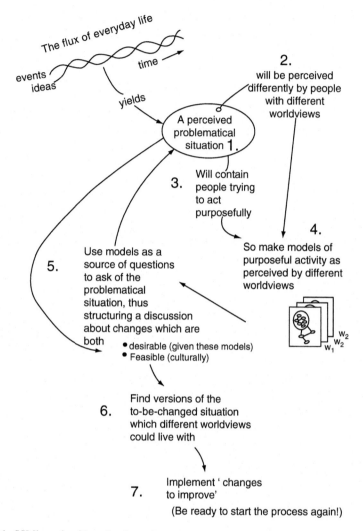

Fig. 15.1 SSM's cycle of learning for action

References

Checkland, P.B. (1980). The systems movement and the 'Failure' of 'Management Science'. *Cybernetics and Systems, 11*(4), 317–324.

Checkland, P. B. (1981). *Systems thinking, systems practice*. Chichester: John Wiley.

Checkland, P.B. (1985). From optimizing to learning: A development of systems thinking for the 1990s'. *Journal of the Operational Research Society 36*(9), 757–767.

Checkland, P. B., & Holwell, S. E. (1998a). *Information, systems and information systems – making sense of the field*. Chichester: John Wiley.

Checkland, P.B., & Holwell, S.E. (1998b). Action research: Its nature and validity. *Systemic Practice and Action Research, 11*(1), 9–21.

Checkland, P.B. (2000a). Soft systems methodology: A thirty year retrospective. *Systems Research and Behavioral Science, 17*(S1), S11–S58.

Checkland, P.B. (2000b). New maps of knowledge. *Systems Research and Behavioral Science, 17*(S1), S59–S75.

Checkland, P.B., & Poulter, J. (2006). *Learning for action: A short definitive account of soft systems methodology and its use for practitioners, teachers, and students*. Chichester: John Wiley.

Flood, R.L. (2000). A brief review of Peter B. Checkland's contribution to systemic thinking. *Systemic Practice and Action Research, 13*(6), 723–731.

Mingers, J. (2000). An idea ahead of its time: The history and development of Soft Systems Methodology. *Systemic Practice and Action Research, 13*(6), 733–755.

Winter, M. (2000). The relevance of soft systems thinking. *Human Resource Development International, 3*(3), 377–383.

Chapter 16
Werner Ulrich

Werner Ulrich has carried out pioneering work on a critical approach to systems thinking for over 25 years. Most importantly, he has developed a highly important and useful method for applying this approach, Critical Systems Heuristics (CSH). He has carried out his work in both academia and in government, and applied his ideas to issues as diverse as public planning, evaluation, reflective practice, the concept of citizenship and civil society, and environmental discourse. While acknowledging a "personal bias towards a more philosophically based, critical kind of systems thinking" (Ulrich 2005a, p. 8), his work is deeply practical. His goal may perhaps be summed up by the title of one of his articles: "systems thinking as if people mattered" (Ulrich 1998).

CSH, Ulrich's major contribution to the systems field, is especially notable in two ways. First, it is a practical working-through of some of the major ideas of West Churchman, in a form that is usable by many different kinds of people (including those with little awareness of the field of systems thinking). Second, it was one of the first methods to take an explicitly emancipatory approach and thus to advance the growing field of critical systems thinking. As Jackson (2003, p. 213) argues, Ulrich's book on CSH "describe[d], for the first time, a systems approach that takes as a major concern the need to counter possible unfairness in society by ensuring that all those affected by decisions have a role in making them".

Ulrich was born in 1948 in Bern, Switzerland. He holds two doctorates – firstly from the University of Fribourg (Switzerland) in 1975, in Economics and Social Science; then from the University of California at Berkeley in 1980, in Philosophy of Social Systems Design. As well as a deep immersion in the ideas of West Churchman, his time at Berkeley led to a study of the philosophy of Immanuel Kant, especially Kant's "critique of pure reason". It was these influences taken together (as well as an interest in the work of Jürgen Habermas), which resulted in his book *Critical Heuristics of Social Planning* (Ulrich 1983), the core work on CSH.

On returning to Switzerland, Ulrich "decided to submit his work on critical systems heuristics to the double test of professional practice and of academic teaching and research" (Ulrich 2002a). He became professor of social planning and evaluation research at the University of Fribourg, and also founder and head of the office of evaluation research within the Department of Public Health and Social Welfare in the Canton of Bern. He has been a visiting professor at the universities of Hull, Lincoln and the Open University in the UK and the university of Canterbury at Christchurch, New Zealand. His dual role as academic and practitioner can be seen in the nature of his writing, which is generally led by theory but also accessible. His ideas have also been shaped by the fact that his professional practice has been in government rather than private sector management. This has led to a considerable awareness of social and political issues – among other areas, he has conducted research into poverty and citizenship. Many of the results of his evaluation and social research have only been published in German – his English-language publications tend to focus on more academic concerns.

Ulrich's work has been heavily shaped by the five years he spent working with West Churchman in Berkeley, although it is a mistake to suggest (as do some commentators) that Ulrich's ideas are derived directly from Churchman with little amendment – there are important differences of detail in their ideas and CSH also draws on other thinkers. Ulrich was deeply attracted by Churchman's ideas in the early 1970s and hoped to work with Churchman as a postdoctoral researcher. Unfortunately this was not to be: "West did not exactly invite me to come, though. I wrote several times, expressing my urgent wish to work with him at [Berkeley]. Alas, he did not care to respond. I had to find a different way of 'convincing' him" (Ulrich 2004, p. 203). His way of convincing Churchman was to apply to join his Ph.D. programme, which is how he ended up taking a second Ph.D. at Berkeley. He writes that "five fascinating years followed, of learning and struggling to understand the implications of the systems approach for a critically tenable approach to applied disciplines such as planning and management" (Ulrich 2002a).

Critical Systems Heuristics (CSH), sometimes referred to just as "critical heuristics" in Ulrich's early work on the approach, took two of its key concepts from Churchman's work: the importance of *boundary judgments*, and a set of *categories* defining boundary judgments which form "a necessary set of conditions that must be fulfilled for a system S to be capable of purposeful activity" (Ulrich 1983, p. 245).

It is useful to look briefly at what Ulrich meant by the name 'critical systems heuristics', as this gives important indications as to his intentions and the ways in which his ideas are distinct from those of other systems thinkers. Ulrich states in his book that he intends all three words of the phrase 'critical systems heuristics' to be understood in the way they were used by Immanuel Kant, the great eighteenth century German philosopher of the Enlightenment. Thus by being *critical*, he means "to become self-reflective in respect to the presuppositions flowing into one's own judgments" (Ulrich 1983, p. 20), a much more reflective and less explicitly political concept than the Habermas' understanding of critical theory which forms the basis of Mike Jackson's use of the term 'critical'. Ulrich's understanding of *systems* "does not presuppose that we can know 'the whole system', but only that we can undertake a critical effort to reflect on the inevitable lack of comprehensiveness in our understanding of and design for (social) systems" (Ulrich 1983, p. 21) which as Ulrich has later observed is a quite different view of comprehensiveness from Churchman's concept of 'sweeping-in' every possible perspective into a systems analysis.

Lastly, by referring to *heuristics*, Ulrich means approaches which "serve to identify and explore relevant problem aspects, assumptions, questions, or solution strategies, in distinction to deductive (algorithmic) procedures, which serve to solve problems that are logically and mathematically well defined" (Ulrich 2002b, p. 72). This use of the term heuristics is common in professional and technical fields, and has close parallels to soft systems approaches where understanding the nature of the problem is a key part of reaching a (partial) solution. However, Ulrich also observes that for Kant, heuristic approaches produce "a judgment whose empirical or theoretical validity is problematic and therefore remains in need of critical reflection ... heuristics cannot serve as a source of discovery unless it is at the same time considered as a source of deception" (Ulrich 1983, p. 23).

Moving on to CSH as an approach, we will first discuss the important concept of *boundary judgments*. The idea that a system is defined by its boundary and the relationship between the inside and the outside of the boundary (the system's environment), is a core one throughout the history of systems thinking. How we decide what should be the system's boundary is a key issue, and very largely defines the nature of the system. Churchman (1970), himself drawing on the work of Kant, refers to these as "whole systems judgments", a concept that formed the basis for Ulrich's idea of the boundary judgment. Ulrich has taken the idea of boundary judgments further with his concept of boundary critique, a larger process of reflection and critique upon boundary choices and their implications, which he discusses at length in the reading from his work which follows.

The major methodological tool of CSH in its process of boundary critique is a "systemic categorisation of boundary issues" (Ulrich 2005b, p. 7), derived closely from a set of categories developed by Churchman to help define boundary judgments. This systemic categorisation is developed in a set of twelve 'categories', a concept Ulrich borrowed from Kant which refers to "a fundamental issue in the theory of knowledge" (Ulrich 2000, p. 256). The categories are: client, purpose, measure of improvement, decision-maker, resources, decision environment, professional, expertise, guarantee, witness, emancipation, world view. These categories represent four kinds of boundaries: sources of motivation, power, knowledge, and legitimation.

The twelve categories lead quite naturally to twelve *boundary questions* which form the 'tool' aspect of CSH. By systematically asking each of the questions in turn, we can question and critique the major issues around the boundary of a system. The questions are straightforward to use, by both experienced practitioners and ordinary stakeholders alike. The questions may take two forms, asking what *is* actually the case in the situation, or asking what *ought to be* the case. For example, for the decision-maker category, the questions are: "Who is (ought to be) the decision-maker? That is, who is (should be) in a position to change the measure of improvement?" (Ulrich 2000, p. 258).

CSH is often presented as an emancipatory method, i.e. one aiming to give power to the relatively powerless in a decision-making situation. It achieves this in two ways. First, it presents a tool which allows those without power to challenge those in power to justify their boundary judgments (i.e. why they have framed the terms of debate in the way they have), and to work through the full implications for all stakeholder groups of those judgments. Second, because the twelve questions are fairly simple to use (despite their deep philosophical grounding), they do not require special expertise or training but can be picked up by ordinary citizens. The approach has received much praise for both of these points, and has been used in a range of practical situations.

In fact, Ulrich (2002b, p. 73) himself is keen to stress that the approach "should not be misunderstood and used as an emancipatory systems approach only; for its principle of systematic boundary critique is vital for sound professional practice in general, whatever importance may be attached to emancipatory issues". Indeed, in further work he argues that "emancipatory reflection and discourse [are] require-ments of all reflective practice" (Ulrich 2003, p. 339).

In this respect Ulrich's view of his method is rather different to that of Mike Jackson and his colleagues at Hull. Jackson early on recognised the importance of CSH as almost the only systems method which explicitly built emancipation into its goals. However, in Jackson's work, CSH is said only to be applicable to certain kinds of situations, those where issues of coercion (of those with less power) are at the fore. Ulrich has long argued that in fact most situations, in both the workplace and society at large, carry such inequalities of power that these form the norm rather than the exception. Also, as we have already discussed, Ulrich sees a critical approach, based on boundary critique, as a necessary part of effective systems thinking. In fact, as Ulrich (2003) argues, the heart of critical systems thinking (CST) should be thought of as a process of "critically systemic discourse" (based on CSH) rather than the Jackson's approach of methodology choice, which has tended to be dominant in most discussions of CST. This divergence of views has led to heated debate between Ulrich, Jackson and others.

One important difference between these approaches is that while Jackson and most of his colleagues (being based in business schools) focus largely on critical thinking within organisations, Ulrich's has tended to focus on issues at the level of society. One of the first papers on CSH that Ulrich published after his 1983 book lists concerns such as "health care planning, city and regional planning, energy and transportation planning, environmental design" (Ulrich 1987, p. 276), and as already mentioned Ulrich worked for many years in evaluation within government. More recently, Ulrich (2000) has argued for critical thinking, via CSH, to be seen as a core tool for building civil society, and he has noted that even in coercive working settings, "as citizens, we are all part of diverse social systems and fulfil in these different systems various roles of a professional, private and public kind, which together offer a great variety of discursive chances" (Ulrich 2003, p. 330). There are undoubtedly genuine areas of theoretical difference between Ulrich and Jackson, as the two major thinkers within critical systems thinking, but at least some of this can be put down to their areas of concern.

Werner Ulrich is an important figure in the development of critical systems ideas. He presents a very interesting combination of very deep, highly philosophical, thinking with a strong and long-standing commitment to empowering those in large-scale practical situations. His method, CSH, is still among the most widely used approaches to critical systems thinking.

Reading from Ulrich's work

Ulrich W (2005) A Brief Introduction to Critical Systems Heuristics (CSH), ECOSENSUS project, Milton Keynes: The Open University, 14 October 2005. With kind permission Werner Ulrich.
Extract from pages 3–6.

Boundary critique – the methodological core principle of CSH

The basic idea of CSH is to support *boundary critique* – a systematic effort of handling boundary judgments critically. Boundary critique may take two main forms: it can aim at handling boundary judgments self-critically (*reflective practice*), or it can use boundary judgments for critical purposes against those who may not handle them so self-critically (*emancipatory practice*).

The methodological core idea consists in surfacing the unavoidable *selectivity* of claims, in the dual sense of 'partiality' explained above. Boundary judgments are the perfect target for this purpose, for unlike what one might think at first, they reflect a claim's *entire* selectivity regarding both its empirical or normative content. It is important to understand that boundary judgments are not just one (perhaps even minor) among many other sources of selectivity – for example, in the sense that once the reference system is determined, it is then the specific content of our thinking or discussion which determines how 'partial' they are. Rather, *any* partiality can and needs to be understood as amounting to boundary judgments; for any content we do or do not consider, and the way we consider it, implies corresponding boundary judgments. This consequence is the reverse side of the coin of 'clear and valid thinking', as it were; we cannot meaningfully talk about any aspect of a situation or an issue without implying boundary judgments. What a certain aspect means depends on what consequences we anticipate it to have, whose concerns we assume to be affected, what criteria of success or improvement we associate with it, and so on; and all these assumptions and associations embody boundary judgments as to what is to be part of the picture and what is not. Whether these judgments are conscious and deliberate or unintended makes no difference.

Likewise, the argumentative quality of a reflection or discussion reflects itself in boundary judgments. Wanting argumentation, say because we argue incoherently or fail to anticipate side effects and risks of a proposed action correctly, always amounts to modifications of the reference system that we treat as relevant. Thus, if for example we consider some aspect as relevant and perhaps even agree with others that it is important, but then fail to take it properly into account, due to lacking knowledge, to an error of judgment or some communicative misunderstanding or distortion, we have in fact excluded that aspect from our reference system. The same observation applies to the influence of power and other non-argumentative means of buttressing a claim: if those in control of a situation deliberately suppress or ignore some aspect of a problem situation at issue, they actually talk about something else than what they pretend. Those who understand the trick can then challenge them by uncovering the circumstance.

In conclusion, both reflective and emancipatory practice can methodologically be grounded in a systematic process of boundary critique. The question is, can we offer people the conceptual tools they need to identify, discuss or challenge boundary judgment systematically?

The process of boundary critique

A systematic *process of boundary critique* faces the following tasks:

1. It needs to *identify* the sources of selectivity that condition a claim, by surfacing the underpinning boundary judgments.
2. It needs to *examine* these boundary judgments regarding their practical and ethical implications; what difference do they make to the way we see the situation in question?
3. It needs to *find options* for determining the reference system that conditions a claim, by giving alternative answers to some of the boundary questions; for only in the light of alternative reference systems can we fully appreciate the selectivity of the present one.
4. It needs to seek some *mutual understanding* with all the stakeholders concerned regarding their different reference systems. If in the process a shared notion of the relevant reference system can be achieved, so much the better; but even if no agreement can be reached, understanding the way reference systems differ still represents an important gain in communicative rationality. Misunderstandings can be avoided in this way, and mutual tolerance can grow. (Note that identifying the stakeholders to be consulted represents itself a boundary judgment in need of critique, although the previous steps should provide a tentative basis).
5. Finally, when some of the parties handle their own boundary judgments uncritically, either because they take them for granted or try to impose them on others, it may become necessary to *challenge* their claims through the emancipatory use of boundary critique.

CSH offers some guidance for each of these tasks. However, it would be a mistake to conceive of boundary critique as a kind of step-by-step technique for 'boundary setting', that is, as a method to determine 'right' and 'wrong' boundary judgments and to settle conflicts. No kind of theory of methodology whatsoever could claim to know the 'right' answers to boundary issues. All that boundary critique can achieve is to help the parties in appreciating their own boundary assumptions and those of others, so that they can then articulate their concerns in a cogent way. The decision on what boundary judgments should underpin practical action is then a question of *legitimacy* rather than of validity; once the selectivity of claims has been become transparent, democratically institutionalised processes of decision-making can work in a meaningful way.

As a matter of principle, from a critical point of view we can never justify our claims by referring to the methodologies we use or to the theories we rely on. Only institutionalised processes of legitimate decision-making can justify the way our claims may affect the different parties concerned. Hence, boundary critique should be understood – and practised – primarily as a reflective *attitude*, rather than as a technique. That has both advantages and disadvantages: The advantage is that practising boundary critique does not depend on learning yet another problem-solving methodology (few professionals, much less ordinary people, are prepared to learn to master a large array of different problem-solving methodologies). It is quite good enough to understand the role that boundary judgments play and then to 'translate' this understanding into a Socratic attitude of self-reflection regarding one's own claims, and of tolerance (combined with critical appreciation) regarding the claims of others. The disadvantage is that boundary critique is not a self-contained approach but is more useful in combination with other approaches to problem structuring and problem-solving.

Let us briefly characterise the kind of *boundary-critical attitude* that CSH proposes:

- Basically, from now on, when we refer to a 'problem situation' or to any kind of 'real-world' circumstances, it should be clear that we always mean to refer to the *perceived* situation or circumstances *as appreciated through a reference system* of underpinning boundary judgments.

- Likewise, we understand that one of the most important qualities of a claim is its limitations, and hence, its *self-limiting* nature. Obviously, as soon as we recognise the conditioned character of all our perceptions and claims, we can no longer articulate perceptions or raise claims in the same (unqualified) assertive mode that is so characteristic of everyday discussions as well as of the usual practice of 'applied science' and expertise. Rather, the question of how '*scientific*' the findings and conclusions of even the most professional application of scientific tools are, as well as how *credible* our everyday claims are, is now to be measured by the extent to which we make their conditioned character clear to ourselves and to everyone else concerned. Lest we be convicted of relying on undisclosed assumptions and hence, of *claiming too much*, an effort of clarifying and disclosing our boundary judgments is required. Furthermore, such a critical effort also makes sense lest we misunderstand the claims of others or let ourselves be deceived by them.

- A third and last important aspect of a boundary-critical attitude is this. Once we have understood that all our claims are conditioned by boundary judgments, the next step is to realise that this limitation holds just as much for the claims of well-trained experts and decision-makers as for those of ordinary people! The implication is that *when it comes to boundary judgments*, we basically meet as equals. Everyone can question the boundary judgments of others with equal right. This opens up a chance for everyone to acquire a new critical competence, one that is independent from any special knowledge or argumentative skills beyond those available to a majority of ordinary people. The mentioned Socratic attitude thus paves the way for an orientation towards emancipation and democratic self-determination.

Let us now look at the *methodological core principle* embodied in the concept of boundary critique. As we have understood, the basic requirement for developing the required critical competence is grasping the way judgments of fact as well as of value depend on boundary judgments and are connected through them. CSH explains this by means of the *eternal triangle* (Fig. 16.1). Whenever we propose a problem definition or solution or raise any other claim with a practical intent, we cannot help but assert the relevance of *some* facts and norms as distinguished from others. Which facts and norms we should consider depends on how we bound the reference system, and vice-versa; as soon as we modify our boundary judgments, relevant facts and norms are likely to change, too. We are thus caught in an argumentative triangle.

CSH calls the process of thinking through the triangle *systemic triangulation*. It means to consider each corner of the triangle in the light of the other two. For example, what new facts become relevant if we expand the boundaries of the reference system or modify our value judgments? How do our valuations look if we consider new facts that refer to a modified reference system? In what way may our reference system fail to do justice to the perspective of different stakeholder groups? Asking ourselves how the facts that we find relevant, the value considerations we deem adequate, and the context (reference system) that we consider, mutually condition one another is highly relevant for developing a sense of modesty regarding our claims, as well as tolerance regarding those of others who appear to have got their facts and values wrong!

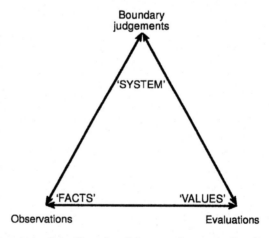

Fig. 16.1 The 'eternal triangle' of boundary judgments, facts, and values (source: Ulrich 2000, p. 252)

References

Churchman, C.W. (1970). Kant – A decision theorist? *Theory and Decision, 1*(1), 107–116.

Jackson, M. C. (2003). *Systems thinking: Creative holism for managers.* Chichester: John Wiley.

Ulrich, W. (1983). *Critical heuristics of social planning: A new approach to practical philosophy.* Bern, Switzerland: Haupt.

Ulrich, W. (1987). Critical heuristics of social systems design. *European Journal of Operational Research, 31*(3), 276–283.

Ulrich, W. (1998). Systems thinking as if people mattered: Critical systems thinking for citizens and managers. Working Paper 23, Lincoln School of Management, University of Lincoln, UK.

Ulrich, W. (2000). Reflective practice in the civil society: The contribution of critically systemic thinking. *Reflective Practice, 1*(2), 247–268.

Ulrich, W. (2002a). A short professional biography of Werner Ulrich. http://www.geocities.com/csh_home/bio.html. Accessed 13 Jan 2009.

Ulrich, W. (2002b). Critical systems heuristics. In H. G. Daellenbach, & R. L. Flood (Eds.), *The informed student guide to management science* (pp. 72–73). London: Thomson Learning.

Ulrich, W. (2003). Beyond methodology choice: Critical systems thinking as critically systemic discourse. *Journal of the Operational Research Society, 54*(4), 325–342.

Ulrich, W. (2004). In memory of C. West Churchman (1913–2004): Reminiscences, retrospectives, and reflections. *Journal of Organisational Transformation and Social Change, 1*(2–3), 199–219.

Ulrich, W. (2005a). Can nature teach us good research practice? A critical look at Frederic Vester's Bio-Cybernetic Systems Approach. *Journal of Research Practice 1*(1), article R2. http://jrp.icaap.org/index.php/jrp/article/view/1/1. Accessed 13 Jan 2009.

Ulrich, W. (2005b). A brief introduction to Critical Systems Heuristics (CSH). ECOSENSUS project, The Open University. http://projects.kmi.open.ac.uk/ecosensus/publications/ulrich_csh_intro.pdf. Accessed 13 Jan 2009.

Chapter 17
Michael Jackson

Michael Jackson is a British management academic. He has made considerable advances in systems thinking and practice, especially in management and organisations, through his development of the Critical Systems Thinking (CST) approach. This approach emphasises the importance of politics and power in organisations. Jackson has been the main champion of CST since its inception, gave it its name, was one of the first to call for such an approach, and has been at the core of the main group developing the approach at the University of Hull. His goal for CST is ambitious but clearly stated: "to reconstitute systems thinking as a unified approach to problem management so that it can again stand at the leading edge in the development of the management sciences" (Jackson 2001, p. 236).

Jackson is usually referred to as Mike Jackson (or Michael C. Jackson) to distinguish him from others of that name, not only the pop singer but particularly also the computer scientist Michael A. Jackson who devised the Jackson Structured Programming and Jackson System Development methods. He was born in 1951, taking his first degree at Oxford University in Philosophy, Politics and Economics and graduating in 1973. He then spent four years working in the civil service as a tax inspector, spending his free time reading Marxist classics and the work of Habermas and Foucault. In 1978, he took the M.A. in Systems in Management at Lancaster University (the programme devised and run by Peter Checkland). He started work as a lecturer in 1979 at the University of Hull, in its then Department of Operational Research (later Management Systems and Sciences), where he gained his Ph.D. He has remained at Hull since that time, becoming a full professor in 1989, except for five years (1994–1999) when he was a professor at the Lincoln campus of the University of Lincolnshire and Humberside (now the University of Lincoln). He is currently director of the Hull University Business School. He has been highly active in the UK and international systems community – he has been president of the UK Systems Society, the International Society for the Systems Sciences and the International Federation for Systems Research, as well as for many years the editor of the journal *Systems Research and Behavioral Science*.

Mike Jackson has developed Critical Systems Thinking in a series of influential publications over a period of 30 years, starting with his M.A. dissertation at Lancaster in 1978, which "was an analysis of applied systems thinking from the point of view of social science and argued for a critical systems approach" (Jackson

2001, p. 235). Several of his articles and books have been very widely read and cited. Following Jackson (2001), we can see the development of CST, mostly through the 1980s, as occurring in four stages: a critique of existing systems approaches; a call for the development of systems methodologies that took an explicitly emancipatory approach; work on a tool to classify the areas within which particular systems methodologies are appropriate; and the development of a meta-methodology for CST.

He first came to prominence through a strongly-worded article (Jackson 1982) criticising soft systems thinking and its three major advocates (Checkland, Ackoff and Churchman) in the same journal published from Lancaster where Checkland and others first outlined most of the major features of soft systems. His analysis drew upon a widely-read book by Burrell and Morgan (1979), who like Checkland were based at the business school at Lancaster University. Burrell and Morgan argue that all social theories used in organisational analysis can be divided into four paradigms, sets of fundamental assumptions about the world – functionalist, inter-pretive, radical humanist and radical structuralist. Checkland (1981) had argued that the approaches he labelled 'hard systems thinking', such as systems engineer-ing and operational research, could be located in the functionalist paradigm. While Jackson accepted that argument, he in turn suggested that soft systems thinking could be located in Burrell and Morgan's interpretive paradigm, which has two main characteristics: it views reality in subjective terms, saying that the social world is constructed by the actions, interpretations and perspectives of the people within it; and it is (at least implicitly) oriented towards consensus and the mainte-nance of existing social order, rather than focusing on conflict between groups and radical change.

This orientation towards social order arises implicitly, in Jackson's view – it is not that soft systems approaches set out to maintain existing social order, and thus to be conservative, rather that their concern is "to understand the social world as it is … there is no interest in radically going beyond the status quo" (Jackson 1982, p. 18). While recognising that all three of Churchman, Ackoff and Checkland had a personal commitment to radical change in the world, Jackson felt that their meth-odologies did not allow for this change to occur and ultimately that "soft systems thinking is most suitable for the kind of social engineering that ensures the contin-ued survival, by adaptation, of existing social elites" (Jackson 1982, p. 28). While these arguments were dismissed at the time by those being criticised, Jackson has continued to argue in later writing (e.g. Jackson 2003) that Checkland's Soft Systems Methodology in particular has a limited domain of applicability due to its focus on building consensus among stakeholders rather than dealing with issues of conflict or coercion.

Jackson followed this critique of existing approaches with an explicit call to take a critical approach to Systems, in particular in "social systems where there are great disparities in power and in resources and which seem to 'escape' the control and understanding of the individuals who create and sustain them" (Jackson 1985, p. 146). By a critical approach, Jackson understood an approach grounded upon critical theory, the post-Marxist social theory associated with the Frankfurt school of sociology, and in particular the work of Jürgen Habermas. In his 1985 paper, Jackson suggests that it might be possible to apply Habermas' theory of the way communication is distorted in the modern world through unequal power distribution, as a means of objectively identifying and correcting inequality within systems approaches. As we shall see later, different aspects of Habermas' work were found to be more useful within CST, but the paper is notable for the strength of its call for a form of Systems based on critical theory and with a clearly emancipatory focus.

A more methodological approach to a critique of systems methodologies came around the same time, in collaboration with Jackson's colleague at Hull, Paul Keys. Starting from the view that different methodologies were appropriate in different contexts, Jackson and Keys (1984) developed the first version of their System of Systems Methodologies (SOSM). This argued that the way systems methodologies understood problem situations could be classified on two dimensions – one concerned with the nature of systems, running from simple to complex; and the other concerned with the relationship between participants, defined as unitary, pluralist or coercive (in later work, this latter dimension would roughly correspond to hard, soft and critical approaches). The SOSM, while imperfect in a number of ways, provided a straightforward tool for examining the relevance of different methodologies to problem situations. It also reinforced Jackson's observation that soft systems approaches were not sufficient to cover all kinds of problem situations; and with its focus on multiple methodologies, acted as a starting point for Jackson's later focus on pluralism as a key feature of critical systems thinking.

The next stage of Jackson's work in developing CST involved work on a meta-methodology that would give practical shape to the concepts. This work was carried out between Jackson and Robert Flood over several years in the late 1980s. Flood was based at City University in London until 1988 when he joined Jackson at Hull. Flood (2001, p. 245) has written about their collaboration that "we experienced a personal and intellectual chemistry that brought together our interests in systemic thinking with our deep concern to improve organisational and societal affairs". The result was a 'meta-methodology' (so called because it assists in the selection and use of other systems methodologies), Total Systems Intervention or TSI.

TSI, designed for assisting in problem situations within organisations was based on a critical perspective in that it "employed critique of different systems approaches, respected the possibility of 'coercive' contexts and was based upon a sophisticated form of pluralism in which methodologies adhering to different paradigms were to be used in the same intervention on the same problem situation" (Jackson 2001, p. 238). It consisted of three phases: creativity, choice and implementation. The methodology was backed up by a very thorough discussion and critique of a number of the major systems methodologies, so that the book which introduced TSI (Flood and Jackson 1991) also acted as a very useful text for understanding each of the methodologies in context.

Jackson has set out five 'commitments' which formed the heart of CST: "it seeks to demonstrate critical awareness; it shows social awareness; it is dedicated to human emancipation; it is committed to the complementary and informed development of all the different strands of systems thinking at the theoretical level; and it is committed to the complementary and informed use of systems methodologies" (Jackson 1991, pp. 184–185). These commitments formed the basis for both CST and TSI – for Flood and Jackson, it was necessary to be observing each to be properly following critical systems thinking and to be properly using the TSI meta-methodology.

We have already discussed most of Jackson's five commitments, but complementarism is worth exploring further. Jackson argued no one systems methodology was sufficient to capture all relevant issues in a problem situation. All methodologies have their strengths and weaknesses (as discussed in detail in the TSI book), and all can be useful in the right setting. What is important is that the methodologies are used in a way that complements each other as appropriate. However, TSI encouraged the complete use of methodologies, arguing that they were designed as coherent wholes (and arose from clearly different paradigms), a matter which formed one of the main criticisms of the approach by subsequent authors. In particular, the multi-methodology approach (Mingers and Gill 1997) argued that it was more productive to design meta-methodologies in ways that combined different parts of methodologies as appropriate to the situation, rather than using the whole methodology.

A further important outcome from Jackson's work in developing CST was the identification of three different types of systems approaches – hard, soft and critical – which continue to be the main groupings in which systems approaches are discussed in the UK and Europe. While this division clearly stems from and extends Checkland's hard–soft distinction, it was given theoretical underpinning through its identification with Habermas' three forms of knowledge interests – technical, practical and emancipatory.

Both Jackson and his colleagues at Hull and Lincoln tried out a variety of ways of taking the basic CST concepts and tools forward in the years that followed. A number of other authors from outside this community also presented critiques, especially of TSI, which ultimately led both Jackson and Flood to reject the meta-methodology in its 1991 form although they each produced quite different revised versions.

This further work on CST is discussed at length in a more recent book by Jackson for practitioners, intended as his update of the TSI book (Jackson 2003). In the latter book, which like the TSI book gives an excellent overview and critique of the major systems methodologies, Jackson presents an updated view of CST in practice, under the name of Critical Systems Practice (CSP). In this approach, Jackson has shifted away from promoting emancipation as the primary goal of his work, and instead locates it as one of four paradigms.

Jackson has continued his critical approach to others' work. He has been involved in a number of long-running debates in academic journals, especially with Peter Checkland, John Mingers and Werner Ulrich, on theoretical and methodological issues. By academic standards, some of these debates have been quite strongly-worded and personal, although Jackson has written that "the dishing out of vociferous criticism can be useful to the recipient and the discipline, as well as being good fun. However, it has to be well-researched and well directed if the recipient is to learn from it and react positively rather than being put, unfairly, on the defensive" (Jackson 1993, p. 209).

Mike Jackson's work is much more focused on methodologies than many of the authors discussed in this book. He has made many important innovations in introducing and developing the concept of Critical Systems Thinking, and in very actively advocating and demonstrating the nature of such an approach. It is clear that his work and that of his colleagues has done much to encourage emancipatory thinking in Systems, and to force those working in other traditions to be much clearer about the way their methodologies can deal with issues of power and politics.

Reading from Jackson's work

Jackson, M.C. "Creative Holism: A Critical Systems Approach to Complex Problem Situations", *Systems Research and Behavioral Science* **23**(5), pp. 647–657 Copyright ©John Wiley 2006. Reproduced with permission of John Wiley and Sons Ltd.
Extract from pages 653–656 (table omitted).

Creative holism

The purpose of creative holism is to learn about and harness the various systems methodologies, methods and models so that they can best be used by managers to respond to the complexity, turbulence and heterogeneity of the problem situations they face today. It shares with critical systems thinking, generally, a basic philosophy that can be described by three commitments – to 'critical awareness' (of the strengths and weaknesses of different systems approaches), 'pluralism' (the use in combination of different systems methodologies and methods) and 'improvement'. This philosophy will not be discussed further here. The critical systems practice it embraces is an enhanced version of 'total systems intervention' (Flood and Jackson 1991). It has four phases – 'creativity', 'choice', 'implementation' and 'reflection'. These phases will be described in turn. [...]

In order to appreciate the complexity and heterogeneity of problem situations, it is essential for the systems practitioner, in pursuing 'creativity', to bring to bear radically different views of the world derived from alternative paradigms. Creative holism suggests that the perspectives of four paradigms – functionalist, interpretive, emancipatory and postmodern – must be considered. In order to achieve this, managers and analysts might explore the paradigms through the use of appropriate metaphors, or employ other creativity enhancing devices. The aim is to take the broadest possible critical look at the problem situation but gradually to focus down on those aspects most crucial to the organisation at this point in its evolution.

Having identified the crucial problems for the organisation, a 'choice' has to be made of suitable systems methodologies and methods to address the problem situation. This is done on the basis of a review of the strengths and weaknesses of the different methodologies and methods, conducted using paradigm analysis, metaphor analysis, past experience, etc. To ensure the broadest possible choice of methodologies, creative holism provides 'generic methodologies', representing each of the four paradigms mentioned above. One advantage is that the theoretical link back to paradigms is made explicit so allowing us to operationalise better, and more obviously, the hypotheses of particular paradigms and to test these in real-world interventions. In practice, the difficulties associated with multi-methodology practice can be managed if an initial choice of 'dominant methodology' is made to run the intervention, with a 'dependant' methodology (or methodologies), reflecting alternative paradigms, in the background. With regard to the methods, models, etc. chosen, creative holism encourages the maximum possible flexibility. It is happy to see existing methodologies 'decomposed' (Midgley 1997), giving the systems practitioner access to the full range of methods to use in combination, as he or she feels appropriate, in support of the generic systems methodologies that are to be employed in the intervention. The existence of the generic methodologies ensures that the methods are not simply 'cut-free' – they can be evaluated as to their usefulness in support of methodology and related theory.

'Implementation' can then proceed by employing the chosen dominant methodology and methods. As intervention progresses, the problems that earlier seemed to be crucial may fade into the background and new ones emerge. This can be catered for by continually cycling round the phases of creative holism, with different systems methodologies (and chosen methods) assuming the role of 'dominant' and 'dependant' in leading the intervention at particular times. Whichever methodology is initially chosen as dominant, the way 'implementation' proceeds will be continually critiqued through the lenses offered by alternative paradigms. Implementation should see highly relevant and co-ordinated change effected, which secures improvement in the problem situation according to the concerns of the different paradigms. Switches in dominant methodology should be common.

'Reflection' seeks to judge how successful the intervention has been in bringing about improvement. It does this by taking into account what each paradigm rates as most significant. The functionalist paradigm prioritises goal-seeking and viability, judging in terms of efficiency and efficacy. The interpretive paradigm prioritises exploring purposes by enhancing mutual understanding, judging in terms of effectiveness and elegance. The emancipatory paradigm seeks to ensure fairness, judging in terms of empowerment and emancipation. The postmodern paradigm values the promotion of diversity, judging in terms of exception and emotion. A highly successful intervention should be able to demonstrate progress on all these fronts. Reflection also seeks to ensure that research, and the generation of new learning, receives the attention it deserves. Any use of creative holism is capable of yielding research findings about: how to manage the relationships between different paradigms; the philosophy and theory that constitutes a paradigm underpinning any generic methodology used; the generic systems methodologies employed; the methods, models, techniques, etc. used; and about the real-world problem situation investigated.

I have, elsewhere (Jackson 2000), compared the critical systems practitioner with a holistic doctor. Confronted by a patient with pains in her stomach, the doctor might initially consider standard explanations, such as over-indulgence, period pains or irritable bowel syndrome. If the patient failed to respond to the usual treatment prescribed on the basis of an initial diagnosis you would expect the doctor to entertain the possibility of some more deep-seated and dangerous malady. The patient might be sent for x-ray, body scan or other tests designed to search for such structural problems. If nothing was found, a thoughtful conversation with the patient might suggest that the pains were a symptom of anxiety and depression. Various forms of counselling or psychological support could be offered. Or, perhaps, a knowledge of the patient's domestic circumstances, and bruises elsewhere on the body, might reveal that the patient was suffering at the hands of a violent partner. What should the doctor do in these circumstances? Finally, perhaps the patient just needs another interest – such as painting or golf – to take her mind off worries at work.

We would expect a 'holistic' doctor to be open to all these possibilities and to have appropriate responses and 'treatments' available. To my mind, the critical systems practitioner, probing with his or her functionalist (positivist and structuralist), interpretive, emancipatory and postmodern perspectives, is similarly taking a holistic approach to organisational and societal problems.

Conclusion

Creative holism, a new development in systems thinking, wants to provide managers with the joint benefits of holism and creativity so that they can do their jobs better. Holism by itself confers many advantages over traditional, reductionist approaches in dealing with complexity, change and diversity. As systems thinking has developed it has discovered a variety of different ways of being holistic, based upon different paradigms and metaphors. We are now able, therefore, to be creative in the way we approach being holistic. Creative holism enables us to use different systems approaches, reflecting alternative holistic perspectives, in combination. Perhaps we cannot use all the various systems approach at once, but they can be employed creatively, over time, to promote together overall improvement in the problem situations managers face. This is the essence of creative holism.

No doubt creative holism will seem 'difficult'. But then, managerial work is becoming more complex, turbulent and diverse. Most managers are likely to find themselves, on a regular basis, confronted by 'messes' made up of interacting issues such as the need to increase productivity, become more market-centred, improve communications, adopt fairer recruitment and promotion strategies, and motivate a diverse workforce. They will also find themselves having to prioritise between the demands made upon them because of lack of time and resources. They cannot tackle them all at once. This all seems like commonsense. Creative holism is in tune with this commonsense. It recognises that excellent organisational performance depends on managers paying attention to improving goal-seeking and viability, exploring purposes, ensuring fairness and promoting diversity.

And it offers critical systems practice, which provides guidelines on how to tackle in an holistic and balanced way, using various systems approaches, the 'messes' that managers so often confront. Creative holism responds to the everyday problem situations that managers have to deal with.

It is one of the satisfactions of systems thinking that its insights translate between levels. If we move beyond the organisational to the societal and world levels, we find that the same imperatives for improvement, highlighted by creative holism, continue to be crucial. We are unlikely to improve things unless we pay attention to efficiency and effectiveness, mutual understanding, fairness and diversity. And we need to understand the interactions between these and treat them holistically. Few of us will get the opportunity to practice our systems thinking on the world stage. Perhaps, though, if we pay attention to each and all of these things, as managers in organisations, our actions will have a resonance beyond our immediate environments and, in some way, contribute to global improvement. This is a nice thought. Most managers, as well as doing a good job, would like to make things better rather than worse for future generations.

References

Burrell, G., & Morgan, G. (1979). *Sociological paradigms and organisational analysis: Elements of the sociology of corporate life.* London: Heinemann.

Checkland, P. B. (1981). *Systems thinking, systems practice.* Chichester: John Wiley.

Flood, R.L., & Jackson, M. C. (1991). *Creative problem solving: Total systems intervention.* Chichester: John Wiley.

Flood, R.L. (2001). Local systemic intervention. *European Journal of Operational Research, 128*(2), 245–257.

Jackson, M.C. (1982). The nature of 'Soft' systems thinking: The work of Churchman, Ackoff and Checkland. *Journal of Applied Systems Analysis, 9,* 17–29.

Jackson, M.C., & Keys, P. (1984). Towards a system of systems methodologies. *Journal of the Operational Research Society, 35*(6), 473–486.

Jackson, M.C. (1985). Social systems theory and practice: The need for a critical approach. *International Journal of General Systems, 10*(2), 135–151.

Jackson, M. C. (1991). *Systems methodology for the management sciences.* New York: Plenum Press.

Jackson, M.C. (1993). The system of systems methodologies: A guide to researchers. *Journal of the Operational Research Society, 44*(2), 208–209.

Jackson, M. C. (2000). *Systems approaches to management.* New York: Kluwer/Plenum.

Jackson, M.C. (2001). Critical systems thinking and practice. *European Journal of Operational Research, 128*(2), 233–244.

Jackson, M.C. (2003). *Systems thinking: Creative holism for managers.* Chichester: John Wiley.

Jackson, M.C. (2006). Creative holism: A critical systems approach to complex problem situations. *Systems Research and Behavioral Science, 23*(5), 647–657.

Midgley, G. (1997). Mixing methods: Developing systemic intervention. In J. Mingers, & A. Gill (Eds.), *Multimethodology: The theory and practice of integrating OR and systems methodologies* (pp. 291–332). Chichester: John Wiley.

Mingers, J., & Gill, A. (Eds.) (1997). *Multimethodology: The theory and practice of integrating OR and systems methodologies.* Chichester: John Wiley.

Later Cybernetics

Applying cybernetics in management, biology, sociology and psychology; and the cybernetics of cybernetics

Chapter 18
Heinz von Foerster

Heinz von Foerster was a physicist and philosopher, who worked extensively in cybernetics, biology and family therapy, although he hated being categorised as belonging to a particular academic discipline. Indeed he once remarked that "I am Viennese. That is the only label that I have to accept. I come from Vienna; I was born there, that's an established fact" (von Foerster and Poerksen 2002, p. 43).

The Vienna that Heinz von Foerster was born into in 1911 was a centre of considerable culture and academic thought, where "in all fields there was a breakaway from the classic and from the standards of the 19th century perspective … everybody was connected and arguing about what art, politics, philosophy, should be" (in Franchi et al. 2005, p. 16). The young von Foerster was strongly influenced by the Vienna Circle of logical positivists (as was Ludwig von Bertalanffy, also from Vienna). This group excited him with their consideration of second-order questions: not just the study of mathematics and philosophy, but the study of the nature of those disciplines through the tools of those disciplines. The philosopher Ludwig Wittgenstein, a friend of the family and an honorary uncle, was also a key early influence (with his focus on language and meaning), and von Foerster quoted passages from Wittgenstein's *Tractatus logico-philosophicus* in much of his subsequent writing. As a teenager, Von Foerster became interested in magic and joined the Magic Circle, a hobby which stayed with him all his life and which influenced his later focus on perception and paradox.

Von Foerster trained as a physicist in Vienna, and worked in a German radar laboratory during World War II. As some of his relatives were Jewish, and his family were well-known in Vienna, when the Nazis came to Austria he moved to Berlin, and throughout the war managed to hide his non-Aryan status. After the war he returned to Vienna where he worked for a few years, but the extreme poverty of the city in that time led him to emigrate to the United States in 1949, where he lived and worked for the rest of his life. He died in California in 2002, followed the next year by his wife Mai, who he married in Vienna in 1939 and from whom he was inseparable.

While in Vienna after the war, he published a study of the nature of memory, using techniques from quantum physics, which hypothesised that memorising and forgetting worked rather like the quantum behaviour of large molecules. Shortly after he arrived in the US, this work came to the attention of Warren McCulloch,

M. Ramage and K. Shipp, *Systems Thinkers*,

who invited von Foerster to Chicago to discuss the work. McCulloch invited von Foerster to the sixth Macy conference on cybernetics, where he presented his work in very faltering English (but as there were a number of German emigrants present, he was able to communicate). The conference's reaction to his presentation was: "What you had to say was extremely interesting, but the way you expressed it was a disaster. In order to help you learn English as quickly as possible we hereby declare you the editor of the reports of our conference" (von Foerster and Poerksen 2002, p. 136). Von Foerster (with help from Margaret Mead and Hans Teuber) thus edited the proceedings of that conference and the four remaining Macy conferences, and he became a core part of the Macy group.

In 1951, von Foerster took up a post at the University of Illinois, where he remained until his retirement in 1976. Initially he held a chair in signal processing and directed an electron tubes laboratory, working on microwaves. In 1958 he established what was to be his primary institutional base, and a key centre for the development of cybernetics in the US – the Biological Computing Laboratory (BCL).

The BCL can readily be seen as a continuation of McCulloch's project of experimental epistemology. Its major themes included "logic and epistemology, language recognition, and communication" (von Foerster and Poerksen 2002, p. 140). It arose at a time when cybernetics was bifurcating, into a comparatively 'soft' side focused on epistemology and biology, and a comparatively 'hard' side focused on computation. The harder side, centred around MIT, gradually dropped the term cybernetics in favour of artificial intelligence. As Krieg (2005, p. 552) describes it, BCL became "the rallying point for the 'soft' side of cybernetics".

The staff and visitors of BCL included many of the key thinkers in cybernetics in the 1960s and 1970s, including Humberto Maturana, Ross Ashby, Francisco Varela, Gordon Pask and Stafford Beer. Many of these thinkers developed some of their key ideas while at the BCL (especially Maturana and Ashby). Von Foerster, as its director, was closely involved in all of the different strands of BCL's work, although he sometimes presented himself simply as a promoter of others' ideas – "it often felt as though the impresario role was the more important one to him, and he would often hide his own achievement behind the work of others who he had promoted" (Glanville 2002, p. 157).

The BCL was dependent on a series of ongoing research grants, mostly funded through the US military, which was a major source of research funding in the 1950s and 1960s to a range of projects with no particular military connection or application. However, protests over the Vietnam war led to growing public concern over the influence of the military on American academia, and the passing of a law in 1970 that the US Department of Defence only fund projects with a specific military impact (Umpleby 2003). Von Foerster was not able to argue that BCL's work had such an impact, and its defence funding was withdrawn. This resulted in the gradual decline of BCL, as it was no longer able to afford the kinds of researchers who had previously worked there, and it closed when von Foerster retired in 1976.

Throughout his time at Illinois, von Foerster's concern and that of BCL was with issues of perception and epistemology, and a keenness to extend cybernetics to include the nature of the observer as well as the system being observed. These ideas gradually coalesced into his greatest intellectual contribution, the concept of *second-order cybernetics*. In a speech in 1974, he defined this as follows: "the cybernetics of observed systems we may consider to be first-order cybernetics; while second-order cybernetics is the cybernetics of observing systems" (von Foerster 2003, p. 285).

It is important to realise that this term 'second-order' is meant logically not historically. It is inaccurate to interpret the phrase in terms of progress, where the second-order is more important than, and drives out, the first-order. Rather, it refers to the taking of cybernetic principles of feedback, information and communication, and their application to the observer as much as to the system being observed – in Scott's terms (2003), a *reflexive* cybernetics. The seeds of this reflexivity can readily be found in Wiener and McCulloch's work, and quite explicitly in that of Bateson, as discussed by Hayles (1999). Interestingly, von Foerster did not publicly name second-order cybernetics until quite late, shortly before the closure of BCL – the perspective of reflexivity and the role of the observer came before the name.

Von Foerster is frequently described as one of the founders of the constructivist approach to philosophy – the view that there is no independent reality, only our understanding of the world which we construct individually and may not match with that of any other individual. This is related to the social construction approach first expressed by Berger and Luckmann (1966), although it is more individualist. Second-order cybernetics, with its focus on the observer and on reflexivity (as well as the approach later described by Maturana as the "biology of cognition") can clearly be seen as being involved with individual constructivism. Segal (2001) argues that von Foerster's constructivism "is concerned with the convergence of two central themes: (1) how we know what we know, and (2) an abiding concern for the present state of the world and its humanity" (p. 1).

As well as his work at BCL, von Foerster made other organisational contributions to cybernetics and systems. He was strongly involved in the founding and early years of the American Society for Cybernetics (ASC), chairing its board of directors for a number of years. When that society became dormant in the 1970s, he joined the Society for General Systems Research (with a number of other key members of the ASC), becoming chair of the SGSR in 1976.

A further contribution of von Foerster's was that he organised the first major conference on self-organising systems, in 1959 at the BCL, with participants including Warren McCulloch, Ludwig von Bertalanffy, Anatol Rapoport, the economist Friedrich von Hayek, Stafford Beer, Ross Ashby and Gordon Pask. Typically iconoclastic, von Foerster (1960) argued at the conference that there was no such thing as a self-organising system. His paper did, however, introduce the concept of 'order from noise', later influential in complexity theory.

When he retired in 1976, he moved to California, from where he continued to write and give lectures until his death in 2002. He and Mai lived near the ocean, on a hill called Rattlesnake Hill from which he spent much time clearing undergrowth, and where they welcomed many visitors during the rest of their lives. Von

Foerster was an inspiration and a dear friend to many people, not least because of his deeply ethical way of being, described by Bessie (2003, p. 199), as based on an attitude that:

> One must always be open; the other is always interesting, a person, not a function. Charm there certainly was, but this was not charm, it was the quintessence of true courtesy, a welcoming of the world. ... The most casual acquaintances seemed to sense a "specialness" in this man, not the effect of a wonderful mind, but the effect of an ethos that welcomed.

In his later work, he became interested in three closely-related topics: the importance of language, questions of ethics and the application of his ideas to family therapy.

Von Foerster's concern for language had two main sources – an interest in precision and in dialogue. The former is perhaps inevitable given his early training through the Vienna Circle and the work of Wittgenstein. He argued that "it is vital that the entire language in second-order cybernetics changes. The references to a world that is independent of an observer are replaced by references to oneself" (von Foerster and Poerksen 2002, p. 110). Much of his later work was conducted via dialogue with one or two others, who would then publish the dialogue as an article or book. He related this closely to his interest in language: "Language for me is an invitation to dance. When we are dancing we are using language to suggest to each other what steps we would like to do. ... Togetherness is the point in a dialogue. And language is an invitation to dialogue and not an invitation to monologue" (von Foerster in Waters 1999, p. 83). He was described by Poerksen (2003) as "the Socrates of cybernetics" but unlike the Socratic dialogues (as represented as Plato), where the dialogue partner's role is simply to agree with the great man, von Foerster's dialogue partners were active participants who disagreed with him and questioned him about his ideas.

Von Foerster took a strong interest in ethics, shaped by his constructivist world-view. For him, ethical positions were essentially individual and were always shaped by the situation within which the ethical question arose: "you can't discuss ethical questions while you are relaxing in your easy chair. They arise in a concrete situation rather than being abstract and being able to be discussed out of context" (von Foerster and Poerksen 2002, p. 148). His ethical stance was strongly based on the importance of enabling human beings to become the best they can be, not constrained by others' negative choices, a view summed up in his saying "act always to increase the number of choices" (von Foerster 2003, p. 295).

Connected both to language and to ethics was von Foerster's connections in later life to family therapy. Especially in the US, this field has been strongly influenced by the cybernetic work of Gregory Bateson on communication and paradox. Von Foerster's second-order cybernetics (and his constructivism) was in many ways a natural extension of this approach, and acted in the 1980s and 1990s as a strong impetus to change within family therapy. He had a strong influence on the Mental Research Institute in Palo Alto (California), on Paul Watzlawick who had worked with Gregory Bateson, and on the school of family therapists in Milan. Cecchin et al. (2005, p. 332), members of the Milan school, summed up von Foerster's influence as follows, in a way very close to his constructivist and dialogic position:

a family comes to you, you talk, and from the questions you ask they construct a set of possibilities, or fantasies. These are maps of unknown territory that are valid for as long as people talk about them. ... If, as a therapist, you become embroiled in a model that claims to have some direct relationship with the 'truth', the model becomes reality, and reality pins you down. The model is useful only until it becomes reality.

In many ways, Heinz von Foerster's contributions to systems parallel those of Peter Checkland. He gave a name to an emerging realignment of the field, ran the main institutional setting for that realignment, and acted as an inspiration to successive colleagues and students. Both were concerned with an epistemological shift, from positivism to phenomenology, and both turned the spotlight on to the observer as well as the observed. In Checkland's case that project resulted in soft systems methodology (at the Systems Department, University of Lancaster); in von Foerster's the result was second-order cybernetics (at the BCL).

Heinz von Foerster had a crucial influence upon cybernetics, shaping its current form through his own research and his support for others' research. Krippendorf (2003, p. 195) described von Foerster as

asking questions that others had not thought of; turning conventional beliefs into puzzling opposites; leading his audiences to consider alternative ways of thinking ... Heinz' greatest strength undoubtedly was his ability to encourage others to be audacious as well, to have the courage to ponder radical questions. Doing this was his cybernetics and it has now become ours.

Reading from von Foerster's work

von Foerster H (1979), "Cybernetics of Cybernetics", in Krippendorf, K. (ed.) *Communication and Control*, New York: Gordon and Breach, pp. 5–8.

Ladies and gentlemen – As you may remember, I opened my remarks at earlier conferences of our Society with theorems which, owing to the generosity of Stafford Beer, have been called "Heinz von Foerster's Theorems Number One and Number Two". This all is now history (Beer 1975; von Foerster 1972). However, building on a tradition of two instances, you may rightly expect me to open my remarks today again with a theorem. Indeed I shall do so but it will not bear my name. It can be traced back to Humberto Maturana (1970), the Chilean neurophysiologist, who a few years ago, fascinated us with his presentation on 'autopoiesis', the organization of living things.

Here is Maturana's proposition, which I shall now baptize "Humberto Maturana's Theorem Number One":

"Anything said is said by *an observer."*

Should you at first glance be unable to sense the profundity that hides behind the simplicity of this proposition let me remind you of West Churchman's admonition of this afternoon: "You will be surprised how much can be said by a tautology". This, of course, he said in utter defiance of the logician's claim that a tautology says nothing.

I would like to add to Maturana's Theorem a corollary which, in all modesty, I shall call "Heinz von Foerster's Corollary Number One":

"Anything said is said to *an observer."*

With these two propositions a nontrivial connection between three concepts has been established. First, that of an *observer* who is characterized by being able to make descriptions. This is because of Theorem 1. Of course, what an observer says is a description. The second concept is that of *language*. Theorem 1 and Corollary 1 connect two observers through language. But, in turn, by this connection we have established the third concept I wish to consider this evening, namely that of *society*: the two observers constitute the elementary nucleus for a society. Let me repeat the three concepts that are in a triadic fashion connected to each other. They are: first, the observers; second, the language they use; and third, the society they form by the use of their language. This interrelationship can be compared, perhaps, with the interrelationship between the chicken, and the egg, and the rooster. You cannot say who was first and you cannot say who was last. You need all three in order to have all three. In order to appreciate what I am going to say it might be advantageous to keep this closed triadic relation in mind.

I have no doubts that you share with me the conviction that the central problems of today are societal. On the other hand, the gigantic problem-solving conceptual apparatus that evolved in our Western culture is counterproductive not only for solving but essentially for perceiving social problems. One root for our cognitive blind spot that disables us to perceive social problems is the traditional explanatory paradigm which rests on two operations: One is *causation*, the other one *deduction*. It is interesting to note that something that cannot be explained – that is, for which we cannot show a cause or for which we do not have a reason – we do not wish to see. In other words, something that cannot be explained cannot be seen. This is driven home again and again by Don Juan, a Yaqui Indian, Carlos Casteneda's mentor (Castaneda 1969).

It is quite clear that in his teaching efforts Don Juan wants to make a cognitive blind spot in Castaneda's vision to be filled with new perceptions; he wants to make him 'see'. This is doubly difficult, because of Castaneda's dismissal of experiences as 'illusions' for which he has no explanations on the one hand, and because of a peculiar property of the logical structure of the phenomenon 'blind spot' on the other hand; and this is that we do not perceive our blind spot by, for instance, seeing a black spot close to the centre of our visual field: we do not see that we have a blind spot. In other words, we do not see that we do not see. This I will call a second order deficiency, and the only way to overcome such deficiencies is with therapies of second order.

The popularity of Carlos Castaneda's books suggest to me that his points are being understood: new paradigms emerge. I'm using the term 'paradigm' in the sense of Thomas Kuhn (1962) who wants to indicate with this term a culture specific, or language specific, stereotype or model for linking descriptions semantically. As you may remember, Thomas Kuhn argues that there is a major change in paradigms when the one in vogue begins to fail, shows inconsistencies or contradictions. I however argue that I can name at least two instances in which not the emergent defectiveness of the dominant paradigm but its very flawlessness is the cause for its rejection. One of these instances was Copernicus' novel vision of a heliocentric planetary system which he perceived at a time when the Ptolemaeic geocentric system was at its height as to accuracy of its predictions. The other instance, I submit, is being brought about today by some of us who cannot – by their life – pursue any longer the flawless, but sterile path that explores the properties seen to reside within objects, and turn around to explore their very properties seen now to reside within the observer of these objects. Consider, for instance, 'obscenity'. There is at aperiodic intervals a ritual performed by the supreme judges of this land in which they attempt to establish once and for all a list of all the properties that define an obscene object or act. Since obscenity is not a property residing within things (for if we show Mr. X a painting and he calls it obscene, we know a lot about Mr. X but very little about the painting), when our lawmakers will finally come up with their imaginary list we shall know a lot about them but their laws will be dangerous nonsense.

With this I come now to the other root for our cognitive blind spot and this is a peculiar delusion within our Western tradition, namely, 'objectivity':

"The properties of the observer shall not enter the description of his observations."

But I ask, how would it be possible to make a description in the first place if not the observer were to have properties that allows for a description to be made? Hence, I submit in all modesty, the claim for objectivity is nonsense! One might be tempted to negate 'objectivity' and stipulate now 'subjectivity'. But, ladies and gentlemen, please remember that if a nonsensical proposition is negated, the result is again a nonsensical proposition. However, the nonsensicality of these propositions either in the affirmative or in their negation cannot be seen in the conceptual framework in which these propositions have been uttered. If this is the state of affairs, what can be done? We have to ask a new question:

"What are the properties of an observer?"

Let me at once draw your attention to the peculiar logic underlying this question. For whatever properties we may come up with it is we, you and I, who have to make this observation, that is, we have to observe our own observing, and ultimately account for our own accounting. Is this not opening the door for the logical mischief of propositions that refer to themselves ("I am a liar") that have been so successfully excluded by Russell's Theory of Types not to bother us ever again? Yes and No!

It is most gratifying for me to report to you that the essential conceptual pillars for a theory of the observer have been worked out. The one is a calculus of infinite recursions (Weston and von Foerster 1973); the other one is a calculus of self-reference (Varela 1975). With these calculi we are now able to enter rigorously a conceptual framework which deals with *observing* and not only with the observed.

Earlier I proposed that a therapy of the second order has to be invented in order to deal with dysfunctions of the second order. I submit that the cybernetics of observed systems we may consider to be first-order cybernetics; while second-order cybernetics is the cybernetics of observing systems. This is in agreement with another formulation that has been given by Gordon Pask (1969). He, too, distinguishes two orders of analysis. The one in which the observer enters the system by stipulating the *system's* purpose. We may call this a 'first-order stipulation'. In a 'second-order stipulation' the observer enters the system by stipulating *his own* purpose.

From this it appears to be clear that social cybernetics must be a second-order cybernetics – a *cybernetics of cybernetics* – in order that the observer who enters the system shall be allowed to stipulate his own purpose: he is autonomous. If we fail to do so somebody else will determine a purpose for us. Moreover, if we fail to do so, we shall provide the excuses for those who want to transfer the responsibility for their own actions to somebody else: "I am not responsible for my actions; I just obey orders." Finally, if we fail to recognize autonomy of each, we may turn into a society that attempts to honor commitments and forgets about its responsibilities.

I am most grateful to the organizers and the speakers of this conference who permitted me to see cybernetics in the context of social responsibility.

References

Beer, S. (1975). *Platform for change*. New York: Wiley.

Berger, P. L., & Luckmann, T. (1966). *The social construction of reality: A treatise in the sociology of knowledge*. Garden City, NY: Doubleday.

Bessie, C. (2003). The man in the room across the hall. *Cybernetics and Human Knowing, 10*(3/4), 197–201.

Castaneda, C. (1969). The reachings of Don Juan: A Yaqui way of knowledge. New York: Ballantine.

Cecchin, G., Barbetta, P., Toffanetti, D. (2005). Who was von Foerster, anyway? *Kybernetes, 34*(3/4), 330–342.

Franchi, S., Güzeldere, G., Minch, E. (2005). From Vienna to California: A journey across disciplines. *Kybernetes, 34*(1/2), 15–32.

Glanville, R. (2002). Heinz von Foerster. *Soziale Systeme, 8*(2), 155–158.

Hayles, N. K. (1999). *How we became posthuman: Virtual bodies in cybernetics, literature, and informatics*. Chicago: University of Chicago Press.

Kuhn, T. (1962). *The structure of scientific revolutions*. Chicago: University of Chicago Press.

Krieg, P. (2005). The human face of cybernetics: Heinz von Foerster and the history of a movement that failed, *Kybernetes, 34*(3/4), 551–557.

Krippendorf, K. (2003). Recollections of Heinz von Foerster, a rhetorical genius. *Cybernetics and Human Knowing, 10*(3/4), 195–196.

Maturana, H. (1970). Neurophysiology of ognition. In P. Garvin (Ed.), *Cognition, a multiple view* (pp. 3–23). New York: Spartan Books.

Pask, G. (1969). The meaning of cybernetics in the behavioral sciences (the cybernetics of behavior and cognition: Extending the meaning of 'Goal'). In J. Rose (Ed.), *Progress in cybernetics*, vol. 1 (pp. 15–44). New York: Gordon and Breach.

Poerksen, B. (2003). Obituary: Heinz von Foerster. *International Journal of General Systems, 32*(6), 519–523.

Scott, B. (2003). Heinz von Foerster – An appreciation (revisited). *Cybernetics and Human Knowing, 10*(3/4), 137–149.

Segal, L. (2001). *The dream of reality: Heinz von Foerster's constructivism* (2nd edition). New York: Springer.

Umpleby, S. (2003). Heinz von Foerster and the Mansfield amendment. *Cybernetics and Human Knowing*, *10*(3/4), 161–163.

Varela, F. (1975). A calculus for self-reference. *International Journal of General Systems*, *2*(1), 1–25.

Von Foerster, H. (1960). On self-organizing systems and their environments. In M.C. Yovits, & S. Cameron (Eds.), *Self-organizing systems* (pp. 31–50). London: Pergamon.

Von Foerster, H. (1972). Responsibility of competence. *Journal of Cybernetics*, *2*(2), 1–6.

Von Foerster, H. (1979). Cybernetics of cybernetics. In K. Krippendorf (Ed.), *Communication and control* (pp. 5–8). New York: Gordon and Breach.

Von Foerster, H., & Poerksen, B. (2002). *Understanding systems: Conversations on epistemology and ethics*. Heidelberg, Germany: Carl-Auer-Systeme Verlag.

Von Foerster, H. (2003). *Understanding understanding: Essays on cybernetics and cognition*. New York: Springer.

Waters, C. (1999). Invitation to dance – A conversation with Heinz von Foerster. *Cybernetics and Human Knowing*, *6*(4), 81–84.

Weston, P.E., & von Foerster, H. (1973). Artificial intelligence and machines that understand. *Annual Review of Physical Chemistry*, *24*, 358–378.

Chapter 19
Stafford Beer

Stafford Beer was a consultant, manager and cybernetician. He was the first person to apply cybernetics to management problems. He combined theory and practice in a highly integrated way, always working as a practitioner but making a number of important contributions in both methodology and theory. His writing was highly inspirational as well as academically rigorous, and he had a profound impact upon those with whom he worked as a consultant and colleague. As Rosenhead (2006, p. 581) has written, "he explored in his work the implications of a holistic approach to organizational and social problems, and exemplified this approach in his own life".

Beer's single greatest contribution to systems thinking was the creation of management cybernetics – the application of cybernetic principles to the management of large organizations. He had a clear professional need for this work as a manager working within several large organizations, but it also derived from his own polymath nature. His longest academic association was with the Manchester Business School, where he was visiting professor for 24 years, although he was a visiting professor at many other universities. He never took a first degree, leaving university after a year to join the army, though he subsequently gained an M.B.A. and a D.Sc. (higher doctorate) as well as several honorary degrees. A number of consultancy firms were established around his ideas and with his involvement.

Anthony Stafford Beer was born in 1926 in the UK and died in 2002 in Canada. He came early to management, appointed at age 18 as a captain in the Gurkha Rifles in India, where he served for three years, and then as an army psychologist in the UK for a further two years. Leaving the army in 1949, he went to work at a branch of United Steel (then the UK's largest steel company) where he set up the company's operational research and cybernetics group. In 1960 he left to set up the UK's first operational research consultancy, SIGMA, where he worked until 1966, after which he spent four years as development director of International Publishing Corporation, then the largest publishing company in the world. From 1970 onwards he worked as an independent consultant and visiting academic. As well as working with commercial organisations, he worked with the governments of a number of Latin American nations, including Mexico, Uruguay and Venezuala, but most famously that of Chile during the Allende government of the early 1970s, discussed in detail below.

M. Ramage and K. Shipp, *Systems Thinkers,*

He learned yoga in India and practiced and taught it subsequently, was a published poet, and had a number of exhibitions of his paintings. He spoke a number of languages, with particular interest in Sanskrit, Greek and Latin (as well as more modern languages including Hindi and Spanish). Beer married twice and subsequently was the partner of Allenna Leonard, herself a cybernetician and president of the American Society for Cybernetics. He had eight children, one of whom, the artist Vanilla Beer, drew covers for a number of his books. Rosenhead (2006, p. 580) described him as follows:

> Stafford Beer was a larger-than-life character. He was tall, broad and brimful of energy, and in later years bearded like an Old Testament prophet. His enthusiasm for life in its many aspects could be over-powering and quite non-Anglo-Saxon. The world of those who encountered him tended to polarize between those who were distrustful of what they saw as his showmanship, and those who were converted into lifelong admirers and supporters. He himself was deeply loyal and affectionate to his friends. It was typical that Stafford spent the year following the Pinochet coup concentrating on helping to find safe places outside Chile for members of the project team.

Beer was a contributor to the systems movement throughout his life. He was the collaborator and friend of many of the key people in systems thinking (notably Warren McCulloch, who he regarded as a mentor, Ross Ashby, Gordon Pask, Heinz von Foerster and Russell Ackoff). He was president of a number of prominent international associations: the Society for General Systems Research, the Operational Research Society, and the World Organisation of Systems and Cybernetics. Although he was not at the Macy conferences, he did attend the first international conference on cybernetics in Namur, Belgium in 1956 and many subsequent important conferences.

The basis of Beer's management cybernetics was a strong belief that both commercial organisations and society as a whole needed to become significantly more flexible and able to change, as reflected in the reading below. As described by Pickering (2004, p. 499), as early as 1959 Beer argued that "the important thing for organisations was that they should be adaptive – light on their feet and ready to accommodate themselves to the new situations which would arise faster and faster as time passed". This strikingly modern view was one found among a number of other systems thinkers of the time (including Donald Schön and Eric Trist) but not prevalent in wider management circles until several decades later. Adaptability to change has been emphasised as a key theme of cybernetics (and later of complexity theory) since the work of Ross Ashby, and Beer's work was crucial in demonstrating how adaptability could work in practice for the design of organisations and society.

Management cybernetics was centred around Beer's development of the Viable System Model (VSM). The purpose of this model is "to explain how systems are viable – that is, capable of independent existence ... [and] to elucidate the laws of viability in order to facilitate the management task" (Beer 1984, p. 7). The model was at first developed in mathematical terms (using set theory), secondly in neurophysiological terms, and latterly in more simple mathematics using a topological version of the original set-theoretic model – that is, a set of rigorous diagrams modelling the nature of a viable system.

The VSM is based on the principle of recursion, "that any viable system contains and is contained in a viable system" (Beer 1984, p. 8). This is important because it means that a system can be viable whatever level it exists at (individual, group, organisational, or societal). Beer's concept of a viable system, whatever its level, contains five subsystems, with the functions of implementation, coordination, control, planning and policy-making (Espejo 1989). These five roles do not necessarily belong to different people, and it is important they not be mapped on to a hierarchical model of the organisation, but Beer defines a clear set of communication and monitoring channels between the five subsystems. Thus according to the VSM, a system is viable to the extent that it meets the model. The VSM can be seen as a way of designing the organisational adaptability discussed earlier – as Pickering (2004, p. 511) argues, "despite the seeming paradoxicality of it, one can indeed construct adaptive systems, systems that adapt to and transform themselves in the face of the unknown, as in Beer's implementations of the VSM".

The VSM has been widely used and discussed in the management literature, both positively and negatively. Jackson (1989) sums up the debate very clearly:

> Its advocates would claim that it is of immeasurable value to managers trying to design and operate goal-seeking, adaptive systems. It provides a sophisticated organisational model which embodies great explanatory power and is readily applicable. ... To its critics, however, the VSM is of dubious value even as a tool for increasing efficiency and effectiveness. The emphasis it places on organisational design may preclude proper attention being given to the generation of shared perceptions and values; to 'organisational culture'. Further, the imposition of a particular design may become fixed and prevent necessary adaptation.

Beer's experiences in Chile demonstrate his ideas and values clearly. In 1970, the democratically-elected Marxist government of Salvador Allende came to power in Chile. One of Allende's ministers (Fernando Flores, a professor of management science) invited Beer to Chile in November 1971. Over the next two years, Beer became intimately involved in the governing of the country, using an early version of the Viable Systems Model.

Through working with a small group within Chile, and talking to a wide range of influential people, after eight days of work he formulated a "plan for the cybernetic regulation of the social economy of Chile" (Beer 1981, p. 248). The plan would have two key features – it would regulate the social economy in real time, and it would support the decentralised decision-making that distinguished Allende's form of Marxism from the Soviet model. The project to do this was called Cybersyn (from 'cybernetic synergy'), and the intention was to implement "a preliminary system of information and regulation for the industrial economy" (Beer 1981, p. 251) by March 1972 – four and a half months after the plan was formulated. The problem was large: there were insufficient resources to make computing power available locally, so computation of the cybernetic model was carried out centrally; but the only telecommunications system available was a basic telex system that ran down the length of the country (3,000 miles). Before Beer left Chile at the end of his first visit, he met with Allende, and discussed with him a model of the Chilean industrial economy as a viable system.

The preliminary design of the Chilean industry economy using the VSM was completed by Beer following his return to London, along with a group based in

Chile. In due course, Project Cybersyn was widened to cover the whole country, and Beer was appointed as Scientific Director of the project, working largely in Chile. The project was largely completed, although the political instability meant continual change in the nature of the system being used. However, the effect was short-lasting, since in September 1973, there was a military coup, Allende was killed, and the government fell.

Beer was working in London at the time of the Chilean coup, so escaped its physical impact, but its effect on him was considerable. He renounced his material possessions in 1974 and moved to a small remote cottage in mid-Wales where he lived alone for ten years. Subsequently, and for the rest of his life, he divided his time between mid-Wales and Toronto, the home of Allenna Leonard.

Beer was an early advocate of Humberto Maturana's work and wrote a preface to his key book *Autopoiesis and Cognition* (Maturana and Varela 1980). He used the concept of autopoiesis (see Chapter 20) in a management context in a most interesting way. Beer coined the term "pathologically autopoietic" to refer to organisations (such as hospitals and universities) where "the staff slides into the error of paying more and more attention to those matters that explicate relationships than to healing or teaching – so that in the end a cured patient or an educated student were only the product of self-help and good luck" (Beer 1987).

In the final years of Beer's life, his chief interest was in a methodology for effective and democratic group processes which he called Team Syntegrity. Using a mixture of mathematics, cybernetics and architecture, the process specifies the way that groups of 30 people can make collective decisions on complex topics that involve all of them. The process is based on Buckminster Fuller's designs for very large, highly stable domes using the icosahedron (a shape with 20 faces and 30 edges) and the observation that if the edges of the icosahedron are taken to represent the members of a team, then each team member will be connected equally to every other team member. Around this model Beer and his collaborators have built up a process that allows a group connected in such a way to make decisions.

Team Syntegrity illustrates the strengths and weaknesses of Beer's work clearly. It derives from well-developed concepts from a range of different disciplines, especially cybernetics, and it exists because of Beer's deep concern for the state of the world and the importance of democracy. Team Syntegrity has both theoretical rigour and strong practical validity – as Pickering (2004, p. 515) argues, it is "a practical sub-political set-up in which democratic deliberation and planning could be conducted in a completely open-ended fashion developed through practice". On the other hand, it is very complex and rather prescriptive in the requirements it places on both facilitators and clients – it is not hard to argue that the organisation must conform to the model rather than the other way around. It also requires both great skill from the facilitators and a high degree of technological back-up. This clearly resembles Jackson's analysis of the VSM, in both good and bad ways.

Stafford Beer was a prolific writer, highly-skilled practitioner and consultant, and originator of many important concepts within management cybernetics. He was a man of deep learning, considerable practical ability, and great passion. Allenna Leonard (2002) described him as a true pathfinder; curious about almost everything and under no illusions about the implications of our accelerating rate of change. He read widely and sought out people to learn from to educate himself in intellectual matters; he pursued spiritual development all his life; at first in the context of the church and later by study and meditation.

Leonard also noted Beer's fondness for the poetry of Antonio Machado, whose work he often quoted. In particular, the following lines sum up Stafford Beer's intellectual journey and his understanding of the importance of adaptability, both by individuals and by structures:

Walker, there is no road

The road is made as you walk.

Reading from Beer's work

Extract from pages 1–7.

The little house where I have come to live alone for a few weeks sits on the edge of a steep hill in a quiet village on the western coast of Chile. Huge majestic waves roll into the bay and crash magnificently over the rocks, sparkling white against the green sea under a winter sun. It is for me a time of peace, a time to clear the head, a time to treasure.

For after all, such times are rare events for today's civilized man. We spend our days boxed in our houses, swarming in and out of office blocks like tribes of ants, crammed into trains, canned in aeroplanes, locked solid in traffic jams on the freeway. Our unbiblical concern for what we shall eat, what we shall drink, and what we shall put on is amplified and made obsessional by the pressure to consume – way, way beyond the natural need. All this is demanded by the way we have arranged our economy. And the institutions we have built to operate that economy, to safeguard ourselves, protect our homes, care for and educate our families, have all grown into large and powerful pieces of social machinery which suddenly seem not so much protective as actually threatening.

Mankind has always been in battle with his environment. But until quite recently in history his battles were on a reasonable scale, a human scale. He could alter his house, if he would brave the weather: he did not have to take on the whole city planning department and the owners of his mortgage and his overdraft. He could dress his children as he pleased, teaching them what he knew and how to learn: he was not flattened in this natural enterprise by educational authorities, attended by boards of experts. When he fought with danger, he matched his strength and skill with another animal of similar size to his: he was not unexpectedly knocked flying by two tons of steel travelling at sixty miles an hour. And if he faced the fact of death, that also was a personal encounter, win or lose: he did not live under the stress of a remotely threatened genocide or nuclear extermination. Bur this is how it is for us. We do not think much about it. When things go badly, there is all of this to blame, and not ourselves: perhaps that is some sort of consolation.

Do we indeed even want to think about such things? I believe that people increasingly do begin to question the assumptions of our society – and not because of any characteristic that I have so far mentioned. Most people alive today in urban societies settled long ago for the role of pygmy man amidst the giants of his own institutions, and for the reason that it meant apparent advance – a higher standard of living, as measured by the gross national product per head. But in the last decade or two something has come through to public consciousness. It is the doubt as to whether the whole apparatus of our civilization *actually works* any longer. Is it beginning to fail?

The evidence for this suspicion is plentiful. I instance the decay of previously rich and healthy cities from the centre outwards, creating ghettos and all the social frightfulness that goes with them, stark inequalities, private penury, social squalor, a rise in crime, a rise in violence. I instance pollution on a world-wide scale: the poisoning of the atmosphere, of seas and lakes and rivers. Then there is the widening chasm between luxury and starvation, whereby we somehow manage to concentrate more wealth with the already wealthy, and more deprivation with the already deprived. I will not go on with this baleful list, because conscientious people are already aware of these problems. The question I would like us to address in these lectures is just *why*? Because if we can fathom that, maybe we can also conduct a fruitful search for answers.

The first point to establish is the most difficult; and it is the most difficult because it sounds so easy. It is to say that all these institutions we have been contemplating – the homes, the offices, the schools, the cities, the firms, the states, the countries – are not just things, entities we recognize and label. They are instead *dynamic and surviving systems*. Well, I did say it sounds so easy. Obviously these entities are systems; because they consist of related parts, and the relations – the connexions – between those parts. Obviously, too, they are dynamic. No-one believes that these institutions are just sitting there brooding; they are all 'on the go'. Finally, if they were not surviving, they would not be there. And having taken the point that we are talking about such systems, it is too natural to pass it by – to pass over the point, pass around the point, pass through the point – without ever grappling with the real meaning of the point at all.

Although we may recognize the systemic nature of the world, and would agree when challenged that something we normally think of as an entity is actually a system, our culture does not propound this insight as particularly interesting or profitable to contemplate. Let me propose to you a little exercise, taking the bay I am looking at now as a convenient example. It is not difficult to recognize that the movement of water in this bay is the visible behaviour of a dynamic system: after all, the waves are steadily moving in and dissipating themselves along the shore. But please consider just one wave. We think of that as an entity: a wave, we say. What is it doing out there, why is it that shape, and what is the reason for its happy white crest? The exercise is to ask yourself in all honesty not whether you know the answers, because that would be just a technical exercise, but whether these are the sorts of question that have ever arisen for you. The point is that the questions themselves – and not just the answers – can be understood only when we stop thinking of the wave as an entity. As long as it is an entity, we tend to say well, waves are like that: the facts that our wave is out there moving across the bay, has that shape and a happy white crest, are the signs that tell me "It's a wave" – just as the fact that a book is red and no other colour is a sign that tells me "That's the book I want".

The truth is, however, that the book is red because someone gave it a red cover when he might just as well have made it green; whereas the wave cannot be other than it is because a wave is a dynamic system. It consists of flows of water, which are its parts, and the relations between those flows, which are governed by the natural laws of systems of water that are investigated by the science of hydrodynamics. The appearances of the wave, its shape and the happy white crest, are actually *outputs* of this system. They are what they are because the system is organized in the way that it is, and this organization produces an inescapable kind of behaviour. The cross-section of the wave is parabolic, having two basic forms, the one dominating at the open-sea stage of the wave, and the other dominating later. As the second form is produced from the first, there is a moment when the wave holds the two forms: it has at this moment a wedge shape of 120°. And at this point, as the second form takes over, the wave begins to break – hence the happy white crest.

Now in terms of the dynamic system that we call a wave, the happy white crest is not at all the pretty sign by which what we first called an entity signalizes its existence. For the wave, that crest is its personal catastrophe. What has happened is that the wave has a systemic conflict within it determined by its form of organization, and that this has produced a phase of *instability*. The happy white crest is the mark of doom upon the wave, because the instability feeds upon itself; and the catastrophic collapse of the wave is an inevitable output of the system.

I am asking "Did you know?" Not "did you know about theoretic hydrodynamics?" but "did you know that a wave is a dynamic system in catastrophe, as a result of its internal organizational instability?" Of course, the reason for this exercise is to be ready to pose the same question about the social institutions we were discussing. If we perceive those as entities, the giant monoliths surrounding pygmy man, then we shall not be surprised to find the marks of bureaucracy upon them: sluggish and inaccurate response, and those other warning signs I mentioned earlier. That is what these entities are like, we tend to say – and sigh. But in fact these institutions are dynamic systems, having a particular organization which produces particular outputs. My contention is that they are typically moving into unstable phases, for which catastrophe is the inevitable outcome. And I believe the growing sense of unease I mentioned at the start derives from a public intuition that this is indeed the case. For people to understand this possibility, how it arises, what the dangers are, and above all what can be done about it, it is not necessary to master socio-political cybernetics. This is the science that stands to institutional behaviour as the science of hydrodynamics stands to the behaviour of waves. But it is necessary to train ourselves simply to perceive what was there all the time: not a monolithic entity, but a dynamic system; not a happy white crest, but the warning of catastrophic instability.

So far we have spoken a little of the nature of dynamic systems; but the other qualification that I used at the start was the word 'surviving'. The wave is not a *surviving* dynamic system, because its destruction is built into its organization. However we certainly regard our institutions as survival worthy. After all, they have survived until now, because they are capable of a trick we call *adaptation*, which waves are not. So why should there now be a fuss about instability and impending catastrophe?

Our institutions have already proven that they can survive, says the argument, and we can have confidence that they will continue to adapt successfully to change. Indeed, we insist that they must – for our institutions enshrine everything we hold most dear. Beginning with the family unit, based on love and mutual support; extending through the school – and perhaps that alma mater the university; bound together in the cohesion of the neighbourhood, the community, and the churches; ramifying into business and the growth of prosperity for all; exemplified, protected, and projected by the state; this – our society – is an entity that survives, albeit by adaptive change. And if this society embodied in its institutions is threatened by too rapid change, then the answer that many serious and concerned people give is to reinforce the rules of the societary game, strengthen the institutions, tighten up the criminal, social, and moral laws, and weather the storm. That is the conservative attitude. It is not mine. It is not going to work much longer.

Indeed, we ought to face the fact that this theory does not work now. People convince themselves that it does, because they see society as an entity, and its main characteristic is to be held most dear. Then they grit their teeth and declare that whatever is wrong with it must and can be put right again. Broken barriers, swept away by permissive morality, can be repaired. Departed children can be summoned home to eat the fatted calf. The majority of people, who do not attend a church, are still (surely to goodness?) fundamentally Christian. The starving two-thirds of the world will eventually be fed (well, not those two-thirds dying right now, but their descendants). And somehow a finite planet, with exhaustible resources, will be made indefinitely to support more and yet more growth. Oh no: this only even looks possible if we are dealing with a fixed entity, a society or a way of life that is held to enshrine eternal values, a golden ideal. If this has become rather tarnished, then it can be reburnished with a little elbow grease. So some people, and especially some politicians, seem to think.

But if society is a dynamic system all these phenomena are not simply blemishes – they are its outputs. These unpleasing threats to all we hold most dear are products of a system so organized as to produce them – to produce *them*, and not their contraries. These are not accidental; and they are not mistakes. They are the continuing output of a systemic conflict which is due to specific modes of organization. And those modes of organization have currently arrived at a stage in their inexorable pattern of behaviour which, like the wedge-shaped wave of 120°, is incipiently unstable – on the verge of catastrophic breakdown. Or so I think.

These dire predictions I am making have to come about, which is why I said they were inexorable, if – but only if – we continue to support modes of organization into which these outcomes are inbuilt. We do not have to do that. We really can change the whole thing. But to succeed, we must first perceive the nature of dynamic surviving systems, and the conditions they must meet to remain stable yet adaptive.

References

Beer, S. (1974/1995). *Designing freedom*. Chichester: John Wiley.

Beer, S. (1981). *Brain of the firm*. Chichester: John Wiley.

Beer, S. (1984). The viable system model: Its provenance, development, methodology and pathology. *Journal of the Operational Research Society, 35*(1), 7–26.

Beer, S. (1987). Holism and the Frou-Frou Slander. *Kybernetes, 17*(1), 23–31.

Espejo, R. (1989). The VSM revisited. In R. Espejo, & R. Harnden (Eds.), *The viable system model revisited: Interpretations and applications of Stafford Beer's VSM* (pp. 77–100). Chichester: John Wiley.

Jackson, M. C. (1989). Evaluating the managerial significance of the VSM. In R. Espejo, & R. Harnden (Eds.), *The viable system model revisited: Interpretations and applications of Stafford Beer's VSM* (pp. 407–439). Chichester: John Wiley.

Leonard, A. (2002). Stafford Beer: September 25 1926 – August 23 2002. http://www.vanillabeer.org/staffordbeer.htm. Accessed 13 Jan 2009.

Maturana, H. R., & Varela, F. J. (1980). *Autopoiesis and cognition: The realization of the living*. Dordrecht, Netherlands: Reidel.

Pickering, A. (2004). The science of the unknowable: Stafford Beer's cybernetic informatics. *Kybernetes, 33*(3/4), 499–521.

Rosenhead, J. (2006). IFORS operational research hall of fame: Stafford Beer. *International Transactions in Operational Research, 13*(6), 577–581.

Chapter 20
Humberto Maturana

What is the nature of life? How do our cognitive processes relate to our perception of the world? These are big questions of both biology and philosophy, and answering them is the life-work of Humberto Romesín Maturana. His work has been massively influential in systems thinking, and has been applied to many other fields. It is deeply philosophical in its implications, but has a strong biological grounding. Although Maturana's name is most closely associated with the theory of autopoiesis (self-producing systems), work that he carried out with his student and close collaborator Francisco Varela, his work is more general than the ideas of autopoiesis. It can best be summed up in the title of an early paper (reprinted in Maturana and Varela, 1980) – the *biology of cognition*.

Maturana's work is not easy. His writing style is complex, the ideas he describes are complex, and their implications are significant for our understanding of life and cognition. They have been described and applied by a number of other writers in systems thinking, but also in areas as diverse as law, sociology, family therapy, artificial intelligence, organisational theory and environmental change. John Mingers, who has written extensively on the theory of autopoiesis and its applications, argues "I believe that it will stand as an example, if not the example, of outstanding work in the field of systems per se. It is founded on genuine knowledge of the relevant domains – biology and neurophysiology – but this is molded within a strong systems perspective which supplies genuinely new insights" (Mingers 1995, p. 4).

Humberto Maturana was born in 1928 in Santiago de Chile, where he has lived and worked for most of his life. His initial degree from the University of Chile was in medicine (as it was not then possible to study biology, his preferred subject, at degree level in Chile). He spent a brief time in England in 1954, at University College London, and then moved to the United States. He received his Ph.D. from Harvard in 1958, subsequently working at the Massachusetts Institute of Technology (MIT). He returned to the University of Chile in 1960, where he has remained since, running a research centre on the Biology of Knowledge. He was a visiting professor at the University of Illinois from 1968–1969. He is currently the co-director of the Instituto de Formación Matríztica in Santiago, which studies "the biological matrix of human existence" (from the Institute's website).

© The Open University 2009. Published in association with Springer-Verlag London Limited

Maturana was present in Chile for the great political events of the early 1970s – the government of Salvador Allende and subsequent military coup and dictatorship. He was not involved in the Allende government – when Stafford Beer came to Chile as a consultant to that government, he asked to meet Maturana (as a fellow cybernetician), and nobody in the government had heard of him. Following the 1973 coup, Maturana decided to remain in Chile during the period of the Pinochet dictatorship (unlike many academics who fled the country in fear of persecution), feeling a responsibility to stay and represent a democratic way of life. He also sought to know what it meant to live under a dictator (in the way that his close colleague Heinz von Foerster had previously done), and to observe how it was possible in a dictatorship to "retain one's own capabilities of vision and perception" (Maturana and Poerksen 2004, p. 168).

Maturana has been concerned with issues of life and cognition for the whole of his career. His inspiration for this work came while he was a medical student. He was seriously ill with tuberculosis and confined to a sanatorium with very little reading material, so was put in the position of reflecting upon his condition and the nature of life. While at the sanatorium, he "realized that what was peculiar to living systems was that they were discrete autonomous entities such that all the processes that they lived, they lived in reference to themselves ... whether a dog bites me or doesn't bite me, it is doing something that has to do with itself" (Maturana 2002, p. 6). This concept of autonomy and self-reference (an unusual perspective in biological sciences, which tends to focus on behaviour which relates to others) has formed the foundation of his work ever since.

His first piece of experimental work to advance this concept was conducted at MIT, where he worked with Jerry Lettvin (one of the group inspired by Warren McCulloch), which resulted in the celebrated paper "What the frog's eye tells the frog's brain" (Lettvin et al. 1959). Studying the retinal cells of frogs, they discovered that the information given from the frog's eye does not describe the world as such, but only such aspects of the world as are relevant to the frog at a particular moment. In particular, the frog does not see flies (its foodstuff) but only patterns of moving shadows which enable it to catch flies. Applied to humans, this leads inexorably to the conclusion that our understanding of the world is partial, that we take only from the world that information which we need at the time. The work was carried out in the traditional scientific paradigm, but was widely regarded as highly important at the time. As Hayles (1999, p. 135) puts it, the article "blew a frog-sized hole in realist epistemology".

The further development of the theory of autopoiesis came as the 1960s progressed. In 1963 he demonstrated the "circular closed dynamics of molecular productions that make living systems discrete autonomous molecular systems" (Maturana 2002, p. 7). In 1965, studying the colour vision of pigeons, he concluded that it was not possible to view colours as objective external features of the world, but rather as internal experiences of the world – which for him meant that he had to abandon "the notion that there was an external independent world to be known by the observer" (Maturana 2002, p. 5).

In 1968, Maturana spent most of a year at the Biological Computing Laboratory at the University of Illinois, working closely with Heinz von Foerster, and it was there that these ideas began to coalesce into a formal theory. The work Maturana published there appeared under the title of "Biology of Cognition" (originally 1970, republished in Maturana and Varela 1980). Early in this paper can be found a phrase which has become emblematic for Maturana's work: "anything said is said by an observer" (Maturana and Varela 1980, p. 8). This focus on the observer as a vital part of the system has been crucial both in Maturana's work and more generally in second-order cybernetics. To be aware of the role of the observer (who for Maturana can only be a human being), and to identify them as a clear part of the system, is to deny the concept of objectivity. It transfers the focus of scientific study from the object being observed, which in the traditional realist paradigm is unchanging regardless of the observer, to the combination of object plus observer, which will necessarily change according to the observer.

In the article "Biology of Cognition", Maturana outlined his theory of cognition based on the "self-referring circular organization of the living system" and of living systems which are "capable of making descriptions and of generating, through orienting interactions with other, similar, systems and with itself, both a consensual linguistic domain and a domain of self-consciousness" (Maturana and Varela 1980, p. 48). At this stage, however, Maturana did not have a fully worked-out description of the processes involved, nor did he have a name for this phenomenon. It was when he returned to Chile, and was joined in his laboratory by his younger compatriot Francisco Varela that these ideas were formalised and given a name: the theory of autopoiesis.

The word 'autopoiesis' was coined by Maturana, and means 'self-making' or 'self-producing'. It refers to the phenomenon that Maturana had earlier identified – that living systems are "organised in such a way that their processes produce the very components necessary for the continuance of these processes" (Mingers 1995, p. 11). This circularity is crucial: the nature of the autopoietic system is that it maintains itself solely through its own activities. Autopoiesis, argues Maturana (2002, p. 8), is "the necessary and sufficient condition for the constitution of living systems". Maturana and Varela initially applied this theory to the dynamics of cells, observing that the processes of the cell continually act to recreate the boundary of the cell (its membrane) that separates it from its environment, but it has been applied by them and others to other levels of living system (Mingers 1995; Capra 1996).

The concept of autopoiesis brings with it several important implications. If an autopoietic system is self-producing and maintains its own boundary from the environment, it may sound as if autopoiesis is only at work in closed systems. This is not so. Maturana and Varela distinguish between the *organisation* and the *structure* of systems. The former refers to the relationships between components which are necessary to define that system as part of a particular class of systems; the latter to the particular physical form which those components take.

An autopoietic system (such as a cell) is one that can be considered as *organisationally closed* – it retains its organisation regardless of changes from its environment – but *structurally open* to the flow of energy and matter in and out of the system. Capra (1996, p. 167) argues that "this organizational closure implies that a living system is self-organizing in the sense that its order and behaviour are not imposed by the environment but are established by the system itself".

Organisational closure is important because it is a criterion of life – for a living (autopoietic) system to remain alive it must retain its basic organisation. However there must be a process by which the living system relates to its environment, and in the theory of autopoiesis this is termed *structural coupling*. As changes occur in the system's environment, the structure of the system changes to match the environment. This is different from the organism adapting to its environment, because "the environment does not specify the adaptive changes that will occur – they either will occur, and thus maintain autopoiesis, or they will not, and the system will disintegrate" (Mingers 1995, p. 35).

We have largely described autopoiesis so far as a physical phenomenon, applying to cells in the first instance and more generally to other living systems. This is the way that Maturana himself understands the theory – he clearly states that "autopoiesis occurs only in the physical domain" (Maturana 2002, p. 8). However, the theory has been very attractive to writers in a range of domains with an interest in circular, self-referential systems. It is a controversial question whether it is legitimate to apply autopoiesis to social systems, in particular. The attempt has been made by a number of authors, but generally by extending the concept, regarding it as a metaphor, or by applying it to abstract ideas such as messages or communications (the approach taken by Niklas Luhmann).

While Maturana is resistant to the application of autopoiesis to social systems, his more general theories on cognition clearly apply to individual human beings and as a collection of human beings, to social systems. In particular, he has written at length of the importance of language. He has extended his celebrated remarks on the observer to note that "we human beings operate as observers, that is, we make distinctions in language" (Maturana 1988, p. 26). Language is crucial to our process of observing and interacting with the world – and it is an active process, one that Maturana calls 'languaging'. Indeed, Maturana refers to a "network of conversation" (Matura 1988, p. 53) which form the dynamics of social systems.

In many ways, Maturana's work is that of philosopher as much as biologist. He is very clear that he sees himself as a biologist, and that that is the foundation of his work. Nonetheless, his ideas have strong philosophical implications, with their focus on the nature of reality. Because of this background as a biologist, Maturana has chosen not to engage directly in philosophical debates, and few references to the philosophical literature can be found in his work. This makes it difficult to situate his ideas in philosophical traditions.

His work is often described as forming a foundation for the theory of constructivism (the idea that we do not observe the world as it is but rather mentally construct the world we inhabit through our observations and actions). This is given credence through statements such as "every act of knowing brings forth a world" (Maturana and Varela 1987, p. 26). However, Maturana is clear that does not regard himself as a constructivist: "I do not consider myself a representative of constructivism, even if I am called a constructivist over and over again" (Maturana and Poerksen 2004, p. 34).

Maturana's view instead is of an active process by which we observe and construct our way of making sense of the world: "our world, as the world which we bring forth in our coexistence with others, will always have that mixture of regularity and mutability, that combination of solidity and shifting sand, so typical of human experience when we look at it up close" (Maturana and Varela 1987, pp. 241). It is not appropriate, Maturana argues, to talk of an objective reality – we should look instead at what we do in observing and acting in the world.

This sense of active engagement in the world is crucial to Maturana's work and his understanding of cognition and human life. As Bunnell (2004, p. 7) argues: "what Maturana has to offer this world is not another way of living in reality, nor the foundations of constructivism, nor a biological argument, but a whole world of awareness of the manner of our living which alters the manner of our living".

Reading from Maturana's work

From *The Tree of Knowledge*, by Humberto R. Maturana, Ph.D, and Francisco J. Varela, Ph.D.
    ©1987 by Humberto R. Maturana and Francisco J. Varela. Reprinted by arrangement with
    Shambhala Publications, Inc., Boston, MA. www.shambhala.com
Extract from pages 42–52; boxes omitted.

How do I know when a being is living? What are my criteria? Throughout the history of biology many criteria have been proposed. They all have drawbacks. For instance, some have proposed as a criterion chemical composition, or the capacity to move, or reproduction, or even some combination of those criteria, that is, a list of properties. But how do we know when the list is complete? For instance, if we build a machine capable of reproducing itself, but it is made of iron and plastic and not of molecules, is it living?

We wish to give an answer to this question in a way radically different from the traditional listing of properties. This will simplify the problem tremendously. To understand this change in perspective, we have to be aware that merely asking the question of how to recognize a living being indicates that we have an idea, even if implicitly, of its *organization*. It is this idea that will determine whether we accept or reject the answer given to us. To prevent this implicit idea from entrapping and blinding us, we must be aware of it when we consider the answer that follows.

What is the makeup or organization of anything? It is both very simple and potentially complicated. 'Organization' signifies those relations that must be present in order for something to exist. For me to judge that this object is a chair, I have to recognize a certain relationship between the parts I call legs, back, and seat, in such a way that sitting down is made possible. That it is made of wood and nails, or plastic and screws, has nothing at all to do with my classifying it as a chair.

This situation, in which we recognize implicitly or explicitly the organization of an object when we indicate it or distinguish it, is universal in the sense that it is something we do constantly as a basic cognitive act, which consists no more and no less than in generating classes of any type. Thus, the class of 'chairs' is defined by the relations required for me to classify something as a chair. The class of 'good deeds' is defined by the criteria that I establish and that must apply between the actions done and their consequences for considering them good.

It is easy to point to a certain organization by naming the objects that make up a class; however, it can be complex and hard to describe exactly and explicitly the relations that make up that organization. Thus, as regards 'chairs' as a class, it may be easy to describe the organization of a 'chair'; however, it is not so with the class of 'good deeds', unless there is a considerable amount of cultural agreement.

When we speak of living beings, we presuppose something in common between them; otherwise we wouldn't put them in the same class we designate with the name 'living'. What has not been said, however, is: what is that organization that defines them as a class? Our proposition is that living beings are characterized in that, literally, they are continually self-producing. We indicate this process when we call the organization that defines them an *autopoietic organization*. Basically, this organization comes from certain relations that we shall outline and view more easily on the cellular level.

First, the molecular components of a cellular autopoietic unity must be dynamically related in a network of ongoing interactions. Today we know many of the specific chemical transformations in this network, and the biochemist collectively terms them 'cell metabolism'.

Now, what is distinctive about this cellular dynamics compared with any other collection of molecular transformations in natural processes? Interestingly, this cell metabolism produces components which make up the network of transformations that produced them. Some of these components form a boundary, a limit to this network of transformations. In morphologic terms, the structure that makes this cleavage in space possible is called a membrane. Now, this membranous boundary is not a product of cell metabolism in the way that fabric is the product of a fabric-making machine. The reason is that this membrane not only limits the extension of the transformation network that produced its own components but it participates in this network. If it did not have this spatial arrangement, cell metabolism would disintegrate in a molecular mess that would spread out all over and would not constitute a discrete unity such as a cell.

What we have, then, is a unique situation as regards relations of chemical transformations: on the one hand, we see a network of dynamic transformations that produces its own components and that is essential for a boundary; on the other hand, we see a boundary that is essential for the operation of the network of transformations which produced it as a unity (Fig. 20.1).

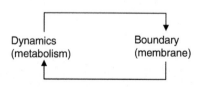

Fig. 20.1   Dynamics and boundary in relation

Note that these are not sequential processes, but two different aspects of a unitary phenomenon. It is not that first there is a boundary, then a dynamics, then a boundary, and so forth. We are describing a type of phenomenon in which the possibility of distinguishing one thing from a whole (something you can see under the microscope, for instance) depends on the integrity of the processes that make it possible. Interrupt (at some point) the cellular metabolic network and you will find that after a while you don't have any more unity to talk about! The most striking feature of an autopoietic system is that it pulls itself up by its own bootstraps and becomes distinct from its environment through its own dynamics, in such a way that both things are inseparable.

Living beings are characterized by their autopoietic organization. They differ from each other in their structure, but they are alike in their organization.

Autonomy and autopoiesis

By realizing what characterizes living beings in their autopoietic organization, we can unify a whole lot of empirical data about their biochemistry and cellular functioning. The concept of autopoiesis, therefore, does not contradict these data. Rather, it is supported by them; it explicitly proposes that such data be interpreted from a specific point of view which stresses that living beings are *autonomous* unities.

We use the word 'autonomy' in its current sense; that is, a system is autonomous if it can specify its own laws, what is proper to it. We are *not* proposing that living beings are the only autonomous entities. Certainly they are not. But one of the most evident features of a living being is its autonomy. We *are* proposing that the mechanism that makes living beings autonomous systems is autopoiesis. This characterizes them as autonomous systems.

The question about autonomy is as old as the question about the living. It is only contemporary biologists who feel uncomfortable over the question of how to understand the autonomy of the living. From our standpoint, however, this question is a guideline to understanding the autonomy of living beings: to understand them, we must understand the organization that defines them as unities. Being aware that living beings are autonomous unities helps to show how their autonomy – usually seen as mysterious and elusive – becomes explicit, for we realize that what defines them as unities is their autopoietic organization, and it is in this autopoietic organization that they become real and specify themselves at the same time.

Our intention, therefore, is to proceed scientifically: if we cannot provide a list that characterizes a living being, why not propose a system that generates all the phenomena proper to a living being? The evidence that an autopoietic unit has exactly all these features becomes evident in the light of what we know about the interdependence between metabolism and cellular structure.

That living beings have an organization, of course, is proper not only to them but also to everything we can analyze as a system. What is distinctive about them, however, is that their organization is such that their only product is themselves, with no separation between producer and product. The being and doing of an autopoietic unity are inseparable, and this is their specific mode of organization.

Like any organization, autopoietic organization can be attained by many different types of components. We have to realize, however, that as regards the molecular origin of terrestrial living beings, only certain molecular species probably possessed the characteristics required for autopoietic unities, thus initiating the structural history to which we ourselves belong. For instance, it was necessary to have molecules capable of forming membranes sufficiently stable and plastic to be, in turn, effective barriers, and to have changing properties for the diffusion of molecules and ions over long periods of time with respect to molecular speeds. Molecules from silicon layers, for instance, are too rigid for them to participate in dynamic unities (cells) in an ongoing and fast molecular interchange with the medium.

It was only at that point in the Earth's history when conditions were right for the forming of organic molecules such as proteins, which have enormous complexity and pliancy, that conditions were right also for the forming of autopoietic unities. In fact, we can assume that when all these sufficient conditions were present in the Earth's history, autopoietic systems formed inevitably.

That moment is the point we can refer to as the moment when life began. This does not mean that it happened in one instance and in one place only; nor can we specify a date for it. All the available evidence leads us to believe that once conditions were ripe for the origin of living systems, they originated many times; that is, many autopoietic unities with many structural variants emerged in many places on the Earth over a period of perhaps many millions of years.

The emergence of autopoietic unities on the face of the Earth is a landmark in the history of our solar system. We have to understand this well. The formation of a unity always determines a number of phenomena associated with the features that define it; we may thus say that each class of unities specific a particular phenomenology. Thus, autopoietic unities specify biology phenomenology as the phenomenology proper of those unities with features distinct from physical phenomenology. This is so, not because autopoietic unities go against any aspect of physical phenomenology – since their molecular components must fulfill all physical laws – but because the phenomena they generate in functioning as autopoietic unities depend on their organization and the way this organization come about, and not on the physical nature of their components (which only determine their space of existence).

Thus, if a cell interacts with molecule X and incorporates it in its processes, what takes place as a result of this interaction is determined not by the properties of molecule X but by the way in which that molecule is 'seen' or taken by the cell as it incorporates the molecule in its autopoietic dynamics. The changes that occur therein as a result of this interaction will be those changes caused by the cell's own structure as a unity. Therefore, inasmuch as the autopoietic organization causes biological phenomenology by bringing about living beings as autonomous unities, a biological phenomenon will be any phenomenon that involves the autopoiesis of at least one living being.

References

Bunnell, P. (2004). Foreword: Maturana Revisited. *Cybernetics and Human Knowing, 11*(2), 5–11.

Capra, F. (1996). *The web of life: A new scientific understanding of living systems.* New York: Anchor Books.

Hayles, N. K. (1999). *How we became posthuman: Virtual bodies in cybernetics, literature, and informatics.* Chicago: University of Chicago Press.

Lettvin, J.Y., Maturana, H.R., McCulloch, W.S., Pitts, W.H. (1959). What the frog's eye tells the frog's brain. *Proceedings of the Institute for Radio Engineers, 47*(11), 1940–1959.

Maturana, H.R. (1988). The search for objectivity or the quest for a compelling argument. *Irish Journal of Psychology, 9*(1):25–82.

Maturana, H.R. (2002). Autopoiesis, structural coupling and cognition: A history of these and other notions in the biology of cognition. *Cybernetics and Human Knowing, 9*(3–4), 5–34.

Maturana, H.R., & Poerksen, B. (2004). *From being to doing: The origins of the biology of cognition.* Heidelberg, Germany: Carl-Auer-Systeme.

Maturana, H. R., & Varela, F. J. (1980). *Autopoiesis and cognition: The realization of the living.* Dordrecht, Netherlands: Reidel.

Maturana, H. R., & Varela, F. J. (1987). *The tree of knowledge: The biological roots of human understanding.* Boston, MA: Shambhala.

Mingers, J. (1995). *Self-producing systems: Implications and applications of autopoiesis.* New York: Plenum Press.

Chapter 21
Niklas Luhmann

Niklas Luhmann was a theoretical sociologist, who built a unified theory of society based on systems theory. He particularly drew upon the tools of second-order cybernetics, notably the theory of autopoiesis. He was extremely prolific, publishing over 50 books and several hundred articles. His research programme, as stated when he took up his professorship in 1968, was "the theory of modern society. Duration 30 years; no costs" (Arnoldi 2001, p. 1). As he died in 1998, having published a theory of modern society the previous year, he achieved this programme precisely.

Luhmann was born in 1927 in Lüneburg, northern Germany. His initial education was in law (at Freiburg in 1949), following which he became a lawyer and then a civil servant. His work allowed him plenty of time for intellectual reading, and eventually led him in 1960 to take a year-long sabbatical at Harvard University where he worked with the American sociologist Talcott Parsons. On returning to Germany, Luhmann moved into an academic career, holding several positions before being appointed as professor of sociology at the newly-formed University of Bielefeld, where he remained until his retirement in 1993 and (as an emeritus professor) until his death in 1998.

Luhmann's work is highly regarded in German social science. On his death, a large number of obituaries were published in mainland European newspapers and magazines, describing him as "the most important social theorist of the 20th century" (Bechmann and Stehr 2002, p. 67). Yet in English-speaking countries his work is not at all well known. This is complicated by language. His two most important books were published in German in 1984 and 1997. One took ten years to appear in English (*Soziale Systeme*, translated as *Social Systems*, Luhmann 1995); the other, widely described as Luhmann's greatest work and the culmination of his efforts to produce a theory of society, is still not available in English (*Die Gesellschaft der Gesellschaft*, 'The Society of Society', Luhmann 1997). For this latter work, those unable to read German are still dependent on secondary sources.

However, even without the issue of language, his work is highly complex. In the introduction to the English translation of *Social Systems*, he himself acknowledges that "the theory's design resembles a labyrinth more than a freeway off into the sunset" (Luhmann 1995, p. lii). Part of the reason for this labyrinthine structure was the way his theory developed, on a very large collection of cross-referenced file-cards (his *Zettelkasten*). Luhmann said that he "spent more time arranging and rearranging his system of file cards than writing books" (Vandenberghe 1999, p. 54), and the non-linear, hypertextual, nature of this way of working can be seen in his ideas, where one flows into another with few breaks. Luhmann's file-card collection was so important to him that he declined professorships at overseas universities on several occasions, afraid that the collection could be lost in an accident while moving (Baecker 2008).

Although Luhmann was passionately devoted to building his theory of society, a colleague recounted that "beyond being a great theorist, he was a great person. He had a lot of patience, towards his topics of study as well as towards his students and friends. Many friends and colleagues appreciated and enjoyed his sense of humour and his contagious smile" (Hornung 1999).

Luhmann's body of work divided into two distinct phases, separated by the publication of *Soziale Systeme* in 1984. Prior to this book, his major influence within systems theory came from Parsons' work (although in a modified form). After this publication, while he still used Parsons' ideas, he was much more strongly influenced by autopoiesis and other concepts connected with second-order cybernetics, especially the work of the logician George Spencer Brown (1969) on the concept of distinction. For reasons of space and its difficulty, we will not discuss Luhmann's use of distinction here. It is well summarised by Seidl and Becker (2006).

In this discussion, we shall largely focus on the post-1984 Luhmann (and especially his use of autopoiesis). He regarded the earlier work as simply a starting point for these later developments, seeing *Soziale Systeme* as "his first real book, the previous ones being part of his 'zero series'" (Baecker 2008). Nonetheless, it is worth briefly mentioning his use of Parsons' ideas. Talcott Parsons, an American, was the first sociologist to make systems theory the centre of his work, with his structural-functionalism. While very influential in the 1950s and early 1960s, Parsons' theory was later widely rejected by sociologists for its lack of account of individual choice and its conservatism. Luhmann retained the concept of function – the division of society into a number of subsystems with different purposes – but replaced Parsons' focus on the conservation of the *structure* of society with a focus on the conservation of the *relationships* within society. While some sociologists still see Luhmann's work as tainted with the technocratic notion of system found in Parsons, for many others Luhmann has rehabilitated systems thinking within sociology.

Luhmann drew on the long Germanic tradition of sociology and social philosophy from Kant onwards. In particular, the work of the phenomenologist Edmund Husserl was crucial to Luhmann's work, especially the centrality he placed on the concept of *meaning* – our understanding and interpretation of ideas. For Luhmann, meaning was the "basic concept" of sociology (Luhmann 1990, p. 21) and indeed of the social sciences and humanities more generally. Strikingly, however, he argued that meaning applies to social systems as well as to individual human beings, as distinct from most social theorists who would argue that only individuals can possess meaning.

This feature of 'meaning' is important given a further key, and controversial, feature of Luhmann's theory. As with many systems thinkers, he makes a clear distinction between different types of systems, and in particular distinguishes four types – machines, organisms, social systems and psychic systems. (The last of these, with its slightly odd sound to the English-speaking reader, refers to the individual human being as a system, as understood through their mind – their 'psyche'.) Social and psychic systems, while highly interdependent, are separate and non-overlapping – each sits in the environment of the other. As Luhmann (1995, p. 59) put it, "persons cannot emerge and continue to exist without social systems, nor can social systems exist without persons". Nonetheless, it is crucial that they are treated as different, and that individuals are not seen as a constituent part of social systems. Luhmann strongly denied that this was an anti-humanist step, but along with his use of Parsons' theories it has led to some of the criticisms of his work.

When Luhmann began to use autopoiesis in his work, Luhmann's approach was not crudely to apply autopoiesis (in Maturana and Varela's original, biological, form) to social systems but rather first of all to abstract the concept of autopoiesis away from the biological realm and then to apply this abstracted concept to social systems. Luhmann argued that living systems are only one form of autopoietic system; others include social and psychic systems. In each case the basic element of the system – that which it continually reproduces to preserve its fundamental organization (the key criterion for autopoiesis) – will vary. For psychic systems, Luhmann argues, this will be thought; for social systems, it will be *communication*. That is, Luhmann treats communication as the fundamental aspect of any kind of social system (including organizations, face-to-face interactions, and society as a whole including its constituent parts).

Communication is an unusual basis for a theory of society, and indeed the only other major social theorist to have used it is Jürgen Habermas (whose debates with Luhmann we will discuss later), although it is the basis of the work of two of the thinkers in this book, Gregory Bateson and Paul Watzlawick. It fits with two of Luhmann's concerns – the importance of meaning (which any communication both creates and is sustained by), and the recasting of Parsons' work away from structure and towards relationship. Any social system, Luhmann argues, exists to communicate and maintains its existence by communicating – when it ceases to communicate it ceases to exist.

In the classical use of the term (that of Claude Shannon), communication refers to the process by which a sender transfers information to a receiver. Luhmann instead used a definition involving three parts: the information (the 'what', the content of the message), the utterance (the 'how' and 'why' – the manner in which it is sent and the intention behind the message), and the understanding (the meaning attributed to it by the receiver). These three parts cannot be separated, and all three must be present for a communication to be said to be occurring.

Luhmann's definition of communication does not include either the sender or the receiver as elements of the communication, although it presupposes the existence of such individuals. Indeed, because both the intention behind the message and the meaning that is understood by the receiver are parts of the communication, more than one individual must be involved in a communication. As Seidl and Becker (2006, p. 19) argue, drawing upon Luhmann (1997), "communication constitutes an *emergent* property of the interaction between *many* (at least two) psychic systems".

Luhmann had a number of critics, within both sociology and systems thinking. His most prominent opponent in sociology was Jürgen Habermas, the key advocate of critical social theory from the late 1960s onwards. Habermas and Luhmann had much in common – similar in age, both highly theoretical, both deeply embedded in the German tradition of sociology with its strong links to two centuries of philosophy. Their initial disagreement arose from Habermas' suspicion that the use of systems concepts would entail a technocratic form of social engineering, as reflected in the title of their initial volume of debates (never translated into English), "Theory of Society or Social Technology?" (Habermas and Luhmann 1971).

There was also a political element to their debates – Habermas' critical theory was clearly left-wing, while Luhmann's work, argues Arnoldi (2001, p. 2) was "very far from being critical theory. It is often described as dispassionate or neutral, and at times tends towards the conservative". This was partly related to the conservatism that we have already discussed in Parsons' ideas but also from Luhmann's own stance on the maintenance of society. Luhmann was not part of the political right either, however, and became increasingly interested in environmental issues: his work on ecological communication (Luhmann 1989) had a big influence on the Green Party in Germany.

The debates between Luhmann and Habermas had a strong influence on the thinking of both. Habermas shifted his position to incorporate some aspects of systems theory in the second volume of his greatest work (Habermas 1987). For Luhmann's part, the Parsonian view of systems theory reflected in their debates was already one that Luhmann was moving away from, and the dialogue with Habermas helped him to move further, until he reached the stance reflected in *Social Systems*. Given Habermas' fame, especially in the English-speaking academic world, the debates also brought Luhmann to the attention of a wider public.

Luhmann's use, and adaptation, of autopoiesis has also brought criticism from within the systems community. Humberto Maturana once said to Luhmann, "thank you for having made me famous in Germany … but I disagree with the way in which you are using my ideas" (Maturana and Poerksen 2004, p. 106). Specifically, he disagreed with Luhmann's use of communication as a central concept and his treatment of the psychic system as separate from the social system, arguing that "autopoiesis takes place in a domain in which the interactions of the elements constituting it bring forth elements of the same kind … communications, however, presuppose human beings that communicate" (Maturana and Poerksen 2004, p. 107). Luhmann's partial reply to this was that communication "is genuinely social insofar as it presupposes the involvement of a multitude of psychic systems [i.e. individual human beings] but, or better because of that, it cannot be attributed as a unit to a single psychic system" (Luhmann 1997, translated by Seidl and Becker 2006, p. 19).

It is clear from the above criticisms that Luhmann's work was somewhat controversial in places, and that his project to create a complete theory of society based on systems concepts was not seen as successful by everyone. His work was highly theoretical and fairly difficult. Nonetheless, he reached further in the field of social systems than any thinker before him, and left a set of highly important ideas for understanding society. Summarising Luhmann's work cannot be done briefly, but a colleague summarised key aspects of his life and personality as follows (Hornung 1999):

> Luhmann spent most of his life in the plains of Northern Germany, not on the coast, but at Lüneburg, Hannover, Münster, and Bielefeld, where the sea is beyond the horizon, sending the winds to sweep up the skies, blue and grey. Horizons, after all, become one of the key concepts in his theory. It seems they were a key concept in his life too, as again and again he moved towards new challenges.

Reading from Luhmann's work

Luhmann, N. (1993). Ecological Communication: Coping with the Unknown. *Systems Practice*, 6(5), 527–539. Copyright ©Springer.
Extract from pages 531–534.

I have used recent developments in systems theory, particularly those ideas associated with how a system produces and reproduces itself in order to achieve an understanding of society. A system does not have an own essence; it should not be treated as an object exhibiting its own peculiar characteristics. Rather, it should be seen as something which, through its own operations, produces and reproduces a difference between the system and an environment. It continues to produce this difference by using the distinction itself, which allows it to distinguish what is internal to the system and what is external. By using this approach it is possible to rewrite the theory of evolution by explaining those systems that emerge and, in the course of achieving this, are able to maintain themselves successfully. One such system is life itself. The biochemistry of life can reproduce life within a living cell or within a living organism, using its own components to produce continually those components and constitute in the space where they exist the boundaries of the system. Life is indeed a good example. The biochemistry of life forms the operation which makes a difference between an organism and its environment.

With this theoretical structure in place, the nagging question becomes 'Are we able to find a similar type of operation which produces a social system?' It is my opinion that only communication can be considered as a serious candidate accounting for the production and reproduction of social systems. We cannot rely on the concept of action because this depends too much on the process of attribution and constantly sees the individual as a determinant actor. Communication, on the other hand, is inherently social and thus it follows that society is composed of communications among human beings.

We can define society as the all-encompassing social system that orders all possible communications. This necessitates that we must exclude everything but communications from our concept of society. This means the exclusion not only of such natural facts as islands, oceans, and technologies, etc., but also of human beings, i.e., concrete individuals and their conscious processes. These aspects all belong to the environment of the social system of society. They must remain aspects of the environment; otherwise we could not formulate communication as the fundamental social operation which accounts for the production and reproduction of society. If we are going to analyze the environmental relations of the system of society, we cannot include psychical processes and individual conscious activities as definitive parts of society. Nor is this particularly necessary since communication can take place without us knowing what is happening in the minds of those with whom we choose to communicate.

Social systems use communications by highly selective processes. With the use of communications, we can question and answer, understand and misunderstand. Again, this type of thinking has links with research in neurophysiology and research concerning the biochemistry of cells. If we consider the concept of operational closure which has been explained in cognitive theory, we can appreciate that operational closure is an achievement of system building. This is not to say that operational closure allows us to isolate a system so as to study it and generalize about its regularities through the observation of its inputs and outputs. We might have cause to attribute many different regularities and causal relations, but only the system itself can produce its own operations. The system is sovereign with respect to the construction of identities and differences.

My next step in this argument requires a decisive conceptual innovation because we have to ask, 'How under the conditions described above can we think about the relationship between a system and an environment?' There is a concept in the writings of Humberto Maturana (1982) which allows us to appreciate the relationship between a system and its environment. It is the very technical concept of structural coupling. It is vital because it can explain how organisms are able to survive given the physical conditions imposed by the earth. For instance, if temperatures were slightly different, or if the planet was either very large or very small, then we could not survive. This way of thinking should not imply that our movement is determined by physical forces in a deterministic way. Certainly, we can decide where to go so long as it satisfies the condition of structural coupling. And it follows that if we drastically change the nature of this structural coupling, then we might endanger ourselves to the point where we are unable to survive. This is roughly what Maturana's work tells us, and I would like to add the important dimension that structural couplings are highly selective, including but also excluding influences of the environment on the system.

If this type of thinking is applied to ideas about communication, it prompts the question – What are the structural couplings of communication? We have already argued to the effect that psychical and conscious activity is not part of the social system. This allows us to reformulate a theory of society in terms that dictate that the processes of societal communication depend upon structural coupling with consciousness. To reiterate, consciousness is not part of the system; it is an essential environmental condition. We can certainly acknowledge that conscious activity operates in all communications, but it does not determine communication – it can only irritate communication processes.

Normally we think that conscious activity tells us what to say and what not to say, but the theory I am proposing here suggests that communication itself decides what can be communicated. The human conscious aspect exists to irritate or to make problems for the system. It forces the system to adapt or preadapt to potential irritations. For instance, I have to adapt my argument to the possibilities of it being understood. There may indeed be difficulties in being understood, but the system somehow arranges itself in view of these irritations provoked by consciousness. It is difficult to assume that a human can communicate as an actor; for example, you might consider that the way in which I am now communicating to the reader would definitively make me the communicating subject. But to explain the process of communication in this way is unsatisfactory. It makes use of a rather artificial and causal assumption, adjudging me as the communicating actor. This is difficult because the recipient of communication knows nothing of my personality and can tell little of what I am actually thinking. Nevertheless, we can continue to communicate, and during this process we will inevitably produce understandings and misunderstandings.

So far there are two important aspects to this evolving theory. First, I mentioned that structural coupling can explain why consciousness can irritate but not determine communication processes. And second, because we know that communication is structurally coupled with consciousness, this tells us something about selectivity. It suggests that there is a vast environment which has no access to communicative processes. In fact there are only two accessible routes by which communication can be accessed or 'changed'. One, of course, is through the idea of irritation; the other is destructive of possible communications. For instance, we can spill ink on a manuscript, but this does not create any new text; it just makes existing text illegible. Similarly our libraries might be burned down but in the ashes we do not find any new messages. It seems that there is a great deal that can destroy communication processes, though we still have recourse to the irritation of such processes via structural couplings with consciousness.

With this theory in place, we can see how society might possibly react to such areas of concern as ecological problems. I have explained how society organizes and restricts itself to particular communications. Individuals have the opportunity to irritate these societal communications, but bearing in mind that the population of the planet amounts to some 5 billion people, we need to understand something of the content of these communications and who actually communicates them. Evidently it is a question of how an individual can communicate the communications that he or she sees. At this juncture I will elaborate a little more on the notion of structural coupling and the implications of operational closure.

Consciousness can be said to be coupled tightly to the brain. The brain constantly requires living cells, and these in turn require a working organism to continue, and so the organism is structurally coupled with its environment, and so on. The point is that these relationships are highly selective and are the result of evolution. In point of fact, the relationships between systems and their environments are much more complex and much more artificial or improbable. This is of course a long way from the conventional idea that human beings can get together and talk about action and then reflect on the quality of this action.

References

Arnoldi, J. (2001). Niklas Luhmann: An introduction. *Theory, Culture and Society, 18*(1), 1–13.

Baecker, D. (2008). Niklas Luhmann. International Society for the Systems Sciences. http://projects.isss.org/Main/NiklasLuhmannByDirkBaecker. Accessed 13 Jan 2009.

Bechmann, G., & Stehr, N. (2002). The legacy of Niklas Luhmann. *Society, 39*(2), 67–75.

Habermas, J. (1987). *The theory of communicative action vol. 2: Lifeworld and system: A critique of functionalist reason.* Cambridge: Polity Press.

Habermas, J., & Luhmann, N. (1971). *Theorie der Gesellschaft oder Sozialtechnologie: Was leistet die Systemforschung?* Frankfurt am Main: Suhrkamp.

Hornung, B. (1999). Obituary: Niklas Luhmann. *Bulletin of the International Sociological Association,* 78–79.

Luhmann, N. (1989). *Ecological communication.* Cambridge, UK: Polity Press.

Luhmann, N. (1990). *Essays on self-reference.* New York: Columbia University Press.

Luhmann, N. (1993). Ecological communication: Coping with the unknown. *Systems Practice, 6*(5), 527–539.

Luhmann, N. (1995). *Social systems.* Stanford, CA: Stanford University Press.

Luhmann, N. (1997). *Die Gesellschaft der Gesellschaft.* Frankfurt am Main: Suhrkamp.

Maturana, H. R. (1982). *Erkennen: Die Organisation und Verkoperung von Wirklichkeit.* Braunschweig, Germany: Vieweg.

Maturana, H. R., & Poerksen, B. (2004). *From being to doing: The origins of the biology of cognition.* Heidelberg, Germany: Carl-Auer-Systeme.

Seidl, D., & Becker, K. H. (2006). Organizations as distinction generating and processing systems: Niklas Luhmann's contribution to organization studies. *Organization, 13*(1), 9–35.

Spencer Brown, G. (1969). *Laws of form.* London: Allen and Unwin.

Vandenberghe, F. (1999). Niklas Luhmann, 1927–1998: Systemic supertheorist of the social. *Radical Philosophy, 94,* 54–56.

Chapter 22
Paul Watzlawick

Paul Watzlawick made significant advances in applying a systems approach in a number of related fields: family therapy, communications theory, and change management. His ideas were firmly rooted both in theory and in practical experience, especially as a psychotherapist. His many writings included several books which are highly engaging and easily read. A colleague summed up his work and personality as follows (Ray 2007, p. 416):

> Through his writings and countless teaching seminars, this gentle man brought a clear and unequivocal message about the relational and contextual nature of human behaviour. Articulate and charming with old-school bearing, this brilliant yet unassuming man was the ideal ambassador to the world for the interactional view pioneered by the Palo Alto Group.

Watzlawick was born in 1921 in Villach, Austria, studying philosophy and modern languages at the University of Venice, where he gained his Ph.D. in 1949. He then moved to Zürich where he studied psychotherapy at the C.G. Jung Institute and subsequently worked as a therapist. From 1957 to 1960 he taught psychotherapy and psychiatry at the University of El Salvador and at Temple University in Philadelphia. In 1960, he met Don Jackson, who had founded the Mental Research Institute (MRI) in Palo Alto, California in the previous year, and Watzlawick moved to work at MRI, where most of his major ideas developed. He continued to work with MRI until shortly before his death. From 1967, he was also professor of psychiatry (later emeritus) at Stanford University. Watzlawick died in 2007 in Palo Alto.

The Mental Research Institute was formed as an offshoot of the projects led by Gregory Bateson on human communication and schizophrenia. Many of the key staff from Bateson's projects were involved in the forming of MRI – Don Jackson, its founder, had been Bateson's clinical consultant. Bateson played no formal part in MRI, although his ideas were foundational to its work.

The work of the MRI on family therapy, with a very strong systemic orientation, was to become extremely important in the field, and is often referred to as the *strategic* school (or simply the Palo Alto school) of family therapy. The term strategic refers to "any therapy in which the clinician actively designs interventions to fit the problem" (Hoffman 1981, p. 271). Those working at MRI approached this form of therapy with the tools of cybernetics, especially in the forms discussed by Bateson,

M. Ramage and K. Shipp, *Systems Thinkers,*
© The Open University 2009. Published in association with Springer-Verlag London Limited

such as information, communication, feedback and homeostasis. As Wilder (1979, pp. 172–173) notes, contrasting the approach with the individualistic perspective of Freudian psychoanalysis, "the focus of [MRI's] model is interactional, i.e. it considers the individual within the nexus of his or her most important relationships, most typically the interactional system of the family".

It is important to note that while Watzlawick was one of the key members of MRI, he was by no means its only important member. Other staff of MRI who made an important contribution to family therapy, communications theory and psychotherapy in general included Richard Fisch, Jay Haley, Virginia Satir, Janet Beavin and John Weakland, as well as Don Jackson. Watzlawick has made many important contributions, but it would be misleading to suggest that he is the sole originator of some of the ideas we will discuss on family therapy.

Family therapy is also a wider movement than the work of the MRI. Many therapists have had the idea that if they are to understand and improve an individual's psychological problems, then they need to investigate that individual's key relationships, especially their family. This concept crystallised into a movement in the 1960s in the United States, and from its start has been tied up with the use of systems ideas. In particular, the family is treated as an open system (Jones 1993), with the characteristics of wholeness (interdependence between family members), non-summativity (that the whole is great than the sum of the parts), feedback (behaviour from members of a family feeding into future behaviour of the family) and equifinality (where the same endpoints can be reached from many different starting points).

Two major schools of family therapy that are frequently identified in addition to the strategic school of MRI are the structural school and the Milan school. We will discuss the Milan school below, as it has interesting similarities and differences to Watzlawick's approach. The structural school, associated with the therapist Salvador Minuchin of Philadelphia, considers the structure of the family as a system (its boundaries, key subsystems and hierarchies) and looks for weaknesses in that structure. There are also many approaches associated with individual therapists and their immediate colleagues which we will not consider here.

Returning to Watzlawick's own work, it can be summed up in three themes, each associated with some of his major publications (often co-authored) – human communication, change management and brief therapy, and constructivism.

His work on communication theory, summarised in the book *Pragmatics of Human Communication* (Watzlawick et al. 1967), was ground-breaking and widely read. It presents an approach to the understanding of human communication, derived explicitly from Bateson's work (and thus in cybernetics) but also with a strongly therapeutic background. It emphasises the importance of 'metacommunication', our communication about communication – that all human communications have aspects of relationship built into them as well as the ostensible message we are conveying. Thus "one cannot *not* communicate" (Watzlawick et al. 1967, p. 51) as all human interaction, even ignoring someone, sends a message to other people.

Watzlawick and his co-authors argued that family interactions are ongoing open systems, similar to the definitions of Jones (1993) discussed above but with a stronger emphasis on the role of feedback and of homeostasis (the goal of maintaining the system in a steady state). They also emphasised the importance of paradox – putting an individual in a state where they are required to simultaneously believe in two or more mutually contradictory items of information, at different levels, and to act accordingly. A clear example of a paradox is the injunction to 'Be Spontaneous!' which if obeyed explicitly invalidates itself (as to obey would not be a spontaneous act) – see the reading below from Watzlawick's work. Paradox is considered, in the MRI approach, to be the source of much that is harmful in the dynamics of family systems. Identifying and 'solving' paradoxes is one of Watzlawick's key themes across a number of his works, although in *Pragmatics of Human Communication* and later work he emphasises that paradox can also be used by the therapist as a form of intervention.

It is worth noting that, as with Bateson, the Palo Alto group generally were not seeking simply to discuss communication in situations where it was not working, but rather to discuss communication is general. As Wilder (1979, p. 171) notes, "the emphasis on pathologies serves primarily to gain an understanding of the process by focusing upon the extremes". It is also notable that, while the work of *Pragmatics of Human Communication* draws quite explicitly on Bateson, and credits him on many occasions, it was not at all to Bateson's liking. Stagoll (2005, p. 1036) has written that

> Bateson also felt pre-empted by his research team with the publication of 'Pragmatics of Human Communication' in 1967. This book went on to become the classic text explicating the new ideas of communication theory. [Jay] Haley reported Bateson saying the book 'stole thirty of his ideas'. *Pragmatics* presented communication theory and practice in isolation from its larger cultural and evolutionary contexts. This did make the ideas very clear but was anathema to Bateson.

The second major theme of Watzlawick's work concerned change and how to handle it effectively. This work arose in the context of brief therapy, the idea of creating short (a small number of sessions) but effective psychotherapeutic interventions. Brief therapy was pioneered at MRI by Richard Fisch, one of Watzlawick's co-authors on the book *Change: principles of problem formation and problem resolution* (Watzlawick et al. 1974) which first reported and extended lessons learnt from brief therapy that apply to a wide range of change situations.

Drawing on Russell and Whitehead's theory of logical types (as did Bateson for his work on levels of learning), Watzlawick et al. distinguish between two types of change: "one that occurs within a given system which itself remains unchanged, and one whose occurrence changes the system itself" (Watzlawick et al. 1974, p. 10). They refer to these two types as first- and second-order change. There is also a clear parallel with Ashby's two types of feedback loops, which formed the basis for the work of Argyris and Schön on double-loop learning, and Watzlawick et al. briefly discuss links to Ashby's work.

For Watzlawick et al., second-order change is much more important in therapeutic situations. They argue that it "is applied to what in the first-order change perspective appears to be a solution, because in the second-order perspective this 'solution' reveals itself as the keystone of the problem whose solution is attempted"

(Watzlawick et al. 1974, p. 82). However, second-order change can only occur from a perspective outside the system (as it changes the rules of the system) and it "usually appears weird, unexpected, and uncommonsensical" (Watzlawick et al. 1974, p. 83). One of the key techniques they draw upon for second-order change is reframing: changing the fundamental ways in which a situation is understood, intellectually and emotionally, so that the assumptions of those involved become quite different. These concepts of second-order change and reframing are useful in many different interventions beyond therapy, and are applicable in any kind of change management situation – they have been widely used for organisational change.

The third major theme of Watzlawick's work has been that of constructivism – the concept that reality, or at least all the ways human beings can approach it, is constructed through human perceptions, sense-making and interaction. This concept, which is also discussed in the chapters on Heinz von Foerster and Humberto Maturana, sounds highly philosophical. In Watzlawick's use, it is extremely practical, and strongly linked to therapy (as well as resting on his earlier work). In the foreword to *How Real is Real?* (Watzlawick 1976, p. xi), he talks of "the way in which communication creates reality" and argues that:

> our everyday, traditional ideas of reality are delusions which we spend substantial parts of our daily lives shoring up ... the most dangerous delusion of all is that there is only one reality. What there are, in fact, are many different versions of reality, some of which are contradictory, but all of which are the results of communication and not reflections of eternal, objective truths.

He expanded upon this theme through an exploration of how confusion (involuntary breakdowns of communication) and disinformation (deliberate withholding of information) can lead people to understanding the world in the ways that lead to bizarre or harmful results. His approach in this book, as in a number of his later books, is anecdotal and very readable: he tells stories and recounts relevant passages of literature, in the same way that Bateson did in his later work. He developed these therapeutically into what he described as "the therapy of the as-if", drawing on the early twentieth century philosopher Karl Vaihinger, who argued that we generally work on the basis of a large set of interrelated assumptions about the world – *as if* the world were a particular way. In an interview, Watzlawick described his method as:

> I always assume that a person coming to see me lives in a [personal] reality, which has, for some reason or other, become a source of suffering. All of a sudden, the world has lost its meaning, the personal constructions have collapsed or are no longer functioning. I try to change these distressing constructions by interventions and to replace them by less painful or even pleasant or joyful ones. (Poerksen 2004, p. 183).

As well as his own development of constructivist ideas, Watzlawick played an important role in bringing together others involved in this perspective. His edited book *The invented reality* (Watzlawick 1984) was one of the first collections of papers on constructivism and is still widely cited. It was also through Watzlawick that Heinz von Foerster, after having retired from the University of Illinois and moved to California, became involved with MRI and with family therapy more widely. Von Foerster's work was to have considerable influence in family therapy, and for this reason he often said in later life (only semi-flippantly) that he "was an invention of Paul Watzlawick" (Broecker 2005, p. 323).

We have already mentioned the Milan school of family therapy, the work of which makes for interesting comparisons with that of Watzlawick. This school, originally consisting of four therapists led by Mara Selvini Palazzoli, began its work in the mid-1970s, and has been very influential in Europe, especially the UK. It originally stressed issues of paradox, communication, circularity and the neutrality of the therapist – ideas developed both from and in reaction to those of the Palo Alto School. As the 1980s progressed, the Milan school split into a number of groups with different views, some of whom became more influenced by the work of von Foerster and Maturana, drawing explicitly upon second-order cybernetics (with a focus on the observer and on subtle interventions) instead of the first-order cybernetics of the early Palo Alto work (with its focus on maintaining homeostasis). Some of this group have been very critical of the early Palo Alto work, and especially the early books of Watzlawick. In fact, Watzlawick's later views, with their strongly constructivist flavour, became much closer to those of the Milan school.

Paul Watzlawick consistently sought to ask questions about the nature of communication between individuals (both healthy and pathological), the ways in which people understand the world; and to help people through the many interesting answers he has discovered to those questions. While his intent was deeply serious and humanistic, his means of expressing it was highly accessible. Through a description of his Austrian compatriots, he described his own understanding of the world and way of working as follows (Watzlawick 1983, p. 9):

> In the heart of Europe there was once a great empire. It was composed of so many and so widely different cultures that no commonsense solution to any problem could ever be reached, and absurdity became the only possible way of life…. The great empire is now a tiny country, but absurdity has remained its inhabitants' outlook on life, and the author of these pages is no exception. For all of them, life is hopeless, but not serious.

Reading from Watzlawick's work

Sometimes confusion is inherent in the structure of the message itself. This is best introduced by examples:

1. According to a very ancient story, which has vexed philosophers and theologians alike, the devil once questioned God's omnipotence by asking Him to create a rock so enormously big that even God Himself could not lift it. What was God to do? If He cannot lift the rock, He is no longer omnipotent; if He can lift it, He is unable to make it big enough.

2. When asked what he thought that Mona Lisa smiled about, an eight year-old is supposed to have said, "Well, one evening when Mr. Lisa came home from work, he asked her, 'What kind of a day did you have, dear?' And Mona Lisa smiled and said, 'Imagine, Leonardo da Vinci came and painted my portrait.'"

3. There is a popular bumper sticker that reads: "My convictions are not for public display".

4. "I'm glad I don't like cauliflower, because if I did, I'd eat it, and I hate the stuff." (Anonymous)

5. The philosopher Karl Popper claims, tongue in cheek, that he once sent the following letter to a colleague:

Dear M.G.,

Kindly return this card to me, but make sure to write "Yes", or to put some other mark of your choice, in the blank rectangle to the left of my signature if, and only if, you feel justified in predicting that, upon its return, I shall find this space still empty.

Yours sincerely,

K. R. Popper (1963)

If by now the reader feels a strange paralysis creeping into his mind, he has already had a direct experience of this form of confusion. Let us look at still another example, this one from *Mary Poppins*, by Pamela L. Travers. Mary Poppins, an English nanny, has taken her two little charges, Jane and Michael, to a gingerbread shop owned by Mrs. Corry, a tiny, witchlike old woman with two large, sad daughters, Fannie and Annie. The following conversation develops:

"I suppose, my dear" – she turned to Mary Poppins, whom she appeared to know very well – "I suppose you've come for some gingerbread?"

"That's right, Mrs. Corry", said Mary Poppins politely.

"Good. Have Fannie and Annie given you any?" She looked at Jane and Michael as she said this.

"No, Mother", said Miss Fannie meekly.

"We were just going to, Mother –" began Miss Annie in a frightened whisper.

At that Mrs. Corry drew herself up to her full height and regarded her gigantic daughters furiously. Then she said in a soft, fierce, terrifying voice:

"Just going to? Oh, *indeed*! That is very interesting. And who, may I ask, Annie, gave you permission to give away my gingerbread?"

"Nobody, Mother. And I didn't give it away. I only thought –"

"You only thought! That is *very* kind of you. But I will thank you not to think. I can do all the thinking that is necessary here!" said Mrs. Corry in her soft, terrible voice. Then she burst into a harsh cackle of laughter. "Look at her! Just look at her! Cowardy-custard! Crybaby!" she shrieked, pointing her knotty finger at her daughter.

Jane and Michael turned and saw a large tear coursing down Miss Annie's huge, sad face, and they did not like to say anything, for, in spite of her tininess, Mrs. Corry made them feel rather small and frightened. (Travers 1934).

Within half a minute Mrs. Corry has managed to block poor Annie in all three areas of human functioning: acting, thinking and feeling. She first implies that to give the children some gingerbread would have been the right thing to do. When her daughters are about to apologize for not having done this yet, she suddenly denies their right to take that action. Annie tries to defend herself by pointing out that she did not actually do it, but only thought of doing it. Mrs. Corry promptly lets her know that she is not supposed to think. The way the mother expresses her displeasure leaves no doubt that this is an important matter and her daughter had better be sorry about what happened. With this she manages to drive Annie to tears and then immediately ridicules her feelings.

Let us not make the mistake of shrugging off this story because it is fiction, and children's fiction to boot. Research into the communication styles of families with a member who has been diagnosed as psychiatrically disturbed or into larger human conflicts shows that this pattern appears very frequently (Bateson et al. 1956). It is called a double bind. What a double bind and the earlier examples have in common is that they are all structured like the paradoxes, or antinomies, in formal logic. But while for most of us formal paradoxes are merely amusing recollections from our school days, the paradoxes contained in communication are of stark practical importance. Very much as in the Mary Poppins story, there are three basic variations of the paradoxical theme:

1. If an individual is punished for correct perception of the outside world or of himself by a significant other (e.g., a child by a parent), he will learn to distrust the data of his senses. A predicament of this kind arises when, say, an alcoholic father demands that his children see him as a gentle, loving parent, even or especially when he comes home drunk and threatens them all with violence. The children are then forced to perceive reality not as it looks to them, but as their father defines it for them. A person who has repeatedly been exposed to this kind of confusion will find it very difficult to behave appropriately in many life situations and may spend inordinate amounts of time trying to find out how he 'should' see reality. Examined out of its interpersonal context, his behavior would satisfy the diagnostic criteria of schizophrenia.

2. If an individual is expected by a significant other to have feelings different from those he actually experiences, he will eventually feel guilty for being unable to feel what he is told he ought to feel in order to be approved of by the other person. This guilt may itself be labeled one of the feelings he should not have. A dilemma of this kind arises most frequently when a child's occasional normal sadness (or disappointment or fatigue) is construed by a parent as a silent imputation of parental failure. The parent typically reacts with the message "After all we have done for you, you ought to be happy". Sadness thus becomes associated with badness and ingratitude. In his fruitless attempts not to feel unhappy, the child displays behavior which, examined out of context, satisfies the diagnostic criteria of depression. Depression also occurs when an individual feels, or is held, responsible for something over which he has no control (e.g., marital conflict between his parents, the illness or failure of a parent or sibling, or his

own inability to meet parental expectations that exceed his physical and/or emotional resources).
3. If a significant other gives injunctions that both demand and prohibit certain actions, a paradoxical situation arises in which the individual (again, notably a child) can obey only by disobeying. The prototype of this is: "Do what I say, not what I would like you to do". This is the message given by a mother who wants her teen-age son to be both law-abiding and a daredevil. The likely result is behavior that, examined out of context, satisfies the social definition of delinquency. Other examples are parents who place great value on winning by any means, fair or foul, but tell the child that "one should always be honest"; or a mother who begins to warn her daughter at a very early age of the dangers and ugliness of sex, but insists that she be "popular" with boys.

There is a fourth variation of this theme, and it is probably the most frequent in human interaction. It occurs whenever somebody demands of another person behavior that by its very nature must be spontaneous but now cannot be because it has been demanded. 'Be spontaneous' paradoxes, as they are called, range in intensity from mild nuisances to tragic traps, depending on the importance of the need expressed through them. It is one of the shortcomings of human communication that there is no way in which the spontaneous fulfillment of a need can be elicited from another person without creating this kind of self-defeating paradox. A wife who needs a sign of affection from her husband eventually tells him, "I wish you would sometimes bring me flowers". The request is quite understandable, but by making it, she has irreversibly ruined her chances of getting what she wants: if her husband disregards her request, she will feel dissatisfied; if he now brings her flowers, she will also be dissatisfied, because he did not do it of his own accord.

Very much the same impasse arises between a child and his parents when they think he is not assertive enough. In one way or another they signal: "Don't be so obedient". Again this leaves only two alternatives, both unacceptable: either the child remains unassertive (in which case the parents will be dissatisfied because he is not obeying them) or he becomes more assertive (in which case they will be discontent because he is doing the right thing for the wrong reason – that is, he is obeying them). A person in this situation cannot win, but neither can the originator of the paradoxical request.

(A variation of the 'Be spontaneous' theme, or rather its converse, considered a 'nice touch' by certain hotel managers, is shown on the opposite page [a drawing of an unhappy waitress wearing a badge expressing pleasure at the customer's presence]. Not only is the welcome expressed by the lapel button disqualified (contradicted) by the waitress's facial expression, but the statement itself, "We're glad you're here", is further disqualified by the way it is communicated. A welcome is meaningful only if it is given individually and spontaneously. But as a written message, worn by every employee of the hotel as part of the uniform, it is not simply meaningless, it gives the guest a good idea of the kind of 'personalized' service he can expect. Here the paradox is contained not in a *demand* for spontaneous behavior, but in the indiscriminate, blanket *offer* of such behavior.)

The 'Be spontaneous' pattern is a universal paradox. As recent advances in logic, especially in the computer sciences but also in pure mathematics, have shown, many seemingly unambiguous concepts are ultimately paradoxical (e.g., computability, provability, consistency, probability). The same holds true for more general concepts, such as spontaneity, trust, sanity or even power.

References

Bateson, G., Jackson, D.D., Haley, J., Weakland, J.H. (1956). Toward a theory of Schizophrenia. *Behavioral Science, 1*(4), 251–264.

Broecker, M. (2005). Introduction: Continuing the magic. *Kybernetes, 34*(3/4), 321–329.

Hoffman, L. (1981). *Foundations of family therapy: A conceptual framework for systems change.* New York: Basic Books.

Jones, E. (1993). *Family systems therapy: Developments in the Milan-Systemic therapies.* Chichester, UK: John Wiley.

Poerksen, B. (2004). *The certainty of uncertainty: Dialogues introducing constructivism.* Exeter, UK: Imprint Academic.

Popper, K.R. (1963). A comment on the new prediction paradox. *British Journal for the Philosophy of Science, 13*(1), 51.

Ray, W. (2007). In Homage to Paul Watzlawick. *Family Process, 46*(3), 415–417.

Stagoll, B. (2005). Gregory Bateson (1904–1980): A reappraisal. *Australian and New Zealand Journal of Psychiatry, 39*(11–12), 1036–1045.

Travers, P. L. (1934). *Mary Poppins.* New York: Harcourt Brace.

Watzlawick, P., Beavin, J. H., Jackson, D. D. (1967). *Pragmatics of human communication: A study of interactional patterns, pathologies, and paradoxes.* New York: W.W. Norton & Company.

Watzlawick, P., Weakland, J.H., Fisch, R. (1974). *Change: Principles of problem formation and problem resolution.* New York: W.W. Norton & Company.

Watzlawick, P. (1976). *How real is real? Confusion, disinformation, communication.* New York: Random House.

Watzlawick, P. (1983). *The situation is hopeless, but not serious: The pursuit of unhappiness.* New York: W.W. Norton & Company.

Watzlawick, P. (Ed). (1984). *The invented reality: How do we know what we believe we know? Contributions to constructivism.* New York: W.W. Norton & Company.

Wilder, C. (1979). The Palo Alto Group: Difficulties and directions of the interactional view for human communication research. *Human Communication Research, 5*(2), 171–186.

Complexity Theory

Modelling highly complicated and interconnected physical and human systems, focusing on self-organisation and emergence

Chapter 23
Ilya Prigogine

Ilya Prigogine was a chemist and physicist. He made enormous advances in the field of thermodynamics, historically the study of the behaviour of energy, heat and work in physical systems. His theory of dissipative structures, which describes the self-organising activity of systems 'far from equilibrium', has been foundational in complexity theory. He both drew upon systems theory and advanced it in important ways, particularly regarding systems in the physical world. His ideas have also been applied to human systems in several disciplines. McMillan (2004, p. 27) describes his work as follows: "Instead of a world where systems ran down and were subject to an ongoing deterioration, he showed that systems were essentially non-linear, dynamic and able to transform themselves into new states of being."

Prigogine was born in January 1917 in Moscow, shortly before the Russian revolution. His family "had a difficult relationship with the new regime" (Prigogine 1977), being both Jewish and merchants, and left Russia in 1921, initially for Germany but settling in Belgium in 1929. Prigogine was educated and lived the rest of his life in Brussels, becoming a Belgian citizen in 1949. His university education was at the Université Libre de Bruxelles (Free University of Brussels), where he took his Ph.D. in chemistry in 1941, and where he became a professor for the rest of his life. He died in 2003 in Brussels, at the age of 86.

Prigogine had two major academic affiliations for most of his working life. He was director of the International Solvay Institutes for Chemistry and Physics in Brussels from 1959 onwards. He was also based in the USA, as professor of physics and chemical engineering at the University of Texas in Austin, where in 1967 he founded the Centre for Statistical Mechanics. He continued to direct both institutes until his death. He was active in many scientific societies, and in 1988 served as president of the International Society for Systems Sciences.

He received many awards. Most notably, he was awarded the Nobel prize for chemistry in 1977, for his work on dissipative structures. This led to enormous popularity in Belgium – it is said that "no restaurant in Brussels would allow him to pay for a meal" (Brennan 2003) – and he was granted the title of Viscount in 1989 by the King of Belgium. He also received many other scientific and political awards from countries including the UK, Sweden, Spain, Russia, France, Japan and Italy. He was awarded the Norbert Wiener Gold Medal by the World Organisation of Systems and Cybernetics in 1999.

Prigogine had wide interests beyond the purely academic. He was a keen piano player and collector of art (especially ancient Chinese and pre-Columbian American). A colleague writing an obituary called him "a modern equivalent of a humanist of the Renaissance period" (Goldbeter 2003, p. 259), and in his autobiography for the Nobel prize, he wrote that:

> as I left [high school], my interest was more focused on history and archaeology, not to mention music, especially piano. According to my mother, I was able to read musical scores before I read printed words. And, today, my favourite pastime is still piano playing, although my free time for practice is becoming more and more restricted. (Prigogine 1977).

Prigogine's work was extensive and wide-ranging within the physical sciences, and this discussion will only touch on aspects of it which are most relevant to systems ideas. His contribution to systems thinking was very significant: he carried on the *scientific* tradition of general systems theory, and gave this respectability through his Nobel prize. Just as Ludwig von Bertalanffy was strongly inspired by thermodynamics in the formulation of general systems theory, so Prigogine's work on thermodynamics drew upon and extended Bertalanffy's theory of open systems.

Most important for our purposes is the theory of dissipative structures. Classical thermodynamics deals with the behaviour of energy in closed systems in a state of equilibrium (or close to it). It is in this context that the second law of thermodynamics – that entropy (disorder) always increases through the dissipation of energy – was described. However, many physical systems are open to energy entering and leaving from beyond the system; and many are in a non-equilibrium state. These were studied by a number of scientists in the first half of the twentieth century, notably by Théophile de Donder, Prigogine's mentor and Ph.D. supervisor.

Prigogine's interest was in the thermodynamics of systems that are 'far from equilibrium' –those where the energy levels are constantly changing and which are characterised by instability rather than stability. Open systems that are far from equilibrium are constantly dissipating energy to their environment, which leads to their self-organisation into complex forms of order (as opposed to increasing disorder as happens with dissipation in a classic thermodynamic closed system). This combination of constant change with emerging order, which might seem paradoxical, is summarised by the term 'dissipative structure'. As Capra (1996) remarks, this combination of terms in many ways resembles Ludwig von Bertalanffy's coining, in general systems theory, of the key term *Fliessgleichgewicht* (usually translated 'dynamic equilibrium', but literally 'flowing balance') which similarly puts together concepts of flux and constancy. Prigogine and Stengers (1984, p. 12) comment that:

> In far-from-equilibrium conditions we may have transformation from disorder, from thermal chaos, into order. New dynamic states of matter may originate, states that reflect the interaction of a given system with its surroundings. We have called these new structures *dissipative structures* to emphasise the constructive role of dissipative processes in their formation.

An example of a dissipative structure from everyday life is given by Capra (1996): the 'whirlpool' caused when a bathtub is emptying. Water is constantly flowing out of the whirlpool down the drain, yet a consistent structure is maintained. In fact the structure (the classic whirlpool shape) arises because of the outflow of water through the structure, and arises spontaneously as a result of complex feedback processes that have their origins in the rotational velocities of the water (as well as other factors such as air currents and the exact shape of the drainpipe). There are many similar phenomena in nature which are also dissipative structures (albeit with much greater complexity and many more forces in operation) – examples include tornadoes and the Great Red Spot, the continually changing storm system on the planet Jupiter.

Some living systems can also be described as dissipative structures, notably cells. In Kauffman's words (1995, p. 21), "cells hum along as complex chemical systems that persistently metabolize food molecules to maintain their internal structure and to reproduce. Hence cells are nonequilibrium dissipative structures." Indeed, Capra (1996) links the behaviour of a cell quite explicitly to that of the whirlpool, but with the key difference that the instabilities which lead to the dissipative structure of the whirlpool arise from mechanical causes, based on the rotary motion of the water, but the instabilities in cells which lead to their structures arise from chemical processes.

The constantly changing state of a dissipative structure is crucial to understanding its nature. It is not the case that such a system reaches a particular structure and then remains in that structure. Rather, a dissipative structure is constantly maintaining its current form and/or changing into different forms. Prigogine describes it as going through a series of 'bifurcation points', where the system can either stay as it currently is, move to a new form, or collapse altogether into chaos. It is not possible to predict in advance what will happen at any given bifurcation point, and the behaviour of the system is extremely sensitive to very small changes in its environment.

We have discussed the concept of the dissipative structure in terms of physical and biological systems, where it has its origins and direct application. However, the concept has great application to a variety of other situations, in particular human systems. Prigogine and his collaborators applied the concept directly to traffic patterns in urban settings and to the activities of termite mounds. It has been used as part of the opening up of family therapy to complex dynamic settings far beyond the equilibrium sought by early therapists (Elkaïm et al. 1982).

As with many concepts linked to complexity theory, dissipative structures have also found considerable application in organisational theory (largely in a metaphorical way). Sice and French (2006, p. 858) argue that managers "can exploit the chaotic characteristic of behaviour by looking for conditions that will allow small efforts to produce a significantly variable spectrum of appropriate behaviours". Mitleton-Kelly and Papaefthimiou (2000, p. 2) discuss the importance of bifurcation points in organisations:

> In human systems, far-from-equilibrium conditions operate when a system is perturbed away from its established norms, or away from its usual ways of working and relating. When it is thus disturbed (e.g. after restructuring or a merger) it may reach a 'bifurcation' point and either degrade into disorder, loss of morale, loss of productivity, etc., or create a new order and organisation – i.e. find new ways of working and relating – and thus create a new coherence.

While dissipative structures are an important concept in their own right, they also form a key mechanism by which self-organisation – the "spontaneous emergence of order" (Capra 1996, p. 84) – occurs in a range of systems. This concept is at the heart of complexity theory, which examines the way in which highly complex phenomena arise from apparently simple rules along with tiny fluctuations in initial conditions. Stacey (2003, p. 226) clearly describes the link between the two concepts:

> self-organisation is a process that occurs spontaneously at certain critical values of a sys-tem's control parameters and it involves the system organising itself to produce a different pattern without any blueprint. ... The different pattern that emerges is a dissipative structure in that it easily dissolves if the system moves away from critical points in its control parameters. An equilibrium structure requires no effort to retain its structure and great effort to change it, while a dissipative structure requires great effort to retain its structures and relatively little to change it.

The concept of self-organisation is generally attributed to Ross Ashby and was further developed by Heinz von Foerster and Stuart Kauffman, as described in the chapters of this book on each author, and thus largely has its roots in cybernetics. Although Prigogine makes considerable use of the concept of self-organisation, he does not draw upon the cybernetics tradition at all (his few brief references even to Wiener are often critical), and his basis for discussing self-organisation comes instead from the physical sciences. This can be said to strengthen the concept of self-organisation, as it can be seen to have two independent justifications from quite different traditions. Given his work on self-organisation, it is appropriate to regard Prigogine as one of the key founders of modern complexity theory, and indeed the subject of complexity was of considerable interest to him and his collabo-rators (e.g. Nicolis and Prigogine 1989, has the title *Exploring Complexity*).

Prigogine was keenly aware that his work had significant philosophical impli-cations, both for the nature of science and for the relationship between science and society. These stemmed from the importance he placed on the role of time in physical science. In much of the traditional physical sciences (especially Newtonian physics and classical thermodynamics), he argued, time is irrelevant: the focus has been on phenomena which are reversible, in principle able to occur in the opposite direction. However, many phenomena can be observed, especially in chemistry, which are irreversible: if we mix together two liquids (say by pouring milk into a cup of coffee and stirring it), it is not subsequently possible to separate them. This applies equally strongly to dissipative structures.

By concentrating on irreversibility, Prigogine argues that we are able to introduce the concept of time – and thus related concepts of evolution and fluctuation – into physical science. This is the major theme of Prigogine's popular work *Order out of chaos*, co-authored with Isabelle Stengers: "where classical science used to emphasise permanence, we now find change and evolution" (Prigogine and Stengers 1984, p. 214). We have noted above that the second law of thermodynamics (entropy always increases) is only applicable to closed systems close to equilibrium. By contrast, Prigogine sought to reconcile the apparent contradiction between the principles of evolution (increasing order) and entropy (increasing disorder), by using this to introduce the concept of evolution into physics, in discussing "open systems that evolve to higher and higher forms of complexity" (Prigogine and Stengers 1984, p. 298).

As mentioned above, Prigogine had a strong interest throughout his life in the arts, and was also keenly aware of the application of his theories to social systems. By focusing on time and irreversibility, he hoped to bring together the physical and human sciences. Prigogine and Stengers (1984, p. xxvii) begin their book by arguing that "our vision of nature is undergoing a radical change toward the multiple, the temporal, and the complex", and that this change is much more amenable to the human sciences than the deterministic approach usually emphasised in the physical sciences. The original French title of their book (published in 1979) was *La Nouvelle Alliance*, the new alliance, to reflect this hope. In his autobiographical summary, Prigogine (1977) wrote that:

> All these problems have a common element: time. Maybe the orientation of my work came from the conflict which arose from my humanist vocation as an adolescent and from the scientific orientation I chose for my university training. Almost by instinct, I turned myself later towards problems of increasing complexity, perhaps in the belief that I could find there a junction in physical science on one hand, and in biology and human science on the other.

Prigogine's work was scientifically and philosophically radical in many areas. As one might expect with such radicalism, he received criticism from a number of others for his ideas and the way he expressed them, both in terms of the science itself and his application of the science to philosophical contexts. One reviewer summed up these criticisms in discussing *Order out of chaos*: "while this book contains much that is new and correct, all too often that which is correct is not new and that which is new is not correct" (Pagels 1985, p. 97).

Nonetheless, his ideas have been widely accepted and applied across a range of disciplines, and are highly important in our understanding of both physical and human systems. In an obituary, Goldbeter (2003, p. 259) wrote:

> In his last public lecture, given in Brussels in November 2002 on the occasion of a celebration of the 25th anniversary of his Nobel prize, he simply declared: "Astonishment leads to creativity". These words sum up well his relentless, creative questioning of the world.

Reading from Prigogine's work

Reprinted from "The Philosophy of Instability", *Futures*, Prigogine, I. August 1989, with permission from Elsevier.

The word 'instability' has a strange fate. It is sometimes used with a slightly negative connotation, as if it is something which must be transcended. In fact, its usage is quite recent. The word is used occasionally in physics, where it describes an elementary phenomenon: if I swing a pendulum, holding it so that the weight is at the bottom, it will eventually stop with its centre of gravity as low as possible – this is a stable phenomenon. But it is common knowledge that if I hold it upside down it could fall to the right or the left, and very small vibrations will be sufficient to make it fall one way rather than the other.

This phenomenon is obviously very elementary and has probably been known for thousands of years; indeed, early work in mechanics shows that everyone studied the movement of the pendulum in great detail. Very little, however, has been written about the upside-down pendulum. The notion of instability has in some way been ideologically suppressed, for the phenomenon of instability leads naturally to very important, serious problems.

The first of these is the problem of forecasting. Clearly, if I take a stable pendulum and agitate it, I can predict what will happen: it will return to a minimum swing. If, on the other hand, I hold it upside down, it is very difficult to predict whether it will fall to the right or to the left – this depends on fluctuations. So we have on one hand something that is forecastable, and on the other something that is not. This is where the problem of determinism comes in. The pendulum on its minimum swing is a deterministic object: we know what will happen. In contrast, the problem of the pendulum turned on its head involves a non-deterministic object.

[...]

Man and nature

Firstly, there is the question of why in science today the talk is of instability, whereas previously people talked about determinism. Instability has in some way replaced determinism. The introduction of instability allows us a clearer view of human activity within nature, and hence enables us to incorporate humankind more fully into nature. The introduction of instability and non-forecastability, and hence ultimately of time as the essential variable, is highly significant in reducing the cultural fragmentation which currently exists between social science and pure science.

Why does this concept change man's relationship to nature? In a deterministic world nature is controllable, it is an inert object susceptible to our will. If nature contains instability as an essential element, we must respect it, for we cannot predict what may happen.

Secondly, in introducing the concept of instability, we arrive at a more global concept of science, embracing more of the cultural context of the seventeenth century when Western science was born. In this way, science leads to a more universal message, more respectful of the cultural traditions of other civilizations.

[...]

Order and disorder

Today, we know that increase in entropy is not an increase in disorder, for order and disorder are created simultaneously. If we take two containers and put two gases in them, for example hydrogen and nitrogen, and if we heat one and cool the other, we find that there is more hydrogen in one container and more nitrogen in the other, due to the difference in temperature. Here we have a dissipative phenomenon which creates disorder, while the flow of heat also creates order: hydrogen on one side, nitrogen on the other. Order and disorder are intimately connected – one implies the other. This is the change we are witnessing in our perception of the universe today.

Our view of the universe has long been partial. It has been like the view we have from the aeroplane when we arrive in, say, Venice; we see the magnificent buildings and squares, and say: 'What an extraordinary structure'. But when we are in Venice, we see that there is also pollution, and mosquitoes – we see both aspects. Interestingly, in contemporary cosmology the universe is to a large extent – I would even say essentially – formed by disorder, in which order floats.

We know today that for every billion thermal photons in disorder, there is one elementary particle supposed to be able to transmit ordered structures. Our perception of the universe has become dualistic – the two aspects of order and disorder coexist and give us a different vision of the universe. Not only does non-equilibrium lead to both order and disorder, but it also leads to events, because more possibilities appear than do in a state of equilibrium. In a situation far from equilibrium, equations become non-linear, and non-linear equations usually have more than one solution. We now know that at any given moment, new solutions are emerging; it is the phenomenon of bifurcation which leads to new solutions which imply a new spatio-temporal organization. For example, a chemical clock is something in which all the molecules become blue at the same time, then red a little later, then blue, then red.

So molecules can communicate. Coherence far from a state of equilibrium acquires huge dimensions in comparison with what happens in a state of equilibrium. In equilibrium each molecule can see only its immediate neighbours. Out of equilibrium the system can see the totality of the system. One could almost say that matter in equilibrium is blind, and out of equilibrium it starts to see. Hence there are events, fluctuations which prepare for an event, amplification, sensitivity to the external world, historical perspectives due to other successive forms of organization, and the appearance of a series of new categories of phenomena, called attractors.

If we pick up a pendulum which has been left to itself, it returns to one point – this is a punctual attractor; but in the case of chemical clocks, we are talking about periodic attractors. Subsequently much more complicated attractors have been discovered, strange attractors which correspond to numerous points. The system moves from one point to another   it is a mixture of stability and instability. What is curious, and central to the interest of many physicists, chemists, meteorologists and ecologists, is that our environment, our climate, our ecology, and even our nervous system can only be understood in the light of such systems, which are both stable and unstable. They are determined by strange attractors and hence by a mixture of stability and instability; it is therefore difficult to forecast what will happen.

Respect, not control

Of course, this does not mean that these systems elude science; we have not chosen the world we describe, we are born into a certain world and we must take account of this world as it is, reducing as far as possible our *a priori* feelings. This world is unstable – this is not a capitulation, but on the contrary an encouragement to combine new experimental and theoretical research which takes account of this unstable character. The world is not a victim offered up for us to dominate; we must respect it. The world of unstable phenomena is not a world which we can control, any more than we can control human society in the sense that extrapolation in classical physics led us to believe. [...]

We need to be aware that our knowledge is still a limited window on the universe; because of instability we must abandon the dream of total knowledge of the universe. From our window, we must extrapolate and guess what the mechanisms could be. An unstable world means that although we may know the initial conditions to an infinite number of decimal points, the future remains impossible to forecast.

There is a close analogy with a work of literature: in its first chapter a novel begins with a description of the situation in a finite number of words, but it is still open to numerous possible developments and this is ultimately the pleasure of reading: discovering which one of the possible developments will be used. Similarly, in a Bach fugue, once the theme has been given it allows a great number of developments out of which Bach has chosen. This world is very different from the classical world, and it extends to all of physics and cosmology. Instability leads to a new rationality, which puts an end to the idea of absolute control, and with it an end to any possible idealization of a society under absolute control. The real is not controllable in the sense which science claimed.

[...]

Risk and responsibility

Obviously there is no risk in a deterministic universe. There are risks in a universe which we see differently, particularly in a human universe. I will not discuss this problem in more detail here, but it is clear that in going back to the very foundations of science from this viewpoint, humankind necessarily has choices, and choice means ethical responsibility. Valéry wrote: "Time is construction". I believe this is precisely right. Time is not something already made, which would appear unfolded before a supra-human consciousness. It is something which is constructed at each moment. Humankind can participate in this construction.

References

Brennan, D. (2003). Obituary: Ilya Prigogine. *The Guardian*, 18 June 2003, p.23.
Capra, F. (1996). *The web of life: A new scientific understanding of living systems.* New York: Doubleday.
Elkaïm, M., Prigogine, I., Guattari, F., Stengers, I., Denenbourg, J.-L. (1982). Openness: A round-table discussion. *Family Process, 21*(1), 57–70.
Goldbeter, A. (2003). Ilya Prigogine (1917–2003). *Journal of Biosciences, 28*(6), 657–659.

Kauffman, S. (1995). *At home in the universe: The search for the laws of self-organisation and complexity*. London: Penguin.

McMillan, E. (2004). *Complexity, organizations and change*. London: Routledge.

Mitleton-Kelly, E., & Papaefthimiou, M.-C. (2000). Co-evolution of diverse elements interacting within a social ecosystem. FEAST 2000 International Workshop on Feedback and Evolution in Software and Business Processes. London: Imperial College

Nicolis, G., & Prigogine, I. (1989). *Exploring complexity: An introduction*. New York: W.H. Freeman.

Pagels, H.R. (1985). Is the irreversibility we see a fundamental property of nature? *Physics Today, 38*(1), 97–99.

Prigogine, I. (1977). Autobiography. Nobel Foundation. http://nobelprize.org/nobel_prizes/chemistry/laureates/1977/prigogine-autobio.html. Accessed 13 Jan 2009.

Prigogine, I., & Stengers, I. (1984). *Order out of chaos: Man's new dialogue with nature*. Toronto: Bantam Books.

Prigogine, I. (1989). The philosophy of instability. *Futures, 11*(4), 396–400.

Sice, P., & French, I. (2006). A holistic frame-of-reference for modelling social systems. *Kybernetes, 35*(6), 851–864.

Stacey, R. (2003). *Strategic management and organisational dynamics: The challenge of complexity*. Harlow: Pearson Education.

Chapter 24
Stuart Kauffman

Stuart Kauffman is a theoretical biologist and one of the founders of complexity theory. Through a series of highly detailed computer models, he has explored the nature of evolution and self-organisation – the ways in which order and organisation can spontaneously arise in biological systems. His research is driven by the goal to prove a hypothesis he first felt intuitively at the age of 24: "there is 'order for free' out there, a spontaneous crystallisation of order out of complex systems, with no need for natural selection or any other external force" (quoted in R. Lewin 1999, p. 25). His work on this hypothesis has led to many important advances.

Kauffman, an American whose father was a wealthy Romanian immigrant, was born in 1939. He had a strong teenage interest in science and was very inspired by Einstein's view of science as a quest for "the secrets of the Old One" (i.e. God). However, this led him initially towards a study of human nature, first briefly as a playwright ("instead of writing comedies or tragedies I created a third form: I wrote three atrocities" – quoted by Boucher 2005) and then as a philosopher. He took degrees in philosophy first at Dartmouth College and then, via a Marshall scholarship, at Oxford, specialising in the philosophy of science and mind.

Kauffman is very articulate and creative, "like a composer whose mind was endlessly aboil with melody ... [and] a very high ratio of talking to listening" (Waldrop 1992, p. 101), but he distrusted these qualities in himself. This led him to attend graduate school in medicine, reasoning that "I figured somewhere I had to learn a bunch of facts, and if I went to medical school, the bastards would make me learn a lot of facts" (quoted by Regis 2000). He graduated from medical school in 1968, but only worked as a hospital doctor for a year before entering academia as a theoretical biologist, initially in mathematical biosciences at Chicago. In 1975 he moved to the University of Pennsylvania, where he became professor of bioscience and biophysics until his retirement in 1995. While at Pennsylvania, he became a founding member of the Santa Fe Institute (discussed further below), of which he remains an external faculty member. Following a period as an entrepreneur, he re-entered academia in 2004 as a professor of Biocomplexity and Informatics at the University of Calgary, where he is currently based.

While he was still a medical student, Kauffman became interested in the question of how order arose in biological systems. Using recently-published work that showed how certain genes acted as regulators of other nearby genes, and switched on or off in a binary fashion, he was able to model a series of binary genetic networks and show order spontaneously arising above a certain level of complexity in the network. He wrote about this work to Warren McCulloch at the Massachusetts Institute of Technology, as it bore a strong resemblance to McCulloch's own early work in neural networks, and McCulloch invited him to spend the summer of 1966 at MIT. As with many others previously, Kauffman was inspired, supported by and introduced to many important contacts by McCulloch. He would later say that "Warren literally catapulted me into the world that I've lived in ever since" (quoted in Waldrop 1992, p. 116); and McCulloch in turn said that he "regarded Kauffman as his most important collaborator since [Walter] Pitts" (Hayles 1999, p. 241). McCulloch's influence on Kauffman demonstrates the way in which Kauffman has served as a bridge between cybernetics and complexity theory.

The cybernetic concept of feedback and the use of computer modelling were to become vital in Kauffman's subsequent work. He has continued to use binary networks as the basis of his models – a series of nodes which can take the values of 'on' or 'off', each connected to a number of other nodes. The number of nodes and the ways in which they are connected vary, as do the rules which govern the behaviour of the network – whether a node should switch on or off according to the value of its connected nodes. By varying these different aspects, Kauffman has built networks which can model many kinds of highly complex and interconnected situations. The model starts with a set of initial values at the nodes, but the rules for switching lead to changing patterns across the network, exhibiting many different kinds of emergent behaviour. Because the key parameters of the network are the number of nodes (N) and the average number of inputs to each node (K), Kauffman refers to these models as NK networks.

He has particularly used these networks to model fitness landscapes – a map of the evolutionary strength of particular organisms (or other kinds of agents), where the peaks of a landscape represent high ability to survive and the valleys represent low survival. NK networks are also the basis of Kauffman's theory of autocatalytic sets – interlinked collections of objects (such as living cells), forming a self-reinforcing network, which act to catalyse the formation of the other objects in the network. In particular, Kauffman has applied autocatalytic sets to the question of the origins of life, and argued that life "is the natural accomplishment of catalysts in sufficiently complex nonequilibrium chemical systems" (Kauffman 1995a, p. 51).

In 1986, Kauffman became one of the founding members of the Santa Fe Institute, in New Mexico, USA, perhaps the most important centre for the development of complexity theory. The Institute arose from two related sources – an awareness by a number of eminent physical scientists that there was a growing convergence of research in a range of fields into nonlinear dynamics and self-organisation, for which traditional reductionist and disciplinary methods were inadequate; and the growing power of computer technology with the capacity to model highly complex problems.

The Santa Fe Institute was largely established by researchers connected to the Los Alamos National Laboratory, the major research centre for nuclear weapons in the US, who wanted to pursue issues of nonlinearity and complexity in a highly interdisciplinary environment and were also keen to carry out work that was not connected to the military. The Institute's work is characterised by the use of detailed computer models of large numbers of adaptive agents, where simple rules are established as to the interactions of the agents and complex behaviour is seen to emerge with no further intervention from the model's designers. Kauffman's NK networks are one example, along with a number of other models such as cellular automata. These models display such high levels of emergent self-organisation that they have led to the creation of a field, related to artificial intelligence, known as 'artificial life'.

Although Kauffman had originally intended to spend perhaps a month in each year at the Santa Fe Institute, personal circumstances led to him spending much more time in Santa Fe, and becoming one of the key people in the Institute. He described the Institute as

> a brand new enterprise comprised of an interdisciplinary group of extremely smart people who started a new science called complexity. None of us knew exactly what this new science was but we all knew it was very important ... our mixture of passion and utter confusion drove our creativity for a decade as we struggled to invent this new area of science (quoted in Boucher 2005).

The work of the Santa Fe Institute has led to many important developments in complexity theory, particularly the concepts of complex adaptive systems and the edge of chaos, both of which Kauffman helped to develop. It has also drawn on, and made popular, the general systems theory concept of emergence (and related it closely to self-organisation), which Kauffman (2006b) describes as the view that "new entities with their own properties and causal powers arise and are part of the furniture of the universe".

Complex adaptive systems are systems which are made up of many interconnected parts that are constantly self-organising and adapting in response to their environment. The concept has been applied widely to natural systems such as the brain and insect colonies, to organisations and societies, and to economies. The adaptiveness which they exhibit has been the subject of much of Kauffman's modelling work, drawing quite explicitly on Ross Ashby's research within cybernetics in the 1950s on adaptive behaviour (discussed in Chapter 5).

A further major contribution which Kauffman has made to complexity theory is his work on the concept of the 'edge of chaos' (which he and a number of other researchers at Santa Fe, notably Chris Langton who is a pioneer of 'artificial life', independently discovered). This concept observes that in many systems, there is a narrow zone between total order (which is stagnant and lifeless) and total disorder (which is chaotic and uncontrollable). It is within this zone – the edge of chaos – that life and creativity can exist, as Kauffman vividly describes in the reading which follows.

Kauffman has applied his ideas quite widely both to business and to economics. In particular, he started a consultancy company, Bios Group, in 1996 in Santa Fe (along with a partner of the accountancy firm Ernst & Young), to apply NK networks and other models of complexity to practical problems within business. A key early client was Procter & Gamble (P&G), who wanted to examine the streamlining

of their supply chain. Through a series of large-scale computer models of the supply chain, Bios were able to create "a policy space with lots of knobs you can tune"
(Kauffman, quoted in Regis 2000). For example, Kauffman and his colleagues
observed that P&G's intuitively sensible policy that all trucks leaving distribution
warehouses should be full was creating bottlenecks in their supply chain which
could be removed if trucks were allowed to leave warehouses with only partial
loads. Similar techniques were applied to a number of other organisations in various sectors.

While this application of Kauffman's ideas directly uses NK networks to model
business situations, he has also drawn upon his ideas to discuss a number of issues
in relation to business and economics. He has written extensively on the importance
of coevolution between species interacting in a particular ecosystem, and particularly the phenomenon known to biologists as the 'Red Queen effect' (after a character in *Alice in Wonderland*) where "species keep changing in a never-ending race
simply to sustain their current level of fitness" (Kauffman 1995b, p. 125). He draws
a clear analogy between this phenomenon and the way in which technologies, and
the organisations which develop and depend on them, evolve in relation to other
technologies. However, he sees the connection as going beyond analogy, believing
that "biological coevolution and technological coevolution, the increasing diversity
of the biosphere and of the 'technosphere', may be governed by the same or similar
fundamental laws" (Kauffman 1995b, p. 129).

Kauffman's work has significant philosophical implications as well as purely
scientific ones. In relation to the origin of life, he has used phrases such as "we the
expected" and "at home in the universe" (Kauffman 1995a) to indicate the importance
of self-organising living systems within the world, as distinct from the neo-Darwinian
view of natural selection occurring at random. Indeed he has argued that "natural
selection cannot be the sole source of the order we see in the world" (Kauffman 1995a,
p. viii). In the highly-charged context of contemporary America, this view has drawn
him into the debates on 'intelligent design', the quasi-creationist argument that some
kind of designer must be necessary to explain the complexity of the universe. While
Kauffman agrees with the intelligent design advocates in arguing that neo-Darwinism
is insufficient, his solution of self-organisation is quite different, and he has very
publicly distanced himself from intelligent design (Kauffman 2006a).

The philosophical aspect of Kauffman's work has also led him to consider the
nature of agency, the capacity for organisms to act on their own behalf and to
attribute meaning to their actions and those of others. This is a key concept both in
biology and in sociology. In his view, agency is present in very tiny organisms – he
has suggested that "a minimal molecular agent is a system which can reproduce
itself and carry out at least one work cycle in the thermodynamic sense" (Kauffman
2006b). If this is true, it would mean that the capacity for independent action, and
to some extent thought, would be present not just in humans and the higher animals
but even in many bacteria, something that has profound philosophical implications.
Ultimately, he suggests, his understanding of the universe is essentially a spiritual
one, that "points to a new vision of our co-creating reality, that it invites precisely
an enhancement of our sense of spirituality, reverence, wonder, and responsibility,

and can form the basis of a trans-national mythic structure for an emerging global civilization" (Kauffman 2006b).

Stuart Kauffman has made enormous contributions to the way we view complex systems and evolution. His work has far-reaching consequences, and his methods of modelling intricate networks of interacting agents are useful in a wide range of settings. His is a truly original and innovative mind.

Reading from Kauffman's work

Kauffman, S. (1995) *At Home in the Universe: The Search for the Laws of Self-Organization and Complexity*, London (Penguin) & New York (OUP). Copyright © Stuart Kauffman 1995. Reproduced by permission of Penguin Books Ltd and Oxford University Press. Extracts from pages 23–28.

The vast mystery of biology is that life should have emerged at all, that the order we see should have come to pass. A theory of emergence would account for the creation of the stunning order out our windows as a natural expression of some underlying laws. It would tell us if we are at home in the universe, expected in it, rather than present despite overwhelming odds.

Some words or phrases are evocative, even provocative. So it is with the word *emergent*. Commonly, we express this idea with the sentence, The whole is greater than the sum of its parts. The sentence is provocative, for what extra can be in the whole that is not in the parts? I believe that life itself is an emergent phenomenon, but I mean nothing mystical by this. [Later], I shall be at pains to give good reasons to believe that sufficiently complex mixes of chemicals can spontaneously crystallize into systems with the ability to collectively catalyze the network of chemical reactions by which the molecules themselves are formed. Such collectively autocatalytic sets sustain themselves and reproduce. This is no less than what we call a living metabolism, the tangle of chemical reactions that power every one of our cells. Life, in this view, is an emergent phenomenon arising as the molecular diversity of a prebiotic chemical system increases beyond a threshold of complexity. If true, then life is not located in the property of any single molecule – in the details – but is a collective property of systems of interacting molecules. Life, in this view, emerged whole and has always remained whole. Life, in this view, is not to be located in its parts, but in the collective emergent properties of the whole they create. Although life as an emergent phenomenon may be profound, its fundamental holism and emergence are not at all mysterious. A set of molecules either does or does not have the property that it is able to catalyze its own formation and reproduction from some simple food molecules. No vital force or extra substance is present in the emergent, self-reproducing whole. But the collective system does possess a stunning property not possessed by any of its parts. It is able to reproduce itself and to evolve. The collective system is alive. Its parts are just chemicals.

[...]

The network within each cell of any contemporary organism is the result of at least 1 billion years of evolution. Most biologists, heritors of the Darwinian tradition, suppose that the order of ontogeny is due to the grinding away of a molecular Rube Goldberg machine, slapped together piece by piece by evolution. I present a countering thesis: most of the beautiful order seen in ontogeny is spontaneous, a natural expression of the stunning self-organization that abounds in very complex regulatory networks. We appear to have been profoundly wrong. Order, vast and generative, arises naturally.

The emergent order seen in genomic networks foretells a conceptual struggle, perhaps even a conceptual revolution, in evolutionary theory. In this book, I propose that much of the order in organisms may not be the result of selection at all, but of the spontaneous order of self-organized systems. Order, vast and generative, not fought for against the entropic tides but freely available, undergirds all subsequent biological evolution. The order of organisms is natural, not merely the unexpected triumph of natural selection.

[...]

This is a massive and difficult theme. We are just beginning to embrace it. In this new view of life, organisms are not merely tinkered-together contraptions, bricolage, in Jacob's phrase. Evolution is not merely "chance caught on the wing", in Monod's evocative image. The history of life captures the natural order, on which selection is privileged to act. If this idea is true, many features of organisms are not merely historical accidents, but also reflections of the profound order that evolution has further molded. If true, we are at home in the universe in ways not imagined since Darwin stood natural theology on its head with his blind watchmaker.

Yet more is presaged by self-organization. I said we must encompass the roles of both self-organization *and* Darwinian selection in evolution. But these sources of order may meld in complex ways that we hardly begin to understand. No theory in physics, chemistry, biology, or elsewhere has yet brokered this marriage. We must think anew. Among the progeny of this mating of self-organization and selection may be new universal laws.

It is perhaps astonishing, perhaps hopeful and wonderful, that we might even now begin to frame possible universal laws governing this proposed union. For what can the teeming molecules that hustled themselves into self-reproducing metabolisms, the cells coordinating their behaviors to form multicelled organisms, the ecosystems, and even economic and political systems have in common? The wonderful possibility, to be held as a working hypothesis, bold but fragile, is that on many fronts, life evolves toward a regime that is poised between order and chaos. The evocative phrase that points to this working hypothesis is this: life exists at the edge of chaos. Borrowing a metaphor from physics, life may exist near a kind of phase transition. Water exists in three phases: solid ice, liquid water, and gaseous steam. It now begins to appear that similar ideas might apply to complex adapting systems. For example, we will see that the genomic networks that control development from zygote to adult can exist in three major regimes: a frozen ordered regime, a gaseous chaotic regime, and a kind of liquid regime located in the region between order and chaos. It is a lovely hypothesis, with considerable supporting data, that genomic systems lie in the ordered regime near the phase transition to chaos. Were such systems too deeply into the frozen ordered regime, they would be too rigid to coordinate the complex sequences of genetic activities necessary for development. Were they too far into the gaseous chaotic regime, they would not be orderly enough. Networks in the regime near the edge of chaos – this compromise between order and surprise – appear best able to coordinate complex activities and best able to evolve as well. It is a very attractive hypothesis that natural selection achieves genetic regulatory networks that lie near the edge of chaos. Much of this book is bent on exploring this theme.

Evolution is a story of organisms adapting by genetic changes, seeking to improve their fitness. Biologists have long harbored images of fitness landscapes, where the peaks represent high fitness, and populations wander under the drives of mutation, selection, and random drift across the landscape seeking peaks, but perhaps never achieving them. The idea of fitness peaks applies at many levels. For example, it can refer to the capacity of a protein molecule to catalyze a given chemical reaction. Then peaks of the landscape correspond to enzymes that are better catalysts for this reaction than all their neighboring proteins – those in the foothills and, worst of all, those in the valleys. Fitness peaks can also refer to the fitness of whole organisms. In that more complex case, an organism with a given set of traits is fitter – higher on the landscape – than all its near variants if, roughly speaking, it is more likely to have offspring.

We will find in this book that whether we are talking about organisms or economies, surprisingly general laws govern adaptive processes on multipeaked fitness landscapes. These general laws may account for phenomena ranging from the burst of the Cambrian explosion in biological evolution, where taxa fill in from the top down, to technological evolution, where striking variations arise early and dwindle to minor improvements. The edge-of-chaos theme also arises as a potential general law. In scaling the top of the fitness peaks, adapting populations that are too methodical and timid in their explorations are likely to get stuck in the foothills, thinking they have reached as high as they can go; but a search that is too wide ranging is also likely to fail. The best exploration of an evolutionary space occurs at a kind of phase transition between order and disorder, when populations begin to melt off the local peaks they have become fixated on and flow along ridges toward distant regions of higher fitness.

The edge-of-chaos image arises in coevolution as well, for as we evolve, so do our competitors; to remain fit, we must adapt to their adaptations. In coevolving systems, each partner clambers up its fitness landscape toward fitness peaks, even as that landscape is constantly deformed by the adaptive moves of its coevolutionary partners. Strikingly, such coevolving systems also behave in an ordered regime, a chaotic regime, and a transition regime. It is almost spooky that such systems seem to coevolve to the regime at the edge of chaos. As if by an invisible hand, each adapting species acts according to its own selfish advantage, yet the entire system appears magically to evolve to a poised state where, on average, each does as best as can be expected. Yet, as in many of the dynamical systems we will study in this book, each is eventually driven to extinction, despite its own best efforts, by the collective behavior of the system as a whole.

As we shall see, technological evolution may be governed by laws similar to those governing prebiotic chemical evolution and adaptive coevolution. The origin of life at a threshold of chemical diversity follows the same logic as a theory of economic takeoff at a threshold of diversity of goods and services. Above that critical diversity, new species of molecules, or goods and services, afford niches for yet further new species, which are awakened into existence in an explosion of possibilities. Like coevolutionary systems, economic systems link the selfish activities of more or less myopic agents. Adaptive moves in biological evolution and technological evolution drive avalanches of speciation and extinction. In both cases, as if by an invisible hand, the system may tune itself to the poised edge of chaos where all players fare as well as possible, but ultimately exit the stage.

The edge of chaos may even provide a deep new understanding of the logic of democracy. We have enshrined democracy as our secular religion; we argue its moral and rational foundations, and base our lives on it. We hope that our heritage of democracy will spill out its abundance of freedom over the globe. And in the following chapters we will find surprising new grounds for the secular wisdom of democracy in its capacity to solve extremely hard problems characterized by intertwining webs of conflicting interests. People organize into communities, each of which acts for its own benefit, jockeying to seek compromises among conflicting interests. This seemingly haphazard process also shows an ordered regime where poor compromises are found quickly, a chaotic regime where no compromise is ever settled on, and a phase transition where compromises are achieved, but not quickly. The best compromises appear to occur at the phase transition between order and chaos. Thus we will see hints of an apologia for a pluralistic society as the natural design for adaptive compromise. Democracy may be far and away the best process to solve the complex problems of a complex evolving society, to find the peaks on the coevolutionary landscape where, on average, all have a chance to prosper.

References

Boucher, G. (2005). Q & A with Stuart Kauffman. *OnCampus*, University of Calgary, 22 April 2005. http://www.ucalgary.ca/oncampus/weekly/april22-05/kauffman.html. Accessed 13 Jan 2009.

Hayles, N. K. (1999). *How we became posthuman: Virtual bodies in cybernetics, literature, and informatics*. Chicago: University of Chicago Press.

Kauffman, S. (1995a). *At home in the universe: The search for the laws of self-organization and complexity*. London: Penguin.

Kauffman, S. (1995b). Technology and evolution: Escaping the Red Queen effect. *McKinsey Quarterly, 1995*(1), 118–129.

Kauffman, S. (2006a). Intelligent design, science or not? In J. Brockman (Ed.), *Intelligent thought: Science versus the intelligent design movement*. New York: Vintage.

Kauffman, S. (2006b). Beyond reductionism: Reinventing the sacred. *Edge: The Third Culture*. http://www.edge.org/3rd_culture/kauffman06/kauffman06_index.html. Accessed 13 Jan 2009.

Lewin, R. (1999). *Complexity: Life at the edge of chaos* (2nd edition). Chicago: University of Chicago Press.

Regis, E. (2000). Greetings from Info Mesa. *Wired 8*(6), 337–345.

Waldrop, M. M. (1992). *Complexity: The emerging science at the edge of order and chaos*. New York: Simon & Schuster.

Chapter 25
James Lovelock

James Lovelock is an unusual figure in the sometimes rather homogeneous world of science. In a scientific community founded on team working and institutions, he works alone from his rural home. While many start from others' work and are content to make advances through small steps, he is deeply committed to starting from experimental data and drawing his own, often radical, conclusions. Lovelock writes in a highly accessible, almost poetic fashion, and is famous for his adoption of a vivid metaphor (Gaia) to describe his ideas; yet he has worked for decades carrying out detailed experimental science and even designing and building innovative instruments for his experiments. He is one of the UK's most eminent scientists, has been a Fellow of the Royal Society since 1974 and received several prestigious international awards, yet he is regarded by some of the scientific establishment as something close to a crank. He is deeply involved in the environmental movement and has inspired many people in it, but he is also held in considerable suspicion by many environmentalists.

Lovelock's greatest contribution is in the development of Gaia theory – that the Earth (including the physical planet and all living organisms) can be considered as a single self-organising system. He has derived the theory from studies of the behaviour of the Earth's atmosphere, by comparisons with other planets, and backed it up by computer modelling. He has applied this theory to how humans need to behave to preserve conditions that make life possible on Earth, describing himself as "a planetary physician whose patient, the living Earth, complains of fever" (Lovelock 2006, p. 1).

Lovelock's work is an excellent example of applying a systems approach to a very large-scale situation, resulting in both a well-founded theory and clear recommendations for action. In its blend of cybernetics and physical science, and its focus on self-organisation, it has clear connections with complexity theory. Indeed, in his book on complex biological and ecological systems, Capra has described Gaia theory as "perhaps the most surprising and most beautiful expression of self-organisation" (Capra 1996, p. 100). Capra also draws a close parallel between Gaia theory and autopoiesis, arguing that Gaia is self-bounded, self-generating and self-perpetuating, as does Lovelock's colleague Lynn Margulis (1997, p. 280), who has written that "life does not 'adapt to' a passive

M. Ramage and K. Shipp, *Systems Thinkers,*

physiochemical environment, as the neo-Darwinists assume; Rather, life actively 'produces and modifies' its surroundings".

James Ephraim Lovelock was born in 1919 in Letchworth, UK, and grew up in Brixton, south London, at the time an area of heavy pollution from coal fires, something that would shape his later environmental awareness. On leaving school, he initially worked as an apprentice to a firm carrying out chemical work under contract to a range of organisations, during which he learned many experimental skills and a sense of himself as a problem-solving scientist. He took a degree in chemistry at Manchester University, graduating in 1941. During the Second World War, he was a registered conscientious objector. After graduating, he started work for the Medical Research Council at the National Institute for Medical Research in London, where he worked for the next 20 years (apart from a spell of five years at the Common Cold Research Unit in Salisbury and two sabbatical years in the USA). During this time he took his Ph.D. at the London School of Hygiene and Tropical Medicine, in 1948; he also later gained a D.Sc. degree from London University.

Lovelock's work as a medical researcher was concerned with many topics, notably the effects of air pollution and the preservation of blood cells through freezing. A constant theme, however, was his development of scientific equipment – a large range of instruments to detect various chemicals in the air and elsewhere. Most notable of these was the electron capture detector (ECD), the development of which he has described as "perhaps the most important event in my life as a scientist" (Lovelock 2000, p. 191).

The ECD is an extraordinary device – it is small, easy to build, and when developed in the late 1950s, it was thousands of times more sensitive than other available detectors in its field of gas chromatography. It is especially sensitive to the presence of certain polluting chemicals, such as DDT and CFCs. This device had a crucial impact upon the establishment of a sound scientific basis for the environmental movement. Data collected using the ECD (by Lovelock and others) was foundational in establishing the case put forward in the 1960s by Rachel Carson in her book *Silent Spring* (Carson 1962) for the banning of DDT as a pesticide, and later for establishing the effect of CFCs on the ozone layer and the subsequent worldwide ban of CFCs in aerosols and refrigerators. Lovelock however was sceptical for some years about the impact of CFCs and even acted as a consultant to the chemical industry during the 1970s when scientific debates on the ozone layer were at their height. Despite the ECD's considerable success, Lovelock received no money from its patent, as he developed it in its final form and first published a paper on its working while on sabbatical at Yale University, and the US government demanded that he assign the patent rights to them.

On leaving the National Institute for Medical Research in 1961, Lovelock was based for three years in the USA, at Baylor University in Houston, while conducting much of his research in California, at NASA's Jet Propulsion Laboratory (JPL). He saw his time in Houston as a stepping-stone to the practice of independent science, and he has worked independently from his own home since then. His work has been funded through a series of consultancies, with organisations including NASA, the Chemical Manufacturers Association, Shell (for whom he was a scientific consultant for 30 years), Hewlett-Packard (who develop many scientific instruments and were interested in his ECD work), and the UK Ministry of Defence (for whom he worked on chemical detectors used for tracking by the security services).

He has described as his motivation for working as an independent scientist that "science was and is my passion and I wanted to be free to do it unfettered by direction from anyone, not even by the mild constraints of a university department or an institute of science" (Lovelock 2000, p. 2). He did, however, keep close academic links, in particular as a visiting professor at the Department of Cybernetics at Reading University for 25 years, and also at the University of Houston, and Green College, Oxford. Independent working and a fiercely independent mind go hand-in-hand for Lovelock; both have allowed him the freedom to challenge long-held beliefs and come to radical conclusions. However, his independence has also led to considerable distrust at times from those who are used to scientists being part of established research institutions.

Lovelock spent much of his time at the Jet Propulsion Laboratory working on instruments for planned NASA missions to the Moon and Mars. It was while he was working on the detection of life on Mars that he had the initial insight that led to the development of Gaia theory. One afternoon in the autumn of 1965, he was given new data giving a detailed analysis of the chemical composition of the atmospheres of Mars and Venus. These atmospheres exist in a state of complete chemical equilibrium – in the absence of life, all possible chemical reactions have already happened. The atmosphere of the Earth, by contrast, is very different. Much later, Lovelock described his initial perception in poetic language:

> Chance favoured me with a view of the Earth from space and I saw it as the stunningly beautiful anomaly of the solar system.... I saw it as a planet that has always, since its origins nearly four billion years ago, kept itself a fit home for the life that happened upon it and I thought that it did so by homeostasis, the wisdom of the body, just as you and I keep our temperature and chemistry constant. In this view the spontaneous evolution of life did more than make Darwin's world: it started a joint project with the evolving Earth itself. (Lovelock 2000, p. 2)

Lovelock's initial perception was that the Earth formed some kind of self-regulating system with organisms on the planet forming a key part in the process of regulation – in his early formulation, the Earth is "a cybernetic planetary system with homeostatic tendencies" (quoted in Sagan and Margulis 1997, p. 202). It took a number of years for this initial concept to develop further, through his own studies of the atmosphere and through his work with the biologist Lynn Margulis, who contributed a deep understanding of life on earth, especially micro-organisms. Putting these insights from biology and chemistry together enabled Lovelock and Margulis to form what was referred to as the Gaia hypothesis: that "the temperature, oxidation state, acidity, and certain aspects of the rocks and waters are at any time kept constant, and that this homeostasis is maintained by the organisms at the Earth's surface" (Lovelock 1995, p. 19).

The Gaia hypothesis was initially published in a series of papers in fairly obscure scientific journals. It became widely known when Lovelock published the work in a book, *Gaia* (Lovelock 1979), which was read both in scientific circles and more broadly by environmentalists and the general public. The concept became quickly taken up and widely accepted by the environmental movement, for whom it was a way of describing the Earth as a whole entity, deeply interconnected – an equivalent of the image of the planet from space that had appeared from early space missions (and which had also inspired Lovelock).

In the scientific community, the Gaia hypothesis was very controversial. Although it has many respectable scientific antecedents, beginning with the pioneering eighteenth century geologist James Hutton, it was seen as very radical. The biologists Ford Doolittle and Richard Dawkins published very strong attacks on Lovelock's book. This was partly due to the holistic nature of the theory, so very different from the reductionism that was at the core of the then-dominant strands in biology – neo-Darwinism and molecular biology. It also reflected what Lovelock was later to acknowledge as an error in the hypothesis, which sought to locate the regulatory part of the planetary system (that is, its control system) solely in the living parts of the Earth. This is too limited, and makes too much of a separation between organisms and their planetary environment. As Lovelock later wrote, "the worst thing that can happen to a new theory is for it to be ignored … [these criticisms] hurt at the time – 1979 to 1982 – but they made me think and tighten what had been a loose hypothesis into a firm theory" (Lovelock 2000, p. xii).

The controversy over the Gaia hypothesis led Lovelock and Margulis to develop Gaia theory in two important ways. First, through further experiments they widened the scope of the control system so that it included the wider planetary environment, such as the atmosphere and rocks, in a series of richer and more complex feedback loops. Second, Lovelock constructed a computer model, Daisyworld, of a planet where life consists only of white and black daisies existing on various zones of the planet and evolving in tandem with the planetary ecosystem. Daisyworld resembles closely the computer models of complex systems built by Stuart Kauffman and others at the Santa Fe Institute (described in the chapter on Kauffman) and clearly demonstrates the way in which complex interactions between life and the physical aspects of a planet can arise as an emergent property from very simple initial starting conditions.

An important aspect of the scientific, and wider, reaction to Gaia theory has been the name. Gaia was the name of the Greek goddess of the Earth, and the commonality of names has led some to believe that Lovelock is claiming that the Earth should be regarded as divine, or at least as having a personality. For some in the New Age movement, this is seen as positive and inspiring; for others, including many scientists, it is somewhat disturbing. The name is in fact intended to be a vivid metaphor. It was suggested to Lovelock by his friend and one-time neighbour, the novelist William Golding, who on a walk the pair had in 1969 said that "for so grand an idea you need a grand name. You must call it Gaia" (quoted in R. Lewin 1999, p. 113). Even some of those who favour the theory in principle object to the name. Partly due to this dissatisfaction, and partly due to the incorporation of other concepts, Gaia theory is now often known as Earth Systems Science, or sometimes as geo-physiology. Notwithstanding the name, Gaia theory – or at least the concept of the complete Earth forming a self-regulating system – has become increasingly respected within the scientific community.

Lovelock has a very mixed relationship with the environmental movement. Gaia theory, with its strong message of interconnection and consequent need for respect for the Earth, has been deeply inspiring to environmentalists; and as discussed above the ECD was fundamental to a number of important and successful environment campaigns. In recent years, however, he has become unpopular for his championing of nuclear power. He argues that climate change is so problematic and so urgent that nuclear power has become inevitable, producing as it does much lower carbon emissions than electricity generated from coal, oil or gas. He has summed up his view in a book on humanity's response to climate change, where he writes that "I am a green and would be classed among them, but I am most of all a scientist; because of this I entreat my friends among greens to ... drop their wrong-headed objection to nuclear energy" (Lovelock 2006, p. 11). Given the importance many environmentalists place on opposition to nuclear power, this view has caused considerable discomfort in the environmental movement.

Lovelock's stance on nuclear power illustrates well a key aspect of his personality: his strong individualism. He has long lived and worked in small rural English villages, valuing their combination of isolation and community – indeed he moved from Wiltshire to the border between Devon and Cornwall as his beloved village of Bowerchalke turned from "a village community ... [to] little more than a gentrified nest of middle-class strangers" (Lovelock 2000, p. 314). His independence of mind can also be seen in his constant striving and arguing for what he perceives as the truth, and his unwillingness to adhere to any form of received wisdom or group pressure. This has served him well in very many ways and allowed him to express issues, invent devices and formulate theories far beyond the accepted norms. James Lovelock is a truly individual and innovative thinker, whose work has contributed deeply to our understanding of the interconnected living world.

Reading from Lovelock's work

Lovelock, J. (2002) "What is Gaia?" *Resurgence* no.211/Planet Syndication.

In 1925 the American scientist Alfred Lotka published a small but important book, *Physical* Biology. In it he wrote: "It is not so much the organism or the species that evolves, but the entire system, species and environment. The two are inseparable." As a follower of Lotka, I want to consider extinction in the context of an evolutionary science that is as much about the rocks and oceans as about the living things that inhabit them. In this view what evolves is an 'Earth system' that can move gradually for long periods under an ever-warming sun. But as it evolves, sudden changes punctuate its gradual evolution: such as the appearance of oxygen, a glaciation, a species like humans, or the impact of tiny planets. Whether internally or externally driven, these events change the whole system.

Lotka's view of evolution passed almost unnoticed in his time and it was not until the National Aeronautics and Space Administration (NASA) in the 1960s began exploring our planetary neighbourhood that this broader, transdisciplinary, view of the Earth was revisited. As part of NASA's exploration team, it led me to propose, in a paper in *Nature* in 1965, that life and its environment are so closely coupled that the presence of life on a planet could be detected merely by analysing chemically the composition of its atmosphere. This proposal is now part of NASA's astrobiology programme and they aim to use it in the search for life on extra-solar planets.

When we look at the Earth we see an atmosphere that, apart from the noble gases, has a composition almost wholly determined by the organisms at the surface. If some catastrophe removed all life from the Earth without changing anything else, the atmosphere and surface chemistry would rapidly – in geological terms – move to a state similar to those of Mars or Venus. These are dry planets with atmospheres dominated by carbon dioxide and close to the chemical equilibrium state. By contrast, we have a cool wet planet with an unstable atmosphere that stays constant and always fit for life. The odds against this are close to infinity.

Science is about probabilities, so we are forced to consider the difficult but more probable alternative: something regulates the atmosphere. What is it? It has to be something connected with life at the surface, because we know that the atmospheric gases, oxygen, methane and nitrous oxide, are almost wholly biological products, while others, nitrogen and carbon dioxide, have been massively changed in abundance by organisms. Moreover, the climate depends on atmospheric composition and there is evidence that the Earth has kept a fairly comfortable climate ever since life began, in spite of a 30% increase in solar luminosity. Together these facts led me to propose, in a 1969 paper in the JAAS (*Journal of the American Astronautical Society*), that the biosphere was regulating the atmosphere in its own interests. Two years later I started collaborating with Lynn Margulis and we published a paper in *Tellus* where we stated: "The Gaia hypothesis views the biosphere as an active adaptive control system able to maintain the Earth in homeostasis".

This idea was so contradictory to the views of evolutionary biologists that it was not long before Ford Doolittle, Richard Dawkins and other biologists challenged it. They pointed out that global regulation by the organisms could never have evolved, because the organism itself was the unit of selection, not the Earth. In time I found myself agreeing with them. They were right: there was no way for organisms by themselves to evolve so that they could regulate the global environment. But, I wondered, could the whole system, organisms and environment together, evolve self-regulation? In 1981 I redrafted the hypothesis as an evolutionary model, 'Daisyworld', that was intended to show that self-regulation can take place on a planet where organisms evolve by natural selection in a responsive environment. Following the model, the Gaia hypothesis was restated as follows: "The evolution of organisms and their material environment proceeds as a single tight-coupled process from which self-regulation of the environment at a habitable state appears as an emergent phenomenon".

At about the same time, Andrew Watson, Mike Whitfield and I discovered the first mechanism for climate control by the Earth system, namely the biologically assisted reaction between atmospheric carbon dioxide (CO_2) and calcium silicate in soil and on rocks. This process can regulate both climate and CO_2 at a level comfortable for plants. Soon other putative regulation mechanisms were discovered, such as the connection between ocean algae, dimethyl sulphide gas, clouds and climate. By the end of the 1980s there were sufficient evidence and models of the hypothetical system to justify calling it Gaia Theory.

Despite this, in the biological community Gaia Theory was almost wholly rejected, and Earth system science was ignored so far as evolution was concerned. Then in the mid-1990s William Hamilton became interested in Gaia theory. He accepted what was by then the strong evidence that the environment was regulated at a state comfortable for the biota. He saw it as a challenge to explain how this could be a consequence of evolution through natural selection. He published (with Tim Lenton) one paper on the cloud algal system, and his colleague Peter Henderson continues to model systems of biological evolution that include the material environment.

So what bearing does this new view of evolution have on the current mass extinction and what practical use is it?

1. It draws our attention to the biological infrastructure of the Earth, namely the micro-organisms. Lynn Margulis first pointed out their significance and that they still play an important, if not major part, in planetary regulation. Bacteria were the whole biosphere for 3 billion years before multi-cellular organisms such as humans and trees came on the scene.
2. In the real world, organisms grow in a material environment where growth is strongly constrained by the laws of physics and chemistry. When these constraints are included in evolutionary biology models, it becomes possible to build a wide range of stable model systems. These models offer insight into the nature of the Earth system and into the need for biodiversity. Biodiversity is usually valued for its aesthetic or human medicinal qualities; *we* think that biodiversity is an important part of planetary self-regulation.
3. We see the interglacial period that we are now in as a pathological state of the Earth system and see the ice ages as the normal state of the Earth system. In the present interglacial, all of the regulation systems we have so far discovered appear to be in positive feedback towards climate change. This means that any change, either to hotter or colder, is amplified not resisted. This is true of the mechanisms for pumping down CO_2 from the atmosphere, for cloud production by algae, and for the Daisyworld-like behaviour of the boreal and tropical forests. In addition, geophysical feedbacks, such as the effect of ice cover, are positive. An interglacial like now is a period when regulation has temporarily failed and is certainly no time to add more greenhouse gases or deplete biodiversity.

We are living in the midst of a great extinction, where the number of species is declining at a rate comparable in intensity with the extinctions that punctuate the geological record, such as that when the dinosaurs died out 65 million years ago. There is concern about the disappearance of plant and animal species from the equatorial regions, which are sometimes taken as representative of the natural state of the Earth. These tropical regions are indeed biodiverse, but I wonder if, instead of regarding this as a natural state, we should regard biodiversity as an indication that the Earth itself is continuously, but gently, perturbed. Even the single environmental variable, temperature, is perturbed on the short timescale of diurnal change, and through the yearly march of the seasons, to the alternation of glaciations with warm periods like now.

Models that Stephan Harding and I have made suggest that biodiversity is a symptom of perturbation during a state of comparative health. What seems important for sustenance is not so much biodiversity as such, but potential biodiversity, the capacity of a healthy system to respond through diversification when the need arises. In tropical forest and other regions under threat, destroying diversity will reduce the numbers of rare species. Among them may be those able to flourish and sustain the ecosystem when the next large environmental change takes place. It is the loss of diversity and the loss of the potential of the region to sustain biodiversity, that makes the large-scale replacement of natural ecosystems with farmland so dubious an act.

Gaia theory is not contrary to Darwin's great vision; it is like neo-Darwinism, a new look at Darwin's evolutionary theory. I suspect it will be some time before biologists and geologists collaborate closely enough for us to see the emergence of a truly unified Earth system science. William Hamilton, in a television interview, referred to the Gaian view of evolution as Copernican, but he added, "We await a Newton to explain how it works."

References

Capra, F. (1996). *The web of life: A new scientific understanding of living systems*. New York: Doubleday.

Carson, R. (1962). *Silent spring*. Boston: Houghton Mifflin.

Lewin, R. (1999). *Complexity: Life at the edge of chaos* (2nd edition). Chicago: University of Chicago Press.

Lovelock, J. (1979). *Gaia: A new look at life on earth*. Oxford: Oxford University Press.

Lovelock, J. (1995). *The ages of Gaia: A biography of Our Living Earth* (2nd edition). Oxford: Oxford University Press.

Lovelock, J. (2000). *Homage to Gaia: The life of an independent scientist*. Oxford: Oxford University Press.

Lovelock, J. (2002). What is Gaia? *Resurgence, 211*, 6–8.

Lovelock, J. (2006). *The revenge of Gaia: Why the earth is fighting back – and how we can still save humanity*. London: Allen Lane.

Margulis, L. (1997). Big trouble in biology: Physiological autopoiesis versus mechanistic neo-Darwinism. In L. Margulis, & D. Sagan (Eds.), *Slanted truths* (pp. 265–282). New York: Copernicus.

Sagan, D., & Margulis, L. (1997). A good four-letter word. In L. Margulis, & D. Sagan, *Slanted truths* (pp. 201–206). New York: Copernicus.

Learning Systems

Systems of learning in individual practice, groups and organisations

Chapter 26
Kurt Lewin

Kurt Lewin was a visionary and deeply original thinker. He was highly committed both to social change and to developing theories about human behaviour, summing up the connection between the two in saying that "there is nothing so practical as a good theory" (Lewin 1951, p. 169). The list of ideas that he originated is long, notably including group dynamics and action research; he also had a huge impact through institutions he founded, projects he worked on, and students he taught. Often described as the founder of social psychology, Lewin can also been seen as a key bridge between Gestalt psychology (a predecessor to systems thinking), and several early traditions in systems thinking. Burnes (2004, p. 981) has summed up his interests and values as follows:

> Lewin was a humanitarian who believed that only by resolving social conflict, whether it be religious, racial, marital or industrial, could the human condition be improved. Lewin believed that the key to resolving social conflict was to facilitate learning and so enable individuals to understand and restructure their perceptions of the world around them.

Lewin was born in 1890 in the village of Moglino, then part of Germany but now in Poland; his family moved to Berlin when he was 15. He was Jewish, at a time when anti-Semitism was growing within Germany. His personal experience of anti-Semitism gave him a lifelong passion for minority rights and also instilled in him a desire for social change. As a student he became involved in the socialist movement, working for stronger rights for Jewish people and women and for the democratisation of German institutions. At this time he also became involved in adult education for working-class men and women. Many of these concerns would stay with him for the rest of his life.

Most of Lewin's university studies were in psychology at the University of Berlin (following studies at the Universities of Freiberg and Munich in medicine and biology). He graduated with his Ph.D. in 1916, although his studies were interrupted by the First World War – he served the whole war in the German army, during which time he was injured and was awarded the Iron Cross.

Lewin's Ph.D. supervisor was Carl Stumpf, founder of the Psychological Institute at the University of Berlin and a pioneer of experimental psychology, and Lewin carried on to teach and research at the Psychological Institute. Among Stumpf's other doctoral students were the founders of Gestalt psychology – Max

Wertheimer, Kurt Koffka and Wolfgang Köhler – all of whom were working in Berlin at the same time as Lewin.

Gestalt psychology emphasised the patterns (*Gestalten* in German) through which psychological phenomena – notably perceptions – were organised in the mind. The Gestalt theorists held that these patterns of organisation were much more important than the individual elements, that when we perceive (say) a collection of dots we see the pattern of the dots more readily than the individual dots. Gestalt psychologists demonstrated these phenomena experimentally, using tools such as the famous 'figure-ground' images which shift back and forwards between two different interpretations (e.g. a vase and two faces in profile). Gestalt theory can readily be taken as a precursor to systems thinking, with its emphasis on the whole rather than the parts and on the organisation of the whole (a theme later taken up at length by Ludwig von Bertalanffy). Indeed, Koffka (1935, p. 176), building on Aristotle's famous saying that the whole is greater the sum of its parts, wrote that "It has been said: The whole is more than the sum of its parts. It is more correct to say that the whole is something else than the sum of its parts, because summing up is a meaningless procedure, whereas the whole-part relationship is meaningful."

Lewin worked closely with the Gestalt theorists, and is often considered among their number, but had somewhat different interests from the mainstream of Gestalt theory. While he shared their basic view of the importance of pattern and organisation, he was more interested in human needs and motivations than perception, and in the application of psychology to practical problems rather than studies for their own sake. As early as 1920, Lewin wrote an article on the 'socialization of the Taylor system' (the highly mechanistic work of Frederick Taylor on workplace efficiency, later called scientific management), arguing in favour of the involvement of workers in the planning of their work; and in the mid-1920s he carried out two lengthy field studies, in a wallpaper firm and in a textile mill (John et al. 1989). While Lewin continued to carry out laboratory-based experiments as well throughout the 1920s, the use of studies in real settings was firmly established in his work.

The result of Lewin's early work was the development of a highly innovative approach to psychological dynamics, known as field theory. A field is "the totality of coexisting facts which are conceived of as mutually interdependent" (Lewin 1951, p. 240) – all the factors in the environment of an individual or group which influence their behaviour. Lewin saw individual behaviour as a function both of the person and of the environment in which it occurred, expressed in his celebrated formula $B = f(P,E)$. A key aspect of field theory is its use of detailed diagrams, derived from the mathematical principles of topology, to represent the different regions of an individual's personality. More broadly, Lewin referred to the combination of the individual and the environment affecting their personality and behaviour as their life space. Lewin also used diagrammatic forms – force-field diagrams – to represent the forces relating to change in a given situation, both 'driving forces' and 'resisting forces'. Force-field analysis, the approach of analysing driving and resisting forces in a change situation, has been used considerably in management consulting, forming one of the key elements of scenario planning.

Although Lewin's quasi-mathematical use of formulae and diagrams has largely fallen out of favour in social psychology, many of the concepts he introduced through field theory, including his use of boundary, dynamics and life space, have become widely used. An important and influential aspect of field theory was its holistic research method: to start from a description of the whole situation (such as in a diagram) and progressively to analyse the parts of that description, as opposed to the more traditional scientific method of building up from an analysis of the individual parts to a synthesis of the whole. Lewin described this method as being one "that seeks truth by successive approximations" (Argyris 1989, p. 97).

As the 1920s moved into the 1930s, Germany became an increasingly difficult place to be Jewish, and following a brief sabbatical in the United States, Lewin moved there in 1933 (the year Hitler became Chancellor). He was initially based as a refugee scholar at Cornell University, but moved in 1935 to Iowa University where he was to spend the next ten years and where he would develop some of his most influential work.

While at Iowa, he became increasingly concerned with applying field theory to the behaviour of groups as much as of individuals, an approach to which he gave the name group dynamics. This was a logical extension of his earlier observation of the importance of the environment upon an individual's behaviour. Taking as an example the position of Jews in various countries, Lewin observed that "it is not similarity or dissimilarity of individuals that constitutes a group, but rather interdependence of fate" (Lewin 1948, p. 165). Group dynamics was also strongly connected for Lewin with the development of democracy in groups: one of the most famous studies carried out in his time at Iowa (along with his students Ronald Lippitt and Ralph White) demonstrated that children in play groups learnt and behaved much better under democratic styles of adult leadership as opposed to autocratic or laissez-faire styles (White and Lippitt 1960).

The rise of group dynamics reflected Lewin's preferred way of working as well as his research interests. In both Berlin and Iowa, he gathered around him a group of students with whom he worked in a highly collaborative manner based on free discussion of research ideas, usually at a local restaurant or café. In Berlin, this group was known as the *Quasselstrippe*, from the German for 'rambling strings'; in Iowa, it was called the Hot Air Club. As Pratkanis (1989, p. 565) notes, "often research ideas and proposals would emerge, prompting Lewin to frequently claim that he could think only in a group". In this context, rather than in a formal lecture, he was a highly popular and influential teacher, and many of his students in both Germany and the United States were themselves later at the forefront of social psychology. Schellenberg (1978, pp. 77–78) observes that this way of working "expressed as well a key element in his personal belief system. He had a profound faith in democracy, which to him was … a way of life, based on mutual participation and continual interaction in decision making."

Three factors in the conditions of the time in the United States led Lewin to formalise his lifetime goal of social change through social research: the difficult status of minorities (notably Jews and blacks) in a society so keen to espouse democratic values; the high value placed in American culture on applied research, in both society and industry; and the involvement of social theorists in a range of applied, interdisciplinary, projects in the Second World War. Notable projects in this area, among many others, included work (with Margaret Mead) on changing food habits to discourage eating of scarce foods during the war; the training of leaders in inter-group relations (especially involving minority ethnic groups) on behalf of the Connecticut State Inter-Racial Commission; and the setting up of the Commission of Community Interrelations on behalf of the American Jewish Congress, to study and influence racial and religious prejudice.

It was from these experiences that Lewin coined the term 'action research'. Projects of this kind could be characterised, Lewin (1947, p. 150) argued as "a comparative research on the conditions and effects of various forms of social action, and research leading to social action – research that produces nothing but books will not suffice". Thus theory led to action, and action led to theory. The research involved was not necessarily field-based – it could and even should involve laboratory experiments – but it was clearly the case for him that "the problem of our own values, objectives, and of objectivity are nowhere more interwoven and more important than in action-research" (Lewin 1947, p. 153). Indeed, he summed up the basic conception of action research in the saying that "you cannot understand a system until you try to change it" (quoted by Schein 1996).

The cycle of activities that Lewin outlines for action research was later taken by David Kolb as the basis for his learning cycle, widely used in education. This model describes learning as a four-stage feedback cycle: concrete experience, observations and reflections, formations of abstracts concepts and generalisations, and testing implications of concepts in new situations. While this basic model is often referred to as the Kolb learning cycle, Kolb (1984, p. 21) himself refers to it as "the Lewinian experiential learning model".

Lewin's concern for social change led him to develop a three-step model of how to change the behaviour of a group or organisation: *unfreeze* the group from its current 'quasi-stationary equilibrium' (Lewin's term for the current state of a field with its driving and restraining forces); *move* the group to a new state through action research; and *refreeze* it at a new quasi-stationary equilibrium so it cannot return to its original state. This model became widely applied in organisational change, and later widely criticised – for example Orlikowski & Hoffman (1997, p. 11) argue that it treats change "as an event to be managed during a specified period [which] may have been appropriate for organizations that were relatively stable and bounded" which is less relevant in today's complex and turbulent situations. In fact, as Burnes (2004) observes, for Lewin the three-step model is necessarily bound up with a very subtle understanding of behaviour through field theory and group dynamics, and with the method of action research; thus the criticisms apply more to the way Lewin's model has been taken up unthinkingly and without this wider background.

Lewin died suddenly of a massive heart attack, aged 57, in 1947. The final two years of his life were an extremely busy time of institution building and consolidation of his ideas. In 1945, he moved to the Massachusetts Institute of Technology, where he founded the Research Center for Group Dynamics (which continued and moved to the University of Michigan after his death, although the harsh political climate in the US in the late 1940s and early 1950s made social action much harder for his successors). He was very supportive of the founders of the Tavistock Institute of Human Relations in London (notably Eric Trist): "at least in the minds of the initial staff, Kurt Lewin was a 'shadow founder' of the Institute" (Neumann 2005, p. 119); plans were in place for him to spend the academic year 1947–1948, its first full year of operation, at the Tavistock. With colleagues at the Tavistock, he co-founded the important interdisciplinary journal of social science, *Human Relations*, although the first articles by him in that journal appeared posthumously.

The work he led at the Connecticut State Inter-Racial Commission in 1946 led to a breakthrough – the concept of leadership training incorporating reflective feedback sessions, based on dialogue between training staff and group participants, on the experience of being in the group. Drawing on the Connecticut experience, Lewin was involved in the design and planning for a National Training Laboratory in Group Development, which took place in Bethel, Maine in the summer of 1947 (although Lewin himself had died by the time the event began). The success of this laboratory led to the formation of the National Training Laboratories (NTL) as an institute, through which many important innovations in organisational development took place, such as the 'T-group' (based directly on the training groups in Connecticut) and even the invention of the flipchart! Lewin's influence and inspiration can clearly be seen throughout the development of the NTL. The involvement of Chris Argyris with NTL and the inspiration he took from Lewin are described in the chapter on Argyris.

Lewin attended the first two Macy conferences on cybernetics in 1946, and was highly influenced by the developing concept of feedback. His formulation of action research (which first appeared in print in 1946) has a strongly cybernetic flavour. Indeed, Lewin's use of the term feedback in the group dynamics work that led to the NTL was the source of the popular, somewhat inaccurate use of the term (as in 'I must give you some feedback'), as discussed in the chapter on Margaret Mead.

Kurt Lewin was an extraordinary innovator both in terms of theoretical and methodological development, and of social change. His twin passions were summed up by his wife, in an introduction to a posthumous collection of his papers (G. Lewin, in Lewin 1948, p. xv):

> Kurt Lewin was so constantly and predominantly preoccupied with the task of advancing the conceptual representation of the social-psychological world, and at the same time he was so filled with the urgent desire to use his theoretical insight for the building of a better world, that it is difficult to decide which of these two sources of motivation flowed with greater energy or vigour.

Reading from Lewin's work

Lewin, K. "Action Research and Minority Problems," *Journal of Social Issues* **2**, pp. 34–36.
Reproduced with permission of Blackwell Publishing Ltd.

In the last year and a half I have had occasion to have contact with a great variety
of organizations, institutions, and individuals who came for help in the field of
group relations. They included representatives of communities, school systems,
single schools, minority organizations of a variety of backgrounds and objectives;
they included labor and management representatives, departments of the national
and state governments, and so on.

Two basic facts emerged from these contacts: there exists a great amount of
good-will, of readiness to face the problem squarely and really to do something
about it. If this amount of serious good-will could be transformed into organized,
efficient action, there would be no danger for inter-group relations in the United
States. But exactly here lies the difficulty. These eager people feel themselves
to be in the fog. They feel in the fog on three counts: (1) What is the present
situation? (2) What are the dangers? (3) And most important of all, what shall
we do?

We have been conducting an interview survey among workers in inter-group
relations in the State of Connecticut. We wanted to know their line of thinking, their
line of action, and the major barriers which they encounter. Not a few of those
whose very job is the improvement of inter-group relations state that perhaps the
greatest obstacle to their work is their own lack of clarity of what ought to be done.
How is economic and social discrimination to be attacked if we think not in terms
of generalities but in terms of the inhabitants of that particular main street and those
side and end streets which make up that small or large town in which the individual
group worker is supposed to do his job?

One of the consequences of this unclearness is the lack of standards by which to
measure progress. When the inter-group worker, coming home from the good-will
meeting which he helped to instigate, thinks of the dignitaries he was able to line
up, the stirring appeals he heard, the impressive setting of the stage, and the good
quality of the food, he cannot help feeling elated by the general atmosphere and the
words of praise from his friends all around. Still, a few days later, when the next
case of discrimination becomes known he often wonders whether all this was more
than a white-wash and whether he is right in accepting the acknowledgment of his
friends as a measuring stick for the progress of his work.

This lack of objective standards of achievement has two severe effects:

1. It deprives the workers in inter-group relations of their legitimate desire for
   satisfaction on a realistic basis. Under these circumstances, satisfaction or
   dissatisfaction with his own achievements becomes mainly a question of
   temperament.
2. In a field that lacks objective standards of achievement, no learning can take
   place. If we cannot judge whether an action has led forward or backward, if we

have no criteria for evaluating the relation between effort and achievement, there is nothing to prevent us from making the wrong conclusions and to encourage the wrong work habits. Realistic fact-finding and evaluation is a prerequisite for any learning. Social research should be one of the top priorities for the practical job of improving inter-group relations.

Character and function of research for the practice of inter-group relations

The research needed for social practice can best be characterized as research for social management or social engineering. It is a type of action-research, a comparative research on the conditions and effects of various forms of social action, and research leading to social action. Research that produces nothing but books will not suffice.

This by no means implies that the research needed is in any respect less scientific or 'lower' than what would be required for pure science in the field of social events. I am inclined to hold the opposite to be true. Institutions interested in engineering, such as the Massachusetts Institute of Technology, have turned more and more to what is called basic research. In regard to social engineering, too, progress will depend largely on the rate with which basic research in social sciences can develop deeper insight into the laws which govern social life. This 'basic social research' will have to include mathematical and conceptual problems of theoretical analysis. It will have to include the whole range of descriptive fact-finding in regard to small and large social bodies. Above all, it will have to include laboratory and field experiments in social change.

Integrating social sciences

An attempt to improve inter-group relations has to face a wide variety of tasks. It deals with problems of attitude and stereotypes in regard to other groups and to one's own group, with problems of development of attitudes and conduct during childhood and adolescence, with problems of housing, and the change of the legal structure of the community; it deals with problems of status and caste, with problems of economic discrimination, with political leadership, and with leadership in many aspects of community life. It deals with the small social body of a family, a club or a friendship group, with the larger social body of a school or a school system, with neighborhoods and with social bodies of the size of a community, of the state, a nation and with international problems.

We are beginning to see that it is hopeless to attack any one of these aspects of inter-group relations without considering the others. This holds equally for the practical and the scientific sides of the question. Psychology, sociology, and cultural anthropology each have begun to realize that without the help of the other neither will be able to proceed very far. During the last five years first timidly, now very clearly, a desire for an integrated approach has become articulated. What this integration would mean specifically is still open. It may mean an amalgamation of the social sciences into one social science. It may mean, on the other hand, merely the co-operation of various sciences for the practical objective of improving social management. However, the next decade will doubtless witness serious attempts of an integrated approach to social research. I am of the opinion that economics will have to be included in this symphony if we are to understand and to handle inter-group relations more effectively.

[…]

The function and position of research within social planning and action

At least of equal importance to the content of the research on inter-group relations is its proper placement within social life. When, where, and by whom should social research be done?

[…]

Rational social management [proceeds] in a spiral of steps each of which is composed of a circle of planning, action, and fact-finding about the result of the action.

With this in mind, let us examine for a moment the way inter-group relations are handled. I cannot help feeling that the person returning from a successful completion of a good-will meeting is like the captain of a boat who somehow has felt that his ship steers too much to the right and therefore has turned the steering wheel sharply to the left. Certain signals assure him that the rudder has followed the move of the steering wheel. Happily he goes to dinner. In the meantime, of course, the boat moves in circles. In the field of inter-group relations all too frequently action is based on observations made 'within the boat' and too seldom based on objective criteria in regard to the relations of the movement of the boat to the objective to be reached.

[…]

The idea of research or fact-finding branches of agencies devoted to improving inter-group relations is not new. However, some of them did little more than collect newspaper clippings. The last few years have seen a number of very significant developments. About two years ago the American Jewish Congress established the Commission on Community Interrelations. This is an action-research organization designed primarily to function as a service organization to Jewish and non-Jewish bodies in the field of group interrelations. It is mainly interested in the group approach as compared to the individual approach on the one hand and the mass approach by way of radio and newspaper on the other. These latter two important lines are the focus of attention of the research unit of the American Jewish Committee.

Various programs try to make use of our educational system for betterment of inter-group relations. [...] I cannot possibly attempt to discuss the many projects and findings which are emerging from these research undertakings. They include surveys of the methods which have been used until now, such as reported in Watson (1946); studies of the development of attitudes in children; studies of the relation between inter-group attitudes and such factors as political belief, position in one's own group; experiments about how best to react in case of a verbal attack along prejudice lines; change experiments with criminal gangs and with communities; the development of many new diagnostic tests; and last but not least, the development of more precise theories of social change.

References

Argyris, C. (1989). Integrating theory and practice. *Academy of Management Review, 14*(1), 96–98.

Burnes, B. (2004). Kurt Lewin and the planned approach to change: A re-appraisal. *Journal of Management Studies, 41*(6), 977–1002.

John, M., Eckardt, G., Hiebsch, H. (1989). Kurt Lewin's early intentions. *European Journal of Social Psychology, 19*(2), 163–169.

Koffka, K. (1935). *Principles of Gestalt psychology.* New York: Harcourt-Brace.

Kolb, D. (1984). *Experiential learning: Experience as the source of learning and development.* Englewood Cliffs, NJ: Prentice-Hall.

Lewin, K. (1946). Action research and minority problems. *Journal of Social Issues, 2*(4), 34–46.

Lewin, K. (1947). Frontiers in group dynamics II: Channels of group life; Social Planning and Action Research. *Human Relations, 1*(2), 143–153.

Lewin, K. (1948). *Resolving social conflicts.* New York: Harper & Row.

Lewin, K. (1951). *Field theory in social science.* New York: Harper & Row.

Neumann, J. (2005). Kurt Lewin at The Tavistock Institute. *Educational action research, 13*(1), 119–136.

Orlikowski, W.J., & Hofman, J.D. (1997). An improvisational model for change management: The case of Groupware Technologies. *Sloan Management Review, 38*(2), 11–21.

Pratkanis, A. (1989). Review of *The Lewin Legacy. American Journal of Psychology, 102*(4), 563–567.

Schein, E. (1996). Kurt Lewin's change theory in the field and in the classroom: Notes towards a model of management learning. *Systems Practice, 9*(1), 27–47.

Schellenberg, J. (1978). *Masters of social psychology.* New York: Oxford University Press.

Watson, G. (1946). *Action for unity.* New York: Harper and Brothers.

White, R. K., & Lippitt, R. (1960). *Autocracy and democracy: An experimental inquiry.* New York: Harper & Bros.

Chapter 27
Eric Trist

One of the greatest contributions made to a humanistic approach to work organisation started with a coal mine. In the late 1940s, Eric Trist, social psychologist and deputy chairman of the Tavistock Institute in London was supervising a postgraduate industrial fellow called Ken Bamforth, a former miner. The fellows were encouraged to return to their former industries and report on developments. When Bamforth did this, Eric Trist later said, "he came back to London very excited and said, 'You must come and see what is happening up there, because I think it has something to do with us.' So I went up with him to Yorkshire, went down the mine, and came up a different man" (Fox 1990, p. 260).

The research that Trist carried out in the light of his Yorkshire coal mine experience was to become known as the sociotechnical systems approach, and it had considerable impact on the way work is organised in a number of countries. It reflected Trist's personality: passionately committed to social justice and to being active in the world, but also deeply grounded in academic knowledge and in the detail of the situation he was studying. As one former colleague recalled, he displayed "a tremendous sense of fun, a tremendous sense of seeing the enjoyment in life – and really engaging with real life in a personal way and not only, as it were, in thinking or in conceptual terms" (Bridger et al. 1994, p. 21).

Trist both pioneered and embodied action research – an interplay between his deep interaction with real problems in organisations, and the forefront of academic thought in social science. In each of his many projects – from jute mills in Dundee through coal mines in Yorkshire to an entire manufacturing town in New York State – he was an active contributor to both theory and practice. He said that "I used to look with longing at what I called the 'white-coated peace', the tranquillity of the white-coated scientists working in the lab. But that was not for me. I didn't have a white lab coat. I was in the messy, ambiguous, problematic stuff that you have to endure if you are going to be a psychologist" (Fox 1990, p. 263).

Eric Lansdown Trist was born in 1909 in Dover, UK and died in 1993 in Carmel, California. He studied English and psychology for five years at Cambridge University, graduating in 1933. His most significant influences at Cambridge were the important scholar of literary criticism I.A. Richards (who later attended one of the Macy conferences on cybernetics) and the psychologist Frederick Bartlett, who developed a highly active theory of memory that continues to be important.

M. Ramage and K. Shipp, *Systems Thinkers,*   269
© The Open University 2009. Published in association with Springer-Verlag London Limited

Towards the end of his time at Cambridge, Trist became interested in the work of the social psychologist Kurt Lewin. One afternoon, he shared his deep excitement over an article of Lewin's on scientific method with his professor, Frederick Bartlett, which "went against me – young Trist had shown himself guilty of enthusiasm, of being uncritically over-impressed, not detached enough, too involved" (Trist 1993). He met Lewin briefly at Cambridge (while Trist was showing him around the city, Lewin almost missed his train because he was too excited by the statue of Isaac Newton at Newton's own college, Trinity), and later for a longer period in the United States. Trist became deeply influenced by Lewin's work, and indeed Evered (1994, p. 8) argues that "Lewin's principle that behaviour is a function of both the person and the environment is brought to fruition in Trist's work. Eric Trist is surely the true heir of Kurt Lewin's life work".

After Cambridge, Trist was awarded a Commonwealth Fellowship and went to Yale University. While there, he was particularly inspired by Edward Sapir, the great linguistic anthropologist who argued that personality and culture were strongly intertwined (a view he shared with fellow-anthropologist Margaret Mead). Sapir's concept of culture as something active, which each person interacts with individually, was greatly important to Trist's developing sense of the importance of the environment (the context in which they live) on the individual, and he later described Sapir as "the biggest influence on my intellectual life, ever" (Trist 1993). His time in the US confirmed his identity as a social psychologist.

However, British psychology of the time did not favour the social view, and Trist found it hard to obtain a job when he returned to the UK in 1935. Eventually he found a research post based at the University of St Andrews, studying the psychological effects of long-term unemployment in the nearby city of Dundee. This work built on and enhanced his growing social consciousness, also gained in the US through observing the terrible effects upon people of the Depression. This project was one of the very first examples of an action research approach, with Trist living in the community he was studying and establishing with them in advance that there would be mutual benefit both for the researchers and for the community.

Trist's career took a new turn with the outbreak of the Second World War, as a clinical psychologist at the Maudsley Psychiatric Hospital in London, which gave him considerable new experience of clinical psychology and of psychoanalysis. His experience at the Maudsley led him, after two years, to move into the British army to join the work being carried out by a group of psychiatrists from the Tavistock Clinic who were working on the effective use of human resources in the army. With Jock Sutherland and Wilfred Bion, psychiatrists strongly aligned with psychoanalysis (Bion later became famous for his work on group dynamics), Trist developed the form and methods of the War Office Selection Boards, the direct antecedents of the 'assessment centres' widely used in recruitment. Trist's final main work in the war, again with the Tavistock group, was as chief psychologist to the Civil Resettlement Units, therapeutic communities for prisoners of war returning to the UK, which he described as "probably the most exciting single experience of my professional life ... a tremendous success and broke very new ground" (Trist 1993).

The successes of the Tavistock Clinic and its associates in the war led them to an awareness that the methods they had developed would have a role in the post-war world well beyond that of individual psychiatry. This led to the formation of the Tavistock Institute of Human Relations as a distinct entity in 1946, of which Trist became the deputy chairman. The Tavistock was strongly influenced by psychoanalysis, particularly the work of Melanie Klein, and all their staff were required to enter training analysis. However, Klein's interest in the impact of the environment on the individual was waning while the Tavistock "paid major attention to the environment, and became interested in social applications of psychoanalysis" (Trist 1993).

The importance of the environment, and the interdisciplinary nature of the work it required, was to become quickly important for the nascent Tavistock Institute: while it had initially received project funding from the Medical Research Council, and seed funding from the Rockefeller Foundation, both ran out at the end of the 1940s. The Institute therefore had to fund itself by industrial consultancy, with clients including Unilever (for whom they applied the work on War Office Selection Boards to their management development programme) and Mars (for whom they carried out consumer studies). The Tavistock's industrial and interdisciplinary focus made it hard for them to publish in traditional academic journals, so in 1947 they established the journal *Human Relations* along with Kurt Lewin and his colleagues (the journal continues to this day and has published many important articles).

It was in this context that Trist had his revelation at the Haighmoor coal mine in Yorkshire. What he saw there was that technological developments had enabled miners to work in small autonomous groups, with each person responsible for a range of tasks, rather than the highly specialised and routinised production-line approach then common in industry. Further studies in coal mining and in other industries over the next few years revealed similar experiences with autonomous work groups enabled by new technologies, although the Tavistock group experienced considerable resistance from industry (with the National Coal Board threatening to cut off all access if they published on autonomous groups).

During the early 1950s, Trist began a research collaboration with Fred Emery that would last the rest of their lives and shape both of their ideas considerably. Emery was an Australian who began as a natural scientist, became a psychologist during his doctorate, and made great contributions to organisational development and to systems thinking (working later with Russell Ackoff as well as with Trist), notably through his 'search conference' workshop design for looking at desirable futures for an organisation. He was attracted to the Tavistock because he wanted to "do real science in important practical social matters" (quoted by Heller 1997, p. 1212), and worked there for a decade.

In due course, Trist and Emery put together a solid theoretical perspective from the Haighmoor experiences. They built on Bion's and Lewin's different theories of group dynamics, which both "emphasised the capacity of the small group for self-regulation, an aspect of systems theory which received increasing attention as cybernetics developed" (Trist 1981). They also drew extensively on von Bertalanffy's

(1950) work on open systems, with its emphasis on the importance of the role of the environment in the development of a system. Taken together, this work became the sociotechnical systems approach.

The basic goal of sociotechnical systems design is one of "the joint optimization of the social and technical systems" (Emery, quoted in Trist 1981). Strongly linked with this goal has been the development of a theory of work design that is based on the study of the whole work system, organised in terms of self-regulating groups and multi-skilled individuals. This approach developed through a large number of international projects at the Tavistock, largely led by Trist. Perhaps the most notable was the Norwegian Industrial Democracy Project in the early 1960s which ultimately led to legislation in Norway (later emulated throughout Scandinavia) which "gave workers the right to demand jobs conforming to sociotechnical principles of good work practice – variety, learning opportunity, own decision power, organizational support, social recognition and a desirable future" (Mumford 2006, p. 325). The focus on industrial democracy became increasingly important in sociotechnical systems through the 1960s, although discomfort with the particular phrase in some large corporations, especially American, led to the rebranding of this approach as 'quality of working life' at a conference in 1972.

Trist carried out many other research projects at the Tavistock, notably on group dynamics with Wilfred Bion. He became chairman of the Tavistock in 1956 (when the founding chairman, Tommy Wilson, left to join Unilever) and continued in that role for ten years. Under Trist's leadership, the Tavistock began important work in group relations training (the Leicester conferences), family therapy (which led to the semi-autonomous Institute of Marital Studies) and operational research (which again led to a semi-autonomous Institute of Operational Research, with the considerable involvement of Russell Ackoff). In each of these pieces of work (and many others), Trist was more than a manager – he was deeply involved in their conceptualisation and their practical implementation. Building effective institutions, often taking a networked form, was something very important to him.

In 1966, Trist left the Tavistock Institute and moved to California, partly due to the health of his wife Beulah and partly because of splits and differences within the Tavistock. He was based in North America for the rest of his life – for three years at the University of California at Los Angeles, from 1969 until 1978 at the University of Pennsylvania (where he worked closely with Russell Ackoff) and from 1978 until 1985 at York University in Toronto. Although ill health forced him to retire from his active university post (at the age of 76), he carried on working on a three-volume anthology of papers from the Tavistock.

Trist's work in North America continued to be strongly focused on action research, "which expresses the social engagement of social science, compels the research worker to make interdisciplinary combinations in order to understand the many-sided real life situations being dealt with" (Trist 1990, p. 539). Notably, he carried out a sociotechnical project on a whole town in Jamestown, New York State, allowing him to go up a systemic level and look at a much larger work system.

His later work took him to a further systemic level, though building on many of the same principles. Working with Fred Emery again, Trist also expanded his work to cover what they the termed 'social ecology' – the changing nature of the environment around systems (unrelated to the ecology of the natural world). It arose from a set of projects carried out in the early 1960s with very large organisations working in rapidly changing situations, such as the National Farmers Union and a manufacturer of aircraft engines. Emery and Trist argued in a classic paper that it was necessary to go beyond general systems theory, and consider not just the elements of a system's environment that impact upon the system but the processes of change within the environment which will in future come to affect the system. In particular, they identified a certain class of environments as 'turbulent fields', with rapid change and significant interdependencies between elements in the environment: "the dynamic properties arise not simply from the interaction of the component organizations but also from the field itself – the 'ground' is in motion" (Emery and Trist 1965, p. 26).

This led Trist and Emery to a series of further studies and publications around the ways organisations need to behave in turbulent fields (published as Emery and Trist 1972). In industrial societies, organisations have succeeded through structuring themselves mechanistically, competing with each other, and controlling their environments. In a more turbulent post-industrial world, organisations need to learn to plan for the long term, work in a co-ordinated and co-operative way, and structure themselves organically around networks. This also led Trist into future studies, the role of flexibility in organisations and the use of methods such as action learning and Emery's 'search conference' workshops. In the 1990s and 2000s, an awareness of turbulence, complexity and the deeply interconnected globalised environment, and the consequent use of techniques such as scenario planning and organisational learning have become widespread. It shows Trist's extraordinary far-sightedness that he was able to see the need for these approaches, from working closely with real organisations, 30 years before they become common.

Eric Trist made an enormous set of contributions to organisations, systems and psychology. He developed many important new ideas and techniques; he founded several significant organisations; and he was passionately committed to social change. He achieved a great deal with his life, and was never afraid to go beyond accepted wisdom. It is not really possible to sum up all of Trist's contributions, but his values were clear, and those stand as his greatest tribute and lasting impact, as one colleague recalled (Evered 1994, p. 7):

> His life stands as an example of what is possible in working *with* others. He was a collaborator, someone whose power was working with others as colearners and cocreators. He has shown us all how to do social science that has real human consequences, that both makes a difference to people's lives and provides us with the means to more richly understand the nature of organisational life.

Reading from Trist's work

Trist, E. (1981) "The Evolution of Socio-Technical Systems", *Perspectives on Organizational Design and Behavior*, Van de Ven, A. H and Joyce, W. F. (eds.), Copyright ©1981. New York: John Wiley. Reproduced with permission of John Wiley & Sons Inc.
Extract from pages 20–25.

The sociotechnical concept arose in conjunction with the first of several field projects undertaken by the Tavistock Institute in the British coal-mining industry. The time (1949) was that of the post-war reconstruction of industry in relation to which the Institute had two action research projects. One was concerned with group relations in depth at all levels (including the management-labor interface) in a single organization, an engineering company in the private sector. The other project focused on the diffusion of innovative work practices and organizational arrangements that did not require major capital expenditure but which gave promise of raising productivity. The former project represented the first comprehensive application in an industrial setting of the socioclinical ideas concerning groups being developed at the Tavistock. For this purpose a novel action research methodology was introduced. The book describing the project became a classic (Jaques 1951). Nevertheless, it approached the organization exclusively as a social system. The second project was led, through circumstances described below, to include the technical as well as the social system in the factors to be considered and to postulate that the relations between them should constitute *a new field of inquiry*.

Coal being then the chief source of power, a plentiful and cheap supply of it was important for industrial reconstruction. But the newly nationalized industry was not doing well. Productivity failed to increase in step with increases in mechanization. Men were leaving the mines in large numbers for better opportunities in the factories. Among those who remained, absenteeism averaged 20%. Labor disputes were frequent despite improved conditions of employment. Some time earlier the National Coal Board had asked the Institute to make a comparative study of a high producing, high morale mine and a low producing, low morale, but otherwise equivalent mine. Despite nationalization, however, our research team was not welcome at the coal face under the auspices of the Board.

There were at the Institute at that time six postgraduate Fellows being trained for industrial field work. Among these, three had a trade union background and one, the late Ken Bamforth, had been a miner. After a year, the Fellows were encouraged to revisit their former industries and report any new perceptions. Bamforth returned with news of an innovation in work practice and organization taking place in a new seam in the colliery where he used to work in the South Yorkshire coalfield. The seam, the Haighmoor, had become possible to mine 'shortwall' because of improved roof control. I can recall now the excitement with which I listened to him. I lost no time in going up to visit this colliery where, since we were introduced by him, the local management and union readily agreed to our researching their innovation with a view to its diffusion to other mines. The Area General Manager, who managed some 20 mines, welcomed the idea. The technical conception of the new scheme was his, though the men, with union support, had proposed the actual working arrangements.

The work organization of the new seam was to us a novel phenomenon consisting of a set of relatively autonomous groups interchanging roles and shifts and regulating their affairs with a minimum of supervision. Cooperation between task groups was everywhere in evidence; personal commitment was obvious, absenteeism low, accidents infrequent, productivity high. The contrast was large between the atmosphere and arrangements on these faces and those in the conventional areas of the pit, where the negative features characteristic of the industry were glaringly apparent. The men told us that in order to adapt with best advantage to the technical conditions in the new seam, they had evolved a form of work organization based on practices common in unmechanized days when small groups, who took responsibility for the entire cycle, had worked autonomously. These practices had disappeared as the pits became progressively more mechanized when 'longwall' working had been introduced. This had enlarged the scale of operations and led to aggregates of men of considerable size having their jobs broken down into one-man-one-task roles, while coordination and control were externalized in supervision, which became coercive. Now they had found a way at a higher level of mechanization, of recovering the group cohesion and self-regulation they had lost and of advancing their power to participate in decisions concerning their work arrangements. For this reason, the book which overviewed the Tavistock mining studies was subtitled "The Loss, Rediscovery and Transformation of a Work Tradition" (Trist et al. 1963).

The transformation represented a change of direction in organizational design. For several decades the prevailing direction had been to increase bureaucratization with each increase in scale and level of mechanization. The organizational model that fused Weber's description of bureaucracy with Frederick Taylor's concept of scientific management had become pervasive. The Haighmoor innovation showed that there was an alternative.

Those concerned with it had made an *organizational choice* (Trist et al. 1963). They could, with minor modifications, have extended the prevailing mode of working. They chose instead to elaborate a major design alternative. It was not true that the only way of designing work organizations was to conform to Tayloristic and bureaucratic principles. There were other ways, which represented a discontinuity with the prevailing mode. The technological imperative could be disobeyed with positive economic as well as human results. As became clearer later, what happened in the Haighmoor seam gave to Bamforth and me a first glimpse of "the emergence of a new paradigm of work" (Emery 1978) in which the best match would be sought between the requirements of the social and technical systems.

Some of the principles involved were as follows:

1. The *work system*, which comprised a set of activities that made up a functioning whole, now became the basic unit rather than the single jobs into which it was decomposable.
2. Correspondingly, the *work group* became central rather than the individual jobholder.

3. *Internal regulation* of the system by the group was thus rendered possible rather than the external regulation of individuals by supervisors.
4. A design principle based on the *redundancy of functions* rather than the redundancy of parts (Emery 1967) characterized the underlying organizational philosophy, which tended to develop multiple skills in the individual and immensely increase the response repertoire of the group.
5. This principle valued the *discretionary* rather than the prescribed part of work roles (Jaques 1956).
6. It treated the individual as *complementary* to the machine rather than as an extension of it (Jordan 1963).
7. It was *variety-increasing* for both the individual and the organization rather than variety-decreasing in the bureaucratic mode.

Conceptually, the new paradigm entailed a shift in the way work organizations were envisaged. Under the old paradigm, engineers, following the technological imperative, would design whatever organization the technology seemed to require. This was a rule accepted by all concerned (Davis et al. 1955). The 'people cost' of proceeding in this way was not considered. [...]

The idea of separate approaches to the social and the technical systems of an organization could no longer suffice for one who had experienced, as I had, the profound consequences of a change in social-technical relations such as had occurred in the Haighmoor development. Work organizations exist to do work – which involves people using technological artifacts (whether hard or soft) to carry out sets of tasks related to specified overall purposes. Accordingly, a conceptual reframing was proposed in which work organizations were envisaged as sociotechnical systems rather than simply as social systems (Trist 1950). The social and technical systems were the substantive factors, that is, the people and the equipment. Economic performance and job satisfaction were outcomes, the level of which depended on the goodness of fit between the substantive factors.

[...]

From the beginning the sociotechnical concept has developed in terms of systems, since it is concerned with interdependencies. It has also developed in terms of open system theory, since it is concerned with the environment in which an organization must actively maintain a steady state. von Bertalanffy's (1950) paper on "Open Systems in Physics and Biology" became available at the time that the sociotechnical concept was being formulated. It influenced both theory-building and field projects, compelling attention alike to self-regulation and environmental relations.

References

Bridger, H., Burgess, S., Emery, F., Hjelholt, G., Qvale, T., van Beinum, H. (1994). Eric trist remembered: 1. The European years. *Journal of Management Inquiry*, 3(1), 10–22.
Davis, L.E., Canter, R.R., Hoffman, J. (1955). Current job design criteria. *Journal of Industrial Engineering*, 6, 5–11.

Emery, F. (1967). The next thirty years: Concepts, methods, and anticipations. *Human Relations,* *20*(3), 199–237.

Emery, F. (1978). *The emergence of a new paradigm of work.* Canberra: Centre for Continuing Education, Australian National University.

Emery, F., & Trist, E. (1965). The causal texture of organizational environments. *Human Relations, 18*(1), 21–32.

Emery, F., & Trist, E. (1972). *Towards a social ecology: Contextual appreciation of the future in the present.* London: Plenum.

Evered, R. (1994). Editor's introduction. *Journal of Management Inquiry, 3*(1), 6–9.

Fox, W. (1990). An interview with Eric Trist, Father of the Sociotechnical Systems Approach. *Journal of Applied Behavioral Science, 26*(2), 259–279.

Heller, F. (1997). Frederick Edmund Emery. *Human Relations, 50*(10), 1211–1214.

Jaques, E. (1951). *The changing culture of a factory.* London: Tavistock.

Jaques, E. (1956). *Measurement of responsibility: A study of work, payment, and individual capacity.* New York: Dryden.

Jordan, N. (1963). Allocation of functions between man and machines in automated systems. *Journal of Applied Psychology, 47*(3), 161–165.

Mumford, E. (2006). The story of socio-technical design: Reflections on its successes, failures and potential. *Information Systems Journal, 16*(4), 317–342.

Trist, E. (1950). The relations of social and technical systems in coal-mining. Paper presented to the British Psychological Society, Industrial Section.

Trist, E. (1981). The sociotechnical perspective. In A. H. Van de Ven, & W. F. Joyce (Eds.), *Perspectives on organizational design and behavior* (pp.19–75). New York: John Wiley.

Trist, E. (1990). Culture as a psycho-social process. In E. Trist, & H. Murray (Eds.), *The social engagement of social science: A Tavistock anthology,* vol. 1 (pp. 539–545). Philadelphia: University of Pennsylvania Press.

Trist, E. (1993). Guilty of enthusiasm. In A. G. Bedeian (Ed.), *Management laureates,* vol. 3. Greenwich, UK: JAI Press.

Trist, E., Higgin, G. W., Murray, H., Pollock, A. B. (1963). *Organizational choice: Capabilities of groups at the coal face under changing technologies: The loss, rediscovery and transformation of a work tradition.* London: Tavistock Publications.

Von Bertalanffy, L. (1950). The theory of open systems in physics and biology. *Science, 111*(2872), 23–29.

Chapter 28
Chris Argyris

Chris Argyris is a theorist and practitioner of organisational development. For more than 50 years, he has written, taught and acted as a consultant in helping people and organisations to learn. He has published over thirty books and a large number of articles, many written with a high degree of scientific rigour, but his focus has always been on research that can be applied within organisations – a strong "commitment to the development of actionable knowledge" (Argyris 2003, p. 1190). He has described the starting point of his work as follows:

> I began my career with a dedication to reducing injustices. The injustices that intrigued me were those that inhibited the expansion of liberating alternatives. Soon I narrowed my focus even further to those injustices created by human beings when they were acting to reduce the injustices. The more that I studied these phenomena, the more I found myself studying processes that were self-sealing, compulsively repetitive, and non-interruptible and changeable by the very people who created them. (Argyris 2003, p. 1178).

Argyris was born in 1923 in New Jersey, USA, of Greek-American origin. He took his B.A. degree (1947) in Psychology at Clark University, where he met Kurt Lewin, the founder of group dynamics and action research (two of Argyris' greatest interests), who had a huge influence on his work (Woodell 2003, p. 67). His Ph.D. (1951) was from Cornell University in Organizational Behaviour, where his supervisor was William Foote Whyte, author of the classic ethnography of urban life, *Street Corner Society* (Whyte 1943). He has largely worked at two universities – Yale, from 1951 to 1971 as a professor of Administrative Science; and Harvard from 1971, as a professor of Education and Organizational Behaviour. For a number of years, he was a fellow of the National Training Laboratories (NTL), which carried on the work of Lewin after his early death and founded the field of organisational development through its T-group method; and he is a director of the Monitor Group, a consultancy organisation linked to the Harvard Business School.

Early in his academic career, Argyris shifted his concern from studying individuals to studying organisations. His first widely-read work (Argyris 1957) discussed the impact of hierarchical organisations with their classic pyramid structures upon the people who worked in them. He concluded that "if hierarchies had their way, they would create work worlds for human beings that were consistent with the features of infancy ... those workers who valued adult-like work settings would likely experience a conflict and would likely be frustrated" (Argyris 2003, p. 1182).

This led him to look for ways to change this situation but he "could find no approach, at that time, which was both powerful and efficient enough to do the job – after all, you can't put thousands of employees through therapy" (Woodell 2003, p. 68). It was only through working as a trainer with NTL that he "felt that I had finally found a way to integrate the individual and the organisation" (Woodell 2003, p. 68). Argyris was particularly effective in working with T-groups, the intensive training groups developed at NTL based on Kurt Lewin's work on feedback and participant observation. Kleiner (1996, p. 230) describes Argyris' work with NTL:

> The [T-]group confronted people with the direct record – Argyris called this the 'data' – of their own conversations, so that they could see how they had been locked into destructive ways of thinking and relating. Nobody could confront a group with its 'data' the way Argyris could. He was fearless in the facilitator's role; he seemed oblivious to whether people might be offended or have their feelings hurt, as long as they were learning. Listening to the conversation, his eyes would brighten and intensify until he was like a bird of prey, perching at the edge of the table, alert to the nuance in every phrase. Then, suddenly, he would pounce.

In 1971, Argyris moved from Yale to Harvard and stopped working with NTL. Although Argyris was based jointly in the graduate schools of education and business, and initially preferred to work on effective learning within schools, he found that schoolteachers were not receptive to his ideas, and thus moved to work with business executives (Crossan 2003).

It was also at Harvard that his long collaboration began with Donald Schön, of the Massachusetts Institute of Technology (MIT), with whom several of his major academic contributions developed. For 15 years, they worked closely together in teaching, researching and consultancy about the nature of effective organisational learning. Their collaboration led to two major joint books, *Theory in Practice* (Argyris and Schön 1974) and *Organizational Learning* (Argyris and Schön 1978, 1996). The latter was the first published use of the term organisational learning (Fulmer and Keys 1998), at a time when it was not of obvious interest to academics or managers, despite its later importance through the works of Peter Senge and others on the learning organisation. Argyris and Schön each brought important contributions to this joint work, as discussed in the chapter on Schön, and they later took their joint ideas forward in different ways.

Argyris and Schön's first piece of joint research was a study of educational administrators. Their starting point was around theories of action: "a set of rules that individuals use to design and implement their own behaviour as well as to understand the behaviour of others" (Argyris 1991, p. 103). They distinguished between two forms of theories of action: espoused theories, which people believe in, advocate, and claim to be those which govern their actions; and theories-in-use, which in real situations actually govern a particular individual's actions. The former are explicit and articulated, the latter are implicit and can only be inferred from an individual's behaviour. There is frequently a discrepancy between the two forms of theory – that is, we frequently behave in ways other than our self-image or the image we project to others. This discrepancy is not a matter of hypocrisy, but it is important for an individual to understand that the two theories of action may be different, and to be able to make sense of their own theory-in-use.

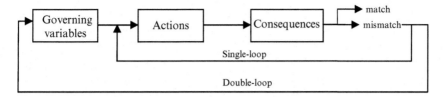

Fig. 28.1 Single- and double-loop learning. From Argyris (1992) with permission Wiley-Blackwell

Argyris and Schön (1974) defined theories-in-use according to three linked elements: governing variables (the assumptions we make in our theories and the things we seek to keep at acceptable levels), action strategies (the ways we act in order to keep our governing variables within our appropriate levels), and consequences (the results of actions, both intended and unintended). It is the relation between these three elements that leads to their distinction between single-loop and double-loop learning (see Fig. 28.1 below). This concept derives from a long antecedence in cybernetics. Argyris and Schön explicitly credit Ross Ashby (1960) for this distinction – as discussed in the chapter on Ashby, he referred to the process of 'double feedback' – as well as drawing on Gregory Bateson's work on levels of learning.

The distinction between single-loop and double-loop learning is thus concerned with what changes as a result of a mismatch between the expected and actual consequences of one's actions. If observing those consequences just results in changes in future actions (better to meet the sought-for values of the governing variables), that is single-loop learning; if observing the consequences of actions results in changes in assumptions about what outcomes are desirable, that would be double-loop learning.

It is not the case that single-loop learning is necessarily inferior to double-loop learning. Argyris and Schön (1996, p. 22) observe that single-loop learning is "concerned primarily with effectiveness: how best to achieve existing goals and objectives, keeping organisational performance within the range specified by existing values and norms", and this is frequently both appropriate and necessary. However, it is clear that double-loop learning brings about results which are not possible with single-loop learning, and that any sort of significant transformation within organisations requires this deeper form of learning.

Double-loop learning is hard for both individuals and organisations – and especially for successful ones – in that it appears to challenge the very factors that led to their success. This creates a form of defensive behaviour which has been the subject of much of Argyris' work. He has observed it operating within organisations (Argyris 1990), among highly-skilled professionals (Argyris 1991) and even among researchers studying the nature of defensive behaviour (Argyris 2003).

The source of this defensive behaviour is found in Argyris and Schön's (1974) work on theories-in-use. They distinguish between two typical patterns of theories-in-use. The first of these, Model I, is closely linked to single-loop learning: its values include being in unilateral control of situations, striving to win rather than losing, suppressing negative feelings in oneself and others, and acting rationally. By contrast, Model II behaviour is linked to double-loop learning: its values include utilizing valid information, promoting free and informed choice, and assuming personal responsibility to monitor effectiveness (Fulmer and Keys 1998, p. 25).

Argyris has observed through a number of studies that "the use of Model I is consistent, regardless of gender, race, culture, education, wealth, and type of organization" (Argyris 2002, p. 212). He acknowledges that both espoused theories and the way that theories-in-use are actually implemented vary widely, but that when theories-in-use are examined, Model I behaviour is extremely prevalent.

Model I behaviour creates the phenomenon of defensive reasoning: "individuals keep their premises and inferences tacit, lest they lose control; they create tests of their claims that are self-serving and self-sealing" (Argyris 2002, p. 212). In turn this defensive reasoning creates a set of additional negative phenomena – skilled incompetence, where skilful people act below their capabilities in order to maintain patterns of comfortable behaviour; and organisational defensive routines, which act in the same manner at an organisational level: "any action, policy, or practice that prevents organizational participants from experiencing embarrassment or threat and, at the same time, prevents them from discovering the causes of the embarrassment or threat" (Argyris 2002, p. 213). The use of Model I behaviour inhibits the capacity of organisations and individuals towards double-loop learning.

It is important to realise that Argyris does not blame those who exhibit defensive routines for their behaviour, although he is highly critical of those defensive routines and their effects. Rather, he seeks to help individuals and organisations shift towards Model II theories-in-use, those he refers to as "productive routines" (Argyris 2002, p. 214). How to enable this shift to Model II has been the subject of much of Argyris' work – he has worked on the question theoretically but also worked with many people through his teaching and consultancy to enable them to achieve this shift themselves. Senge (1990, p. 183) describes an experience of Argyris in action, carrying out this work:

> Within a matter of minutes, I watched the level of alertness and 'presentness' of the entire group rise ten notches – thanks not so much to Argyris's personal charisma, but to his skilful practice of drawing out … generalizations. As the afternoon moved on, all of us were led to see (sometimes for the first time in our lives) subtle patterns of reasoning which underlay our behaviour; and how those patterns continually got us into trouble.

Chris Argyris has made many contributions to theories about the effective working of organisations. He writes that his goal has always been "to emphasize the importance of theory and to connect the theory with my deepest feelings" (Argyris 2003, p. 1190). Seen as a whole, his work emphasises themes of the relationship between the individual and organisations, the importance and difficulty of real learning, and the ways in which research must be applicable to be considered valid. He exhibits a deep congruence between the way he thinks and the way he acts, and demands that congruence of others. Tsoukas (2002) summarises these strands and relates them to other systems work:

> Argyris invites knowledge workers to undertake a primarily moral, not just technical, task: to be open to criticism, to be willing to test their claims publicly against evidence, to accept that they too are partly responsible for the problems they are confronted with. … In that sense, as well as being an influential organisational psychologist and an implicit moral philosopher,

Argyris is a systemic theorist, not too different from his own hero Gregory Bateson: we partly create the problems we face, he says, and we have a responsibility for this.

Reading from Argyris' work

How professionals avoid learning

For 15 years, I have been conducting in-depth studies of management consultants. I decided to study consultants for a few simple reasons. First, they are the epitome of the highly educated professionals who play an increasingly central role in all organizations. Almost all of the consultants I've studied have MBAs from the top three or four U.S. business schools. They are also highly committed to their work. For instance, at one company, more than 90% of the consultants responded in a survey that they were "highly satisfied" with their jobs and with the company.

I also assumed that such professional consultants would be good at learning. After all, the essence of their job is to teach others how to do things differently. I found, however, that these consultants embodied the learning dilemma. The most enthusiastic about continuous improvement in their own organizations, they were also often the biggest obstacle to its complete success.

As long as efforts at learning and change focused on external organizational factors – job redesign, compensation programs, performance reviews, and leadership training – the professionals were enthusiastic participants. Indeed, creating new systems and structures was precisely the kind of challenge that well-educated, highly motivated professionals thrived on.

And yet the moment the quest for continuous improvement turned to the professionals' *own* performance, something went wrong. It wasn't a matter of bad attitude. The professionals' commitment to excellence was genuine, and the vision of the company was clear. Nevertheless, continuous improvement did not persist. And the longer the continuous improvement efforts continued, the greater the likelihood that they would produce ever-diminishing returns.

What happened? The professionals began to feel embarrassed. They were threatened by the prospect of critically examining their own role in the organization. Indeed, because they were so well paid (and generally believed that their employers were supportive and fair), the idea that their performance might not be at its best made them feel guilty.

Far from being a catalyst for real change, such feelings caused most to react defensively. They projected the blame for any problems away from themselves and onto what they said were unclear goals, insensitive and unfair leaders, and stupid clients.

[...]

Defensive reasoning and the doom loop

What explains the professionals' defensiveness? Not their attitudes about change or commitment to continuous improvement; they really wanted to work more effectively. Rather, the key factor is the way they reasoned about their behavior and that of others.

It is impossible to reason anew in every situation. If we had to think through all the possible responses every time someone asked, "How are you?" the world would pass us by. Therefore, everyone develops a theory of action – a set of rules that individuals use to design and implement their own behavior as well as to understand the behavior of others. Usually, these theories of actions become so taken for granted that people don't even realize they are using them.

One of the paradoxes of human behavior, however, is that the master program people actually use is rarely the one they think they use. Ask people in an interview or questionnaire to articulate the rules they use to govern their actions, and they will give you what I call their 'espoused' theory of action. But observe these same people's behavior, and you will quickly see that this espoused theory has very little to do with how they actually behave. For example, the professionals on the case team said they believed in continuous improvement, and yet they consistently acted in ways that made improvement impossible.

When you observe people's behavior and try to come up with rules that would make sense of it, you discover a very different theory of action – what I call the individual's 'theory-in-use'. Put simply, people consistently act inconsistently, unaware of the contradiction between their espoused theory and their theory-in-use, between the way they think they are acting and the way they really act.

What's more, most theories-in-use rest on the same set of governing values. There seems to be a universal human tendency to design one's actions consistently according to four basic values:

1. To remain in unilateral control
2. To maximize 'winning' and minimize 'losing'
3. To suppress negative feelings
4. To be as 'rational' as possible – by which people mean defining clear objectives and evaluating their behavior in terms of whether or not they have achieved them

The purpose of all these values is to avoid embarrassment or threat, feeling vulnerable or incompetent. In this respect, the master program that most people use is profoundly defensive. Defensive reasoning encourages individuals to keep private the premises, inferences, and conclusions that shape their behavior and to avoid testing them in a truly independent, objective fashion.

Because the attributions that go into defensive reasoning are never really tested, it is a closed loop, remarkably impervious to conflicting points of view. The inevitable response to the observation that somebody is reasoning defensively is yet more defensive reasoning. [In one case study], for example, whenever anyone pointed out the professionals' defensive behavior to them, their initial reaction was to look for the cause in somebody else – clients who were so sensitive that they would have been alienated if the consultants had criticized them or a manager so weak that he couldn't have taken it had the consultants raised their concerns with him. In other words, the case team members once again denied their own responsibility by externalizing the problem and putting it on someone else.

In such situations, the simple act of encouraging more open inquiry is often attacked by others as 'intimidating'. Those who do the attacking deal with their feelings about possibly being wrong by blaming the more open individual for arousing these feelings and upsetting them.

[...]

Learning how to reason productively

If defensive reasoning is as widespread as I believe, then focusing on an individual's attitudes or commitment is never enough to produce real change. And [neither] is creating new organizational structures or systems. The problem is that even when people are genuinely committed to improving their performance and management has changed its structures in order to encourage the 'right' kind of behavior, people still remain locked in defensive reasoning. Either they remain unaware of this fact, or if they do become aware of it, they blame others.

There is, however, reason to believe that organizations can break out of this vicious circle. Despite the strength of defensive reasoning, people genuinely strive to produce what they intend. They value acting competently. Their self-esteem is intimately tied up with behaving consistently and performing effectively. Companies can use these universal human tendencies to teach people how to reason in a new way – in effect, to change the master programs in their heads and thus reshape their behavior.

People can be taught how to recognize the reasoning they use when they design and implement their actions. They can begin to identify the inconsistencies between their espoused and actual theories of action. They can face up to the fact that they unconsciously design and implement actions that they do not intend. Finally, people can learn how to identify what individuals and groups do to create organizational defenses and how these defenses contribute to an organization's problems.

Once companies embark on this learning process, they will discover that the kind of reasoning necessary to reduce and overcome organizational defenses is the same kind of 'tough reasoning' that underlies the effective use of ideas in strategy, finance, marketing, manufacturing, and other management disciplines. Any sophisticated strategic analysis, for example, depends on collecting valid data, analyzing it carefully, and constantly testing the inferences drawn from the data. The toughest tests are reserved for the conclusions. Good strategists make sure that their conclusions can withstand all kinds of critical questioning.

So too with productive reasoning about human behavior. The standard of analysis is just as high. Human resource programs no longer need to be based on 'soft' reasoning but should be as analytical and as data-driven as any other management discipline.

Of course, that is not the kind of reasoning the consultants used when they encountered problems that were embarrassing or threatening. The data they collected was hardly objective. The inferences they made rarely became explicit. The conclusions they reached were largely self-serving, impossible for others to test, and as a result, 'self-sealing', impervious to change.

How can an organization begin to turn this situation around, to teach its members how to reason productively? The first step is for managers at the top to examine critically and change their own theories-in-use. Until senior managers become aware of how they reason defensively and the counterproductive consequences that result, there will be little real progress. Any change activity is likely to be just a fad.

Change has to start at the top because otherwise defensive senior managers are likely to disown any transformation in reasoning patterns coming from below. If professionals or middle managers begin to change the way they reason and act, such changes are likely to appear strange – if not actually dangerous – to those at the top. The result is an unstable situation where senior managers still believe that it is a sign of caring and sensitivity to bypass and cover up difficult issues, while their subordinates see the very same actions as defensive.

The key to any educational experience designed to teach senior managers how to reason productively is to connect the program to real business problems. The best demonstration of the usefulness of productive reasoning is for busy managers to see how it can make a direct difference in their own performance and in that of the organization. This will not happen overnight. Managers need plenty of opportunity to practice the new skills. But once they grasp the powerful impact that productive reasoning can have on actual performance, they will have a strong incentive to reason productively not just in a training session but in all their work relationships.

References

Argyris, C. (1957). *Personality and organization*. New York: Harper Brothers.
Argyris, C. (1990). *Overcoming organizational defenses: Facilitating organizational learning*. Boston: Allyn and Bacon.
Argyris, C. (1991). Teaching smart people how to learn. *Harvard Business Review, 69*(3), 99–109.
Argyris, C. (1992). *On organizational learning*. Oxford: Blackwell.
Argyris, C. (2002). Double-loop learning, teaching, and research. *Academy of Management Learning and Education, 1*(2), 206–218.
Argyris, C. (2003). A life full of learning. *Organization Studies, 24*(7), 1178–1192.

Argyris, C., & Schön, D. A. (1974). *Theory in practice: Increasing professional effectiveness*. San Francisco: Jossey-Bass.

Argyris, C., & Schön, D. A. (1978). *Organizational learning: A theory of action perspective*. Reading, MA: Addison-Wesley.

Argyris, C., & Schön, D. A. (1996). *Organizational learning II: Theory, method and practice*. Reading, MA: Addison-Wesley.

Ashby, W. R. (1960). *Design for a brain: The origin of adaptive behaviour* (2nd edition). London: Chapman & Hall.

Crossan, M. (2003). Altering theories of learning and action: An interview with Chris Argyris. *Academy of Management Executive, 17*(2), 40–46.

Fulmer, R.M., & Keys, J.B. (1998). A conversation with Chris Argyris: The father of organizational learning. *Organizational Dynamics, 27*(2), 21–32.

Kleiner, A. (1996). *The age of heretics: Heroes, outlaws, and the forerunners of corporate change*. London: Nicholas Brealey.

Senge, P. M. (1990). *The fifth discipline: The art and practice of the learning organization*. New York: Doubleday.

Tsoukas, H. (2002). Vulnerability, moral responsibility, and reflexive thinking. *Reflections, 4*(2), 14–15.

Whyte, W. F. (1943). *Street Corner Society: The social structure of an Italian slum*. Chicago: University of Chicago Press.

Woodell, V. (2003). An interview with Chris Argyris. *Organization Development Journal, 21*(2), 67–70.

Chapter 29
Donald Schön

Donald Alan Schön was a pre-eminent scholar of professional practice and learning. He is most celebrated for his work on the reflective practitioner and on organisational learning. He made significant contributions to the fields of education, management, urban planning, and design. His original intellectual home, however, was philosophy and throughout his career he regarded himself as a "displaced philosopher" (Waks 2001, p. 37). He wrote his Ph.D. thesis on the philosopher John Dewey's theory of inquiry, and as Sanyal (1998, p. 6) notes, "the Deweyian notion that all knowledge derives from practice remained at the heart of Don's formulation of the epistemological foundation of effective practice".

Schön was born in Boston in 1930 and lived in the city most of his life. Schön was educated in philosophy at Yale University (undergraduate) and Harvard University (Ph.D.), and in the clarinet at the Paris Conservatoire. After his Ph.D. and a short spell in the army, he worked for 15 years as a practitioner: in new product development at the consultancy Arthur D. Little, in government at National Bureau of Standards, and in a small enterprise as the co-founder and director of the Organization for Social & Technical Innovation (OSTI). In 1972, Schön became professor of Urban Studies and Education at the Massachusetts Institute of Technology (MIT), where he remained until his death in 1997.

Schön blended practice and theory throughout his life, as an academic, consultant and practitioner. While working as a practitioner, he made significant contributions to theory: three of his eight major books were written outside academia, and his invitation to give the BBC Reith Lectures in 1970 (the highly prestigious annual lecture series of ideas at the forefront of current thought) came when he was working at OSTI. When he became an academic, he remained involved as a consultant (as well as a researcher into professionals of many kinds).

Three facets of Schön's character stand out. First, he felt a close affinity with a giraffe: "long-necked, graceful, curious, aloof" (Warsh 1997, p. F1). Waks (2001, p. 37) describes the comparison as insightful, observing that "he also looked down upon the world of practice – learning its ways and assisting its denizens to make life a little better – from the inquisitive but distanced perspective of the philosopher". After his death his wife Nancy created a set of sculptures called "The Reflective Giraffe" in his honour (pictures of which can be seen on her website, N. Schön, n.d.).

© The Open University 2009. Published in association with Springer-Verlag London Limited

Second, he was a highly accomplished musician. Trained in the clarinet, he played daily, both chamber music and jazz. Both these forms had a profound influence on his work. As Smith (2001) remarks, "this interest in improvisation and structure was mirrored in his academic writing, most notably in his exploration of professionals' ability to 'think on their feet'". Music was crucial throughout Schön's life, right up to the moment of his death. Sanyal (1998, p. 7), drawing on accounts by Don's son Andrew, writes that "it was a fitting farewell for his family to stand surrounding his bed holding hands and singing rounds of songs ... as Don's eyes closed for the last time, the family members lowered their voices in sorrow only to be urged by Don who raised his right palm to request them to continue singing so he could listen to his favourite Brahms as he gently embraced death".

Third, he was devoted to his family. He was married to sculptor Nancy Schön, and they had four children and many grandchildren. At the time of his death, he was preparing one grandson for his barmitzvah (Schön was Jewish) and building a puppet theatre for his grandchildren, "who he taught the essence of reflection by having them critically conceive a theory of how a puppet theatre ought to work" (Richmond 1998, p. 3).

Schön's many contributions can be viewed in three, highly interconnected, major areas.

The first of these areas was his work on change. Schön's second book (1967) was subtitled *The New Heraclitus*. Schön had much in common with Heraclitus, the Greek philosopher of change from the sixth century BC, who discussed the constancy of change and argued that stability is a temporary phenomenon. The phrase "one can never step in the same river twice" is often attributed to Heraclitus (in fact it is a later paraphrase of his words) to indicate his view that stability in one area of the world – the river – is only achieved through rapid change in another area – the water that flows in it. In the same way, Schön argued from early in his work that change, partly delivered through technology and partly through society, is an ever-present feature in today's world.

Schön's clearest expression of his understanding of change came when he was invited to give the BBC Reith Lectures in 1970, at the time the youngest-ever person to have done so. The lectures were the basis of his classic and influential book *Beyond the stable state* (Schön 1971), which "sent unexpected tremors down the airwaves as he spoke about the loss of the stable state in society, and its implications for our major institutions" (Weil 1997). In this work, he argues that we have lost a situation where our society and its institutions can remain in their current form, and that they will need to keep continuously changing in the future. This requires us to understand and guide the transformations in our society and institutions, but also to transform them in a different way: "we must invent and develop institutions which are 'learning systems', that is to say systems capable of bringing about their own continuing transformation" (Schön 1971, p. 30).

In this work, he applied his concept of a learning system both to business organisations and to society and governments – the basis both for his later work on organisational learning but also for the concept of a 'learning society'. However, as he discussed, organisations have a significant tendency to fight to preserve their structures and identity – that is, they exhibit 'dynamic conservatism', in Schön's term. As he observed, "social systems resist change with an energy roughly proportional to the radicalness of the change that is being threatened" (Schön 1971, p. 38). Dynamic conservatism is not entirely negative – it is the process "through which social systems keep from flying apart at the seams … our systems need to maintain their identity, and their ability to support the self-identity of those who belong to them, but they must at the same time be capable of trans-forming themselves" (Schön 1971, p. 60).

This work on change led to Schön's second major contribution, his work on learning. Much of this work was conducted with Chris Argyris, and is discussed in more detail in the chapter on Argyris. In their two major books, *Theory in Practice* (Argyris and Schön 1974) and *Organisational Learning* (Argyris and Schön 1978), they introduce a number of major concepts as well as that of organisational learning, notably the idea of a theory of action, the distinction between espoused theory and theory-in-use, and the concepts of single and double loop learning.

Much of the concept of organisational learning was present in Schön's work predating his collaboration with Argyris, although the idea in its mature form arose from the combinations of the ideas of both – Schön's philosophical and industrial experience, and Argyris' work in social psychology and group dynamics. As a former student of the two described his contributions to organisational learning, Schön's "big picture orientation … helped keep the fledgling field from becoming mired in micro-issues (analysis of linguistics and conversational patterns)" (Tomasko 1997). The same author comments on the differences in styles of interaction between Schön and Argyris, from a time when they were jointly teaching: "his warm and nurturing nature served as a great foil to Chris' sometime prickliness [although] … Chris could certainly be extremely warm and generous, and Don rigorous and judgmental when the situation called for it" (Tomasko 1997).

Schön's third major contribution was in the concept of reflective practice (and its parallel concept of the reflective practitioner). The starting point for this work was a study of professionals and their learning, and the observation of a "crisis of confidence in professional knowledge" (Schön 1984, p. 3). This crisis arises from a mismatch between the needs of professionals working in real situations, and the skills they learn through traditional education processes. In a vivid image (Schön 1984, p. 42), drawing on Russell Ackoff's use of the term 'mess', he wrote that:

> In the varied topography of professional practice, there is a high, hard ground where practitioners can make effective use of research-based theory and technique, and there is a swampy lowland where situations are confusing 'messes' incapable of technical solution. The difficulty is that the problems of the high ground, however great their technical interest, are often relatively unimportant to clients or to the larger society, while in the swamp are the problems of greatest human concern.

However, Schön argues, professional education is ill-suited for the problems of the 'swamp' – it is dominated by a model of "technical rationality", which stresses "instru-mental problem solving made rigorous by the application of scientific theory and technique" (Schön 1984, p. 21). The importance of this approach to professional edu-cation arises from a lack of self-confidence in university departments educating professionals – especially applied professions such as social work, education, architecture and town planning. Comparing themselves with the certainties and academic ground-edness of traditional university disciplines and long-established professional schools in medicine and law, these professions seemed at their founding less rigorous and well-founded. The Faustian bargain that resulted was that the education of these professionals would stress first the scientific foundations of the field, then a set of rigorous and instrumental techniques derived directly from those foundations, and only finally issues of the practice of these techniques and their relation to real-world situations. Thus in the process of trying to become more academically acceptable, these professional educators have removed themselves a long way from the things which will be valuable to professionals following their education.

The solution which Schön put forward followed on from his earlier work with Argyris on theories of action, as well as a number of other bodies of work, including his earlier interest in Dewey's understanding of knowledge, Vickers' appreciative systems (described in the chapter on that author), among others. He observed that much of what we know is only exhibited when it is enacted, which he referred to as knowing-in-action – a form of knowledge that is distinct from that which is learnt in the classroom and later applied. This knowledge leads to the process that Schön described as reflection-in-action: that when professionals act, and are faced with an unfamiliar situation, they improvise on the basis of past experience and their knowing-in-action. Someone who reflects-in-action "is not dependent on the categories of established theory and technique, but constructs a new theory of the unique case" (Schön 1984, p. 68).

A reflective practitioner, therefore, is one who habitually reflects-in-action, and who cultivates their ability to do so. This latter process may well involve reflection-*on*-action, that is reflection on the action taken, after the event (post-hoc). However, these two processes are quite distinct. This is important to stress because it is post-hoc reflection which is the more familiar form – the quiet minutes at the end of the day, or the use of a journal. Some of those who have taken up Schön's call for reflective practice have stressed post-hoc reflection as the key activity for the reflective practitioner, and it clearly has a role, but it is not the heart of the concept as expressed by Schön, who stresses reflection in the midst of action. Schön frequently used jazz as an image of reflection-in-action: the process of improvisation in the moment based on a response to the situation (what other musicians are playing, the audience's response etc.), to the established rhythm and melody of the piece, and also on one's own abilities and enthusiasms.

The concept of the reflective practitioner can be seen as largely individual. Its focus is on how the individual practitioner learns and reflects, and it has been criti-cised by a number of authors for having a weak focus on power and politics. Verma (1998, p. 9) has defended this aspect of Schön's approach: "Don was deeply inter-ested in issues of power – not the power of holding a gun over someone, but a subtle form of intellectual power that grips us and forces us to act in particular ways … in its consequences it is as dangerous as more conventional forms of power. It can marginalise, dominate, and force particular outcomes."

Later in his life, Schön did apply concepts of reflection to questions of public policy – in one of his last major books he discussed the concept of frames ("underlying structures of belief, perception and appreciation" – Schön and Rein 1994, p. 23) created within an institutional context. They ask the question to what extent is it possible to change frames in a manner akin to reflection-in-action, observing that "policies are sometimes reframed in action, and their reframing sometimes results from the actors' reflection on frame conflicts that arise in the evolving, politically coloured process of policy design" (Schön and Rein 1994, p. viii).

Schön's major focus was on change in many forms and settings. As his colleague Jeanne Bamberger (2000, p. 10) summed up his concerns: "Don's persistent and abiding belief in the permanence of change, of evanescence, and transience was, I think, an underlying, moving force – it was the foundation upon which the multi-faceted puzzle of his several lives-in-one was built, and in its paradox, also knit together a life that worked as one vibrant whole."

Reading from Schön's work

Educating the Reflective Practitioner: toward a new design for Teaching and Learning in the Professions, San Francisco: Jossey-Bass ©1987. Reproduced with permission of John Wiley & Sons Inc.
Extract from pages 26–31.

When we have learned how to do something, we can execute smooth sequences of activity, recognition, decision, and adjustment without having, as we say, to 'think about it'. Our spontaneous knowing-in-action usually gets us through the day. On occasion, however, it doesn't. A familiar routine produces an unexpected result; an error stubbornly resists correction; or, although the usual actions produce the usual outcomes, we find something odd about them because, for some reason, we have begun to look at them in a new way. All such experiences, pleasant and unpleasant, contain an element of *surprise*. Something fails to meet our expectations. In an attempt to preserve the constancy of our usual patterns of knowing-in-action, we may respond to surprise by brushing it aside, selectively inattending to the signals that produce it. Or we may respond to it by reflection, and we may do so in one of two ways.

We may reflect *on* action, thinking back on what we have done in order to discover how our knowing-in-action may have contributed to an unexpected outcome. We may do so after the fact, in tranquility, or we may pause in the midst of action to make what Hannah Arendt (1978) calls a 'stop-and-think'. In either case, our reflection has no direct connection to present action. Alternatively, we may reflect in the midst of action without interrupting it. In an *action-present* – a period of time, variable with the context, during which we can still make a difference to the situation at hand – our thinking serves to reshape what we are doing while we are doing it. I shall say, in cases like this, that we reflect-*in*-action.

Recently, for example, I built a gate out of wooden pickets and strapping. I had made a drawing and figured out the dimensions I wanted, but I had not reckoned with the problem of keeping the structure square. As I began to nail the strapping to the pickets, I noticed a wobble. I knew the structure would become rigid when I nailed in a diagonal piece, but how could I be sure it would be square? There came to mind a vague memory about diagonals: in a rectangle diagonals are equal. I took a yardstick, intending to measure the diagonals, but I found I could not use it without disturbing the structure. It occurred to me to use a piece of string. Then it became apparent that, in order to measure the diagonals, I needed a precise location at each corner. After several trials, I found I could locate the centre point at each corner by constructing diagonals there [...] I hammered in a nail at each of the four centre points and used the nails as anchors for the measurement string. It took several minutes to figure out how to adjust the structure so as to correct the errors I found by measuring. And then, when I had the diagonals equal, I nailed in a piece of strapping to freeze the structure.

Here, in an example that must have its analogues in the experiences of amateur carpenters the world over, my intuitive way of going about the task led me to a surprise (the discovery of the wobble), which I interpreted as a problem. In the midst of action, I invented procedures to solve the problem, discovered further unpleasant surprises, and made further corrective inventions, including the several minor ones necessary to carry out the idea of using string to measure the diagonals. We might call such a process 'trial and error'. But the trials are not randomly related to one another; reflection on each trial and its results sets the stage for the next trial. Such a pattern of inquiry is better described as a sequence of 'moments' in a process of reflection-in-action:

- There is, to begin with, a situation of action to which we bring spontaneous, routinized responses. These reveal knowing-in-action that may be described in terms of strategies, understandings of phenomena, and ways of framing a task or problem appropriate to the situation. The knowing-in-action is tacit, spontaneously delivered without conscious deliberation; and it works, yielding intended outcomes so long as the situation falls within the boundaries of what we have learned to treat as normal.
- Routine responses produce a surprise – an unexpected outcome, pleasant or unpleasant, that does not fit the categories of our knowing-in-action. Inherent in a surprise is the fact that it gets our attention. For example, I might not have been surprised by the wobble in my gate because I might not have attended to it; the structure might not have ended up square, and I might not have noticed.
- Surprise leads to reflection within an action-present. Reflection is at least in some measure conscious, although it need not occur in the medium of words. We consider both the unexpected event and the knowing-in-action that led up to it, asking ourselves, as it were, "What is this?" and, at the same time, "How have I been thinking about it?" Our thought turns back on the surprising phenomenon and, at the same time, back on itself.
- Reflection-in-action has a critical function, questioning the assumptional structure of knowing-in-action. We think critically about the thinking that got us into

this fix or this opportunity; and we may, in the process, restructure strategies of action, understandings of phenomena, or ways of framing problems. In my example, the surprise triggered by my observation of the wobble led me to frame a new problem: "How to keep the gate square?"

- Reflection gives rise to on-the-spot experiment. We think up and try out new actions intended to explore the newly observed phenomena, test our tentative understandings of them, or affirm the moves we have invented to change things for the better. With my measuring-string experiment, I tested both my understanding of squareness as equality of diagonals and the effectiveness of the procedures I had invented for determining when diagonals are equal. On-the-spot experiment may work, again in the sense of yielding intended results, or it may produce surprises that call for further reflection and experiment.

The description I have given is, of course, an idealized one. The moments of reflection-in-action are rarely as distinct from one another as I have made them out to be. The experience of surprise may present itself in such a way as to seem already interpreted. The criticism and restructuring of knowing-in-action may be compressed into a single process. But regardless of the distinctness of its moments or the constancy of their sequence, what distinguishes reflection-in-action from other kinds of reflection is its immediate significance for action. In reflection-in-action, the rethinking of some part of our knowing-in-action leads to on-the-spot experiment and further thinking that affects what we do – in the situation at hand and perhaps also in others we shall see as similar to it.

The distinction between reflection- and knowing-in-action may be subtle. A skilled performer adjusts his responses to variations in phenomena. In his moment-by-moment appreciations of a process, he deploys a wide-ranging repertoire of images of contexts and actions. So a baseball pitcher adapts his pitching style to the peculiarities of a particular batter or situation in a game. In order to counter an opponent's changing strategies, a tennis player executes split-second variations in play. We can say, in cases like these, that the performer responds to *variation* rather than *surprise* because the changes in context and response never cross the boundaries of the familiar.

However, in a kind of process that may look from the outside like the ones described above, a skilled performer can integrate reflection-in-action into the smooth performance of an ongoing task. I recently heard the story of a cellist who had been called to join in performing a new piece of chamber music. Because of illness, he missed the first few rehearsals and finally put in an appearance the day before the performance was to take place. He sat down with the other musicians and sight-read his way through the difficult part, playing it so well that the conductor had no need to reschedule the performance. As the cellist sight-read the score, he could not have known for certain where the piece was heading. Yet he must have sensed at each moment the direction of its development, picking up in his own performance the lines of development already laid down by others. He must have encountered surprises in response to which he formed, online, an interpretation guided by his emerging sense of the whole. And the execution of this feat left him with a newly developed understanding of the piece and how to play it that he would reveal as knowing-in-action on the day of the performance.

When good jazz musicians improvise together, they similarly display reflection-in-action smoothly integrated into ongoing performance. Listening to one another, listening to themselves, they 'feel' where the music is going and adjust their playing accordingly. A figure announced by one performer will be taken up by another, elaborated, turned into a new melody. Each player makes on-line inventions and responds to surprises triggered by the inventions of the other players. But the collective process of musical invention is organized around an underlying structure. There is a common schema of meter, melody, and harmonic development that gives the piece a predictable order. In addition, each player has at the ready a repertoire of musical figures around which he can weave variations as the opportunity arises. Improvisation consists in varying, combining, and recombining a set of figures within a schema that gives coherence to the whole piece. As the musicians feel the directions in which the music is developing, they make new sense of it. They reflect-in-action on the music they are collectively making – though not, of course, in the medium of words.

Their process resembles the familiar patterns of everyday conversation. In a good conversation – in some respects predictable and in others not – participants pick up and develop themes of talk, each spinning out variations on her repertoire of things to say. Conversation is collective verbal improvisation. At times it falls into conventional routines – the anecdote with side comments and reactions, for example, or the debate – which develop according to a pace and rhythm of interaction that the participants seem, without conscious deliberation, to work out in common within the framework of an evolving division of labor. At other times, there may be surprises, unexpected turns of phrase or directions of development to which participants invent on-the-spot responses.

In such examples, the participants are *making* something. Out of musical materials or themes of talk, they make a piece of music or a conversation, an artifact with its own meaning and coherence. Their reflection-in-action is a reflective conversation with the materials of a situation.

References

Arendt, H. (1978). *The life of the mind, vol. 1: Thinking*. New York: Harcourt Brace Jovanovich.

Argyris, C., & Schön, D. A. (1974). *Theory in practice: Increasing professional effectiveness*. San Francisco: Jossey-Bass.

Argyris, C., & Schön, D. A. (1978). *Organizational learning: A theory of action perspective*. Reading, MA: Addison-Wesley.

Bamberger, J. (2000). Unanswered questions. *Cybernetics and Human Knowing, 7*(2–3), 9–16.

Richmond, J. (1998). Donald Schön – a life of reflection. *Journal of Planning Literature, 13*(1), 3–5.

Sanyal, B. (1998). Learning from Don Schön – A tribute. *Journal of Planning Literature, 13*(1), 5–7.

Schön, D. (1967). *Technology and change: The new Heraclitus*. Oxford: Pergamon.

Schön, D. (1971). *Beyond the stable state: Public and private learning in a changing society*. London: Temple Smith.

Schön, D. (1984). *The reflective practitioner: How professionals think in action.* Aldershot, UK: Ashgate.

Schön, D. (1987). *Educating the reflective practitioner: Toward a new design for teaching and learning in the professions.* San Francisco: Jossey-Bass.

Schön, D., & Rein, M. (1994). *Frame reflection.* New York: Basic Books.

Schön, N. (n.d.). Great reflective giraffe. http://www.schon.com/public/giraffe.php. Accessed 13 Jan 2009.

Smith, M. K. (2001). Donald Schön: Learning, reflection and change. *The encyclopedia of informal education.* http://www.infed.org/thinkers/et-schon.htm. Accessed 13 Jan 2009.

Tomasko, R. M. (1997). In memory of Don Schön. Learning-org mailing list posting LO15112. http://www.learning-org.com/97.09/0301.html. Accessed 13 Jan 2009.

Verma, N. (1998). Donald Schön's reflection-*in*-action. *Journal of Planning Literature, 13*(1), 8–10.

Waks, L.J. (2001). Donald Schön's philosophy of design and design education. *International Journal of Technology and Design Education, 11*(1), 37–51.

Warsh, D. (1997). The giraffe. *The Boston Globe,* 28 December 1997, F1.

Weil, S. (1997). Obituary: Donald Schön: Tremors down the airwaves. *The Guardian,* 17 October 1997, 22.

Chapter 30
Mary Catherine Bateson

Mary Catherine Bateson is a social anthropologist and linguist. She has written about topics including cross-cultural issues, social and individual learning, women's life patterns, ageing, family dynamics, AIDS, and the nature of knowledge. Her work is suffused with systems ideas, especially a highly-developed form of cybernetics. It is deeply humanitarian, and combines a strong respect for the individual with an awareness of wider forces to which they relate. She exhibits what might be called 'documented embodiment', as an individual who has taken systems ideas so deeply into herself that they influence all of her thinking and writing, and who has written at length about that process.

Her work is broad but she has characterised it as all being connected with learning, writing that "the underlying challenge [of her work] has to do with becoming aware of the process that defines our humanness: we are not what we know but what we are willing to learn" (MC Bateson 2004, p. 8).

Catherine Bateson – she is usually known by her middle name – is the daughter of two of the other thinkers in this book, Gregory Bateson and Margaret Mead. She has written on several occasions about the lives of her parents, worked on a number of projects with her father in particular, and remains the literary executor of both her parents. Her experience with having two very interesting parents made some of her early works of particular note, but she also has much important work of her own and is by no means in her parents' shadows. She has written that "if you're going to have a famous parent, have two" (MC Bateson 2007), and she clearly has attributes and research areas taken from each of her parents. She has also observed that "in my family, we never simply live, we are always reflecting on our lives" (MC Bateson 1984, p. 11). This constant reflection is clearly a pattern of living that she shares with both her parents, and demonstrates to great effect – many of her publications draw upon her own life experiences.

Bateson was born in 1939 in New York, and is still an active researcher. Her early childhood was characterised both by the frequent absences of her parents on war work, and by the extent to which her childhood was studied by them – they recorded and photographed her in great detail. This partly reflected their anthropological experience, and partly Margaret Mead's keenness to innovate with child-rearing methods. Catherine's paediatrician was Benjamin Spock – she was the first on-demand breastfed baby he had encountered, an approach he was later to make famous in his books on childcare. Her parents separated in 1947 (divorcing in 1950), and Catherine grew up in a series of households shared with other families and children: "I had a rich and unusual childhood, with many adult caretakers, and I made my own synthesis from the models offered by my parents and the others I saw around me" (MC Bateson 1989, pp. 12–13).

Catherine Bateson's adult life has been characterised by a series of encounters with other cultures. She had her first encounter with life in another country in her final year of high school, which she spent in Israel. She took her degrees at Radcliffe College in Cambridge, Massachusetts (B.A. in Semitic languages in 1960) and Harvard University (Ph.D. in linguistics in 1963, specialising in Arabic poetry), became an instructor in Arabic at Harvard and wrote a number of books and articles on Arabic. After three years teaching at Harvard, her husband, Barkev Kassarjian (whom she married in 1960) took a job in Manila in the Philippines and Bateson moved there with him. As she later wrote, "that was the end of that career, like getting a degree in tropical medicine and going to Siberia. Arabic linguistics just didn't hack it in Manila. This is a very common situation of women who move following their husbands' careers" (MC Bateson 2004, p. 328). This might be considered ironic in the light of her later insightful writings on developments in women's lives, but in another sense it reflects precisely a theme of much of her work – that "women suffer a great many interruptions and discontinuities, and have to start again" (MC Bateson 2004, p. 328).

Because of the lack of demand for her linguistic skills, she took a job in Manila teaching anthropology, something she had initially resisted given her parents' fame in the field but a logical enough step given the close connection between linguistics and anthropology. She has worked as an anthropologist rather than a linguist since that time: she has never written a traditional ethnography (a large-scale monograph describing another culture in great detail) but follows the anthropological tradition of being a participant observer in that she has written at length about the several different cultures in which she has lived and worked. She has written of her many experiences of living overseas that each "was followed by a period of considering American society with new eyes, realizing that the same lessons were available here, for a rapidly changing society embracing many cultures and traditions – multiple systems of meaning – is a school of life" (MC Bateson 1994, pp. 238–239).

On leaving Manila in 1968, she returned to the United States, where she taught until 1971 at Northeastern University in Boston. She then followed her husband's work again, moving in 1972 to Iran, where she was based until the Islamic Revolution of 1979, working at a number of Iranian universities, culminating in her appointment as dean of social sciences and humanities at a university in northern Iran. After the revolution (when Westerners were generally expelled from Iran), she returned to the United States, where she spent three years as dean of the faculty at Amherst College, moving in 1987 to George Mason University where she worked as professor of anthropology and English until her retirement in 2001. Her further shift of subject reflected her increasingly narrative and personal writing style, developed in a series of books, which had as much a literary as a social scientific flavour.

Our discussion of Bateson's major contributions to systems thinking will consider three main areas (in many ways interlocking): her parents' legacy, her work on life histories, and her work on learning. Most of our focus will be on her books, of which she has written many and in which she has developed her ideas clearly and at length.

She worked on a number of projects with her father during his life. She appears as the 'daughter' character in Gregory Bateson's celebrated metalogues (collected in G Bateson 1972). Her first adult collaboration with her father was her role as rapporteur for the major conference on the 'Effects of Conscious Purpose on Human Adaptation', on the theme of environmental change, human systems, and epistemology, that Gregory Bateson organised in Austria in 1968. Her book discussing the conference, *Our Own Metaphor* (MC Bateson 1972), is one of the most readable accounts of an academic conference ever produced, focusing on the people and their emotions (including her own) rather than providing a set of papers. In this it is sharply different from the much more conventional proceedings of the Macy conferences, in which both Gregory Bateson and Margaret Mead were participants, as Hayles (1999, p. 76) remarks:

> Catherine assumes that *of course* the observer affects what is seen, so she takes care to tell her readers about her state of mind and situation at that time.... She takes care to tell her readers not only what ideas were exchanged but also how the people looked and her interpretation of how they were feeling.

Catherine Bateson was to continue to work with her father in shaping his final two books (G Bateson 1979; G Bateson and MC Bateson 1987), in the latter explicitly bringing out her own voice while respecting that of her father. After her parents' death, she produced a memoir of their lives, and her life with them, *With a Daughter's Eye* (MC Bateson 1984), which is one of the best accounts of both of her parents' lives. The memoir also carried further Catherine Bateson's use of her own life and emotions as anthropological data.

Bateson has taken forward her parents' work in other ways. She has been president since 1980 of the Institute for Intercultural Studies (IIS), set up by Margaret Mead in 1944 to advance intercultural relations. Through the IIS, she organised celebrations of the work of both parents in the centenary years of their birth (2001 for Mead, 2004 for Bateson), including many events and publications such as special issues of journals. She is keen, however, that her championing of her parents' work not be over-protective: about her father's work, she has written that

> I decided very early on that I was not going to accept the position of Anna Freud, a woman of undoubted brilliance and conscientiousness, who became protector and arbiter of orthodoxy for the work of her father, Sigmund Freud. The creation of an orthodoxy around Freud's work was a misapprehension of the way he wove ideas and of the way he developed and expressed them, which has had a negative effect on psychoanalysis (MC Bateson 2008, p. 17).

The second major strand of her work has concerned issues of age and gender, specifically by focusing on life histories. This work was especially prominent in her book *Composing a Life*, which discusses the way that five women (herself and four friends) have shaped their lives: "each of us has worked by improvisation, discovering the shape of our creation along the way, rather than pursuing a vision already defined" (MC Bateson 1989, p. 1). This concept of improvisation is core to the book, as a way of describing the lives of modern women, "constantly trying to make something coherent from conflicting elements to fit rapidly changing settings" (MC Bateson 1989, p. 3), constantly involved in new beginnings and changes, where "fluidity and discontinuity are central to the reality in which we live" (MC Bateson 1989, p. 13) and yet we must make sense of those discontinuities and weave together a pattern as we live our lives. She draws analogies between living life and creating portmanteau works of art, such as jazz and quilt making, that entail improvisation (as does Donald Schön). The book is rich and powerful, and again takes Catherine Bateson's own life trajectory (especially in this case her unhappy exit from the deanship at Amherst College) as a key part of its story. It is one of her most widely read books, used by many readers going through major life changes as a way of reflecting upon their own life journey, and cited by academics in a range of human-centred fields such as nursing, social work, education, psychoanalysis and organisation studies (e.g. Kimble Wrye 1994; Weick 1998).

The success and effectiveness of *Composing a Life*, together with her work on her parents' lives, has led Bateson to take this work further. At George Mason University, she taught for several years a course on life histories. She also taught this course at a historically black women's college in Atlanta, Spelman College, in 1996, at the invitation of its president, Johnetta Cole (one of the women that appear in *Composing a Life*). This experience led to a further book about the life histories of some of the participants in that course (all black women of various ages), focusing on experiences of race and age as well as gender, *Full Circles, Overlapping Lives* (MC Bateson 2000). Bateson's personal experience of ageing has led her to further developments in this field, organising a movement of 'Granny Voters' during the US elections in 2004 and planning further work along the lines of *Composing a Life* about older people. She has noted with regard to her earlier book that she was deliberately challenging society's preconceptions by focusing on women's lives:

> our society tends to regard women as exceptions to the full human condition and men as representative, so it was somewhat mischievous of me to write a book about human beings in the form of a book about women, and some men have complained that they gained valuable insights about themselves from the book but would not have read it on their own (MC Bateson 1994, p. 239).

As we mentioned at the start of this chapter, Bateson sees all her work as being concerned with learning throughout life, but some of her work is quite explicitly focused on this issue, and forms the third major strand of her work. She has especially done this in two books. The first was *Peripheral Visions*, a book about learning from experience (again, with many illustrations from her own life in different cultures), of which she observes: "each person is calibrated by experience, almost like a measuring instrument for difference, so discomfort is informative and offers a starting point for new understanding" (MC Bateson 1994, p. 17). Most recently, she has published a book, *Willing to Learn* (MC Bateson 2004) in which she collects together articles, speeches and some book excerpts from throughout her career which cover the broad theme of learning. In a newspaper article discussing this theme, she has argued that "willingness to learn demands respect for others across difference. Puzzling and even disturbing ideas are invitations to curiosity, and the greater the difference the more there may be to be learned.... willingness to learn is a form of spirituality. It is a stance of humility, because there is so much to be learned" (MC Bateson 2005).

An aspect of her work on learning which has been present throughout her career but particularly appears in *Willing to Learn* is a focus on epistemology – ways of thinking and knowing the world, a favourite theme of her father's which she has also taken up. She considers many issues within this theme – participation, transcendence, multiple ways of knowing, ambiguity, ethics, and the implications for our consciousness of AIDS. It is by no means a purely philosophical issue for her, but relates deeply to the way we live our lives, organise society, and (through its relation to environmentalism) manage our world.

Mary Catherine Bateson is a wise and compassionate thinker and writer, who "communicates a strong sense of optimism, hope and multiculturalism" in her writing (Janesick 2005, p. 2). She lives a life that has been examined in depth by herself and others from her earliest childhood, and has served as data for her highly systemic form of anthropology. She writes that "my background has led me to a lifelong search for pattern and its recurrence in different contexts ... this has meant a lifelong rhythm of introspection, connecting personal experiences to more distant phenomena, exploring and testing metaphors and analogies to see what new insight they might reveal" (MC Bateson 2004, p. 3). This approach has brought many new insights, and exemplifies a mature, self-aware and deeply rooted form of systems thinking at its best.

Reading from M.C. Bateson's work

An excerpt from *Willing to Learn: Passages of Personal Discovery*, by Mary Catherine Bateson, published by Steerforth Press of Hanover, New Hampshire.
Copyright ©2004 by Mary Catherine Bateson.
Extracts from pages 399–400 and 409–410.

We have always shared, we human beings, some portion of the nomadic pattern. We evolved in Africa, standing upright and foraging for food, moving on as resources dictated. Mobility demands continuing learning, since the survival of migrants depends on the capacity of adults to cope with the unfamiliar. Mobility also engages one of our most basic characteristics, curiosity. We developed the capacity to learn and the skill to teach that made it possible to travel from continent to continent, adopting new behaviors adapted to every kind of environment. Over time, humans made the inventions that allowed them to settle and to support ever larger numbers. Yet movement – and the idea of movement – have remained part of the human repertoire even among the most adamantly settled of peasants. Few groups have been so profoundly isolated that the notion of learning from strangers is entirely absent – even when the last outsiders are so obscured by time that they are remembered as visiting gods.

We learn from difference, but difference often triggers hostility. A pattern of interdependent adaptations, linked by exchange and trade, recurs on every continent and often alternates with conflict. The nomadic tribes of Arabia, for instance, moved to find water and grazing for their animals – camels, sheep, or horses – but maintained a symbiotic relationship with settled farmers with whom they traded animal products for grain. When populations have exceeded carrying capacity, large numbers have spilled out into surrounding areas, often arriving as invaders but gradually learning to live with new neighbors and blending cultural traditions. The planet is now effectively peopled and interconnected, but surges of migration continue. The search for living space and resources for our elaborate forms of subsistence results in conflict of many kinds as well as learning. And as always, we make war with elaborate rhetoric and refer to different beliefs to underline our separations.

We are a single species with a common origin, but we are not notably good at putting it all back together. In the course of their migrations, local populations of human beings lived for millennia largely cut off from one another, developing the variations in physical characteristics that are referred to as race and building up complex learned systems of language and culture and belief. We remain very much attached to the distinctive traditions that continue to keep us apart, yet we are attracted by both novelty and the idea of uniformity, while curiosity is often at odds with loyalty. So people ask, sometimes in hope and sometimes in horror: Will all human beings eventually speak the same language? Will everyone accept a single religion? Will there be so much intermarriage that everyone will look the same? Probably none of the above.

Today we are nomads of the imagination, increasingly familiar with other cultures. In huge numbers, we travel the globe for recreation as often as for survival. And we are nomads in another sense, constantly moving on in our lives and adjusting to new circumstances even in the place called home, abandoning familiar constancies. Ruth Benedict, an anthropologist who often felt like an outsider in her own culture, imagined that for every temperament there might somewhere be a society that would be hospitable in a distinctive way. Even so, her vision was based on homogeneity within a given society and on the expectation of continuity and consistency over a lifetime. Today, we can begin to live in a world where individuals are able to sojourn with the cultures or religious expressions that most nearly match their deepest longings. That match might vary at particular stages of the life cycle, however, guiding choices that need not be irreversible, just as we are finding time in extended lives for changes in careers and marriages and sexual orientations. Perhaps we will learn to live in a shifting and multicultural world by building on the ancient human patterns and skills of nomads.

[...]

We are perhaps becoming nomads in what we care about, so that change and novelty have come to seem more important than continuity and tradition. If values once learned are to be kept flexible and adaptable, there is a need to learn to modify, question, and reintegrate existing values, not simply to discard them. The experience of learning some new value could be used to provide models for integrating new understandings into existing ones in other new situations. Many Americans can remember that the handicapped were invisible to them until they learned to include them in their thinking; can that memory help them to listen and respond differently to some newly recognized excluded group, and how far can the concept of access be generalized? Is there then deutero-learning (learning to learn) in the area of values? Something that is good in a given context can be a danger when the context changes. Today in particular, we live in a world of change, so that our values or the way they are configured or the way we interpret and implement them must be flexible and changeable.

Everyone has some skills for dealing with the kinds of differences that always exist, even in so-called homogeneous societies, like the interaction across differ-ence that obviously happens between adults and children and leads to learning, but often the adults do not recognize that they too are learning and changing.

Thinking about multicultural societies or societies in the process of change would be less threatening if we would re-examine the assumptions we make about continuity in ourselves. I have argued that we need to reflect on the most intimate kinds of diversity and strangeness – strangeness in the self and strangeness in those we love most. We need to question assumptions about the degree of uniformity needed for society to function also. Honing the skills of dealing with diversity means listening and learning as well as making do. There is a whole history of inventions that make limited mutual understanding tolerable, lingua francas and pidgins for dealing with practical needs, forms of translation like monetization, or seeing everything in zero-sum terms. Sometimes working alliances based on different goals and crude approximations fall apart, but sometimes they mature and deepen.

A multicultural society does require some metavalues, such as those that are embedded in the American Constitution, which has allowed for growth and adaptation. One of these metavalues is what we call 'pluralism'. Pluralism essentially means that, whatever I believe at a moment in time, it is valuable – not just tolerable – to me that there are people around me whose beliefs are different. The concept of a democracy, in which you understand that you benefit from the presence and often success of people with whom you disagree, is analogous to the concept of an ecosystem. Different species, after their order, sometimes compete, some times cooperate, and sometimes live right past and hardly encounter each other. Still, they are present and in the broadest sense interdependent, not each on each but throughout the system. There are interior or spiritual aspects of pluralism. Empathy makes it possible to bridge differences, but one is changed in that process. In fact, if we visualize a con-tinual diverse interaction of points of view and a habit of trying to understand the ideas of others, this becomes a definition of lifelong learning and changing in which the teacher is necessarily a learner, because there is no fixed truth in this fluid world, and the learner is necessarily a teacher, as of course newborn infants are teachers who train their mothers and fathers in the art of being parents.

It's confusing, but *we have a right to be confused*. Perhaps even a need. The trick is to enjoy it: to savor complexity and resist the easy answers; to let diversity flower into creativity. Politicians again and again try to wean people from the effort to understand complexity. They know, for instance, that war is the great simplification that makes it possible to silence dissonant opinions and to decide once and for all that guns are more important than butter instead of seeking a more complex balance.

References

Bateson, G. (1972). *Steps to an ecology of mind.* Toronto: Chandler.

Bateson, G. (1979). *Mind and nature: A necessary unity.* New York: Dutton.

Bateson, G., & Bateson, M. C. (1987). *Angels fear: An investigation into the nature and meaning of the sacred.* New York: Macmillan.

Bateson, M. C. (1972). *Our own metaphor: A personal account of a conference on the Effects of Conscious Purpose on Human Adaptation.* New York: Alfred A. Knopf.

Bateson, M. C. (1984). *With a daughter's eye: A memoir of Margaret Mead and Gregory Bateson.* New York: William Morrow.

Bateson, M. C. (1989). *Composing a life.* New York: Grove Press.

Bateson, M. C. (1994). *Peripheral visions: Learning along the way.* New York: HarperCollins.

Bateson, M. C. (2000). *Full circles, overlapping lives: Culture and generation in transition.* New York: Random House.

Bateson, M. C. (2004). *Willing to learn: Passages of personal discovery.* Hanover, NH: Steerforth Press.

Bateson, M. C. (2005). Learning to teach, teaching to learn. *Philadelphia Inquirer,* 28 August 2005, p.C01.

Bateson, M. C. (2007). Frequently asked questions. Mary Catherine Bateson personal website. http://www.marycatherinebateson.com/faqs.html. Accessed 13 Jan 2009.

Bateson, M. C. (2008). Angels fear revisited: Gregory Bateson's cybernetic theory of mind applied to religion-science debates. In J. Hoffmeyer (Ed.), *A legacy for living systems: Gregory Bateson as precursor to biosemiotics* (pp. 15–26). New York: Springer.

Hayles, N. K. (1999). *How we became posthuman: Virtual bodies in cybernetics, literature, and informatics.* Chicago: University of Chicago Press.

Janesick, V. J. (2005). A moment in history – The Ethnographic Family: Bateson, Bateson, and Mead. *American Educational Research Association Qualitative Research Special Interest Group Newsletter,* VI, p. 2.

Kimble Wrye, H. (1994). Narrative scripts: Composing a life with ambition and desire. *American Journal of Psychoanalysis, 54*(2), 127–141.

Weick, K.E. (1998). Improvisation as a mindset for organizational analysis. *Organization Science, 9*(5), 543–555.

Afterword: The Story Behind This Book

Let me tell you how this book arose.

When Magnus and I joined the systems group at the UK's Open University in September 2000, the group was in the midst of a 'meta project'. The idea was that instead of re-writing all our basic systems teaching each time a new course was written, the group would work together on a set of basic systems materials which would be shared by all our systems courses. The hope was that this would lead to a better quality of teaching on these core topics, alleviating both the pressures on our own time, and the confusion of our students.

Three texts had already been created but the fourth – a set of pieces by key systems thinkers – was missing. I was interested in the omission because – being relatively new to systems thinking, having come into the group primarily as a teacher and practitioner – I was longing to read this fourth text. Like many of our students, I was familiar with basic systems ideas and approaches, but felt lost without a sense of the history and geography – the territory – of the field I was now working in.

While we worked as members of the same course team, the case of the unwritten text remained an issue in the systems group. There had been conversations, attempts to make a start, but nothing had followed. Two problems were mentioned. One was the embarrassing absence of celebrated women writers in the field: you couldn't produce such a text without drawing attention to this, and it didn't sit well with our image of ourselves or of the field. The more intractable problem was the impossibility of reaching agreement on which authors should be included in the book. The introduction has already covered some of the reasons for this, but there was another: we were a group where everyone spoke, everyone had their say. And if everyone had their say about who should or shouldn't be included, the conversation would go on for ever without resolution.

Magnus and I did some preliminary work on the project, thinking about who might appreciate such a collection of readings, and what they might get out of it. We became excited at the idea of a book which would bring together the various strands of systems thinking, so that readers familiar with one systems tradition could discover a breadth in the field that they had perhaps been unaware of, encountering other authors they would value and enjoy.

We also felt it was important that students of systems could begin to gain a sense of ownership of the field – of knowing their way around what can otherwise seem

M. Ramage and K. Shipp, *Systems Thinkers,*
© The Open University 2009. Published in association with Springer-Verlag London Limited

a mysterious and almost unbounded domain – and that such a book could address this need.

Somewhat tentatively we decided to take the project on. We designed a learning process for working together on the book: taking one author a fortnight, finding a good representative piece of their work, studying it and discussing it, before writing a short piece describing the author's contribution to the field. But explicitly with myself in the role of learner and Magnus in the role of guide. It was a neat design: putting together two distinct needs – mine for knowledge and Magnus's for motivation – to create a solution.

We needed the group's agreement to proceed. But when we told them of our plans we were dismayed to find that everyone else wanted to join in. If Magnus was going to do the work of finding the extracts, they too wanted to read them, and to have their say. We knew that if this became a whole-group project the book would never get written. Alongside the issue of reaching agreement on which authors to include, and the politics of deciding who would write what, it raised questions about motivation and quality. We knew that we would be distracted and discouraged if the audience for our early drafts was too wide or too voluble. So we went away to devise a process which would allow everyone to be involved but which would enhance rather than derail the project. Our solution was the systems study group.

The study group, which Magnus and I co-facilitated, met once a fortnight over a period of two and a half years. During that time we studied 50 key systems thinkers. We had expected interest in the project to wane after the first few meetings, but to our surprise a good proportion of the systems group attended, and the numbers remained fairly stable. Given the group's tendency to stray from the topic in hand onto questions of process, and our desire to create a democratic forum where everyone's view was respected, we designed a simple structure for meetings, and chaired them fairly tightly to this structure. This may have frustrated one or two more dominant members, but we felt that the inclusive structure was one of the reasons that interest was sustained over such a long period.

This is how it worked: Magnus made a working list of authors, roughly grouped by school or application area. We didn't publish this in advance because we expected the list to evolve over time; and we found that people seemed to enjoy the suspense of seeing who would come next. For each author in turn, Magnus would painstakingly assemble as much of their work as possible. From this collection we would select a reading, and e-mail details of the author and reading to the group. The project secretary made copies which people could pick up from her office, and everyone had about a week to read it before we met. We had a regular lunchtime slot, lasting an hour and a half.

The meeting would start with Magnus explaining why he'd chosen the author, and a few words about their work and context. Then someone would volunteer to start, and each participant would have a turn to say anything they wanted to: perhaps their thoughts on or reactions to the reading, perhaps making connections and comparisons with other authors, perhaps sharing insights or anecdotes about the author. Once everyone had spoken, people would be itching to respond to points others had raised, and we would go into open discussion – generally animated, stimulating and playful, with widely divergent views.

We had arguments with colleagues about the idea of providing any sort of 'map' of the territory. Of course there is no 'true' map – an individual might lay out the connections between these authors in any number of ways, to reveal a different pattern. By providing a model we emphasise certain connections, but underplay others. Yet to offer no map at all – no structure – is to deny the explorer a vital aid to their journey. Without some sort of map, the learner cannot even start to lay down the interconnections in memory. This map, which over time they will refine, extend, amend, embellish, and colour with their own experiences, preferences and insights can only ever be an approximation, a starting point from which the individual can set out. The categories by which we have grouped our thirty thinkers provide such a structure, represented graphically in the diagram at the start of the book (Fig. 0.1).

Magnus and I knew from the start that we were interested in the individual authors themselves, as well as their work. The study group demonstrated that this interest was echoed in others; we found that discussions dwelled as often on the character and behaviour of the author, their relationships with others or the context of their life, as on their contribution to the field. We felt that developing a sense of ownership of the field entailed having a sense of knowing the significant individuals in the field, as well as knowing what they had written.

By offering insights into an author's life, I think we wanted to support the sense of relationship that a reader can experience after studying an author in depth when, arriving at powerful new understandings which change the way that individual looks at the world, they can feel an enduring connection the author, almost a sense of gaining a mentor or guide they can converse with in imagination.

When Magnus presented a paper on this project at the UK Systems Society conference in 2006, one of the listeners commented with some frustration that it sounded as if it would be a book of 'the dead and the nearly dead'. It seems to me that the learning to which academia aspires moves forward in leaps and dribbles. Most published research doesn't supersede what precedes it, but adds to it by very small steps. Occasionally an idea emerges which is profoundly original, and which sets everyone off in a new direction. This is followed by a period of consolidation, where others draw on the idea, refine it perhaps, relate it to other theory, and put it to practical use.

Of course there is a case for reinterpreting such significant thinking for a new generation – translating it into the language of the day. But there is also a case for returning to the original work to ensure that you have understood the thinking precisely and in all its subtlety, and to search for other nuances and conceptions which may yet remain undiscovered.

And besides, to label a piece of writing uninteresting or irrelevant simply because it is old is to dismiss the whole of academic endeavour. Every fresh and exciting piece of work will be old in a few years time; is all of it then ultimately worthless?

As I write this I'm reminded of a pattern of behaviour I commented on in the study group. Author after author would express – perhaps in a later edition of a seminal work – great frustration that people hadn't properly understood what they had meant. Followers had grasped the gist of it, but hadn't absorbed the full idea in its richness and depth, or with all its implications. This underlined for me the importance of studying the original authors, rather than assuming their ideas could be picked up by reading only more recent writers.

The study group concluded in summer 2005, after which we were able to begin work on the book itself. This required a second cycle of assembling and studying each author's work, together with various secondary materials. In fact we cycled through our set of 30 thinkers at least four more times, as Magnus wrote and revised drafts and I reviewed them. We were often seen in one or other of the campus cafes, absorbed in discussion of the current week's draft.

In all our work, I have tended to be an advocate for the less expert reader, while Magnus has been the one to uphold academic values and to do the painstaking research necessary to construct each chapter. Sometimes I like to think that my name on the cover stands for every unnamed collaborator who has contributed to the thinking attributed to our celebrated authors. Magnus and I have had so many discussions about how ideas evolve in an academic community; about the strangeness of saying that an idea 'belongs' to one individual. We've puzzled over this, trying to understand the nature of the communities and families these thinkers worked amongst. We've tried out stories – based on glimpses from documented comments and conversations, or the personal experience of study group members – of how the relationships may have worked between these individuals and their fellows; this based also on our own experiences of how things go in academia. So much thinking evolves through conversation. And for these conversations to take place there have to be listeners as well as speakers. There have to be meeting organisers, process designers, chairs and facilitators. There have to be believers and promoters. There have to be teachers and communicators to translate the original thinker's dense academic text into a form that can be digested and promulgated more widely. I see these stretched out like a child's cut-out paper-chain of figures, hand in hand, passing the potent ideas along – transforming them, playing with them, showing how they might be understood or applied.

We hope that our book will play its part in this chain of communication, with your participation. The material above gave you a taste of the writing, and an insight into the person, of thirty key systems thinkers. You may have arrived here because you were already familiar with some of them. Our hope is that you have found others to excite and inspire you. And perhaps that by encouraging readers to return to some of these 'original source' authors, and to venture across the boundaries between traditions, the field of systems will be strengthened and enriched, ultimately providing solid ground for the development of powerful new thinking.

Karen Shipp, January 2009

Index